ATHENS AND THE CYCLADES

Athens and the Cyclades

Economic Strategies 540–314 BC

BRIAN RUTISHAUSER

OXFORD
UNIVERSITY PRESS

OXFORD
UNIVERSITY PRESS

Great Clarendon Street, Oxford, OX2 6DP,
United Kingdom

Oxford University Press is a department of the University of Oxford.
It furthers the University's objective of excellence in research, scholarship,
and education by publishing worldwide. Oxford is a registered trade mark of
Oxford University Press in the UK and in certain other countries

First Edition published in 2012

Impression: 1

British Library Cataloguing in Publication Data
Data available

Library of Congress Cataloging in Publication Data
Data available

ISBN 978–0–19–964635–7

Printed in Great Britain by
MPG Books Group, Bodmin and King's Lynn

To my parents, Kurt and Eleanor Rutishauser

Preface

The island group known as the Cyclades offers great potential to historians of Greek antiquity, yet this potential has only been slightly explored. Though not considered among the most powerful of Greek states, these island communities were crucial nodes on ancient sailing routes in the Aegean, and possessed famous local resources. While they were often neglected by our Athenocentric sources, Cycladic *poleis* make tantalizing appearances in the accounts of the late Archaic through late Classical periods in the Aegean. When coupled with the evidence of epigraphy, numismatics, and archaeological excavation and survey, these accounts help form a regional portrait which, though maddeningly lacunose at times, remains one unlike any other in Greek antiquity.

This study approaches these ancient Cycladic islanders as much more than simple subjects oppressed by various hegemons during different periods of antiquity. Though they were often forced to adapt to hegemony, there is reason to believe that on more than one occasion they found a *modus vivendi* under these hegemons which enabled them to achieve a certain level of economic prosperity. Although many details of political history from the late sixth through late fourth centuries BC are covered herein, the focus remains on the reconstruction of economic phenomena and economic strategies of these islanders. Many practices that appear to be connected to what has been called peer-polity interaction surface during two periods on this timeline—the minting of coinage, the operation of warships, and monumental construction of temples and fortifications. One of these periods is the late sixth century, generally considered in modern scholarship as the apex of power for Cycladic communities. The periods of Athenian domination in the fifth and fourth centuries are usually characterized as periods of economic as well as political decline for these islands. However, the late fourth century is another period when similar phenomena reappear. Although conditions of insularity, mainly those derived from geography, always had some effect on the region, the inhabitants of the Cyclades could and did respond to particular circumstances to maximize benefits for their communities. The decisions of the Athenians, moreover, created symbiotic effects that could alter the factors within economic equations.

Chapter 1 discusses past scholarship and previous approaches to these issues, as well as framing Cycladic economies within the larger debate concerning the ancient Greek economy. Chapter 2 sets the geographical stage by discussing such factors as varying definitions of the 'Cyclades' as a region, navigation, and attested trade routes. Chapter 2 also discusses the wide range of sources that will be examined in this study, including literary, epigraphic, numismatic, and archaeological evidence. Chapter 3 covers the Cyclades in the Archaic period (particularly the late sixth century, called herein the period of 'local hegemonies'), while Chapter 4 focuses on the fifth century and the Athenian *arkhē*, from the Persian Wars through the end of the Peloponnesian War. Chapter 5 gives an overview of the period from 404 to 355, when hegemony over the region was more 'fluid' and could shift among various naval powers. Chapter 6 takes the narrative from the end of the Social War to the loss of Athenian control over Delos in 314. Certain phenomena are addressed throughout all periods: the extent to which various hegemons were able to control the Cyclades militarily and affect commerce; changing (and unchanging) trade routes; and possible economic strategies available to the islanders.

I would like to thank my original mentor in ancient history, R. Bruce Hitchner, who introduced me to the field during my undergraduate years at the University of Dayton and sparked my interest in the ancient economy. This project has its roots in my 1998 PhD dissertation completed at the Ohio State University, now greatly revised and expanded. I wish to thank my dissertation committee: Timothy Gregory, Stephen Tracy, and the late Jack Balcer. I am thankful also for the encouragement given to me by Nathan Rosenstein. I would also like to thank all at the American School of Classical Studies in Athens during the 1996–7 year, when much important material that is presented here was gathered. I am also grateful to Mr. Tzones Zervoudakis, the late Evangelos Th. Pantazoglou, and all on Siphnos during my participation in the 1998 and 2002 Sifnean Symposia.

My thanks also to the following who read earlier drafts of this work: Christy Constantakopoulou, John W.I. Lee, Darel Engen, Patrice Brun, Thomas J. Figueira, and the anonymous readers employed by Oxford University Press. In addition, I would like to express my gratitude to others with whom I have discussed aspects of this project over the years: Ronald Stroud, Ken Sheedy, Lina Mendoni, and Charikleia Papageorghiadou-Banis. Their comments and advice have greatly improved the final product and have saved me from a number of errors. Any errors that remain are the sole responsibility of the author.

Thanks also to Hilary O'Shea, Cathryn Steele, and Taryn Campbell at OUP; and to Siran Erysian for producing the maps. Special praise is due to Theresa Delaney, whose tireless efforts in acquiring research materials made the completion of this project possible. I must also extend thanks to the staff of the Classics Library at the University of Cincinnati for their assistance during my many visits.

Closer to home, I must also mention Colette and Brandon, who have endured my obsession with this project with little to no complaint. Finally, all the thanks in the world would be insufficient to express my gratitude to my parents Kurt and Eleanor Rutishauser. Without their support and encouragement, this book would never have seen the light of day—and it is to them that it is respectfully dedicated.

Brian Rutishauser

Fresno City College, California
October 2011

Contents

List of Maps

List of Tables

Abbreviations

ADelt	*Archaiologikon Deltion. Athens, 1961–.*
BNJ	*Brill's New Jacoby. http://www.brill.nl/publications/online-resources/jacoby-online*
CH	*O. Hoover, A. Meadows, and U. Wartenberg (eds.), Coin Hoards.Vol.10: Greek Hoards. Royal Numismatic Society, London, 2010.*
CIG	*Corpus Inscriptionum Graecarum. 4 vols., Berlin, 1825–77.*
FGrH	*F. Jacoby (ed.), Die Fragmente der griechischen Historiker. Berlin, 1923–58.*
IG I^3	*D.M. Lewis, et al. (eds.) Inscriptiones Graecae: Inscriptiones Atticae Euclidis Anno Anteriores. 3rd edn., Berlin, 1998.*
IG II^2	*J. Kirchner (ed.), Inscriptiones Graecae: Inscriptiones Atticae Euclidis Anno Posteriores. 2nd edn., Berlin, 1916–40.*
IGCH	*M.Thompson, O. Mörkholm and C.M. Kraay, An Inventory of Greek Coin Hoards. New York, 1973.*
OCD	*S. Hornblower and A. Spawforth (eds.),The Oxford Classical Dictionary, 3rd edn., Oxford (1996).*
OGIS	*W. Dittenberger. Orientis Graeci Inscriptiones Selectae. 2 vols. Leipzig 1903–5.*
PCG	*R. Kassel and C. Austin Poetae Comici Graeci. Berlin and New York, 1983–.*
RE	*A.F. von Pauly and G. Wissowa, Real-Encyclopädie der klassichen Altertums-wissenschaft. Stuttgart 1893–1963.*
SEG	*Supplementum epigraphicum Graecum. Amsterdam, 1923–.*
$Syll.^3$	*W. Dittenberger, Sylloge inscriptionum Graecarum. 3rd edn., Leipzig, 1915–24.*

All other abbreviations follow the conventions of *L'Année Philologique* and the *OCD* pp. xxix–liv.

A Note on Transliteration: Most Greek names are cited following a closer spelling to the original Greek—examples include Kyrene, Euboia, Boiotia, Aigina, and Ephoros. In a few cases the Latinized form is used to reflect common practice and avoid confusion—the most notable choice here is Cyclades, but other examples include Crete, Corinth, Cyprus, Peiraeus, Diodorus, Herodotus, and Thucydides.

All dates are BC unless otherwise indicated.

1

Introduction

In his *Island Archaeology of the Early Cyclades*, Cyprian Broodbank characterizes the Aegean as an 'inland sea within the Mediterranean.'[1] When one travels through the Cyclades in modern times, it produces the uncanny feeling that one has entered a self-contained universe. Most of the Cyclades are no more than 12 miles apart; many of them are within sight of at least one other of their number (see Figure 1.1).[2]

And yet, this insular microcosm was to varying degrees defined by its connections with the macrocosm of the wider Greek world. The position of these islands on major trade routes between the Greek mainland and the eastern Mediterranean ensured that this would be the case.[3]

From the time of the Persian Wars through the beginning of the Hellenistic period, the Cyclades lacked true political and military power. Many historians consider them to have become pawns in the greater power struggles between Mediterranean hegemons in these eras. Nearly forty years ago, for example, a classic study of the fifth-century BC Athenian *arkhē* downplayed the importance of the Cyclades, stating that these islands were scarce in resources, yet at the same time 'natural prizes' for those states that could exert naval power.[4]

It was this single paragraph that first inspired this project many years ago. The overall impression that Meiggs creates for the region is one of near-irrelevance, with any potential economic prosperity

[1] Broodbank 2000, 41.

[2] For more discussion of islands as 'imagined communities', see Rainbird 1999.

[3] Horden and Purcell 2000, 76 on Melos: 'It is . . . the conflicting pulls of the various other regions whose meeting point is the Aegean that have given shape to the island's history.'

[4] Meiggs 1972, 271–2.

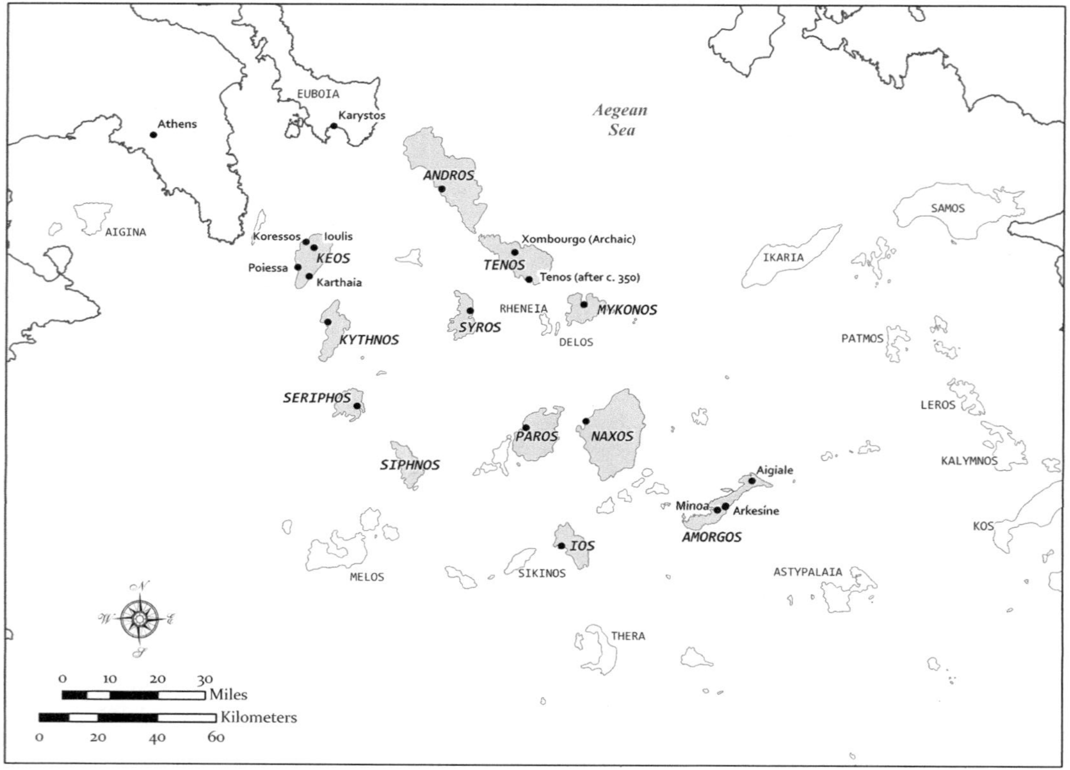

Fig. 1.1. The Cycladic Region

strictly a result of its connections with Athens. Yet, Meiggs's view contains several contradictory statements: that the Cycladic *poleis* were inherently poor, yet were a 'natural prize' for outside powers; and that Athenian protection would have enabled inhabitants of these islands to 'trade securely', yet these same people would have been better served economically by relocation to Athens.

In recent years, there have been a number of important studies that have attempted to reconstruct various aspects of the economic nature of Athens' fifth-century *arkhē*.[5] Discussion of specifics has often focused on the *phoros*, or tribute, levied by Athens on members of the Delian League.[6] Coinage and its possible regulation by Athens has also received attention.[7] The effect of the *arkhē* on commerce remains largely unexplored, but several analyses have been made.[8] Even less-studied, though not completely neglected, has been the effect of Athenian 'imperialism' on the islands of the Aegean.[9] In general, most of these studies have approached these issues from the stand-point of 'oppression' on the part of the Athenians towards their allies.[10]

Compared to the level of interest in the economic nature of Athens' fifth-century *arkhē*, similar studies of Athens and the Aegean world for the fourth-century are more scarce. Most discussions have focused on the Second Athenian League, and whether or not it was as 'oppressive' as the Delian League. The standard view maintains that Athens began the Second League with much fanfare and rhetoric, and assurances that the abuses of the Delian League would not be re-peated; but that their desire to re-create their old hegemony got the better of them, leading to renewed attempts at expansion that resulted

[5] For general discussion see French 1964 and 1972; Erxleben 1969; Schuller 1974; Austin and Vidal-Naquet 1977; Finley 1978; Pečirka 1982; Schmitz 1988; Figueira 1998; Samons 2000; Kallet 2001; Pébarthe 2000 and 2008.

[6] Recent examples include Blamire 2001; Kallet-Marx 1993.

[7] Schönhammer 1993; Figueira 1998, 2003 and 2006; Mattingly 1996; Flament 2007.

[8] Reed 2003; Figueira 2005; Erickson 2005 and 2010.

[9] Brun 1996, esp. 184–92 on island *phoros*; Pébarthe 1999; Constantakopoulou 2007; Wallace and Figueira 2010; Hornblower 2011, 37–42.

[10] A theme still seen in most general treatments of the Delian League: Low 2008; Osborne 2000a; Ma, Papazarkadas, and Parker 2009. McGregor 1987 represents an overly-positive contrast, while Brun 1996 shows the way towards a more balanced assessment.

in the Social War and the loss of the League's most important members.[11] According to this view, Athenian influence in the Aegean was completely moribund after the end of the Social War in 355. While this orthodoxy on the nature of the Second League has not gone unchallenged, it remains the dominant paradigm.[12]

Specific studies of the finances of the Second League are not very numerous,[13] but in the orthodox works the so-called 'failure' of the Second Athenian League is linked to supposed economic hardship among Athens' fourth-century allies, with little evidence demonstrated to support this notion. And no real distinction has yet been made between economic conditions among the allies during the apex of the Second Athenian League (approximately 378–364) compared to other periods of the fourth century.

Several regional histories of specific Cycladic islands have echoed these negative conclusions. One survey of the history of Paros has characterized the fourth century as a time of financial depression and domination of this island by Athens, and a period when the Parians suffered from chronic shortages of cash.[14] A monograph on Andros states that its inhabitants stayed loyal to Athens out of necessity rather than by choice, and that this loyalty had negative effects on the island's prosperity.[15] Similar evaluations for Siphnos, Keos, and Naxos in the fourth century have all been proposed.[16] Recent works

[11] Accame 1941; Cawkwell 1981; Badian 1995; Buckler 2003, 371–83; for more moderate positions see Dreher 1995; Hornblower 2011, 240–6 and 271–4.

[12] Cargill 1981 and 1982 represent the most aggressive attempts at casting the Second League in a more positive light; see also Griffith 1978a; Harding 1995.

[13] Brun 1983; Mitchell 1984a; Dreher 1995; Chankowski 2001 and 2008.

[14] Lanzilotta 1987, 136–9, based on the various loans taken out from the temple of Delian Apollo and from individuals on Chios, considers the Spartan hegemony right after the end of the Peloponnesian War to have been preferable for the Parians: 'risulta infatti che l'isola gode di grande prestigio, prima della battaglia di Cnido, sotto l'egemonia spartana, mentre si trova in grosse difficoltà economiche durante l'alleanza con Atene,come attestano gli indebitamenti che vanno dal 376 al 371.' But see Dreher 1995, 123–9 for a different view of the 'benefits' of Spartan hegemony for Paros. Berranger-Auserve 2000 gives a more balanced picture of Parian conditions in the fourth century, but still implies that Athenian hegemony impacted the island in a negative way financially.

[15] Paschali 1925 [1995], 359–67.

[16] Siphnos: Symeonides 1990, 69–72; Keos: Papageorgiadou-Banis 1997, 68–9; Naxos: Bogaert 1968, 203; for the region in general in the fourth century, see Ceccarelli 1989.

on Delos have also emphasized the notion that the Cyclades were a depressed region during the fourth century.[17]

This concept can also be seen in approaches to the Cyclades during the Hellenistic period. The late third century (the so-called time of 'Delian Independence') has been recently proposed as a time when the region was able to enjoy prosperity.[18] This period was marked by two important phenomena: the lack of an external naval hegemon, and the production of local coinages. According to this view, the Cyclades experienced economic prosperity at this time because of a lack of outside political interference and a lack of commercial integration with areas outside the region. Within this 'vacuum' the inhabitants of the Cyclades created a strong regional economy centred on the island of Delos. The implication is that economic prosperity would only have been possible in the Cyclades if the islands were free of a hegemon.

This analysis of the Cyclades during the third century has some validity. Nevertheless, it involves the supposition that the Cyclades could only be prosperous under one set of historical conditions. Hegemons such as Athens did impose financial and other obligations on the Cyclades, particularly during the fifth century. However, there may have also been economic benefits from close connections with hegemonic states. Moreover, the positioning of the Cyclades on major trade routes, the existence of several good harbours in the region, and the presence of lucrative local resources, could have produced economic prosperity out of proportion to the relative political insignificance of these islands, even under outside hegemony.[19]

In the last two or three decades there have also been several important publications, including archaeological surveys[20] and epigraphical

[17] Reger 1994*a*, 20 states that the Cyclades 'had little to offer a conqueror by the 4th century BC'; Chankowski 2008, 375 implies that the Athenians were not concerned with promoting the prosperity of Cycladic economies in the fourth century.

[18] Reger 1994*a*.

[19] Brun 1993*a* gives a good overview of how reports of poverty in the Cyclades, both from the Imperial Roman period as well as in early modern times, have created a false impression of poverty for other eras. See also Brun 1996, 196–209; 1998 and 2000.

[20] Keos (modern Kea) has been the most intensively surveyed island in the region: Cherry, Davis, and Mantzourani 1991*a*; Cherry and Davis 1998; Whitelaw 1998; Mendoni 1994. For Delos: Brunet 1990; for Rheneia: Charre and Le Dinahet 1999; Melos: Renfrew and Wagstaff 1982; Naxos: Dalongeville and Rougemont 1983 and 1993; Kythnos: Chatzanastasiou 1998.

studies, that offer some support for alternative views of the region during the Classical period.[21] Two general works on the Aegean have appeared by Patrice Brun (Classical through Hellenistic) and Christy Constantakopoulou (Archaic and Classical), both of which include extensive material on the Cyclades.[22] Other studies have proposed that the agricultural productivity of the Cyclades in the Classical period has been underestimated, and that the fourth century might have seen many of the islands at their highest level of population in all of antiquity.[23] Although the use of data and estimates from surveys remains problematic, and comparison of the results of different survey projects is extremely complex, a general statement can be made that many Cycladic landscapes show evidence of extensive settlement and exploitation in the fifth through fourth centuries.[24]

A number of specialized works have also recently appeared which address specific aspects of the economy in the Classical Cyclades. Ken Sheedy has published an important and groundbreaking survey of Cycladic coinage from the late sixth to mid-fifth centuries.[25] Veronique Chankowski has republished many of the important inscriptions from Delos, including the fourth-century loan accounts from the temple of Apollo.[26] The proceedings of the Sifnian Symposia, while focused specifically on the history of Siphnos in various periods, have also added important details to our knowledge of the region.[27]

Yet, many issues remain unexplored. There are important economic phenomena from these periods that have not received major scholarly attention. One is the construction of monumental temples in the Cyclades. The late sixth century was a period of such construction, and several scholars have cited this as one indicator that the late

[21] Reger 2004 (the article on the Aegean in the *Inventory of Archaic and Classical Poleis*) has now become the essential introduction to research on the Cyclades. For the Classical through Hellenistic periods, Brun 1997 and Constantakopoulou 2007, while retaining a larger focus on Aegean islands, also collect much Cycladic material. For Hellenistic Delos and the Cyclades see Reger 1994a, and for the Hellenistic and Roman periods Nigdelis 1990. See also the papers in Lanzilotta and Schilardi 1996 for the Cyclades during various periods in antiquity.

[22] Brun 1996; Constantakopoulou 2007.

[23] Reger 1994*a*, 49 for living space, 272 for agriculture, 108 for population.

[24] For a more detailed discussion of survey archaeology and its relation to Cycladic studies, see Chapter 2, pp. 40–3.

[25] Sheedy 2006.

[26] Chankowski 2008.

[27] Zervoudakis 2000 and 2005.

Archaic period was the time of greatest prosperity for the Cycladic region.[28] Yet there is another period of temple construction in the Cyclades that has largely escaped the notice of scholars, one that occurred during the second half of the fourth century. While not on the same scale as the Archaic constructions, these structures were built on several of the islands during this time and thus represent a recurrence of a regional phenomenon, one which calls for further discussion.[29]

The minting of local coinage follows a similar chronological pattern. Local silver coinages were produced on several of the Cyclades in the late sixth century, despite the apparent ready availability of Aiginetan silver.[30] This minting activity, however, gradually came to a halt by the middle of the fifth century, when Athenian silver owls became common for most transactions. After a long hiatus, local coinages began to be produced in the Cyclades again in the fourth century.[31]

The late sixth century was also a time when Naxos, site of some of the most famous of these temple structures, is credited with the possession of a large fleet of warships.[32] The operation of warships was not limited to Naxos, however. Evidence from authors such as Herodotus indicates that by the early fifth century several of the Cyclades had small numbers of warships (including triremes) that contributed to both the Greek and the Persian sides during the Persian Wars. It will be argued that the possession of warships in the late Archaic period could have enabled a few Cycladic communities to control the passage of merchant shipping through their vicinity.[33] However, we do not see evidence of a recurrence of warships in the Cyclades in the late fourth century, as it was now no longer possible to compete with the superpowers that could deploy major fleets in the Aegean.

All of these factors—minting, monumental construction, and the construction of warships—required financial resources. Moreover, these factors were not limited to one specific period of Cycladic history, but reappeared in various combinations if not necessarily identical conditions. Some recent scholarship proposes that several new economic phenomena appeared in the Greek world during the

[28] See Chapter 3, pp. 64–5.
[29] See Chapter 6, pp. 232–4.
[30] See Chapter 3, pp. 61–3.
[31] See Chapter 6, pp. 229–32.
[32] Hdt. 5.30.4.
[33] See Chapter 3, pp. 70–3.

fourth century.[34] Rather than experiencing a linear development, however, Cycladic economies may in fact have been more characterized by circumstances which continued to recur over a period of several centuries.

This is how the Athenians became an integral factor in Cycladic economies. Their influence on the region can be seen as far back as the time of Peisistratos, who purified Delos and helped install Lygdamis as tyrant of Naxos.[35] With the creation of the Delian League after the Persian Wars, the Cyclades gave up (whether by choice or compulsion) many of the economic practices they had engaged in during the late sixth century: monumental temple construction, the minting of silver, and the operation of warships in local waters. Although the Athenian fleet probably managed to control piracy to some degree and promote commerce, some of the surplus wealth generated by this trade could have been redirected (in tribute, and during the Peloponnesian War through the *eikostē* tax) into the hands of the Athenians.

During the early fourth century, the Cyclades saw a succession of naval powers attempt to exert control over their region. The Spartans, the Athenians again (with the Second Athenian League), and briefly the Thebans, all made their presence known. While the decade of the 360s saw the Athenians unable to fully protect the Cyclades, these islands appear to have stayed loyal during the Social War of 357–355. It is the period of Cycladic history from 355–314 (when Athens finally lost control of Delos and the Cyclades were unified in the First Nesiotic League by the Antigonids) that is the most intriguing, but also most neglected in modern scholarship. The years after 338, which may have seen the revitalized Athenian fleet patrolling the Aegean and suppressing piracy rather than being deployed in imperialistic ventures, may have been a time of prosperity not just for Athens, but for the Cyclades as well. Although precise dating is impossible, after mid-century we begin to see in the Cycladic region the return of several of the economic phenomena attested there during the late Archaic period—namely, monumental temple construction, minting of local coinages (albeit on a smaller scale), and the building of fortification walls. The continuing importance of trade

[34] Descat 1987 and 2006 proposes several different phases of growth and stagnation in the Aegean economy during the fourth century; Burke 1985 and 1992. For criticism see Morris 1994*a*.

[35] See Chapter 3, p. 55.

routes through the Cyclades (especially as one of several conduits of the grain supply to Athens, that from north Africa and the Levant) may also be seen in the re-foundation of the *polis* of Tenos, now moved from its original inland location to a coastal site, and its subsequent rapid growth during this period. Many of the islands, such as Paros and Naxos, had local products that sometimes ended up being exported at great distance from their original sources (such as Parian marble). The policies of the Athenian politicians Euboulos and Lykourgos appear to have resulted in greater revenues for Athens after 355, and peaceable relations with the rest of the Aegean world might have actually contributed to Athenian wealth.[36] The Cyclades may have also profited from the increased level of commerce without having as much of the newly-generated wealth ending up in Athenian hands, as it may have during the *arkhē*. Thus, the presence of a hegemon had effects on local Cycladic economies, but these effects may have been more complex than often assumed, and not necessarily negative in all cases.

If this analysis is correct, it holds interesting ramifications not just for the regional study of the Cyclades, but for the entire 'grand narrative' of Greek Classical history, particularly for the fourth century. The often-trumpeted 'failure' of Athenian hegemony in the fourth century, certainly true in a political sense, may in fact be misplaced where economic history is concerned. It may also be true that Moses Finley's famous denigration of regional studies in ancient Greek history was counterproductive, as the regional level can provide excellent test cases for studying economic phenomena and change in antiquity.[37] Various monographs on specific islands among the Cyclades have not fully taken such a regional perspective into account.[38]

It is hoped that the present study will contribute significantly to regional studies of Greek antiquity. A *caveat* must be kept in mind here, that the majority of our evidence will be '*polis*-based,' particularly in terms of epigraphic evidence. Since we know of so few

[36] Gauthier 1976, 236–7.

[37] Finley 1985, 65–6, a dismissal highlighted by Bissa 2009, 21–4. Recent examples of regional studies include Alcock and Cherry 2004; Bommeljé and Doorn 1987; Foley 1988; Fossey 1989; Nielsen and Roy 1999; Cavanagh, Mee, and James 2005.

[38] Most of the few monographs on island studies in antiquity discuss the Aegean (Brun 1996, Constantakopoulou 2007) or Mediterranean conditions in general (Horden and Purcell 2000), but not the Cyclades exclusively.

Cycladic individuals by name for the Classical period, this study will often necessarily focus on the actions and/or reactions of the Parians, Naxians, Tenians, and so forth as collective entities. This study presumes that Cycladic *poleis* often made decisions on courses of action that would result in increased local economic benefits, even if such benefits were not always evenly distributed. This may strike the reader as an economic version of the 'states as rational actors' paradigm within the Realist school of international relations, a school which has recently found favour among some scholars of antiquity.[39] Although it would not be appropriate to endeavour here upon a full-scale critique of this approach, some aspects of this paradigm may apply to the political situation in the Aegean during the late Archaic period. The concept of states as part of a 'militarized and multipolate anarchy' (to quote Eckstein) does reflect some factors within the Aegean region prior to the creation of Athenian hegemony in the fifth century.[40] Yet, this study will also detail economic decision-making during periods of peace in the Aegean, when fear of interstate violence might not have been an overriding factor.

THE CYCLADES AND THE ANCIENT ECONOMY

Before going further, it will be necessary to briefly discuss how the present work will contribute to the debate on the ancient economy. This has become one of the more contentious areas of inquiry in classical studies ever since the publication of Moses Finley's *The Ancient Economy* in 1973, although the dispute (formerly known as the Bücher–Meyer debate) had already raged for decades when Finley entered the fray.[41] This older debate had centred on whether or not the ancient Greek economy was essentially based on small-scale household production (Bücher) or was closer to a modern market

[39] Eckstein 2006, 12–19 and 37–78 on Classical Greek *poleis* (although mainly focused on Roman Republican expansion); Ma 2000 on the Hellenistic period; Bedermann 2001. For the Realist school in general: Waltz 1959; Aron 1973.

[40] Eckstein 2006, 47–8 and 51.

[41] The literature on this subject is vast. For surveys of the history of the debate see Will 1954; Austin and Vidal-Naquet 1977; Millett 1991; Cohen 1992; Morris 1994*a* and 1999.

economy (Meyer).[42] Rostovtzeff later expanded upon Meyer's conclusions and focused in particular on the Hellenistic period, positing it as one of intensive economic growth in the Greek world.[43]

These conclusions were sharply challenged by Finley, inspired by the work of Johannes Hasebroek and Karl Polanyi. Hasebroek, applying Max Weber's sociological model that characterized ancient economic activity as mainly status-driven, had minimized the importance of trade in ancient Greece and assumed that most such activity was in the hands of low-status non-citizens.[44] Polanyi, for his part, helped create the substantivist position (detailed below) that emphasized the nature of the ancient economy as a social construct.[45] Finley (and his subsequent supporters) created what is still in many ways the most influential paradigm in the field, often simplistically reduced to the label of 'primitivism'. This view states that trade in the ancient world was mainly limited to essential staples such as grain and other agricultural products; that ancient states did not directly supervise economic activity or promote profit-making; and that there was no true 'market economy' in the modern sense or creation of credit for productive purposes.[46]

Those critical of this paradigm, usually styled 'modernists,' take the opposing view that the ancient economy saw large-scale production of goods; active interest from the state in regulating economic activity; and a high level of long-distance commerce for profit. Other concerns of the modernists have included the involvement of elites in commerce, economic rationality, interdependence of markets, and the purpose of coinage, banking, and loans.[47] In fairness, a few scholars have taken pains to counter some of the overly-polemic criticism from the 'modernist' camp by dispelling some misconceptions concerning Finley's ideas. For example, one scholar has noted that Finley did not rule out the existence of commercial markets in antiquity,

[42] Bücher 1912; Meyer 1924.

[43] Rostovtzeff 1941.

[44] Weber 1924 (reprinted 1976); Hasebroek 1933, still essentially followed by recent works such as Reed 2003.

[45] Polanyi 1944. For an overview of the contributions of Weber and Polanyi to Finley's model see Nafissi 2004 and 2005.

[46] Other recent supporters of Finley's model include: Garnsey 1988; Millett 1991; Morris 1994*a* and 1999; Möller 2000.

[47] Examples include Cohen 1992; Burke 1992; Osborne 1996; Bresson 2000, 2007, and 2008; Engen 2001, 2004, 2005, and now 2010.

only of *integrated* markets.[48] Others have recognized that a high volume of trade existed, but still characterize the ancient Greek economy in the Classical and Hellenistic periods as 'underdeveloped' by modern standards.[49]

It now seems clear, however, that Finley underestimated the complexity of the ancient economy. A great deal of evidence, of similar types to those he considered 'exceptional' and that did not conform to his model, has accumulated over the past several decades. Archaeological work, such as the examination of pottery and amphoras as well as the evidence of shipwrecks, indicates a greater level of trade in the Classical Mediterranean than Finley would have admitted.[50] Finley's model also suffers from the assumption that the ancient economy remained an essentially static and unchanging entity throughout all of Greek and Roman antiquity, a view that can no longer be sustained.[51] A growth in population and the increased agricultural exploitation of the countryside,[52] growth in the trade of certain items such as wine, slaves, and grain, the increasing integration of various markets, and an increasing amount of coinage in circulation, can all be seen in the Aegean during the Classical Greek period.[53] This does not necessarily imply that all these factors continued to increase in a linear fashion over time, only that they saw change rather than remaining static. It also does not imply that there was a unified Aegean (much less Mediterranean) market. Rather, it appears that a 'multitude of regional markets' responded to supply and demand, mainly to achieve self-sufficiency.[54]

No real consensus has been reached, and the entire field of ancient economic history was recently (and accurately) described as 'a discourse in search of a method'.[55] Yet it is now abundantly clear that the

[48] Saller 2002, 253; Shaw 2001, 431.

[49] Davies 2007; Reger 2007.

[50] Morley 2007.

[51] See most recently Engen 2010, 20–36; Bissa 2009, 16–18.

[52] Seen on Keos, Kythera, and Praisos on Crete, but also in mainland sites such as Attica: Lohmann 1993; the southern Argolid: Jameson, Runnels, van Andel 1994; Miletus: Lohmann 1999; Kyaneai in Lykia: Kolb 1996.

[53] Descat 2006; Christesen 2003; Shipton 2000. A cautionary note is struck, however, by Migeotte 2009, 174–5 who points out that most elementary information for calculating economic growth is lacking for this period.

[54] Migeotte 2009, 176–7.

[55] Davies 1998, 230.

primitivist/modernist debate deserves to be abandoned in favour of more flexible models.[56]

Recent calls have been made to move discussion to new levels by applying analytical models derived from the social sciences.[57] For example, a formalist/substantivist dichotomy has been proposed as a replacement for the primitivist/modernist distinction. To formalists, the ancient economy was a separate sphere of activity from the rest of ancient society, with its own agenda and logic. Substantivists, on the other hand, hold that the ancient economy was embedded within social and political relations.[58] One major problem with both the formalist and substantivist models, however, is that they assume that modern economies are (in contrast with ancient ones) disembedded, when in fact it would appear that they are also in many ways culturally determined. This is the contention of so-called 'New Institutional' economists, who stress that modern economic activity also operates within its own institutional context, which one cannot separate from other cultural institutions.[59] In particular, the substantivist model, by stressing such 'primitive' phenomena as gift-exchange and reciprocity, runs the risk of distorting the picture.[60]

This calls to mind another distinction, that between the 'public' and 'private' economic spheres. The public sphere is defined as compulsory, one-way movement of goods directed by the leadership of a polity, and sometimes but not always redistributed to the members of the polity.[61] Various polities in the Greek world had different methods of intervention and involvement in economic activity. A *polis*, for example, would not always have the same approach as a Greek kingdom or a non-Greek polity.[62] Any distinction between public and private economic activity must be made cautiously to avoid

[56] Saller 2002; Foxhall 2007, 22 points out the difficulties of shedding modern terminology such as 'capital' and 'entrepreneur' when analyzing the ancient economy.

[57] Morris and Manning 2005*a*, 1–44, and 2005b, 131–59.

[58] Cartledge 1998, 6–7.

[59] Furobotn and Richter 2005; Hodgson 1998. For discussions of this viewpoint in the context of studies of the ancient Greek economy, see Bresson 2007; Foxhall 2007, 23–6, focusing on the nature of olive production and consumption.

[60] Foxhall 2007, 24 and 2005; Kurke 2002; Tandy 1997.

[61] Davies 1998, 242 for a definition of 'public economy' in antiquity, further explored in Davies 2005 and 2007; Möller 2007; von Reden 2007.

[62] This qualification by Bissa 2009 (esp. 22–4 and 227–36) is one the strongest recent contributions to the debate.

oversimplification. For example, the difference between public and private funding is not always so easy to discern.[63]

While all these approaches have their own merits, they are potentially just as hazardous as the primitivist/modernist one in terms of forcing our evidence into neat categories.[64] If anything of value has emerged, it is the realization that the ancient economy was multifaceted, with a mixture of elements (some that could be characterized as either primitive or modern) and subject to dynamic changes over time.[65]

In the past decade, new emphasis has also been given to yet another approach that may lead to a more promising methodology. Connectivity would have been crucial for economic growth in Cycladic *poleis*. Island polities have been characterized as 'uniquely accessible' to pathways of commerce.[66] Economic activity centred on smaller Mediterranean communities was based on the connectivity that enabled networks of distribution to grow.[67] According to a study of the Mediterranean in the Roman period, for example, variations in harvests that were caused by the fragmented geography and climatic contrasts in the Mediterranean area helped stimulate connectivity by attracting merchants to fill local demand for food and other essentials.[68]

This concept is based more upon qualitative (rather than strictly quantitative) study of 'flows' of wealth and goods between various economic centers.[69] One recent study focuses on the Cyclades in the fifth-century Athenian *arkhē* as a textbook case. The elements within this 'flow model' include *bandwidth* (trade routes whose size is determined by their amount of traffic); *motors* (motivating forces for the circulation of goods, such as the Athenian need for imported grain and Aegean naval bases); and *gates* (obstacles to the flow of

[63] Möller 2007; von Reden 2007.

[64] Morley 2006, esp. 36–8.

[65] Engen 2010; Foxhall 2007; Davies 1998 decries the Finleyan model as 'monocolore.' Descat 1987 proposes several different phases of growth and stagnation in the Aegean Greek economy during the fourth century. For Mediterranean islands, Horden and Purcell 2000, 146–7 stress the need to search for common denominators across space and time.

[66] Horden and Purcell 2000, 225.

[67] Ibid. 224–30 for several cases of smaller Mediterranean islands, including Cycladic products such as Parian marble and Keian ruddle.

[68] Garnsey and Saller 1987, 50.

[69] A concept stressed by Davies 2005.

goods, such as Aegean piracy or warfare between states).[70] At issue is finding a middle ground between two interpretive extremes. One groups all regional economies of the Athenian *arkhē* together and thus obscures their differences, while the other focuses too intensively on individual small states as separate economic units isolated from their larger context.[71]

There has also been a new interest in cabotage, which can be described as the 'background chatter' of small-scale shipments throughout different areas of the Mediterranean in antiquity, as opposed to large-scale 'high commerce' between major states, which in fact may have been no more than an intensification of existing trade patterns.[72] We know that some Mediterranean communities, whether island or coastal, were able to prosper due to these networks even when they lacked local resources. An example is the settlement of Aperlai in Lykia. This city thrived from the early Hellenistic period through Late Antiquity, mainly through the production of *murex* dye, which was shipped by caboteurs to the nearby *emporion* at Andriake (a parallel to the Peiraeus), since Aperlai herself lacked a large-scale natural harbour. The monumental tombs and fortifications seen at Aperlai, and the expansion of her urban area in general, testify to the wealth that this small community enjoyed, even though it remained aloof from political events and went largely unmentioned by ancient authors.[73] Another similar example from the medieval period is the port of Amalfi in southern Italy, which lacked a good harbour but was able to ship products to other nearby emporia.[74]

To be sure, this emphasis on 'connectivity' in Mediterranean history has seen its own critics. Some have characterized it as over-simplified and generally unclear, especially in its lack of detail concerning the role played by cities.[75] Others have seen exaggeration in the extent to which smaller communities could link to larger trade networks.[76] Those communities on major shipping routes, for

[70] Davies 2005, 145–51.
[71] Davies 1998, 242; 2005, 142–52.
[72] Horden and Purcell 2000, 366; 2005 and 2006.
[73] Hohlfelder and Vann 2000, 126–35.
[74] Kreutz 1988.
[75] Harris 2005, 10–19 and Alston 2008, 4, citing Horden and Purcell 2000, 89–122.
[76] Pleket 2008, 183.

example, would have been more reliably served than the more isolated centres.[77]

Another 'economic activity' of islanders related to connectivity was piracy, a practice which was considered by some ancient writers to have been just as valid as trade.[78] Several new studies have discussed the nature of piracy in the Mediterranean and, particularly, whether or not Athens was able to keep it in check during her periods of hegemony.[79] Some ancient states eventually became synonymous with this kind of activity, most notably Skyros (suppressed by Kimon in 476)[80] and communities in Kilikia, Pamphylia, and Crete during the Hellenistic and Roman periods. Although the Pamphylian cities were situated along important trade routes, they were apparently not often used as stopovers by merchant shipping.[81] However, none of the islands of the Cyclades developed similar reputations as dens of piracy. What may have been the case in the late sixth century, however, is that Cycladic warships (whether in private hands or operated as public vessels) may have been able to exercise some control over sea lanes in the areas around their home islands.

Most scholars have opined that during the Delian League of the fifth century, the Aegean was relatively free of piratical depredations, due to the strength and regular patrolling of the Athenian navy, while the fourth century was a time when Athenian efforts in this area were not so effective.[82] Of course, the presence of predators indicates the presence of prey, so that it would be misleading to suppose that a high level of piracy alone would have been enough to bring commerce to a standstill.[83] However, *leisteia* may refer more generally to a 'raid mentality,' one that was practised by many states at various times in

[77] Erdkamp 2005, 146–7 and 195.

[78] Arist. *Pol.* 1291b 24; Scott 2000, 99. Ormerod 1924 and Ziebarth 1929 are fundamental discussions.

[79] DeSouza 1999; McKechnie 1989, 101–41; Garlan 1989, 173–201; Jackson 1973, 241–53.

[80] Thuc. 1.98; Plut. *Vit.Cim.* 8.4–5.

[81] Rauh, Townsend, Hoff, and Wandsnider 2000, 152.

[82] De Souza 1999, 28–30 is the exception who claims that even in the fifth century, Athens was largely ineffective in controlling piracy. For the Hellenistic period, an interesting point is made by R. Etienne that since honorific decrees were voted whenever an individual contributed for the ransoming of captives, but never when ships arrived safely, piracy itself is overrepresented in the sources: see his response to Ducrey 1983, 148.

[83] Horden and Purcell 2000, 157.

antiquity.[84] Classical Athens was one of the first to 'nationalize' this phenomenon and turn it into a sort of commodity, a 'protection market'. Under this scheme, the *appearance* of guarding against piracy was more important for a state like Athens than actually achieving success in stopping it—indeed, to suppress it completely would have been detrimental.[85] Hegemons could receive protection money from merchants, and also could benefit from carrying out anti-piratical raids.[86]

It will now be necessary to establish the geographic parameters of the region and the nature of the evidence that will be used to evaluate economic conditions in the Cyclades.

[84] Gabrielsen 2001, 223–4.

[85] Gabrielsen 2001, 226, 232. A similar analysis, in more general terms, is given by Garlan 1989, 194: 'la piraterie a donc joué un rôle complexe et ambigu dans la vie économique des pays méditerranéens: à la fois négatif et positif, d'entrave et de stimulant, selon la nature des modes d'exploitation pratiqués par les différents communautés.' Garlan, however, goes on to repeat the old distinction that Gabrielsen has tried to correct, that an anti-piratical attitude was a more economically 'evolved' one.

[86] Gabrielsen 2001, 235–7. An example from the Hellenistic period is a Rhodian treaty with Hierapytna on Crete *c.*203 (*Syll.*[3] 581).

2

Defining the Cycladic Region

Before beginning an analysis of the Cyclades during various periods of Classical Greek history, it will be important to give a geographical description of the region, and also outline the nature of the evidence that will be used. This chapter will describe the criteria for selecting the islands detailed herein, as well as evidence for trade routes and navigation. Such topics as population and carrying capacity of the islands in the Cyclades, including the evidence from survey archaeology, are also included. Finally, an overview of the sources utilized in the study will address issues of methodology.

The Cyclades are an *archipel*, or sub-region, within the Aegean.[1] There was no strict agreement, even in antiquity, which islands were included in the 'Cyclades'.[2] We possess three separate lists from four authorities and three geographical treatises: Pseudo-Skylax, Strabo, Artemidoros (quoted in Strabo 10.5.3 C485), and the elder Pliny.[3] Despite their differences, all these authors include the following ten islands in the Cyclades: Andros, Keos (modern Kea), Kythnos, Mykonos, Naxos, Paros, Seriphos, Siphnos, Syros, and Tenos.[4] All were Ionian communities, although the Kythnians were unique in having a mixed Ionian and Dryopian population.[5] Epigraphic evidence also

[1] The term is from Brun 1996, 7; cf. Constantakopoulou 2007, 176.

[2] Counillon 2001.

[3] Strabo 10.5.3 C485; Pliny *NH* 4.12.65–67; [Skylax] 48 mentions the Dorian islands opposite Lakedaimon (Melos, Kimolos, Oliaros, Sikinos, Thera, Anaphe, and Astypalaia) and 58 lists the Ionian islands of Delos, Rheneia, Keos, Kythnos, Seriphos, Siphnos, Paros, Naxos, Syros, Mykonos, Andros, and Tenos.

[4] To these, only Artemidoros adds Gyaros, and only Pliny and [Skylax] add Rheneia. Delos is also included, but as will be described below will be considered as separate in this work.

[5] Hdt. 8.46.

supports this grouping. All ten are listed as part of the 'Insular District' on the *aparkhē* lists of the fifth-century Delian League.[6] Most were listed as members of the Second Athenian League in the fourth century (except for Seriphos, Syros, and Naxos, although we will see that there is reason to think that all three were in fact members).[7] Finally, all but one (Kythnos) are extant in the fourth-century loan accounts of the Delian temple of Apollo.[8] However, there are two other islands in the region that display similar characteristics to these ten in terms of their relationships with Athens in the Classical period, and so will be considered along with the ten listed above. Amorgos (an island with three *poleis*—Arkesine, Minoa, and Aigiale), was also listed in the Cyclades by Stephanos of Byzantion.[9] Its cities were grouped as a *synteleia* for the payment of tribute in the Delian League (but included in the Karian District rather than the Insular); and joined the Second Athenian League collectively as well (as 'Amorgians' rather than listed separately as the cities of Keos). They were not listed in the loan accounts of Delian Apollo, however. The island of Ios was in the Insular District, the Second Athenian League, and also contracted loans on Delos. We will thus also take Amorgos and Ios into consideration.

The Cyclades were so named because of their location in a circular pattern around the sacred island of Delos. Delos is a rocky island less than four miles long, yet it has been estimated that fully seventy per cent of it was cultivated in antiquity.[10] Although Delos shared many aspects of the Cycladic paradigm in terms of its position on trade routes and its harbor, it occupied a unique place in the region. Its sanctuary of Apollo made it a religious (and in some ways financial) centre for the Cyclades, and its festival of Apollo provided a major focus for Ionian Greeks.[11] Cycladic connections with the Ionian cult of Apollo on Delos can be traced from the Archaic through the Hellenistic periods.[12] The *Homeric Hymn to Apollo* speaks of the Cyclades as sending dancing girls to the festival called the Delia.[13]

[6] See Chapter 4, pp. 93–5, 119, 121–3 and Table 4.1.
[7] See Chapter 5, pp. 158–9.
[8] See Chapter 5, pp. 170–3 and Table 5.1.
[9] Steph. Byz. *s.v. Amorgos*.
[10] Brunet 1990 and 1999; Reger 1994*a*, 95; Vial 1984, 283–383.
[11] Constantakopoulou 2007, 38–58; Jockey 1996; Gallet de Santerre 1958; Laidlaw 1939.
[12] Thuc. 3.104.6 on the Cyclades as *periktiones* around Delos.
[13] Chankowski 2008, 202–24; Talamo 1996, 241.

Little is known, however, about the actual *polis* of the Delians as distinct from the sanctuary. The Athenians brought the sanctuary under their control at various times in the fifth and fourth centuries, and their treatment of the Delians often provoked hostility. On no other Cycladic island did the Athenians establish such an intrusive presence during the Classical period, even counting the few decades of the fifth century when Athenian klerouchs were placed on Andros and Naxos. As such, it must be considered as separate from our chosen islands for the purposes of this study, although at various points it will appear in the discussion, often by way of contrast with the islands surrounding it.

Of course, any schema for selecting the constituent islands of the Cyclades will be an imperfect one. Attempts to define the Cycladic region must be wary of over-generalization, and also of being overly-restrictive. This situation has been noted by much recent scholarship in insular studies, both Mediterranean and otherwise. It has been asserted that all boundaries denoting groups of islands become 'a fuzzy analytical set' over time,[14] and that island groupings are often shaped by human perception of their geography.[15] Therefore any grouping of islands for analytical purposes is by its very nature subjective.

Melos, for example, is included in some lists of the Cyclades, and many geographical conditions that applied to other islands in the area also applied to it. Yet Melos was a Dorian state, and its inhabitants followed a different historical trajectory. Another example is Nisyros. This island was considered one of the Cyclades by Stephanos of Byzantion, but part of Karia by Pseudo-Skylax.[16] Nisyros was a member of the Delian League, but originally paid tribute along with the Ionian district and only later was included in the accounts for the Insular district.[17] In 394, it was removed from Spartan control at the same time as many of the Cycladic states,[18] yet it is unclear whether it joined the Second Athenian League.

Therefore, the following islands and *poleis* will be the focus of this study:[19]

[14] Broodbank 2000, 263–5. [15] Rainbird 2007, 44–5.

[16] Steph. Byz. *s.v. Nisyros*; [Skylax] 99.

[17] Reger 2004, 763–4.

[18] Diod. 14.83.3.

[19] The following discussion of these Cycladic communities owes much to Sheedy 2006 and Reger 2004.

Amorgos—this was listed by one ancient author as one of the southern Cyclades, and possessed three *poleis* that often cooperated in their dealings with the greater Greek world: *Aigiale* on the eastern side of the island, *Arkesine* on the western side, and *Minoa* just east of Arkesine.[20] These cities issued bronze coinage with a collective ethnic; were grouped together for the payment of tribute in the Delian League (included in the Karian District rather than the Insular, however); and joined the Second Athenian League collectively as well (as 'Amorgians' rather than listed separately as the cities of Keos). Epigraphic evidence indicates that Arkesine had a democratic government in the fifth and fourth centuries, but not much is known of systems in the other two communities.[21]

Andros—this is the northernmost of the Cyclades and the closest to Euboia (which is 6 miles to the north-west). The *polis* of the Andrians was at Palaiopolis, on the southwestern coast near the ancient harbour, and its late Classical fortification walls are well-preserved.[22] Although the Andrians changed their political system several times during the fifth century, an inscription from 357/6 indicates that they had a democracy during that period.[23]

Ios—this island is also on the southern side of the region, approximately halfway between Naxos and Thera. The ancient *polis* was on the northern end at Plakotos (under the modern settlement), and part of the Classical fortifications can still be seen. Ios was included in the Insular District and also appears in the Delian loan accounts. It is not restored on the prospectus of the Second League, but has been proposed as one of the missing names. The epigraphic evidence from the island indicates that its *polis* was a democracy in the fourth century.[24]

Keos (modern Kea)—this island is the closest of all of the Cyclades to the Greek mainland in general and Athens in particular. Athenian influence, one of the main aspects of this study, may have played a major role in shaping the economy of this island in antiquity.[25] Keos

[20] Steph. Byz. *s.v. Amorgos*; Reger 2004, 734–5.

[21] A *boule* and *demos* is attested at Arkesine (*IG* XII.7 1.1 [fifth century] and 2.1 [fourth century]).

[22] Most likely of the fourth century: Reger 2004, 736.

[23] *IG* II^2 123 line 9; Reger 2004, 736.

[24] *IG* XII.5, 1001–1004 for collected decrees; Reger 2004, 743.

[25] Cherry, Davis, and Mantzourani 1991*a*, 5; Sheedy 2006, 21.

had iron mines,[26] and also produced the valuable mineral known as ruddle or *miltos*, which seems to have had a variety of applications.[27] In addition to *miltos*, the island of Keos also was renowned for its wine.[28]

Keos is also unique for our study because it possessed no less than four *poleis* during the Archaic and Classical periods, three of which (Karthaia, Koressos, and Poiessa) were coastal communities. The fourth, Ioulis, was inland. Geographical factors, particularly access to water, probably helped create this dispersed political situation.[29] At certain times in the fifth and fourth centuries, all of these cities except for Poiessa formed a Keian federation.

Karthaia is on the south-east coast, and possessed a good harbour (artificially enhanced with a breakwater) that was well-poised to link the Saronic Gulf with the Cyclades.[30] Although not as fine as the port of Koressos, it has been recently proposed that it was the main commercial node of Keos during the Archaic and Classical periods.[31] This may have changed, however, with the fourth century and the Athenian regulations for the export of *miltos*. Its territory has been estimated at 20.5 square miles (33 km^2).[32]

Koressos was on the north-west coast, and commanded not only the best harbour on the island but also a fertile area near the Elixos River. The site, which occupied a ridge above the bay, has been surveyed, as has the entire north-west of the island in what still amounts to the most extensive such project yet undertaken in the islands of our study (the only other comparable survey in the region has been of Melos).[33] One survey concluded that this *polis* covered 9.3 square miles (15 km^2) and may have boasted up to 1,200 inhabitants in the Classical period.[34]

[26] Mendoni 1985, 181 theorizes that they had been largely exhausted by the fourth century, however.

[27] Photos-Jones, Cottiers, Hall, and Mendoni, 1997. See Chapter 6, pp. 192–4 for full discussion.

[28] Bacchyl. *Od.* 6 and 7; Sheedy 2006, 33.

[29] Sheedy 2006, 22; Reger 1997, 479; Georgiou and Faraklas 1985, 220–1.

[30] Mendoni and Mourtzas 1990, 387–8.

[31] Sheedy 2006, 23.

[32] Mendoni 1994, 150.

[33] Cherry, Davis, and Mantzourani 1991*b*; Whitelaw and Davis 1991; Whitelaw 1998. For Melos: Renfrew and Wagstaff 1982.

[34] Whitelaw 1991, 237; Whitelaw and Davis 1991, 279–80; Sheedy 2006, 28–9.

Ioulis was inland on a plateau, but is attested as having a harbour, of uncertain location. Two modern candidates for the site have been proposed, either at Otzia, or further to the east at Kastri.[35] The site has not seen excavation although the town walls have been studied, and most scholars have pronounced them to be Hellenistic, though this has not been unanimous.[36] Its size is unknown but may have been slightly larger than that of Karthaia.[37] During the Hellenistic period, the city merged with Koressos, which led to the eventual disappearance of the latter.[38]

Poiessa is the most enigmatic of all the Keian *poleis*. Throughout Keian history, the three other cities acted as a unit in many cases, in the form of federations, syntelies for tribute payment, and so forth. But Poiessa seems to have (almost) always followed its own path historically. The territory of Poiessa has been estimated at 12.4 square miles (20 km^2).[39]

Kythnos—this island is located at the entrance of the Saronic Gulf, with the ancient *polis* on the north-west coast. It appears to have been a large settlement due to its extensive fortification walls that may date to the fourth century. However, apart from a single survey, little archaeological investigation has been done.[40] Kythnos did have iron mines that were worked from at least the fifth century.[41]

Naxos—this island is central to the region and is also the largest, at 266 square miles or 428 km^2, and was considered very fertile in antiquity.[42] The harbour was located on the north-west coast and was eventually protected by an artificial breakwater.[43] Naxos had extensive mineral resources in addition to her agricultural productivity. From the seventh century, a distinctive Naxian marble with fine granular crystals was quarried and used to make statues dedicated at such locales as Delos, Sounion, Delphi, and Thasos.[44] Numerous

[35] For Otzia: Merker 1968. For Kastri: Georgiou and Faraklas 1993, 42–3; Sheedy 2006, 27.

[36] For a Hellenistic date: Maier 1958, 6–7 and 1959, 160–2; Georgiou and Faraklas 1993. Sheedy 2006, 27, however, posits that more research must be done before the walls can be firmly dated.

[37] Mendoni 1994, 152; Cherry, Davis, and Mantzourani 1991*b*, 237.

[38] Strabo 10.5.6 C486–487.

[39] Mendoni 1994, 150.

[40] Mazarakis-Ainian 1998.

[41] Brun 1996, 130 and n.55.

[42] Hdt. 5.31; Pliny *N.H.* 4.12.67.

[43] Bent 1885, 337.

[44] Reger 2004, 763; Brun 1997, 407–8; Amandry 1953; Kokkorou-Alevras 1992 and 2000; Fuchs and Floren 1987, 151 and 161; Costa 1997, 131–45; Constantakopoulou 2007, 44–6. It is intriguing, however, that no ancient source actually mentions Naxian

finds on Delos that are associated with Naxians (such as the Nikander dedication, the Lions of the Terrace, and the Oikos of the Naxians), may indicate a high level of influence of Naxians in Delian affairs during the Archaic period.[45] In addition to marble, Naxos was known for its almonds, wine, emery, and iron.[46] A local historian named Aglaosthenes made the claim that the Naxians minted the earliest coins in Greece.[47]

Naxos will figure predominantly in our study, not just as a regional power in the late Archaic period but also because of its often turbulent relationship with Athens in the Classical period. The island famously attempted to secede from the Delian League sometime in the 470s.[48] The government of the Naxians is not well-attested, although a late fourth-century decree indicates some form of democracy in action.[49]

Paros—this island is also central in the region and is the third largest (121 square miles or 194.5 km^2), and although many areas are barren it possesses fertile valleys. Its harbour at Naoussa on the north-eastern side is especially well-suited to shipping, and there are other anchorages on the island as well.[50] Paros, like Naxos, was rich in marble, but of a much finer quality than the Naxian variety. Parian marble began to be used on a wide scale for sculpture and architectural elements throughout the Greek world by the early fifth century, largely replacing Naxian. Its use has been identified on Delos, as well as Delphi, Olympia, and Athens.[51] Greek cities in Sicily and southern Italy also became markets for Parian marble by the early fifth century.

marble: Renfrew and Peacey 1968, 60. Unfinished *kouroi* can be seen at Flerio and Apollonas: Ekshmitt 1993, 201–2. See also Chapter 3, pp. 60–1.

[45] Pedley 1976, 18–37. There may be phases of construction of the Oikos of the Naxians which date as far back as the eighth to seventh centuries, however: Lambrinoudakis 2005, 85–6; Constantakopoulou 2007, 43–4 and n.42.

[46] Almonds and wine: Eupolis *Taxiarkhoi* fr.253 (= *PCG* vol.V, 460 #27); Phrynikhos fr.68 (= *PCG* vol.VII, 424 #73). Iron: Davies 1935, 264. Marble and emery: Herbst 1935, 2079.

[47] Aglaosthenes *FGrH* 499 F7.

[48] Thuc. 1.98.4. See Chapter 4, pp. 89–91.

[49] *SEG* XXXIII. 676.5–6, line 10; Reger 2004, 762.

[50] Heikell 1992, 252–8; Sheedy 2006, 115.

[51] Pliny *N.H.* 36.14 on its quality; Kokkorou-Alevras 2000; Gruben 2000, 126; Herrmann 2000; Fuchs and Floren 1987, 160–72. Tomlinson 2000, 141, theorizes that the Alkmaionidai chose Parian marble for rebuilding the temple of Apollo at Delphi not just because of its quality, but as a political statement, in opposition to the Peisistratid-Lygdamis axis. Neer 2004 proposes that Parian marble was chosen for

Selinos is a prime example, where Parian marble has been identified in sarcophagi and architectural contexts.[52] It should be noted, however, that it is not always easy to distinguish between Parian and Naxian marble, and one scholar has proposed that the term 'lychnites' may have been used interchangeably by ancient authors for marble from either island, in the same manner that modern scholars have used the term 'insular marble'.[53] Even if true, this usage still shows how lucrative the trade in Cycladic marble was during this period. Although many pieces may have been finished in quarries as on Naxos,[54] there are several Parian sculptors, such as Agorakritos in the fifth century and Skopas in the fourth,[55] who were recorded as having travelled to various locales to complete projects.[56]

According to Ephoros, Paros in the early fifth century was 'the most prosperous and greatest of the Cyclades'.[57] The Parians were assessed at up to 18 talents of tribute, one of the highest amounts for the Insular rubric. There is little evidence for governmental structure in the Classical period, it is generally assumed that the Parians had a democracy by the mid-fourth century.[58]

Seriphos—this island is included in the Cyclades by Strabo, although Stephanos of Byzantion places it in the Sporades.[59] Seriphos has little arable land and one harbour, at Livadhi. The location of the *polis* is unclear but probably overlooked this harbour.[60] Little else is known about the island archaeologically, and there are few references in the ancient authors to conditions on the island. Although agriculture is reported on a small scale at certain times in the island's history,[61] it probably possessed fewer resources in antiquity than others in the Cyclades. Yet, it was still able to send a pentekonter to

the Athenian treasury at Delphi to celebrate the victory at Marathon while at the same time denigrating the memory of Miltiades and his failed attack on Paros.

52 Gorgoni and Pallante 2000, 504.

53 Brun 1997.

54 Belli Pasqua 2010, 192.

55 Agorakritos: Stewart 1990, 165 and 269–71; Skopas: Stewart 1977 and 1990, 184–7.

56 Rocco 2010, 161–2; Ohnesorg 2005, 145–8. To Athens: Benson 2000; to Delphi: Partida 2000; to Delos: Berranger 1992, 269 and 271 and *IG* XII.5, 216 (*c*.520).

57 Ephoros *FGrH* 70 F63.

58 Reger 2004, 765.

59 Strabo 10.5.3 C485; Steph. Byz. *s.v. Seriphos*; Reger 2004, 771.

60 Phillippson 1959, 74–6; Bürchner 1923, 1730–1731; Sheedy 2006, 46–7.

61 Liata 1987, 160–8; Sheedy 2006, 47.

the Battle of Salamis.[62] One possible resource on Seriphos was iron ore, although it is unclear whether it was mined in ancient times.[63]

Seriphos became the paradigm for Athenian and even later writers of a destitute and insignificant *polis*.[64] It has been convincingly argued, however, that this judgement derived primarily from its status as an island, and islands by the late fifth century had become synonymous in the Athenian mind with subjection, whatever their level of prosperity.[65] Seriphos was assessed in the Insular District but does not appear in the prospectus of the Second League, though their membership was likely.[66]

Siphnos—this island links the aforementioned western Cyclades to the more central area of the region. The *polis* was located on the eastern side of the island, on a plateau above the coast.[67] This island did not set up dedications at Delos, even though it was an Ionian community. Instead, the Archaic period saw the Siphnians constructing their famous treasury at Delphi.[68] The source of this wealth was silver and gold mines that made them, in the words of Herodotus, the 'richest of the islanders' during the Archaic period.[69] At some indeterminate date, these mines became unproductive. Pausanias states that they were flooded by the sea when the Siphnians ceased to send a tithe to Delphi.[70] Surveys have uncovered evidence that five sites on

[62] Hdt. 8.48. See Chapter 3, p. 76.

[63] Brun 1996, 128 and n.43; Graindor 1903; Freeman 1963, 214; Sheedy 2006, 47.

[64] Ar. *Ach.* 542 compares the Megarian Decrees to the theft of a Seriphian puppy; the original story of Themistokles' denigration of the island of Belbina in Hdt. 8.125 was later altered to Seriphos in Pl. *Resp.* 329e and other sources (including Plut. *Vit.Them.* 18.2–5). See also Plut. *Mor.* 602a–b on Seriphos as a place of banishment. There was also a comedy entitled *The Seriphians* by Kratinos but it is known only from fragments: Constantakopoulou 2007, 105; Brun 1993*a*, 169.

[65] Constantakopoulou 2007, 106 sees the linkage of insularity with subjection as early as the Belbina anecdote in Herodotus, *pace* Brun 1993*a*, 81 and 1998, 658 who proposes that the linkage does not appear until the fourth century in Plato and Isokrates. Constantakopoulou is more likely to be correct since Herodotus wrote when the Athenian *arkhē* was at its height. A similar characterization of Crete appears in Pind. *Ol.* 12, a victory ode for Ergoteles of Knossos: Erickson 2005, 620.

[66] Reger 2004, 772; Cargill 1981, 37; a dissenting voice is Dreher 1995, 245–7.

[67] Sheedy 2006, 51–2.

[68] Daux and Hansen 1987; Neer 2003 on the treasury as a reflection of Siphnian political struggles; Scott 2010, 11–12, 37–9, and 63–6 qualifies Neer's thesis by emphasizing the situation of the treasury in the broader context of Delphic sacred space.

[69] Hdt. 3.57. [70] Paus. 10.11.2.

the island were mined for silver and lead, whereas three south-eastern sites contained gold deposits. One of the first five, the site of Ayios Sostis, is submerged today and might fit the later reports of flooding, but most of the sites are actually inland.[71] Based on identification of pottery sherds and thermo-luminescence studies, it would appear that the high point of exploitation of these mines was the late Archaic period.[72] Nevertheless, Siphnos may still have been producing some gold and silver from its mines in the fifth century.[73] The city also constructed extensive fortifications in the late Archaic period, or perhaps slightly later.[74] As with Naxos and Paros, their government shifted between oligarchy and democracy during the Classical period but democracy is attested in the mid-fourth century.[75]

Syros—the modern port of Ermoupoli covers the ancient site. Despite having one of the finest harbours in the Cyclades, very little is known of Syros during the Archaic and Classical periods. There is a possible reference to the island in Homer, but this is not accepted by all scholars.[76] The site of Galessas on the western coast of the island, however, was active throughout the period covered by our study.[77] The island does not appear in the prospectus for the Second Athenian League, although there is reason to believe that Syros was in fact a member.[78]

Tenos—this mountainous isle is the fourth largest in the Cyclades (194 km^2) and is in the northern part of the region.[79] The original *polis* was located inland at Xombourgo, and during the Archaic period, Tenos appears to have been relatively isolated from the wider Aegean world, perhaps a result of this inland setting.[80] However, after its destruction in the fourth century by Alexander of Pherai,

[71] Wagner and Weisgerber 1979 and 1985; Gale 1979, 36–49; Sheedy 2006, 52.

[72] Wagner, Gentner, Gropengiesser, and Gale 1980, 25–9.

[73] Hdt. 3.57–58. For mines on Siphnos: Phillippson 1959, 78; Brun 1996, 128 and n.47.

[74] Brock and Mackworth Young 1949, 2 posited the late sixth century, followed by Sheedy 2006, 55–6; Brun 2000 favours a late Classical–early Hellenistic date.

[75] Woodhead 1997, #50 lines 9–10 (= *SEG* XVII.19); Reger 2004, 773.

[76] Hom. *Od.* 15.403–14, dismissed by Reger 2004, 775.

[77] Papadopoulos and Smithson 2002, 181 and n.123 propose that the island's importance in antiquity transcends the lack of surviving evidence.

[78] See Chapter 5, p. 159 and n.130.

[79] Étienne 1990, 12–15.

[80] Sheedy 2006, 74.

the Tenians moved to a site on the southern coast and seem to have prospered over the following decades.[81]

TRADE ROUTES THROUGH THE CYCLADES IN ANTIQUITY

The prime sailing season in the Aegean in antiquity ran from May to September.[82] This did not preclude some variation, since shifting wind patterns (including the Etesian winds) could block voyages during the open season and, on occasion, favourable conditions could briefly open up in winter.[83] Such conditions could vary on a daily basis and so travel in the Cyclades was very contingent upon them, and could be potentially dangerous.[84] As examples, the strait between Andros and Euboia, as well as that between Andros and Tenos, could be impassable at certain times due to powerful winds and/or currents.[85]

Yet the seasons did not affect ancient sea travel to the extreme sometimes posited by modern commentators.[86] There is evidence that a certain level of sailing activity persisted throughout the year in the Mediterranean.[87]

Travel was closely tied to various forms of social and economic activity, including the procurement by ship's crews of food, water, and other supplies. An anecdote in Plutarch describes one Dexekreon of Samos, who brought water to vessels plying the waters between Samos and Cyprus.[88] This would suggest that certain islanders in the Cyclades could have developed expertise in seafaring in their home region.[89] Some studies have proposed the opposite and stressed instead that Cycladic populations were more insular and focused on

[81] Étienne 1990, 15–24; Reger 2004, 778. See Chapter 6, pp. 218–24.

[82] Casson 1971, 270–92; Agouridis 1997; Broodbank 2000, 92.

[83] Agouridis 1997, 5–6.

[84] Broodbank 2000, 93–4. This can still be seen in the modern parallel of occasionally-spotty ferry service among the islands.

[85] Constantakopoulou 2007, 25 and n.130; Morton 2001, 38–41 and 90–1.

[86] Pryor 1988, 89.

[87] Horden and Purcell 2000, 143; Abulafia 1990, 132–3 citing 14th-century *ancoratge* documents from Catalan Majorca.

[88] Plut. *Mor.* 303c.

[89] Broodbank 2000, 94; Barber 1987, 18.

their highlands.[90] Yet it is clear that from the early second millennium onward, the Cyclades were part of trade networks that alternately intensified and abated during certain periods.[91] An important trade route is attested in various Classical sources from the Levant and Egypt, past Phaselis, Cyprus, Rhodes, Knidos, Naxos, and Paros, and thence to Athens (see Figure 2.1).[92]

This route was extremely ancient and appears to have been followed by Phoenician traders as far back as the eighth century,[93] and continued to be used throughout antiquity.[94] Some have proposed that a passage in the *Odyssey* mentions the Cycladic island of Syros as a place often visited by Phoenician merchants.[95] Another reference that may point to early Cycladic trade routes comes from Herodotus, in his description of the procession of offerings to Delian Apollo from the land of the Hyperboreans. These offerings are said to have travelled from Dodona, past the Malian Gulf, to Karystos on Euboia, and then to Andros, Tenos, and finally to Delos.[96]

An anonymous work from the Roman Imperial period, entitled the *Stadiasmus Maris Magni*, lists nodes of three major trade itineraries through the Aegean: (*a*) Kos–Kalymnos–Leros–Patmos–Mykonos–Tenos; (*b*) Kos–Leros–Kinaros–Amorgos–Naxos–Delos; and (*c*) Amorgos–Naxos–Kythnos, which then led to the entrance of the Saronic Gulf and the Peiraeus (see Figure 2.2).

This is a problematic source in many ways. It is generally dated to approximately AD 200, although this is not certain, and gives considerably greater detail to the North African coast than it does to the Aegean. But the information it gives on Cycladic routes is in agreement with what we find in other sources. There is also evidence of

[90] Getz-Preziosi 1987, 5.

[91] Broodbank 2000 on the Bronze Age.

[92] Thuc. 2.69, 8.35; [Dem.] 56.9; Lycurg. *Leoc.* 1.18; [Skylax] 15.34. For Pseudo-Skylax now see Shipley 2011; Flensted-Jensen and Hansen 1996. The route would have been easier for ships heading westward, however, due to trade winds and currents, especially those leaving Egypt and the Levant (see below).

[93] Markoe 2000, 173, based on finds of eastern Mediterranean imports; Sherratt and Sherratt 1993, 367.

[94] Reger 1994*a*, 20–1 and n.12. Erickson 2005, 625–6 discusses a similar geographic significance of Crete for Phoenician traders, and proposes that Cretans took the opportunity to sell local products to these merchants.

[95] Hom. *Od.* 15.415–16; Papadopoulos and Smithson 2002, 182, but dismissed by Reger 2004, 775.

[96] Hdt. 4.33.

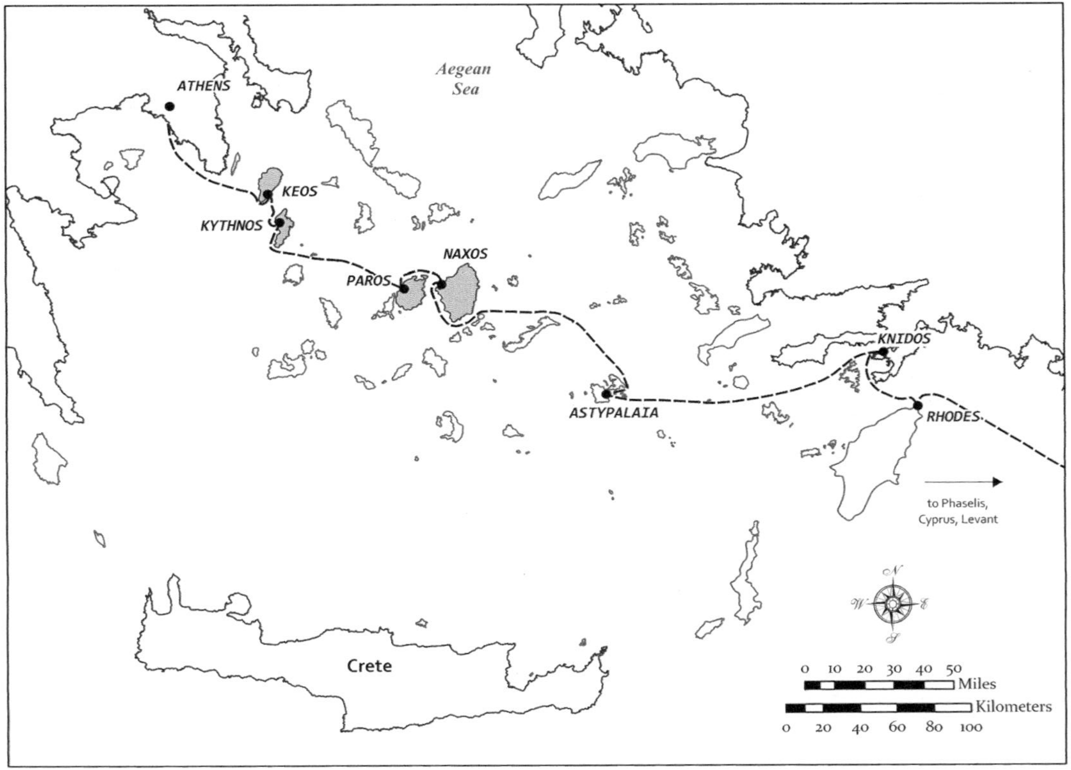

Fig. 2.1. Trade Routes through the Cyclades Attested In Various Classical Sources

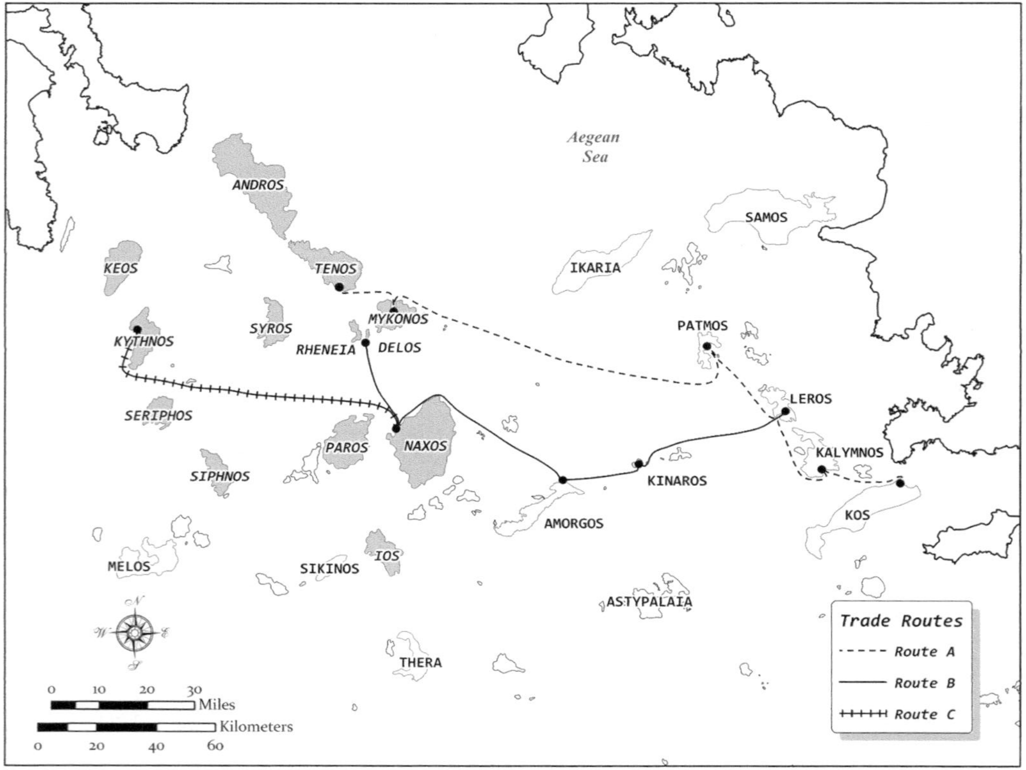

Fig. 2.2. Trade Routes Attested in the *Stadiasmus Maris Magni*

Genoese merchant shipping using these same approximate routes in the Middle Ages, traversing the Aegean on two main paths from Khios: one past Andros and Karystos on Euboia, the other past Naxos and Siphnos.[97]

Thucydides mentions the importance of Kythera (off the south-east coast of the Peloponnese) in linking the Greek mainland with Crete and Egypt.[98] Ships that took this route would have followed prevailing winds (from the north-west during the summer) and currents to return home to the Greek mainland by way of a counter-clockwise route, from Rhodes past Amorgos, Ios, and Melos.[99] Many of these well-travelled routes could have exercised a sort of 'gravitational pull' on shipping that carried products other than grain.[100]

Several Cycladic *poleis* were not just well-oriented towards the centre of the region at Delos, but were also easy stopover points for ships following these routes.[101] It is interesting that Naxos figures as a central node on these itineraries in virtually all periods.[102] Syros is a bit of an enigma, since it is centrally located among the Cyclades and possesses a fine harbour, but is not attested in a great deal of evidence from the Classical period.[103] The importance of certain routes may have waxed and waned under the influence of outside political forces such as Athens. Athenian influence was not limited to the Cyclades but also to many islands elsewhere in the Aegean. For example, a few of the Sporades to the north, such as Peparethos and Skiathos, were

[97] *Stad.Mar.Mag.* 280–2(= Muller 1855, 499–500 with commentary on cxxiii–cxxviii); Bunbury 1883, 665–7 and 672–4; Brun 1996, 140–3. A new translation and commentary is now being prepared by James Ermatinger.

[98] Thuc. 4.53.3.

[99] Balard 1974; Erickson 2010, 284; Fulford 1989, 169–72; Horden and Purcell 2000, 137–43 for a more general discussion of such factors throughout the Mediterranean.

[100] Horden and Purcell 2000, 138–9; Pryor 1988, 91 and 97.

[101] Talbert 2000, 57.

[102] The excellence of Naxos' harbor, Panormos, is mentioned in *Stad.Mar.Mag.* 280–2. There is a reference to a type of merchant vessel known as a *Naxiourgeis* in Ar. *Pax* 143 and schol.; this appears analogous to other location-specific ship names such as *Knidiourgies*, *Kerkyros*, and *Paron*; see Brun 1996, 138; Vélissaropoulos 1980, 61. Andok. 3.9 and Aiskh. 2.175 both mention Naxos as a key Athenian possession in the fifth century, along with Euboia and the Khersonese.

[103] Although Brun 1996, 165–6 points out that Syros discharged her debts to Delian Apollo in the fourth century.

linked to the trade route between Athens and the Hellespont.[104] Yet, except perhaps for Andros, the Cyclades may not have been particularly important for north–south trade from the Hellespont.[105]

Distance has never been much of a factor inhibiting trade in the region, and the Cyclades have always been quite different in this way from other island groups around the globe such as in the Pacific Ocean. There, areas such as Micronesia and the Cook Islands contain many islands more than 2000 km from their nearest neighbours, an isolation that even modern air transport has not fully eradicated.[106] There are certain concepts from insular studies, known as 'effective distance' and the Law of Monotonic Decrement, that are related to this issue. 'Effective distance' refers to all the variables involved in getting to a certain destination by sea (which is different from 'direct distance'). The Law of Monotonic Decrement states that 'frequency of materials from a particular source decreases in a regular, monotonic fashion with increasing distance from the source'.[107] These would only apply to the Cyclades on a limited scale, however, with weather variation constituting the main obstacle to shipping.

One study of the Cyclades in the Neolithic and Bronze Ages has compared the Mediterranean islands geographically to those in the Caribbean and to south-west Oceania in the Pacific, with Melanesia corresponding in some ways to the Aegean.[108] All are archipelagos centrally located between mainland regions, and have a mixture of island sizes. Yet, the inter-visibility between Mediterranean islands and the consequent multiplicity of possible trade and communications links between them makes them unique in comparison to these other island regions of the world.[109] Studies of obsidian trade from the Lipari Islands in the Neolithic period, for example, have demonstrated that many different routes could be used to ship goods from islands to the mainland, not just the most 'direct' route.[110] This is the very pattern that emerges from late medieval Genoese *portolans* for the Cyclades (such as that of Gratiosus Benincasa). These maps detail

[104] Rutishauser 2007.
[105] Etienne 1990, 217–19; Bruneau and Ducat 1983, 97–8; Reger 1994*a*, 21.
[106] Hoyle 1999, 150–2; Evans 1977, 12–13.
[107] Renfrew 1977, 72; Gould 2000, 150–1 (quoted).
[108] Broodbank 2000, 38; Knapp 1990; Brotherston 1992, 10.
[109] Broodbank 2000, 40–1; Braudel 1972, 148–60; Evans 1977, 13–15.
[110] Gould 2000, 150–1, citing Ammermann, Matessi, and Cavalli-Sforza 1978, 191–2.

harbours and coastlines and indicate what has been called with only some exaggeration 'infinitely diverse routes' through this archipelago.[111] An understanding of the history of the Cyclades involves recognition of individual island trajectories, but also of the outside influences that affected them.

MODELS FOR REGIONAL DEVELOPMENT IN THE CYCLADES

A variety of models have been proposed for the development of connections between states within ancient civilizations. The theory of 'peer-polity interaction' has been advocated in some insular studies.[112] Such interaction is defined as the full range of competitive activities, including but not limited to warfare, imitation, and economic exchange, engaged in by autonomous socio-political units (such as early Greek *poleis*) within the same geographic region.[113] Under this system, a situation develops 'in which incentives, material or symbolic . . . intensify production to a degree where state organization became possible'.[114] Local exchanges and contacts are more meaningful than those with areas outside the region, with the result that the constituent states develop at a more or less equal rate.[115] As contacts by sea appear to have been easier and less costly than by land in antiquity, this model may be particularly suitable for maritime states such as the Cyclades, and the religious centrality of Delos has been proposed as an additional force promoting this type of interaction.[116]

Peer-polity interaction within the Cyclades may be especially applicable to the late Archaic period. Several of the islands built warships, minted coinage, and constructed monumental temples and fortification walls.[117] Many had local products, mineral or otherwise,

[111] Pryor 1988, 95 and 97 (quote). For the Genoese records see Motzo 1947, 48–56 and 123–6; Kretschmer 1909, 383–6. Broodbank 2000, 41 calls the Cyclades 'potential stepping-stones from everywhere to everywhere else'.

[112] Renfrew and Wagstaff 1982, 286–9.

[113] Renfrew and Cherry 1971.

[114] Renfrew and Wagstaff 1982, 286.

[115] Renfrew and Wagstaff 1982, 287.

[116] Constantakopoulou 2007, 257.

[117] See Chapter 3, *passim*.

that they exploited and exported. Under such conditions local rivalries would have enjoyed free rein, and it has been proposed that states are partially legitimized by the existence of other states of similar organization and ideology.[118] The model has been particularly applied to Melos, with the notion that state development there could not have occurred in isolation but only in a regional system.[119]

The primary difficulty with the model is that in a sense it 'flattens' the differences between states to a great degree.[120] And in the case of the Cyclades, there are notable differences in the trajectories of various islands in the region in the late Archaic period. Many (such as Naxos and Paros) were wealthy and appear in the literary sources and numismatic record as such; others, such as Andros and Tenos, do not give such indications of wealth. Moreover, it might not have applied to later periods of hegemony by Athens. One study of the cities of the Delian League has declared peer-polity interaction to be too problematic for this period and suggests the use of a different model, that of Early State Modules (ESMs).[121]

Early State Modules are conceived as autonomous political units grouped around central places. These central places tend to be separated by approximately 40 km, which incidentally corresponds to the average distance between the *poleis* of the Cyclades.[122] In archaeological investigations of the ancient Mediterranean world, they have been utilized for both Mycenaean palaces on the mainland and also Minoan centres on Crete.[123] Most ancient civilizations are comprised of about ten such ESMs before unification in an empire, and this also is very close to the number of islands in the Cyclades.[124]

The transition from ESMs to a single unified jurisdiction has been described as the shift from reciprocal trade to redistribution, and the creation of a higher-order central place that dominates the others.[125] The status of the temple of Apollo on Delos as a religious centre for the Cyclades could have provided a focus for peer-polity competition

[118] Renfrew and Wagstaff 1982, 289.
[119] Renfrew and Wagstaff 1982, 286–7.
[120] Cherry 1986, 24.
[121] Nixon and Price 1990, 165–6.
[122] Haggett, Cliff, and Frey 1977, 436–8.
[123] Mycenae: Renfrew 1975 and Hope Simpson and Dickinson 1979; Minoan Crete: Soetens, Sarris, and Vansteenhuyse 2002.
[124] Renfrew 1975, 13–14.
[125] Renfrew 1975, 19.

in the Archaic period, and later Athenian appropriation of the sanctuary in the fifth century could have ended such competition by replacing Delos with the Peiraeus as the new 'higher-order central place', though of course one of a very different nature and magnitude.[126]

Although useful, this analysis should not be pressed too far. In a statistical study of various civilizations that have been proposed as conforming to the ESM model, it has been demonstrated that many of the predictions of the model, including even spacing between the central places, the uniformity of size between the territories they control, and the increased complexity derived from their interaction, do not conform to reality.[127] Variations in the tribute paid by states are just one example of how the model could create a mistaken image of uniformity.[128]

Moreover, the relationship between the Cyclades and Athens during the fourth century may pose similar problems for this 'central-place' concept, since Athens was unable to achieve the same level of lasting political hegemony. And as we will see in Chapter 6, the second half of the fourth century may have actually seen a return of some aspects of peer-polity interaction, though it should be stressed that the model is not a perfect match for either period, and only some aspects are applicable.[129]

CYCLADIC POPULATION ESTIMATES

Most modern estimates of the population of Aegean islands in antiquity have been relatively low. An early study calculated population figures based on the equation of 1 talent paid in *phoros* as equivalent to 800 citizens and 3,200 inhabitants, and then compared the resulting totals with late nineteenth-century census records.[130] This gives such totals as 3,200 for Amorgos, 19,200 for Andros, and 21,330 for Naxos. These correspond to the numbers from 1889 in some cases,

[126] Constantakopoulou 2007, 257. [127] Fisher 1985.
[128] Nixon and Price 1990, 165 and n.49.
[129] See Chapter 6, *passim*.
[130] Ruschenbusch 1984.

but not in others.[131] A more recent work has criticized these figures as being too pessimistic, and cites the example of Boiotia as a region of Greece that appears to have been more densely populated in the fourth century BC than it was in the nineteenth AD.[132] Nevertheless, in a different study the same author has arrived at a similar figure for the population of the island of Aigina in the early fifth century as the earlier one he had computed for Andros and Naxos, around 20,000 inhabitants.[133]

Much of the pessimism regarding the ability of the Cyclades to support large populations derives from an image of poverty that was constructed as a literary *topos* in the Roman imperial period, when they were known as barren places of exile.[134] For some islands, this negative reputation appears even earlier in Classical sources. Seriphos was singled out for particular disdain.[135] But it is obvious that the region enjoyed high productivity and population during certain periods, and suffered from decline during others. The memoirs of the French botanist Tournefort, who travelled through the region in the eighteenth century, reveal diverse levels of population and agricultural exploitation. Those islands described by him as productive include Siphnos,[136] Tenos,[137] Paros,[138] and especially Naxos, which is described by him as very prosperous and rich in several crops, animals, and mineral products, and boasting 18,000 inhabitants.[139] Kythnos was reported by Bent in 1884 as barren, but Charlemont in 1749 had described the same island as 'richly cultivated'.[140]

[131] Reger 1994*a*, 84–5 arrives at the figure of 3,000 by extrapolating from the number of guests at a festival in the *polis* of Arkesine recorded in *IG* XII.7, 22; Hansen 2006*a*, 81–2.

[132] Hansen 2006*a*, 8–10; Nixon and Price 1990, 158–62 are also critical.

[133] Hansen 2006*b*, *pace* Figueira 1981, 22–64, who posits 35,000–45,000 inhabitants.

[134] Brun 1993*a*, 1996, and 1998; Sheedy 2006, 17–19; Constantakopoulou 2007, 99-110 and 133.

[135] Ar. *Ach.* 541–4; Plut. *Mor.* 185c; Freeman 1963, 213–20; Sheedy 2006, 41–2; Constantakopoulou 2007, 104–6.

[136] Tournefort 1718, 135.

[137] Tournefort 1718, 272–3 refers to it as 'the best-manured of any in the Archipelago'; Sheedy 2006, 74.

[138] Tournefort 1718, 158, described as 'well-cultivated'.

[139] Tournefort 1718, 167 and 171.

[140] Bent 1885, 428; Standford and Finopoulos 1984, 102–3 for Charlemont; Brun 1998, 659–61 on the variations in traveller's reports of the region throughout history, echoed by Sheedy 2006, 35.

Population of the islands has fluctuated in more modern times as well. Paros had 9,981 inhabitants in 1928,[141] Naxos had 20,132 in 1940.[142] Keos had 4,900 in 1896.[143] Tenos is recorded as having 12,565 souls in 1879, although it may have reached 18,000 in 1630.[144] Siphnos had 5,000 inhabitants in 1700,[145] although modern figures have been more in the range of 3,000–4,000. Seriphos, low in water supplies and more suited to husbandry than large-scale agriculture, had 2,372 inhabitants in 1940, a figure higher than most estimated for this island in antiquity.[146]

One estimate of the population of Kythnos in the late fourth century proposes between 2,500 and 3,000 inhabitants.[147] Keos has seen widely-varying estimates of its ancient population, from 4,000 to 10,000[148] inhabitants during Classical times. Naxos may have been the most populated in the late Archaic period. Herodotus states that the island had 8,000 available soldiers at the time of the Persian attack in 500, and if modern studies are correct that this would have represented about 20 per cent of the total male population, then one could propose that Naxos had an overall population of over 30,000, though this seems much too high.[149]

Although not generally abundant in water or fertile land, the Cyclades were not barren during antiquity.[150] The available arable land in the Cyclades appears from survey evidence to have been more thoroughly exploited in antiquity, especially in the Classical period, than in more modern times (see below). Terracing to increase the amount of land under cultivation appears to have been practised on a

[141] Kolodny 1974, 794, table VII.

[142] Kolodny 1974, 794, table VII; Sheedy 2006, 86, citing it as 'the highest level I have been able to discover'.

[143] Cherry, Davis, and Mantzourani 1991*b*, 237; Sheedy 2006, 19 states that this is also the maximum known.

[144] Slot 1982, 29; Kolodny 1974, 791, table VII; for 1630, Étienne 1990, 14, also cited by Sheedy 2006, 74 as the highest known figure.

[145] Tournefort 1718, 135; Slot 1982, 27; Sheedy 2006, 52.

[146] Liata 1987, 32–8; Sheedy 2006, 47.

[147] Ruschenbusch 1982, 185.

[148] Cherry, Davis, and Mantzourani 1991*b*, 236–7, who put the peak in the fourth century; Georgiou and Faraklas 1993; Mendoni 1994, 154–7; Sheedy 2006, 32.

[149] Hdt. 5.30.4; Gallant 1991, 4, 28, and 78 estimates that fighting men were 30 per cent of the total population of males; Hansen 1985, 34 favors a lower percentage. Yet, there may have been foreign mercenaries included in the total.

[150] Broodbank 2000, 82–5 discusses various subsistence strategies in the Cyclades, stressing the suitability of Cycladic terrain for the raising of livestock.

wide scale on Keos, with an estimated 84 per cent of the land covered by one archaeological survey in the north-west revealing evidence of this practice.[151] Although the remains of terracing seem to indicate that agriculture was intensively practised in the Cyclades during the Classical period,[152] there is controversy as to whether or not these islands may have been more or less self-sufficient in terms of their grain supply.[153] As an example, Paros is recorded in an Ottoman tax record for 1670 as producing the largest barley crop in the region at 19,000 *medimnoi*.[154] Keos also produced enough barley to export large amounts in the early twentieth century.[155]

CYCLADIC LANDSCAPES AND SURVEY ARCHAEOLOGY

The evidence gathered through archaeological survey on several of the Cyclades is also pertinent, though very problematic to interpret. Out of all the islands covered in this study, Keos has been the most intensively surveyed, with the territories of three of the four *poleis* of the island having seen extensive study. Karthaia, Poiessa, and Koressos all appear to have had a significant number of rural sites active in their hinterlands (identified through pottery finds) during the fifth and fourth centuries.[156] The territory of Ioulis, though not as thoroughly explored, seems to show a similar pattern.[157] The sites on Keos have been interpreted as either: (*a*) independent farmsteads that were the primary residences of their owners; or (*b*) agricultural sites

[151] Whitelaw 1991, 405 and 1998.

[152] Terraces on Keos: Whitelaw 1991; on Amorgos: French and Whitelaw 1999. For ancient Greek terracing in general now see Price and Nixon 2005. For a discussion of terracing on a Greek island outside of the Cyclades, see the article by Frederick at the Kythera Island Project website (http://www.ucl.ac.uk/kip/ga_terrace.php) and Bevan, Frederick, and Krahtopoulou 2003.

[153] Reger 1994*a*, 101–9 gives statistics for several of the islands for population, rainfall, and estimated yields.

[154] Slot 1982, 302–3, table I; Sheedy 2006, 114–15.

[155] Sheedy 2006, 33.

[156] Poiessa: Mendoni 1994, 150; Karthaia: Mendoni 1994, 152; Koressos: Mendoni 1994, 153; Cherry, Davis, and Mantzourani 1991*a*, 327–47.

[157] Cherry, Davis, and Mantzourani 1991*a*, 461; Georgiou and Faraklas 1985 and 1993; Mendoni 1994, 154.

meant for seasonal usage by families who maintained residences in the *astu* of their home *polis*.[158] The second possibility would accord well with some epigraphic testimony concerning the leasing of land at Karthaia from the late fourth century, with a high rate of mobility in tenancies.[159] In any event, it would appear that landholdings near to and far from the *astu* of these cities were worked with similar intensive techniques.[160] In each of the cases of the Keian cities, the period of the greatest number of rural sites in the *chōra* corresponds to the *floruit* of the city centre, as seen from public building and epigraphic evidence.[161] Epigraphic testimony from Ioulis, Koressos, and Karthaia on Keos show a high number of archons during the late Classical and early Hellenistic periods, which implies a large percentage of wealthy inhabitants in these cities.[162] Agriculture appears to have been the main activity of these landowners.[163] Similar epigraphic evidence exists for other Cyclades in the late Classical/early Hellenistic periods (Paros, Naxos, Tenos, Amorgos, and Thera) that indicate a high level of exploitation of arable land.[164]

A very different Classical settlement pattern, however, has been reconstructed by two surveys on Naxos. These have yielded data for this island which appear to indicate a more nucleated settlement pattern during the Classical period, with a smaller number of larger sites than seen in the Keian surveys.[165] It is possible, though by no means certain, that this is an indication of a more intensive rather than extensive use of the landscape. Moreover, this pattern of nucleation is very similar to what has been proposed for Melos during the Classical period by the British School survey, in which a small number of rural settlements were contemporary with a growth in the urban centre.[166] This has been interpreted as a result of the

[158] Cherry, Davis, and Mantzourani 1991*a*, 335–7 and Whitelaw 1998, 230–3 for the former; Mendoni 1994, 153–7 for the latter view.

[159] Osborne 1988 and 1991; Whitelaw 1998, 233. See Chapter 6, p. 219 and n. 211.

[160] Whitelaw 1998, 236, *pace* Cherry, Davis, and Mantzourani 1991, 465, who propose two strategies, with rural sites worked intensively and those closest to the *astu* worked extensively.

[161] Mendoni 1994, 153 for Karthaia, with references.

[162] Mendoni 1998, 156.

[163] Mendoni 1994, 153 and 156.

[164] Nigdelis 1990; Mendoni 1994, 156.

[165] Treuil 1983, 65; Erard-Cerceau 1993, 59–98 (neither of these surveys are mentioned in Reger 2004).

[166] Renfrew and Wagstaff 1982, 142–5 and 254.

Athenian conquest and resettlement in 416/15.[167] Naxos also played host to an Athenian klerouchy in the fifth century, but the locations of the *kleroi* are unknown and it would be premature to try to connect the surveyed area with them.

Comparison of data from different surveys is inherently problematic, due to variations in areas covered, recording methods, and techniques of classification of evidence such as pottery.[168] The interpretation of rural sites remains very controversial, with recent survey publications for other regions of ancient Greece becoming more conservative and neutral in their identification of sites as 'farmsteads', for example.[169] It is difficult if not impossible to know what proportion of sites that once existed in a given area have been located through survey, or exactly how and how often they were used, or their dates of use and/or occupation.[170]

Nevertheless, where we are fortunate enough to have epigraphic evidence on land use in the Cyclades, it often dovetails with what has been found by survey, at least in terms of heavy exploitation of the landscape. It has been proposed for Keos that there was substantial 'investment in the infrastructure of the rural landscape',[171] and this is not an unreasonable supposition. It has also been suggested that the pattern seen in the territories of the Keian cities roughly corresponds to that seen during the Atene deme survey in Attika.[172] It must be stressed that such statements are very tentative, and further survey work needs to be done.

It would also be hazardous to speculate on whether intensive agriculture on the islands would have been necessarily directed towards export of any of its products rather than for the provision of local subsistence needs.[173] Yet, we will see that in the late fourth century on Naxos and Paros some export of wine began,[174] so the

[167] Snodgrass 1987–89, 60; Reger 2004, 759–60.

[168] See the Introduction in Alcock and Cherry 2004.

[169] Cavanagh, Mee, and James 2005.

[170] Cherry, Davis, and Mantzourani 1991a, 16–20 for Keos; Foxhall 2007, 34–5; Pettegrew 2001; Bintliff 2005; Osborne 2004.

[171] Cherry and Davis 1998, 219.

[172] Lohmann 1993 for the Atene survey; Whitelaw 1998, 230; Cherry and Davis 1998, 219.

[173] Acheson 1997, 166–8 and 180–2 treats with skepticism the interpretation of land use in Halieis in the Classical/Hellenistic periods as being driven by the production of crops for export (proposed in Jameson, Runnels, and van Andel 1994).

[174] See Chapter 6, pp. 210–11.

possibility remains that some agricultural products could have been exported from at least a few of the Cyclades.

SOURCES FOR CYCLADIC HISTORY

Most of our source material for the Cyclades, with the exception of some key inscriptions, does not originate from the region. A few local Cycladic historians were active during antiquity, but only fragments of their work have survived. Examples are Philteas of Naxos, Andriskos of Naxos, Eudemos, and Aglaosthenes of Naxos, and Xenomedes of Keos.[175] Thus, we lack the voices and viewpoints of those who actually lived in the Cyclades. A slight exception can be made for Naxos, as it would seem that several of the aforementioned writers of *Naxiaka* were of a patriotic bent, particularly in their description of Naxian participation in the Persian Wars.[176]

More general historians such as Herodotus, Thucydides, and Xenophon did not devote major portions of their narratives to Cycladic history, except when it directly intersected with their wider concerns. As such, it is difficult to write a true 'history of the Cyclades' for the Classical period. Instead, we can only outline the shadows of these communities in the historical record of the Classical period, and focus on certain phenomena.

For the sixth and fifth centuries, Herodotus and Thucydides demonstrate intriguing attitudes towards the islands of the Aegean. Both authors wrote during the late fifth century when Athenian sea power was a reality, and their notion of islands as the natural subjects of such power is understandable. It has been convincingly argued that the methodologies of these writers and their approaches to the Greek

[175] Philteas: *FGrH* 498; dated by Jacoby to the first century (followed by Costa 1997, 197–8 and Constantakopoulou *BNJ*); dated to the fourth century by Consolo Langher 123 n.1. Andriskos: *FGrH* 500; dated by Jacoby to the late fourth/early third centuries. Eudemos: *FGrH* 497; dated by Jacoby to the second half of the fifth century. It is unknown, however, whether he was of Naxos or Paros: Constantakopoulou *BNJ*; Costa 1997, 192–5; Lanzilotta 1987, 17. Aglaosthenes: *FGrH* 499; dated by Jacoby to the second century. Xenomedes: *FGrH* 442, dated by Jacoby to the fifth century.

[176] Jacoby *Komment.* 55. See p. 25 n. 47 above for an example from Aglaosthenes. For discussion of all the fragmentary Naxian historians see Costa 1997, 191–209.

past centered on the idea of thalassocracy.[177] Both authors briefly describe Aegean thalassocracies of the past, with Thucydides focusing on Minos of Crete and Herodotus on Polykrates of Samos as the original holders of the title.[178] In the section of Book One known as the *Archaiologia*, Thucydides sketches a rough timeline of sea power in the Greek world. The legendary king Minos is said by him to have taken control of the Cyclades from the Karians, and to have suppressed piracy in the region.[179] Thucydides later discusses other mythical figures such as Agamemnon, before reaching the sixth century and more securely-attested individuals such as Polykrates of Samos.[180] For Thucydides, Athenian sea hegemony towered above all other past hegemonies, a succession of thalassocracies dating back to Minos.[181]

Admittedly, this aspect of the *Archaiologia* is best understood as a projection of the Athenian fifth-century *arkhē* into the distant past.[182] Nevertheless, there are states mentioned in the *Archaiologia* that also appear as naval powers in Herodotus and other sources. An example is Samos during the rule of Polykrates.[183] For Herodotus, the concept was not as fully developed as his main goal was to contrast the Greek civilization with that of the Persians and other ancient Eastern states. Thus, Polykrates' exaction of tribute from the islands serves as his first real example of thalassocracy.[184]

Another ancient source that is central to this issue also possesses a legendary quality. This is the so-called 'Thalassocracy List', preserved in the *Chronikon* of Eusebius but commonly believed to derive from the lost Book Seven of Diodorus Siculus' *Universal History* (hereafter referred to as the List). It begins with the Phrygians in the seventh century, but from the mid-sixth century the following states are attested as holding dominance over the Aegean:

Samians 540–516
Spartans 516–510

177 Constantakopoulou 2007, 90–7.
178 Minos: Thuc. 1.4; Polykrates: Hdt. 3.122.3.
179 Thuc. 1.4.1.
180 Thuc. 1.13.6.
181 Thuc. 1.1.1; Romilly 1963, 67–8; Hunter 1982, 38; Constantakopoulou 2007, 92.
182 Constantakopoulou 2007, 92.
183 Thuc. 1.13.6.
184 van Wees 2002, 337–43; Constantakopoulou 2007, 93.

Naxians 510–500
Eretrians 500–490
Aiginetans 490–480[185]

Some historians, while expressing reservations about the veracity of the List, have still assumed that it reflects some level of reality concerning sixth-century sea power in certain *poleis*.[186] Others have dismissed it as largely fictional, or have proposed that it represents the same projection of power into the distant past as seen in Thucydides.[187] It is true that the List is simply much too exact in its schema of dates to be taken at face value, but there are references in Herodotus, Thucydides, and other sources to naval power exercised by several of these same states in the broad context of the late sixth and early fifth centuries. Thus the List, if used cautiously, may still provide clues as to the nature of sea power in the late Archaic period and how such phenomena might have affected our region of inquiry, the Cyclades. Various proposals have been made for the sources used by Eusebius, but the List was most likely excerpted from Diodorus Siculus by way of Porphyry.[188]

The problems with our fourth-century sources stem more from a lack of emphasis. The authors tend to ignore states not directly involved in warfare.[189] Xenophon is guilty of being generally unconcerned with naval affairs, and even says so openly when discussing the Corinthian War in his *Hellenika*.[190] Any discussion of Cycladic history is obviously bound intimately to naval concerns, so this presents a real problem. This is not to say that Xenophon ignores naval battles entirely, but his focus tends to be on the personal qualities of commanders (whether on land or at sea) and whether or not they promoted *eutaxia* (discipline or good order) in the forces that they led.[191]

185 Forrest 1969, 105.

186 Myres 1906; Forrest 1969; Miller 1971; Walker 2004 for Eretria.

187 De Souza 1998, 287–8 for strong doubts concerning its authenticity; Constantakopoulou 2007, 91 for the fifth century association.

188 Mosshammer 1979, 66, 135, and 167; Miller 1971, 6–8; Myres 1906 proposes an ultimate source of Periklean date.

189 Bauslaugh 1991, 34–5.

190 Xen. *Hell.* 4.8.1; Figueira 1993, 338–9 and 350 for the Battle of Naxos (see below).

191 Dillery 1995, 28–30. One example is the battle of Notion in 407 (*Hell.* 1.5.14), where he states that a lack of discipline by the Athenian ship crews led to their defeat.

Xenophon also ignores other topics that are important for Cycladic history in the early fourth century, such as details on the formation of the Second Athenian League in 378/7, which included most of the Cycladic islands.[192] A main goal of Xenophon was the glorification of Sparta, particularly the deeds of Agesilaos, and as such his work is not free of bias.[193] But some of his omissions were probably also due to a lack of available information on Athenian affairs rather than deliberate distortion, since these portions of the *Hellenika* were written during his years in exile at Skillous.[194]

Diodorus Siculus is an even more problematic source, but crucial for key points of Cycladic history during the fourth century. This Augustan-era historian has been vilified through the years for his inconsistencies and sloppy chronology.[195] Yet he has also had his recent defenders.[196] Many have noticed that despite his errors, Diodorus has preserved much valuable information that has not survived elsewhere, and the issue is how to separate the wheat from the chaff.

For much of the early fourth century (covered in Books 11–16), Diodorus appears to have primarily utilized and summarized the much more extensive work of Ephoros.[197] Ephoros' work was said to be organized thematically (*kata genos*), and these themes in all likelihood were geographic in nature.[198] Ephoros was noted by Polybios as being ill-informed on military matters on land (Ephoros' description of the Battle of Mantinea in 362 receives particular criticism). However, Polybios also concedes that on naval matters Ephoros was more astute, citing his account of Persian actions against Evagoras of Cyprus and against the Spartans at Knidos.[199] Ephoros

This is in contrast to his description of the battle-readiness of Iphikrates' squadron at Kerkyra in the fourth century (*Hell.* 6.2.27–30).

[192] Cartledge 1987, 61–6; Jehne 2004 proposes that Xenophon's omission of the founding of the Second League was due to his desire to promote the renewed hostility between Athens and Sparta as a result of Theban machinations.

[193] Buckler 1980, 263–8; Kallet-Marx 1985, 129; Dillery 1995.

[194] Anderson 1974, 170–1.

[195] Stylianou 1998, esp. 1–3; Ambaglio 2008; Thomas 2009; Meiggs 1972, 457 claims that 'when Diodorus differs from Thucydides we can usually ignore him'.

[196] Green 2006, esp. 1–47.

[197] Drews 1962, 1963, 1976; Barber 1935, 140–4; Buckler 1980, 268–70; Rubincam 1987; Ambaglio 2008; Parmeggiani 2011.

[198] Drews 1963, 252.

[199] Polyb. 12.25; Barber 1935, 141–4; Gray 1980, 323.

was from the Aiolian city of Kyme, site of a Persian naval base, and was apparently well-informed on Persian naval operations.[200]

It is generally assumed that Diodorus adapted non-annalistic sources to his own annalistic framework, and this adaptation led to frequent errors of chronology.[201] Diodorus' description of the first Athenian attack on Melos incorrectly places the incident two years later than it occurred, in 424.[202] He also credits the Athenian commander Nikias with seizing the island of Kythera in 418, which had actually occurred in 424.[203] But Diodorus occasionally adds important details to our knowledge of naval battles. For example, there is his description of the advantage gained by Syracusan triremes by having lower prows during the engagement with the Athenians in the harbour of Syracuse.[204] And in his account of the battle of Arginousai, Diodorus stresses the contribution made by allied triremes and experienced crewmen to the Athenian side.[205]

His description of the battle of Naxos in 376 is more detailed than Xenophon's,[206] and this may have greater implications as Ephoros has also been accused of possessing a strong pro-Athenian bias that can be seen in some of Diodorus' account.[207] Diodorus has received recognition for his generally more accurate fourth-century chronology,[208] as well as for his information on the foundation of the Second Athenian League (an event wholly absent in Xenophon), which compares favourably with epigraphic evidence from the League prospectus.[209] His coverage of the years 377/6 and 364/3 is particularly

200 Wallinga 1991, 278 and n.6; Kallet-Marx 1985, 132; Barber 1935, 88–101.

201 Barber 1935; Drews 1962; Gray 1980, 319.

202 Diod. 12.65.2; Seaman 1997, 407 n.83.

203 Diod. 12.80.5; cf. Thuc. 3.91.2–3.

204 Diod. 13.10.3, compared to Thuc. 7.36; Stylianou 1998, 124–5 feels that while Diodorus' treatments of naval battles are often brief, they are sometimes superior to Xenophon's accounts, such as Kyzikos and Notion during the Dekeleian War. Bleckmann 1998, 149–82, however, has heavy criticism for Diodorus' description of naval battles during the Dekeleian War and argues for his heavy reliance on the Oxyrhynchos Historian.

205 Bleckmann 1998, 105–7; Diod. 13.97.2.

206 Xen. *Hell.* 5.4.61; Diod. 15.34.4–35.2; Tuplin 1993, 158–9; Figueira 1993, 350–1.

207 Gray 1980, 122 for the glorification of the career of Timotheos among other examples; Barber 1935, 88–101.

208 Drews 1963, 250 n.13.

209 Kallet-Marx 1985, 130–1 compares Diodorus' information on when allies joined the League with their order of inscription on the stone. Diod. 15.29.7–30.1 states that the Euboian cities did not join the League until it was made clear that Athenians would not be able to acquire property in allied states (*IG* II^2 43 lines 25–31

detailed.[210] *Nesiotika* ('Concerning Islands') is the title of his fifth book, which covers some of the same ground as Thucydides and Herodotus (including the tradition of the naval hegemony of the Minoans and Karians).[211] If a certain item of information is only contained in Diodorus, is not contradicted by better evidence, and cannot be shown to be otherwise improbable, then it has a claim to value.[212]

Diodorus is very moralizing when discussing the nature of hegemony in the Aegean, stressing the desirability of *epeikeia* (moderation) on the part of powerful states. He states openly that Athens began to treat its allies in the Delian League unfairly after 421.[213] Similar criticism is levelled against the Spartans for the behaviour after the end of the Peloponnesian War.[214]

Xenophon's account ends in 362, and with it any surviving 'grand narrative' for events in Aegean Greece until the *Anabasis* of Arrian. A narrative for the third quarter of the fourth century must consequently be pieced together from sources such as Diodorus, and the speeches of Athenian orators such as Demosthenes, Aiskhines, and Isokrates. The lack of such a 'grand narrative' may be one of the explanations for why so little scholarly attention has been focused on this period. Yet for these years, additional types of evidence such as numismatics, the remains of temples, and inscriptions can help us reconstruct (although very imperfectly) conditions in the Aegean and the Cyclades.

Many of the Cyclades produced silver coinage in the late sixth century, a phenomenon that continued on some of the islands into the early decades of the fifth century. However, this minting activity came to a halt by the mid-fifth and the apex of the Athenian *arkhē*. Beginning again in the fourth century, Cycladic minting in silver and bronze resumed. The significance of this process for Cycladic prosperity and contact with the Aegean world will be explored, though it draws us into current controversy as to the purpose of ancient Greek coinage. Some scholars have stressed the symbolic and ideological

and 35–46). The Euboians subsequently appear on the stone in a later hand. See also Cawkwell 1973, 47–51; Cargill 1981, 57–61.

[210] For 377/6: Diod. 15.28–35; for 364/3: 15.78–81; Drews 1963, 249 n.15.

[211] Constantakopoulou 2007, 97; Ceccarelli 1989.

[212] Kallet-Marx 1985, 129; Gray 1980.

[213] Diod. 12.76.2–5; Sacks 1990, 42.

[214] Diod. 14.2.1–2; 15.1.1–5; other examples cited in Sacks 1990, 42.

value of such coinage over its commercial aspects.[215] Others have seen its adoption as far back as the seventh century and continue to posit that coinage had a major role in facilitating transactions at all levels of society.[216] The presence of large numbers of smaller fractional coins in very early contexts is one type of evidence used to support this latter view.[217] It seems clear that by the late sixth century coinage in the Greek world helped facilitate long-distance trade, as well as helping to fulfil increased needs for state expenditure. On Rhodes throughout the Classical and Hellenistic periods, for example, coinage may have been produced to cover a wide range of civic payments including the payment of fleet crews and mercenaries.[218] For the Cyclades, payments for the construction of temples and fortifications have been proposed as a major motivation for production of late sixth/early fifth-century coinages on islands such as Siphnos and Naxos, and the operation of warships might be another.[219]

Finally, we have epigraphic evidence. A high percentage of the inscriptions used in this study are Athenian, including decrees such as the settlement of Keian cities after uprisings in the 360s, and also the fourth-century settlement on Paros.[220] As the Cyclades were included in the Insular District for the purposes of tribute collection, the relevant *aparkhē* lists (recording the one-sixtieth of each tribute amount collected that was subsequently dedicated to Athena) are also important.[221] However, many of the years of tribute collection survive only in fragments, and some years are missing altogether.[222] This, of course, assumes that the chronology of the known fragments is fairly secure, but this chronology has been recently called into question.[223] The fourth-century temple accounts of Delian Apollo are another

[215] von Reden 1995 and Kurke 2002 are representative.

[216] Davies 1998, 239 on the 'strong' and 'weak' views of the role of coinage. For Roman history an example of the 'weak' view is Howgego 1995.

[217] Kim 2002, esp. 47–8.

[218] Ashton 2001, 96–8.

[219] Sheedy 2006, 57 and 87.

[220] The author confirmed the readings of these two inscriptions by autopsy in 1997: *IG* II^2 404, and Oliver 1936 (now Rhodes and Osborne 2003, #29).

[221] *IG* I^3 259–89, covering assessments beginning in 454/3 and ending in 416/5.

[222] 449/8, 439/8–435/4, and the years after 425/4 are either missing or extremely fragmentary.

[223] Kallet 2004. See Chapter 4 pp. 119 and 123.

important source of economic information. Yet, these pose similar problems of interpretation as they are also in a fragmentary state.[224]

Several decrees from various Cycladic islands are also referenced in the present study. These are found in the collection *IG* XII, which covers the Aegean islands (including Crete and the Cyclades, but not Delos).[225] An example is the fourth-century collection of *proxenia* awarded by the *polis* of Karthaia on Keos.[226] However, most of the inscriptions collected in *IG* XII date from the Hellenistic and Roman periods. The greatest number of Classical inscriptions hail from Paros and Karthaia on Keos. It is unclear how much the relatively scant epigraphic finds from Cycladic islands reflect accidents of survival, or a less fully-developed 'epigraphic habit' in the region during the Classical period.[227]

All of these sources are to some degree lacking in clarity and problematic to interpret. When direct evidence is lacking, there are attempts made in this study to find comparanda in other regions that may shed light on economic conditions in the Cyclades.

[224] Coupry 1972, now republished in Chankowski 2008.
[225] The inscriptions from Amorgos are included in *IG* XII.7.
[226] *IG* XII.5 542.
[227] See Osborne 2009 for a discussion of Thasos in this regard, with special reference to Paros.

3

Local Hegemonies

The Archaic Cyclades (540–490)

For the purposes of this study, the history of the Cyclades in the Archaic period truly begins in the mid-sixth century, when we can trace the beginnings of naval power in the region. While none of the Cyclades ever approached the level of the great naval hegemons, Naxos was remembered in Greek tradition as a powerful state in the Aegean. While there is little evidence for Cycladic ships travelling long distances in the Aegean or Mediterranean at large, they may not have needed to make such journeys in order to profit from commerce, as their central geographical position played in their favour.

A strategic location on important trade routes, in addition to the possession of warships to compel shipping to use their harbours and pay harbour dues, may have generated increased wealth in the Cyclades. Possible parallels for Cycladic 'thalassocracy' may be seen in the examples of late sixth—century Eretria on Euboia, and of fifth-century Kerkyra as described in the pages of Thucydides, both of which may have exerted some control over local trade routes.

When coupled with the export of local island products, such as precious metals from Siphnos and marble from Naxos and Paros, several of these islands had the resources to mint coinage and invest in infrastructure such as monumental temples and fortification walls. This competition may be characterized as a manifestation of certain aspects of the model of peer-polity interaction. Such interaction and competition, however, was no longer possible after the establishment of the Athenian *arkhē* during the fifth century.

This chapter does not attempt comprehensive coverage of the entire Archaic period in the Cyclades. However, some events prior to the mid-sixth century which may have played a role in encouraging the later competitive activity in the region will be discussed.

ARCHAIC SEA POWER AND 'THALASSOCRACIES' IN THE AEGEAN

The long-held tendency to view Mediterranean history as a 'sequence of achieved thalassocracies' has come under recent criticism.[1] Yet it cannot be doubted that the ancient sources have helped shape such a model. For Thucydides, the Athenian *arkhē* in the Aegean was the end result of a long historical process that involved the establishment of several, lesser thalassocracies in the region. However, it is very problematic to assess the nature of these earlier expressions of sea power, if they did in fact exist.

The earliest references to actions of Cycladic states relate to the so-called Lelantine War. Thucydides states that during this conflict between Khalkis and Eretria, various Greek communities sided with one or the other. The war most likely began in the mid-eighth century, and is said to have ended in the defeat of Eretria *c.*700.[2] While it would be rash to propose, as some modern commentators have done, that the Archaic *poleis* of the Aegean were aligned in two massive 'mercantile' blocs,[3] it would also be counterproductive to dismiss economic motivations for the war entirely.[4]

The meager evidence does not allow us to definitively state which sides were taken by the Cyclades (if they participated at all) during the Lelantine War, and it has been proposed that it might have been in the interest of the islanders to tread a fine line, because of their geographic proximity to Euboia.[5] But a few tentative proposals as to their political alignment have been made. Strabo mentions that Andros, Keos, and Tenos were under the authority of Eretria around this same period.[6] The Amarynthos Stele at the temple of Amarysia

[1] Horden and Purcell 2000, 155.
[2] Burn 1929; Walker 2004, 122–3 and 162–71.
[3] Oliva 1981, 114.
[4] As rightly stressed by Walker 2004, 163 *pace* Starr 1962.
[5] Hdt. 5.28–30; Burn 1929, 20–1; Parker 1997, 149.
[6] Strabo 10.1.10 C448; Murray 1993, 76–80.

on Eretria details Eretrian military units that participated in a festival, listing 3,000 hoplites and 600 cavalry, an indication of substantial military capability if the figures are accurate.[7]

It is difficult to evaluate Strabo's statement, however. Even if he is correct that Eretrian land forces were formidable, this says nothing about potential sea power, which would have been necessary to exert power over the islands. Moreover, evidence for Eretrian influence on the islands mentioned above is somewhat ambiguous. The Eretrian settlement at Zagora on Andros, established around the beginning of the Archaic period, may be an indication of some degree of Eretrian control—but the site was abandoned by 700.[8] Eretrian civic institutions have been noted on Keos, specifically the terms *probouloi* and *khoroi*, but it is unclear just when these terms may have entered Keian usage.[9]

Naxos may have been an ally of Khalkis, since both cities had cooperated in the foundation of the colony of Naxos on Sicily in 734.[10] The Milesians (aided by the Erythraians), allies of Eretria, are also said to have attacked Naxos at some indeterminate date. According to a fragment by a local Naxian historian, this conflict is said to have been won by the Naxians.[11] Paros was friendly to Miletos,[12] and the rivalry between Naxos and Paros during the Archaic period was long-lasting and renowned. The Parian poet Arkhilokhos took part in several conflicts between his home island and Naxos (conflicts in which the Milesians assisted the Parians) that may date to the early to mid-seventh century, and is said to have lost his life fighting a Naxian warrior named Korax.[13]

[7] Walker 2004, 123 favors a late sixth-century date for this stele, coinciding with his thesis (see below) on Eretrian power at that later period.

[8] Walker 2004, 98; Descoeudres 1973, 88.

[9] Dunant and Thomopoulos 1954, 320 favor the early date (tentatively followed by Walker 2004, 123), but Lewis 1962, 2 would date these influences to 411 and the Euboian revolt from the Delian League.

[10] Dunbabin 1979, 8.

[11] Andriskos *FGrH* 500 F1; Plut. *Mor.* 254f; Polyain. *Strat.* 8.36; Burn 1929, 21 n.86 for the possible date.

[12] Kondoleon 1963; Parker 1997, 148, who sees this as an example of the 'enemy of an enemy is a friend'; Burn 1929, 19 would put Paros, Andros, and tentatively Naxos as allies of Khalkis during the conflict, but if this is true Paros had changed sides by Arkhilokhos' time.

[13] Costa 1997, 113–27; Clay 2004; Fox 2008, 388 would put his life about a century earlier.

Andros had founded colonies in the north at Argilos and Stageira,[14] and had joined with the Khalkidians to found settlements at Sane and Akanthos.[15] According to an anecdote in Plutarch, Samos, Paros, and Erythrai awarded Akanthos to the Andrians after a dispute arose with Khalkis over its ownership. The Parian vote for Khalkis' claim, however, created a new dispute between Andros and Paros that annulled marriages between their citizens.[16] Paros had founded Thasos and other colonies in what became the Thasian *peraia*,[17] and also helped Erythrai found Parion in the Hellespontine region.[18]

As we move into the latter half of the sixth century, stronger traditions develop concerning Aegean sea power. Thucydides states that Polykrates, tyrant of Samos, captured many islands, including the Cycladic island of Rheneia, which he symbolically linked to Delos with a chain in 526/5.[19] Herodotus provides more information on his capabilities, stating that Polykrates possessed 100 pentekonters and 1,000 archers (many of whom presumably fought as marines), and that he 'raided and plundered all alike' and 'captured many of the islands and a number of towns on the mainland as well'.[20]

Polykrates is said by Herodotus to have eventually added triremes to his fleet in response to the threat of the Persians.[21] Now Thucydides states that before Xerxes' expedition, there were no major naval powers in the Greek world: 'Aigina, Athens, and others may have possessed a few vessels, but they were principally fifty oars.'[22] He is not fully consistent, since just a few passages earlier in his work, he

[14] Thuc. 4. 88 and 103; Tiverios 2008.

[15] Thuc. 4.107; Diod. 12.68; Plut. *Quaest.Graec.* 30 (= *Mor.* 298a–b).

[16] Burn 1929, 18; Forrest 1982, 251.

[17] Strabo 10.5.7 C487 and 8.6.6 C370; Plut. *Mor.* 604; Ar. *Pax* 1298 and schol.; Owen 2003.

[18] Strabo 13.1.14 C588.

[19] Thuc. 1.13.6 and 3.104.1–2. However, this may actually have been indicative of a confinement of his power to the Cycladic region by the Phoenician fleet under Kambyses: Shipley 1987, 96.

[20] Hdt. 3.39 (translation from Shipley 1987, 94). In the course of an article that has a generally skeptical tone towards Archaic sea power, De Souza 1998, 282–3 nevertheless states that the combination of testimony from both Thucydides and Herodotus does provide support for the existence of some kind of Samian thalassocracy. Whether or not he truly controlled Delos, however, is open to question since there are no real institutional traces: Chankowski 2008, 14 and n.24.

[21] Hdt. 3.45; Haas 1985, 38.

[22] Thuc. 1.14.3 (Crawley translation).

states that after 490 there had been a small number of triremes 'widely distributed' in the Aegean area.[23]

The issue is important, because of the difference in resources required to build and operate different types of ancient warships. *Ploia makra*, or 'long ships,' included galleys that could be used for trade or for warfare, as well as pentekonters ('fifty-oared').[24] Pentekonters were also multi-purpose, but required a greater mobilization of manpower. Triremes (the original Greek term is *trieres,* or 'three-fitted') were highly-specialized warships that necessitated major financial outlays to construct and operate.[25]

It is not clear just how Polykrates was able to afford a fleet of this magnitude. One theory proposes that funding came from Amasis of Egypt as a counter to growing Persian naval power.[26]

Other sources state that Polykrates had been assisted in his takeover of Samos by troops sent by Lygdamis of Naxos.[27] This same Lygdamis is said by Herodotus to have been an ally of Peisistratos of Athens, with Lygdamis aiding him in his third and final seizure of power in 546, after the battle at Pallene.[28] Peisistratos then placed hostages from rival Athenian families on Naxos for safekeeping.[29] This support of Lygdamis, followed by the purification of Delos by Peisistratos, has been proposed as the beginning of Athenian intervention in the Aegean.[30]

In 525, the crews of forty of Polykrates' triremes that had been sent to assist Kambyses in Egypt mutinied. Herodotus says that Polykrates had suspected that these men would revolt, and that was why he had

[23] Thuc. 1.4.1, 3.

[24] Wallinga 1993, 63–4.

[25] For pentekonters see Casson 1971, 58–60. For various theories on trireme development see Wallinga 1993, 104–11; Morrison, Coates, and Rankov 2000, 25–45; Starr 1989, 15–28; Casson 1971, 77–96.

[26] Wallinga 1993, 84–91. His hypothesis that the trireme was in fact invented in Egypt *c.*540–525 (as a modified Egyptian transport), rather than in Corinth, is highly speculative but worthy of consideration.

[27] Arist. *Pol.* 1305a37–41; Ath. *Deip.* 8.348b; Polyain. *Strat.* 1.23.2.

[28] Hdt. 1.62; [Arist.] *Ath.Pol.*15.2 implies that Peisistratos helped put Lygdamis in power *after* the victory at Pallene (followed by de Libero 1996), but it is more likely that this had occurred while Peisistratos was in Eretria: Lavelle 2005, 137 and n.101. Walker 2004, 199 postulates that Eretrian ships helped Peisistratos install Lygdamis.

[29] Hdt. 1.64.2; Costa 1997, 158.

[30] Lavelle 2005, 138–9 and 228–9. On the purification: Hdt. 1.64.2; Thuc. 1.81; Hornblower 1991, 519–20.

dispatched them.[31] After winning a naval battle with Polykrates' forces, but then suffering a defeat on land, the mutineers sailed for Sparta.[32] The Spartans assisted them in a second attack on Polykrates, but this also proved unsuccessful.[33] Now apparently cutting their ties with the Spartans, the Samian mutineers then attempted to borrow ten talents from the inhabitants of Siphnos, but when their request was denied they ravaged the island's territory and cut off the Siphnians from their *astu*, and exacted a hundred talents of silver from them.[34] Herodotus describes how they used this cash to purchase the island of Hydria from Hermione, which they then gave to Troizen. They next planned to take the island of Zakynthos, but instead established themselves at Kydonia in western Crete. For the next five years they preyed on shipping from this base, until they were destroyed by the Aiginetans in 519/18.[35]

Their choice of Kydonia may have been motivated by a desire to insinuate themselves (through piracy or 'legitimate' trade, or a combination of both) into the Peloponnesian trade with North Africa that passed near this site.[36] The later Aiginetan takeover of this site may also have had economic motivations, as the role played by Aiginetans in the movement of Attic pottery[37] is seen in the increase of Attic imports at Kydonia after the end of the sixth century.[38]

At no point does Herodotus state explicitly why the Samian pirates favoured Troizen with their Siphnian spoils, nor why Zakynthos had originally been targeted by them, nor why they then switched their attention to Kydonia. Troizen may have been friendly to the Samians because they were allies of Sparta (due to their fear of Argos).[39] Trade rivalry between Samos and Aigina is likely as the

[31] Although this is difficult to comprehend, since why would the tyrant risk some of his most expensive and powerful warships by assigning them to untrustworthy men?

[32] Hdt. 3.44–45.

[33] Hdt. 3.56.

[34] Hdt. 3.59.

[35] Hdt. 3.59.

[36] Erickson 2005, 634–6, emphasizes the earlier role of Samian merchants as carriers of Lakonian pottery. See also now Erickson 2010, 291–2.

[37] Erickson 2005, 635 and n.121; Boardman 1980, 121 and Roebuck 1950, 238 for evidence of this in Egypt; Johnston 1979, 53 for Italy and Sicily.

[38] Erickson 2005, 635 and now 2010, 291–2 for finds of Aiginetan coins and tombstones utilizing Aiginetan script.

[39] Burn 1929, 17.

overall motivating factor behind attempts to control Kydonia, but much remains unclear.

The sum of a hundred talents shows the kind of wealth that was in the possession of the Siphnians, wealth most likely derived from the island's gold and silver mines. Although no examples of Archaic gold coinage have been definitively linked to Siphnos, an issue of silver drachms on the Aiginetan standard can be approximately dated to 540–525; but this and other Siphnian issues appear to have been on a relatively small scale.[40] Siphnian silver appears instead to have been more commonly exported as bullion and used for minting by other states, the most notable example being the issues of Aigina.[41]

It has been recently proposed that Herodotus' description of the Samian attack reveals a lack of military organization and civic cohesion on Late Archaic Siphnos, also indicated by a lack of interest in issuing large amounts of coinage and by the lack of fortification walls until after 525.[42] According to this thesis, the aforementioned lack of cohesion was due to an aristocratic elitism that provided an obstacle to unity in the Siphnian *polis*. Yet, it is not at all clear that this is what can be drawn from the passage in Herodotus. It seems clear that the Siphnians did not fear the Samians at first, and there may even have been some aristocrats among the Samians who were well known to their counterparts on Siphnos. If the Siphnians were not expecting hostility from the Samians, then forces would not have been gathered against them, and in any case forty triremes would have been difficult, if not impossible, for older-style vessels to defeat.

It is unclear just how the mines of Siphnos were exploited—we do not know if they were leased out to individuals or handled in a more centralized fashion.[43] One wonders why the Siphnians would refuse to part with ten talents, considering the much greater amount that

[40] Sheedy 2006, 48–50, citing this as the earliest known Cycladic coinage. Sheedy's dating of the late Archaic coins of the Cyclades hinges mainly on Greek coins found in the Apadana foundation deposits at Persepolis (*IGCH* #1789 A and B), and the use of the flat-nosed trussel die mount as well as a large skew device on both Aiginetan and Cycladic coins.

[41] Gale and Stos-Gale 1981; Bissa 2009, 39; Di Napoli 2005 also stresses that the Parians could have used Siphnian (as well as the normally-posited Thasian) silver for their more extensive Archaic issues.

[42] Neer 2003, 133.

[43] Sheedy 2006, 55–7. Bissa 2009, 39 proposes that a 'system of diffused exploitation' is more probable, since direct exploitation by the state was more associated with monarchies.

they subsequently lost. The refusal could have been related to their recent expense on their treasury at Delphi, and/or because the mines had begun to be flooded. That process may have already been somewhat advanced by this time.[44]

The attack on Siphnos must have had a strong psychological effect on the entire Cycladic region, in addition to the damage suffered by the Siphnians themselves.[45] Other islands in the Cyclades began to be targeted at this time by outside powers as well. The tyrant Lygdamis was driven out of Naxos by the Spartans and an oligarchy imposed in his place, and although the date of this event is unclear, it probably occurred *c.*514.[46] Other evidence for a period of Spartan naval hegemony is lacking—although there is reason to posit trade links between Sparta and Samos up to mid-sixth century, due to the large number of finds of Lakonian black-figure on Samos dated to the late seventh and first half of the sixth.[47]

The Thalassocracy List attests to a phase of Naxian sea power from 515–505.[48] The Naxian oligarchs were expelled by a democratic uprising around 505.[49] Thucydides says nothing of this event, but Herodotus tells a story that gives Naxos great prominence. After their expulsion, the Naxian oligarchs proceeded to Miletos to ask for aid in regaining control of their home island. The term used by Herodotus for these oligarchs is *οἵ παχέες*, 'the Fat Ones', which he also uses for their counterparts on Aigina, Megara Hyblaia on Sicily, and Khalkis on Euboia.[50]

Aristagoras of Miletos responded favourably to their request, but said that Persian help would be required because the Naxians could

[44] Sheedy 2006, 53 thinks that at least some of them had gone 'dry', but that the amount taken by the Samians may have been hoarded by the Siphnians for some time.

[45] Miller 1971, 32.

[46] Plut. *De Herod.* 21 (= *Mor.* 859d); Schol. Aiskh. 2.77; *Papyrus Rylands* fr.18; Walker 2004, 222 and Andrewes 1966, 123 for the date of 514; Jeffery 1976, 180–1 proposes *c.*517; others prefer to date it to the time of the attack on Polykrates *c.*524: Leahy 1957, 273. Walker 2004, 225–6 points out that Sparta had 'no other known naval tradition', and proposes that the key to their short-lived dominance at sea may have been due to naval assistance from Eretria. For further discussion of Eretrian sea power in the late Archaic period, see below.

[47] Stibbe 1972 and Nafissi 1989, 73–4; Cartledge 1982, 252 and 254.

[48] Diod. 7.11. See Chapter 2, pp. 44–5 for a general introduction to the List.

[49] Hdt. 5.30; Myres 1906, 98; Walker 2004, 270.

[50] Hdt. 6.91.1 (Aigina); 7.156.2 (Megara on Sicily); 5.77.2 (Khalkis); de Ste. Croix 2004, 377. A similar oligarchic class has been reconstructed for Paros around this same time: Lanzilotta 1987, 58–61; Berranger 1992, 328–31.

field 'eight thousand men under arms and many warships'.[51] The Naxian exiles stated that they would pay for the expedition because it was their expectation that Naxos, and even the rest of the Cyclades, would submit to their rule once they appeared with Persian support. Aristagoras then told the Persian satrap Artaphernes that not only Naxos but Paros, Andros, and the rest of the Cyclades, and Euboia as well, could all be taken with a hundred ships.[52] Whatever the truth of what Aristagoras had told him, Artaphernes approved of the plan to attack Naxos, offering 200 ships instead.[53]

Would two hundred triremes really have been necessary to subdue Naxos? It has been pointed out that many of these ships could have been troop transports, and Artaphernes may in fact have had more far-reaching designs than the conquest of a single island.[54] Euboia is also mentioned as a target in Herodotus, and if this is accurate then Eretria's military potential would have had to be taken into consideration by the Persians as well.[55]

It is interesting that an exact figure is given for the number of hoplites, but not the number of ships, that the Naxians could field.[56] As mentioned above, Polyainos tells of Lygdamis assisting Polykrates of Samos with troops.[57] The figure of 8,000 hoplites may represent the resources of Naxos alone,[58] although it is also possible that the Naxians had the power to conscript nearby islanders to military service, or simply had the resources to hire and equip mercenaries.[59] 'Native' members of the hoplite class in Aegean island states were probably relatively few—Aigina contributed only 500 hoplites to the Greek force at Plataia in 479.[60] Other estimates for hoplite classes on

[51] Hdt. 5.30.4; van Wees 2010, 215 considers this figure for military strength to be valid as far back as 540 and the installation of Lygdamis by Peisistratos, but this is unlikely.

[52] Hdt. 5.28–31.

[53] Hdt. 5.31.3–4.

[54] Wallinga 1984, 427–8.

[55] Walker 2004, 271.

[56] Robinson 1997, 118 proposes, however, that Herodotus actually means 'shields' instead of 'hoplites,' and that the figure of 8,000 thus represented all available fighting men.

[57] Polyain. *Strat.* 1.23.2.

[58] Horden and Purcell 2000, 381.

[59] Wallinga 1993, 79 n.40.

[60] Hdt. 9.28.6; de Ste. Croix 2004, 387.

Cycladic islands have been based on evidence from the fourth century from two Keian cities, Ioulis (480 total) and Koressos (154 total).[61]

We will never know for certain, however, if the force was meant only for Naxos. Herodotus says that a siege went on for four months and was ultimately unsuccessful, because Megabates had given the Naxians advance warning of the assault after a quarrel with Aristagoras, so that the Naxians were able to stockpile provisions within their city walls.[62] The Persian forces built a fort as a refuge for the Fat Ones before departing, although Herodotus says nothing further of the fate of these men.[63]

NAXIAN RESOURCES AND SEA POWER

Is the idea of a Naxian thalassocracy in the late sixth century at all historical? Wealth would have been necessary for any island to maintain naval forces.[64] Yet, the possession of wealth did not automatically lead to sea power, since Siphnos was a Cycladic island proverbial for its wealth in the sixth century but was not seen in the tradition as a sea power—and their inability to deal with the attack of the Samian exiles provides support for that evaluation. It will be necessary to examine several factors in order to determine the potential naval power of Naxos.

The most important local resource that the Naxians could have drawn on in the late sixth century was their marble. Lygdamis is said by Aristotle to have exiled many oligarchs from Naxos and then sold their confiscated lands. On these landholdings were unfinished statues destined for temples.[65] It is evident that marble statues were often carved *in situ* at quarries and then shipped to their destination. The block would be purchased by a sculptor from the quarry owner, completed, and then shipped out on behalf of the client.[66] The heavy

[61] *IG* XII.5 609; Cherry, Davis, and Mantzourani 1991*b*, 236–7; Brun 1989, 126–7; Ruschenbusch 1982; Reger 2004, 748–51.

[62] Hdt. 5.33–34; Keaveney 1988.

[63] Hdt. 5.34.3.

[64] De Souza 1998, 284 posits that the sea power of the Phokaians after their relocation to Alalia on Corsica may have been paid for by their trading activities.

[65] Arist. *Oec.* 2.1346b; Costa 1997, 161,

[66] Snodgrass 2006, 19–20 and 25–6.

use of Naxian marble on Delos, including in their treasury and other structures, has even led some to propose that Naxos had control of Delos in the Archaic period, and perhaps even the leadership of some sort of early Ionic amphiktyony in the Aegean.[67]

It has been proposed that confiscations during the tyranny of Lygdamis dealt a 'devastating blow' to the Naxian marble trade.[68] But even if this were the case (and there is no real reason to think that Lygdamis would not have wanted to continue its exploitation in order to reap its financial benefits for his own regime), the Fat Ones could have resumed quarrying once they were back in charge. And marble was not the sole mineral resource of the Naxians, for the island was also renowned for its emery.[69]

The Naxians may also have led the Cyclades in the area of coinage. During the Archaic period, Aiginetan silver coins appear to have been used throughout the Cyclades, and most of the islands that minted their own silver followed the Aiginetan standard.[70] A fragment of a local historian, however, attributes the introduction of coinage in the Cyclades to the Naxians.[71] Although this is problematic, it has been proposed that the earliest Naxian coins (wreathed staters) began to be struck *c.*540–530, during the reign of Lygdamis. However, this was a small issue and Naxian minting did not increase in scale until approximately the last two decades of the sixth century.[72]

During this same period, the Parians minted one of the largest issues of silver coins of any Cycladic state in antiquity.[73] It has been proposed that the increasing complexity of economic activity required the Parian *polis* to mint silver on a larger scale to fulfil its civic projects such as temple construction.[74] The source of the silver, however, is unknown. It is possible that trade with Siphnos provided at least a portion of the bullion used to make these coins,

[67] Costa 1997, 131–45; Constantakopoulou 2007, 44–5. A Naxian dominance of Delos at this time is not accepted by all scholars, however: Chankowski 2008, 25–8.

[68] Kokkorou-Alevras 2000, 145–8.

[69] Pind. *Isth.* 6.73.

[70] Aiginetan coins predominate in such earlier Cycladic hoards as *IGCH* #6 (*c.*500) and #7 (*c.*500–490).

[71] Aglaosthenes *FGrH* 499 F7.

[72] Sheedy 2006, 92.

[73] Sheedy 2000, 118–19 and 2006, 118 for Class C (*c.*500–495).

[74] Sheedy 2006, 117–19.

but silver mines in the possession of the Parian colony of Thasos, located in the Thasian *peraia* on the mainland, are also a likely source.[75] The Thasians maintained an unusually close relationship with their *metropolis* throughout the Archaic period that is attested epigraphically.[76]

Other late Archaic Cycladic issues include those of Siphnos, Seriphos, Karthaia, Koressos, and Ioulis on Keos, and Kythnos (beginning *c*.530–520).[77] This minting activity may have enabled the local economies of the Cyclades to have become more closely integrated with each other and with other areas where Aiginetan coins predominated, such as the Greek mainland and also Egypt.[78] In the early fifth century such connectivity can be seen in the famous Decadrachm Hoard from Lykia (*c*.460), which includes Aiginetan, Parian, and Attic coins as well as those of many other Aegean states.[79]

As mentioned in the discussion of sources in Chapter 2, the purpose of coinage in the Archaic period of ancient Greek history remains controversial.[80] However, by the late sixth-century there is evidence of at least some coinage being used in long-distance trade, and it probably helped to facilitate that trade.[81] It may also have facilitated state expenditures—for monumental temple construction

[75] Hdt. 6.46–47; Pouilloux 1954 and 1982; Graham 1978; Berranger 1992, 170–203; Matthäus 1988; Wagner and Weisgerber 1988; Sheedy 2006, 117. Di Napoli 2005 for Siphnian silver use at Paros; for continuing links between Paros and Thasos see now Osborne 2009; Bissa 2009, 101–2 emphasizes trade rather than more haphazard means of importing silver, such as re-minting or overstrikes. For an ancient statement on the profitability of exporting silver from a *polis*, see Xen. *Por.* 4.1.

[76] The dual archonship of Akeratos on Paros and Thasos: *IG* XII, Suppl. 412 and Berranger 1992, 309–10. For the Parian Tokes and his association with the foundation of Eion: Lazarides 1976. Sheedy 2006, 104 and 117 posits a northern Greek engraver working on Paros due to stylistic similarities with coins from such communities as Stagira, Skione, and Akanthos: Cahn 1973; Price and Waggoner 1975, 40–3.

[77] The following is derived from Sheedy 2006: Siphnos: Series I (*c*.540–525); Seriphos: gorgoneion tetrobols (*c*.470–460); Naxos: wreathed staters (began *c*.540–530); Karthaia: Series I, II, and III (*c*.520–490); Ioulis: Series I (began *c*.515); Kythnos: Series I (*c*.530–500). The dolphins which appear on specimens from all three Keian mints might indicate some sort of monetary union or even federation: Papageorgiadou-Banis 1993, 55; Sheedy 2006, 32.

[78] Figueira 1998, 36–8 with references.

[79] Fried 1987; Sheedy 2006, 131.

[80] See Chapter 2, pp. 48–9.

[81] Davies 1998, 239; for the weaker view of coinage in trade see Howgego 1995; von Reden 1995 stresses the symbolic nature of coinage over its monetary and commercial aspects.

and for warships, particularly triremes.[82] This may also be noted in the construction of fortification walls for *poleis* in the Cyclades. It is intriguing that the three main islands that engaged in these other activities that required capital for state expenditures—Naxos, Paros, and Siphnos—all had such walls by the late sixth century.[83]

If the high point of Naxian silver minting (the unwreathed staters) occurred during the late sixth century,[84] then it is likely that the first construction of triremes on Naxos occurred at roughly the same time.[85] Could Naxian naval power have begun as far back as the tyranny of Lygdamis? There is no specific tradition that he was a builder of warships. However, Polykrates could have provided an example, and he could have also followed the earlier example of the Kypselids of Corinth, confiscating the property of aristocrats in order to fund various projects, such as the construction and deployment of warships.[86] Periander, in particular, is said to have built triremes and employed them in various expeditions.[87]

But where would the Naxians, or the inhabitants of other Cycladic islands, have acquired the necessary timber to build warships? It has been recently proposed that shipbuilding timber is unlikely to have traveled far from its sources of supply, due to difficulties of transport. Instead, such timber was utilized at shipyards (*naupegia*) near the area where this resource was harvested.[88] While this could have been

[82] Trundle 2010, 235–7, esp. 236: 'There is perhaps no coincidence that coined money appeared in the Aegean basin at the same moment as these new three-banked vessels.'

[83] For Naxos: Andriskos *FGrH* 500 F1 and Hdt. 5.34 (though there are scant visible remains today: Reger 2004, 762). For Paros: Hdt. 6.133.2; for modern remains see Berranger 1992, 62–5; Schilardi 1975, 197–203; Reger 2004, 766. For Siphnos: Brock and Mackworth Young 1949, 2; Reger 2004, 773. For the construction of fortification walls in the fourth century see Chapter 5, pp. 179–80 for the Keian cities and Chapter 6, p. 234 for a general phase on several islands in the latter half of the century.

[84] Sheedy 2006, 91. The main evidence for Archaic Naxian coinage are two hoards, *IGCH* #6 and #7.

[85] Costa 1997, 166–8 is somewhat agnostic on when and how Naxian sea power began, but accepts its existence in the later sixth century in broad terms. Walker 2004, 201–2 assumes that Eretria was already a naval power by the mid-sixth century, before the tyranny of Diagoras.

[86] Hdt. 5.92ε.2 and 92η.1; Nic. Dam. *FGrH* 90 F58; Figueira (forthcoming *a*).

[87] Hdt. 3.52.7 and 53.7; Nic. Dam. *FGrH* 90 F58–59.

[88] Bissa 2009, 123–8, 139–40, and 149–1. The only type of shipbuilding supply for which we have strong evidence for its import into Athens is oars (Andok. 2.11; *IG* I^3 89 line 31).

true in some cases, a separate logistical problem would have arisen, in that the new ships would have to be towed, or crewed and sailed to the new 'home' port. The most likely candidate for a source of supply for the Cyclades would have been to the north in Macedon and Thrace. Although the Parians had the strongest ties to this region, there is no reason to think that they were able to actually control the trade in shipbuilding timber from there. While we cannot reconstruct the particulars, it seems obvious that the Cycladic islanders could not have acquired warships without maintaining strong commercial links with areas that produced timber.

The need for coinage for state expenditure may have been increased also by monumental construction, such as the extensive programme of temple-building on Naxos during the late sixth century, including the temple to Apollo Delios at Palati that was the largest such structure in the Cyclades.[89] A similarly extensive programme of temple-building in the late Archaic period is also known on Paros. Three main Ionic temples (including a major Ionic temple to Athena), as well three or four Doric (one to Artemis of Delos) were constructed either in the *polis* centre or nearby.[90] Other temples were built at other sites on the island such as Marmara and Despotiko.[91] Although some have expressed scepticism that temple-building during any period can be used as an absolute marker of prosperity,[92] it is obvious that poorer states could not have undertaken such projects. Other Cycladic communities known for monumental temple construction were Karthaia on Keos[93] and also Siphnos.[94]

It is intriguing to compare this kind of activity with the temple-building that is attested in Ionia at roughly this same time, but on a larger scale of construction. Those of Samos, Ephesos, and Didyma are particularly massive, but smaller structures known from Khios, Myous, Mytilene, and Phokaia can also be included.[95] Not every

[89] Gruben 1982 and 2000 on the temple; Reger 2004, 762; Sheedy 2006, 87 on state expenditures for such purposes.

[90] Gruben and Koenigs 1970; Gruben 1982 and 1997; Schuller 1985 and 1991. For other smaller sites see Reger 2004, 766–7.

[91] Schuller 1985, 332–8 and 353–7; Kourayos 2005.

[92] Osborne 1999.

[93] Apollo Pythios (Mendoni 1985, 163–5) and Athena (Mendoni 1985, 161).

[94] The Siphnians built a *prytaneion* in the late sixth century with Parian marble: Hdt. 3.57.4.

[95] Osborne 1999, 322. The Khian structures at Emborio and Kato Phana have been compared to the Naxian and Parian temples from this same period.

Ionian *polis* built in this manner, and great wealth did not necessarily result in monumental construction. But it has been proposed that 'peer-polity interaction' and competition may have driven such building activity in Ionia, and this may also be applicable to the Cyclades at this time.[96]

It may be instructive to compare Naxos with a known commercial powerhouse of the sixth century, Aigina. The nature of society on Aigina in the Archaic and early Classical periods remains controversial, especially in terms of the social background of its elite. The prevailing modern view is that Aigina was an agriculturally impoverished island that derived most of its wealth through trade in slaves, metals, grain, and small luxury items known as *Aiginaia*.[97] Others have stressed the idea that the Aiginetan aristocracy was a more traditional Archaic landed elite.[98] The most outspoken proponent of the second position still admits that at least some of the wealth of Aigina derived from trade, particularly in grain imported from the Black Sea area, but proposes that it was mainly in the hands of metics.[99] Aiginetan merchants, however, ranged throughout the Aegean and west to Italy and Sicily, and Aigina eventually fielded more warships in 480 than any of the Cyclades.[100] Also, as mentioned above, Aiginetan coins were produced in very large numbers and became common currency not only in the Cyclades but also in the Peloponnese and Crete during the late sixth and early fifth centuries.[101] As mentioned above, many states also adopted the Aiginetan standard for their own coinage.[102]

Naxos, and by extension the Cyclades in general, cannot compare in scale. However, given their geographic position, did the inhabitants of the Cyclades *need* to send whatever ships they had far and wide as

[96] Ibid.

[97] Figueira 1981 and forthcoming *b*; Möller 2000, 76; Lätsch 2005, 107–8 and 149–50.

[98] de Ste. Croix 2004; Winterscheidt 1938; Hansen 2006*b*, 5–18 disputes Figueira's high population figures and posits hired rowers to explain the island's naval potential.

[99] de Ste. Croix 2004, 386–7 and 407. However, metics are not securely attested on Aigina until the fourth century: Figueira 1998, 225–7. See Arist. *Pol.* 1291b 17–25 for an *emporikon* class on Aigina and Khios.

[100] This has been questioned by De Souza 1998, 285, since Thucydides downplays the strength of the Aiginetan navy at 1.14.3. But see Hdt. 6.92.1 for a total of 70 warships.

[101] Figueira 1981, 98–107 and forthcoming *b*.

[102] Figueira 1998, 36–8 and 255–7.

part of their economic strategies? They may have instead been able to control more closely the heavy flow of commerce that already used nearby routes. To understand how this could have worked, we must now turn to a different island in a different region, and roughly a century later in time.

The case of Kerkyra on the eve of the Peloponnesian War may offer clues. Thucydides records speeches given at Athens by both Corinthian and Kerkyraian envoys during the debate of 433. Both sides remark on a curious aspect of Kerkyra's situation, that this state had avoided political alliances in the past but had now been compelled to change this policy. The Kerkyraian envoys stress that giving aid to their *polis* would be in the interests of Athens, since their home island

> lies conveniently for the coast navigation in the direction of Italy and Sicily, being able to bar the passage of naval reinforcements from there to the Peloponnesus, and from the Peloponnesus to there; and it is in other respects most suitably positioned.[103]

The rival Corinthian ambassadors add another related detail about the Kerkyraians:

> their geographical situation makes them independent of others, and consequently the decision in cases where they injure lies not with judges appointed by mutual agreement, but with themselves, because while they seldom make voyages to their neighbors, they are constantly being visited by foreign vessels which are compelled to put in to Kerkyra.[104]

These passages were famously dismissed by Kagan in 1969 as nothing but Corinthian propaganda pitched to the Athenian assembly.[105] However, they provide much fuel for speculation and should not be so lightly dismissed. This discussion will not focus on the standard approach to these Thucydidean passages, which has concentrated on the question of causation of the Peloponnesian War, and the role played by the 'Kerkyraian Affair' in such causation.[106] The goal,

[103] Thuc. 1.36.1–2 (Crawley translation): *τῆς τε γὰρ Ἰταλίας καὶ Σικελίας καλῶς παράπλου κεῖται, ὥστε μήτε ἐκεῖθεν ναυτικὸν ἐᾶσαι Πελοποννησίοις ἐπελθεῖν τό τε ἐντεῦθεν πρὸς τἀκεῖ παραπέμψαι, καὶ ἐς τἆλλα ξυμφορώτατόν ἐστιν*. This is echoed by Xen. *Hell.* 6.2.9–10 (discussing the island's situation in 374).

[104] Thuc. 1.37.3: *ἡ πόλις αὐτῶν ἅμα αὐτάρκη θέσιν κειμένη παρέχει αὐτοὺς δικαστὰς ὧν βλάπτουσί τινα μᾶλλον ἢ κατὰ ξυνθήκας γίγνεσθαι, διὰ τὸ ἥκιστα ἐπὶ τοὺς πέλας ἐκπλέοντας μάλιστα τοὺς ἄλλους ἀνάγκῃ καταίροντας δέχεσθαι.*

[105] Kagan 1969, 211–14.

[106] In addition to Kagan 1969, see Stadter 1983; Crane 1998.

rather, will be to evaluate the truth of this statement in terms of geographic proximity to trade routes and concomitant geopolitical factors that might be applied to the late Archaic Cyclades, particularly Naxos.

It is a fair question to ask whether or not Thucydides has given here an accurate picture of Kerkyra as it was in the 430s. We do have evidence of Kerkyraian connections with other states in the Archaic period that would seem to belie a policy of isolation. An early inscription records a Kerkyraian *proxenos* at Lokris in Italy in the late seventh century.[107] Herodotus relates that at some point in the sixth century, Kerkyra and Knidos had forged ties after the Knidians helped rescue 300 Kerkyraian boys from Periander.[108] These ties included tax exemptions for Knidians on Kerkyra and a joint colonial venture on the island dubbed 'Black Kerkyra', or Korcula, on the Dalmatian coast.[109] These examples could indicate that the image of total political isolation for Kerkyra would have been a false one, although they are all much earlier in time than the 430s and the Kerkyraians may have cut all such links by then.

Economic isolation for Kerkyra, however, would have simply been out of the question, for evidence of major trade in Greek vases across the Adriatic begins in the late sixth century and increases through the fifth at sites such as Spina.[110] It is possible that the Kerkyraians made their harbour into an emporium for both Greek and non-Greek merchants from nearby locales.[111] While not the only potential stop-over for passage between the Greek mainland and Italy, Kerkyra was by far the most convenient.[112] The distance between Kerkyra and the coast of Italy is approximately fifty miles, with land always visible, and could possibly have been crossed by triremes in a single day.[113] Other locales in the Peloponnese, such as Leukas, were further from Italy and ships departing from there would have also passed close by Kerkyra.

[107] Meiggs and Lewis 1989, #4; Hornblower 1991, 80–1.

[108] Hdt. 3.49.

[109] [Skymnos] 421; Strabo 7.5.5 C315; Beaumont 1936, 173–4, who thinks that the colony may have vanished by the 430s.

[110] Kiechle 1979, 173–4; Braccesi 1977, 57.

[111] Gomme, Andrewes, and Dover 1945, 173.

[112] Admitted even by Kagan 1969, 212, and notwithstanding the sentiments of Kiechle 1979, 178.

[113] Wilson 1987, 107.

The isolation spoken of in the envoys' accounts pertained to the resolution of disputes, with such problems handled at Kerkyra instead of being referred to international agreements.[114] While such disputes could at times have had economic ramifications, this does not imply that the Kerkyraians were economically isolated from other Greek states.[115]

Thucydides may in fact have been attempting to draw a contrast between Kerkyra and other island states involved in organizations like the Delian or Peloponnesian Leagues. To Thucydides, naval power *was* imperial power; this is clear from his statement that throughout Greek history until his day 'no warfare on land... resulted in the acquisition of empire'.[116] This is an example of how islands were seen in Athenian sources as natural subjects of the Athenian *arkhē*. Kerkyra was not a member of either league, yet by 435 the Kerkyraians had the second most powerful navy in mainland Greece in terms of ship numbers,[117] 120 warships according to Thucydides.[118] Although the Kerkyraians sent sixty triremes to the Greek side during the war with Xerxes, they remained neutral during the conflict and prepared for either outcome, according to Herodotus.[119] This act may have helped cement their reputation for political isolation.[120] The Kerkyraians may have preserved into the later fifth century a truly antiquated form of island maritime power, a form that was within reach of *poleis* that were suitably positioned and had sufficient wealth to exploit that position. It is possible that in this section of Book One Thucydides was presenting the Kerkyraians as exceptional, because in the 430s they were an unaligned island with their own fleet.

[114] Wilson 1987, 27.
[115] Kagan's focus was on discounting economic motivations among the Corinthians as a reason for war with Kerkyra. At pp. 213–15 he fully admits the importance of Kerkyra as a stopover for shipping to Italy and Sicily, while downplaying the possibility that the Corinthians used it as a stopover on the way north to Illyria, as proposed by Beaumont 1936, 183. Kagan then goes on to contradict his earlier statements by stressing how Kerkyra can be seen as one of several Kypselid colonies in the Adriatic designed to secure commerce.
[116] Thuc. 1.15.2; Constantakopoulou 2007, 85.
[117] Kiechle 1979, 175.
[118] Thuc. 1.25.4; Thiry 2001, 140.
[119] Hdt. 7.168.
[120] Kiechle 1979, 175 and 178.

Just as with Naxos, it is unclear from what source the Kerkyraians would have acquired the timber to build such a fleet of triremes. Illyria to the north is possible, or the mountains of Akhaia and Arkadia could have also sufficed.[121] Southern Italy also had these resources, as seen in a late fifth-century Athenian inventory.[122] The Kerkyraian warships appear to have been owned and operated by Kerkyraian aristocrats and predominantly rowed by slave labour.[123] Despite the doubts of some modern scholars, this is far from the only attested example of servile rowers.[124] It has been proposed that the Aiginetan fleet of the late Archaic period was crewed by rowers who were either slaves, or of manumitted status but still bound to Aiginetan aristocratic shipowners by ties of clientage.[125] The combination of Kerkyraian naval power with a lack of political alignment (what might be called 'convenient neutrality'[126]) may have resulted in Kerkyraian hegemony over the surrounding waters, a hegemony that could have maximized economic benefits for the Kerkyraians. It should be noted that in Thucydides' account, the Epidamnians had become angry since the Kerkyraians would not protect them

[121] Meiggs 1982, 130.

[122] *IG* I^3 386 line 100; Hornblower 2011, 59.

[123] Thuc. 1.54.2 and 55.1 (800 slaves out of 1,050 Kerkyraian prisoners taken); de Ste. Croix 2004, 388 n.46; Welwei 1977, 113–17. Some modern authors have downplayed this testimony: Wilson 1987, 51–2; Wallinga 1993, 178 n.17 simply dismisses it as the result of a 'full-scale mobilization' in Kerkyra. While this is certainly possible, he goes on to say that slaves would have been more likely to have fallen prisoner because 'they couldn't swim' or they 'wanted a better lot', a chance at freedom. There is no reason to think that the Corinthians would have done anything else with these individuals than resell them as booty from their victory, or keep them for their personal property.

[124] At Khios in 412 (Thuc. 8.15.2) and in the Peloponnesian fleet commanded by Gorgopas at Aigina in 388 (Xen. *Hell.* 5.1.11). A recent redating of an Athenian honorary naval catalogue (*IG* I^3 1032) from the Battle of Arginusai to 412, if correct, would indicate that slaves were used in the Athenian navy extensively during the Peloponnesian War: Graham 1992 and 1998; Hunt 2006, 25–9; Papazarkadas 2009, 76 (for the older view that it dated to the Battle of Arginusai see Amit 1965, 31–7; Morrison, Coates, and Rankov 2000. But there have been other dates proposed. Laing 1966 considers it to be early fourth century, followed by Figueira 1981, 59–60 and n.30, so the issue remains unresolved). Just as in the building accounts for the Erechtheion in Athens (Randall 1953), slave rowers and free rowers worked side by side and were paid equal wages: Hunt 2006, 27–8.

[125] Based on Pin. *Ol.* 8.20–30 with schol., and Arist. fr. 475.1 Gigon; Figueira 1981, 35–8 and 59–60; 1993, 207–8.

[126] Kiechle 1979, 177 calls it 'splendid isolation.'

from barbarians who lived nearby.[127] The implication is that the Kerkyraian refusal to protect the Epidamnians was in fact exceptional for them, and that Greek communities in the region may have expected the Kerkyraian fleet to provide protection in the Adriatic.[128]

'Protection', however, may have also extended to compulsion to put into the harbour of Kerkyra, perhaps for the payment of dues. The context of Thucydides' statement on ships being 'compelled to put into Kerkyra' seems to refer to deliberate action and not to weather conditions or some other cause.[129] This raises a larger issue—were ancient navies able to effectively control sailing routes and local waters? Several modern scholars have raised serious doubts that such control was possible, citing the difficulties of operating triremes and other warships for extended periods, due to supply and other logistical problems. Triremes, in particular, were unable to remain at sea for long, and were not particularly suited to the maintenance of blockades or other similar operations. Their design was more applicable to pitched battles at sea, or to amphibious landings against fixed coastal targets.[130]

However, despite these obstacles to the employment of triremes and other warships to control shipping routes, the reality appears to have been more complex. Various ancient Greek sources do report incidents of merchant vessels being successfully intercepted by warships.[131] Moreover, there is also testimony concerning the convoying of merchantmen (generally in wartime).[132] Presumably

[127] Thuc.1. 24–25.

[128] Kiechle 1979, 184.

[129] *Pace* Hornblower 1991, 81.

[130] Gomme 1933; Stroud 1998, 49; Guilmartin 2003, 78–82 and 112–16; Figueira 1993, 332 and n.22, emphasizing the greater suitability of triremes for amphibious assaults.

[131] The Athenians from their base at Naupaktos in the Corinthian Gulf: Thuc. 2.69.1 and 80.1; Athenian ships in the area of the Hellespont take three Spartan troop transports (though twelve more escape to Sestos): Xen. *Hell.* 1.1.35–36; the Spartan commander Teleutias against grain transports and other ships near Sounion: Xen. *Hell.* 5.1.23; Antalkidas with eighty triremes at the Hellespont in 387: Xen. *Hell.* 5.1.25; the Carthaginians against grain ships near Akragas in 396: Diod. 13.88.3–5; the Syracusans against grain ships in 357: Diod. 16.13.3; Evagoras of Salamis against Persian supply ships in 386: Diod. 15.3.3.

[132] Syracusan triremes escorting ships in 396: Diod. 14.64.1; Polyain. *Strat.* 5.13.1 for Corinthian escorts during the Peloponnesian War; Corinthian warships countering the Athenian Naupaktos squadron to allow galleys to successfully leave the Corinthian Gulf and complete the crossing to Sicily: Thuc. 7.17.3–4 and 19.4–5. The separate accounts of the prelude to the Battle of Naxos in 376 can be used either

such precautions would not have been taken unless there was an expectation that galleys *could* be successfully intercepted by hostile vessels. While there is no reason to suppose that interception of vessels at sea was a simple and straightforward endeavour, this does not automatically entail that maritime states would not have attempted it, and at least occasionally (if not regularly) experienced success.[133]

'ACTIVE' AND 'PASSIVE' INSULARITY

In several studies, T.J. Figueira has characterized two types of maritime states in the Archaic period—one type for islands located at the intersection of trade routes and focused on colonization (Corinth and Eretria being two examples), the other for islands located near trade routes and focused more on piracy than colonization (Aigina and Samos being exemplary).[134] According to this approach, 'thalassocracy' to Thucydides meant first and foremost the suppression of piracy.[135] The trireme was the type of warship most suited to such operations, whereas pentekonters were more appropriate for *leisteia*. Thus, Thucydides dismisses Greek fleets before 480 as overly focused on piratical activity and utilizing older types of vessels, with a number of one hundred triremes apparently seen by him as a benchmark for a truly thalassocratic *polis*, and one which would have actively attempted to suppress piracy.[136] Thucydides is not fully consistent with his own definition, however, since Corinth invented the trireme and was the first Greek state to build them in great numbers, but was also known for *leisteia*.[137]

to support the possibility of successful interception of galleys (Xen. *Hell.* 5.4.61) or that of successful protection of such vessels by escorts (Diod. 15.34.3).

[133] See Chapter 6, pp. 225–9 for a discussion of such issues during the fourth century.

[134] Figueira 1981, 192–202; 2002*a*; forthcoming *a*.

[135] Thuc. 1.3.4 (on Minos' activities) and 1.13.5 (on those of the Corinthians). Figueira forthcoming *a* emphasizes the different purposes of Polykrates' trireme fleet (for expansion) and his pentekonter fleet (for *leisteia*).

[136] Figueira forthcoming *a*.

[137] Salmon 1984, 133–5 and 222–5.

Another recent study proposes a distinction between 'active maritime' and 'passive maritime' insularity—by this definition, Kerkyra's naval power and its control of nearby trade routes made it an example of 'active maritime insularity.'[138] Other islands near to Kerkyra such as Kephallenia and Zakynthos, by contrast, tended to exhibit what might be called 'passive maritime insularity'—they stayed out of political connections with the nearby region of the Greek mainland, and they did not build warships in great numbers or engage heavily in commerce.[139]

Thus, according to Thiry's interpretation, thalassocracy might be equated with 'active maritime insularity,' and it need not have meant hegemony on the later Athenian model but simply 'the possession of a fleet and an aim, a concentration of force and purpose.'[140] Polykrates' 'thalassocracy' has been characterized by one commentator as 'a kind of corsair adventuring writ large'.[141] Yet another study has called it a 'centralization of finances—a regular and heavy impost on all merchant vessels using what Polykrates was able to claim as territorial waters'.[142] If Polykrates' naval programme represents a transition between piratical activity and a more organized, 'state-oriented' system of levying transit tolls and harbour dues, then we may see the seed of a concept later put into more effective practice by later states.[143]

Although it is not specifically stated by Thucydides, some of the Cyclades may have fit such a model in the Archaic period because merchant ships used them as stopovers on the east–west route in the Aegean, either out of convenience or because Cycladic warships could force them to stop from time to time. This is not to say that the example of Kerkyra should be pushed too far—most of the Cyclades do not appear to have operated fleets of anything close to a comparable size. Yet a smaller number of vessels might have been sufficient to control local routes and harbours in the Cycladic region. The aforementioned logistical issues of operating warships would have been lessened, due to the proximity of home bases and sources of supply.

138 Thiry 2001, 139 on Kerkyra as an 'île maritime à insularité active.'

139 Thiry 2001, 143 on Kephallenia and Zakynthos.

140 Miller 1971, 45.

141 Shipley 1987, 95.

142 Miller 1971, 23; De Souza 1998, 282–3.

143 De Souza 1998, 272–4; Papalas 1999, 6–7.

Only Naxos, however, constructed warships in such numbers that it entered the Aegean historical tradition of thalassocracy. The parallels between Kerkyra in the 430s and Naxos prior to the Persian Wars are intriguing. In both instances, the islands in question straddled important trade routes.[144] The Kerkyraian use of slave rowers may have also been seen on Naxos—it is otherwise difficult to explain Herodotus' mention of 'many slaves' on Naxos in the same sentence as foot soldiers and warships (although it could simply be a reference to the wealth of the Naxians). It may be that the construction of pentekonters (and later, triremes) by the Naxians and other Cycladic islanders was motivated not by a desire to create a 'thalassocracy' in the traditional sense (of a sea empire that covered a vast area, such as created by Athens in the fifth century), but instead for the *local* control of trade.[145] The Naxians could have deployed a greater number of ships and taken advantage of their central location in the region. Yet, the Naxians were not expansionistic in the same sense as the Samians under Polykrates, so they would have escaped notice in Thucydides based on his definition of naval hegemony. It would appear that Naxos is difficult to fit into either Figueira's or Thiry's typologies in too strict of a fashion, although some correlation can be discerned.

Under such conditions, it would not have been necessary to send Cycladic ships far and wide for trading purposes, or make international agreements for the handling of trading disputes. This is not to say that inhabitants of the Cyclades never travelled abroad. A famous example is Anaxilas of Naxos, commemorated by a funerary inscription found in the Kerameikos in Athens.[146] However, on the macro scale of activity it would seem that Cycladic products were most likely transported by merchants from locales other than the Cyclades themselves.

In addition to the aforementioned mineral and metal resources, several of the islands appear to have been production centers for

[144] See Chapter 2, pp. 30–3 for the number of attested trade routes through the Cyclades that passed by Naxos.

[145] It is possible that some Naxian galleys could have been public warships (this is known from Thasos: Hdt. 6.46) but it is more likely that they were private (Scott 2000, 103).

[146] *IG* I[3] 1357 (*c*.510); *SEG* XXII.79; Willemsen 1963; for discussion of Anaxilas' possible status as a metic at this early date see Baba 1984; Papadopoulos and Smithson 2002, 188–90.

pottery during the late Archaic period, as they had been during the earlier Protogeometric and Geometric periods.[147] Sites of known workshops include Paros, Naxos, Melos, Thera, and especially Siphnos.[148] Cycladic ware from the late sixth century has been found at several sites in eastern Crete such as Olous, Azoria, and Itanos, and also at Tokra in Libya.[149] As will be seen in the discussion for the fifth century, this is intriguing because such trade with Crete breaks off in the early fifth but resumes near the end of that century, perhaps due to a realignment of trade routes during the Peloponnesian War.[150] It is not always easy to determine the point of origin of a specific pottery type, however.[151]

The roots of Naxian sea power could possibly date back to Lygdamis, but the building and operation of warships no doubt continued (and intensified) under the regime of the Fat Ones, and also under the democracy established after their fall.[152] Once democracy was established on Naxos, a possible parallel for changes in fleet organization could come from another nearby example. The so-called 'Laws of Eretria' appear to give details on the payment (apparently by all in the *polis* who could contribute) of some sort of dues to crews on ships sailing beyond certain northern (Cape Kenaion) and southern points (the Petaliai Islands).[153] This payment of a *misthos* to crews is

[147] For Protogeometric and Geometric Cycladic ware a good overview is Papadopoulos and Smithson 2002, esp. 164 and 171–2; Coldstream 1990 for finds of this ware at Knossos.

[148] For general discussion see Papadopoulos and Smithson 2002, 174–7 and nn. 96 and 97. For pottery workshops in the Cyclades see Gautier 1993; Villard 1993; Sheedy 1985; Brock and Mackworth Young 1949; Sutton 1991, 256. At the sanctuary of Aghia Irini on Keos, 70 per cent of the Archaic ware found has been identified as Siphnian, and it has also been found in large amounts at Tokra in Libya: Butt 1977, 304.

[149] Erickson 2010, 294–5 and n.126 for references (this pottery remains unpublished, however). Proposed islands of origin for these finds include Naxos, Paros, and Thasos.

[150] See Chapter 4, pp. 107–8.

[151] Bikakis 1985, 66–7 on the idea that sixth-century 'Melian' ware was actually Parian, and 286–7 on 'Parian skyphoi' that may have also been produced on Naxos.

[152] Did the Fat Ones take any of the triremes with them? None appear to be defending Naxos against Megabates in 500. The question of how the Fat Ones actually left the island is intriguing one. Wallinga 1984, 421 proposes that the expulsion of the Fat Ones may in fact have been at least partially a result of the politicization of the crews as more pentekonters and triremes were built.

[153] *IG* XII.9, 1273 and 1274 (= *SEG* XLI.725). For commentary: Vanderpool and Wallace 1964; Mansfield 1976; Cairns 1991; Walker 2004; van Wees 2008 and 2010. Walker 2004, 192–6 interprets it as dues paid *by* shipping to use the area *between* the two points, while Cairns 1991, 310–12 (followed by van Wees 2010, 208 n.7) proposes that it was actually meant to pay crews for naval expeditions *outside* the straits.

intriguing and may represent a radical departure from normal organization of sea power at the time.[154] If it can be used to support the argument of pushing the advancement of Greek sea power back from the 480s to the late sixth century, as a few scholars have attempted to do, then there may have been other 'laws' of this type elsewhere that escaped preservation. However, one must still be cautious about assuming a single model of naval organization among all states in the late sixth century.[155] The pattern of aristocratic shipowners in the predominantly oligarchic states of the late Archaic Cyclades may have still been the most common structure of naval forces. It remains open to speculation what kind of relationship Eretria and Naxos might have maintained in the late sixth century.[156] Naxos is the only Cycladic island that is mentioned as having participated in the Ionian Revolt, albeit with a small number of either five or six warships.[157] This reference is part of what has been called an 'alternative' historical tradition concerning the Revolt that gave more prominence to Eretria, and that was at odds with Herodotus' glorification of Athens.[158] It is not pertinent to this study to determine whether or not Eretria has been slighted in the Greek historical tradition, but it is intriguing to consider whether the Naxians could have desired revenge for the attack on their island.

Constantakopoulou 2007, 218–19 discounts this inscription as evidence for an Eretrian thalassocracy, but even if the Thalassocracy List is unreliable in many details, this law provides a foundation for a naval reputation at the time that may have been preserved in the List: van Wees 2010, 217.

[154] van Wees 2008, 135–6.

[155] As van Wees 2010, 222–6 concludes. For another cautionary view see Malitz 2008 in the same volume.

[156] van Wees 2010, 217 thinks that Eretria and Naxos were rivals for control of the Cyclades at this time. Walker 2004, 270 says that the Eretrians took control of Andros and Paros away from the Naxians in return for their assistance. Other scholars have stretched this idea beyond belief. Burn 1929, 34 would place Strabo's testimony on Eretrian control over Andros, Keos, and Tenos (Strabo 10.1.10 C448) in this period rather than in the time of the Lelantine War. Myres 1906, 98 n.40 and n.41 even states that when she first became an important naval power after the Persian Wars, Athens attempted to take up 'pieces . . . of the Eretrian *arkhe*' through her assaults on Andros and Paros after the Persian Wars.

[157] For the alternative tradition: Plut. *De Herod.* 24 (= *Mor.* 861b–c) and Ephoros *FGrH* 70 F187; Hellanikos *FGrH* 4 F183. Herodotus says nothing of Naxian ships participating in the revolt: Costa 1997, 179.

[158] Walker 2004, 273–8, who considers the Naxian and Athenian ships sent to the Ionian Revolt to have been mainly troop transports; Myres 1953, 197–200; How and Wells 1975, 58.

The numbers of triremes and pentekonters provided by the Cyclades at the Battle of Salamis in 480 may show echoes of the competition of the late sixth century.[159] Diodorus gives a total of fifty ships from all islanders 'within the area bounded by the Kyanean Rocks, Cape Sounion, and Cape Triopion' augmenting the Persian fleet.[160] Herodotus is a little more geographically specific and says that the Karystians, Andrians, and Tenians, and 'all the rest of the islanders' except for the five that he lists in chapter 46, aided the Persian fleet.[161] Though technically allied with the Persians, an unnamed number of Parian vessels waited at Kythnos to see how the fortunes of Salamis would play out.[162]

Herodotus' list of naval forces on the Greek side at Salamis, on the other hand, is somewhat confusing. He states that Melos, Seriphos, and Siphnos provided pentekonters (2, 1, and 1 respectively), while the rest of the islanders provided triremes.[163] But he also says that the Keians provided two triremes and two pentekonters,[164] as they had at Artemision.[165] The Kythnians sent one trireme and one pentekonter, and Aigina provided the Greek force with no less than thirty of 'their best sailing vessels'.[166] This would seem to imply triremes, although Thucydides states that the Aiginetan fleet at this time had been mainly pentekonters.[167] To further complicate the picture, ships (apparently triremes) from two of the Cyclades are attested as having defected from the Persians to the Greeks—from four to six Naxian[168] and one Tenian.[169]

[159] van Wees 2008, 142 thinks it very unlikely that all triremes (even all the Athenian ones) were built within the decade of the 480s.

[160] Diod. 11.3 (translation in Green 2006).

[161] Hdt. 8.66. Aes. *Pers.* 887 for Andrians; Wallinga 2005, 39 makes the unlikely suggestion that no islander ships were actually present on the Persian side, but that islanders had been pressed into service as rowers.

[162] Hdt. 8.66–67.

[163] Hdt. 8.48.

[164] Hdt. 8.46.

[165] Hdt. 8.1. These are the only Cycladic ships listed by him at this battle.

[166] Hdt. 8.46.

[167] Thuc. 1.14.3; De Souza 1998, 285 supports.

[168] Four in Hdt. 8.46.3; five in Ephoros *FGrH* 70 F187; six in Hellanikos *FGrH* 3B F323a; Plut. *De Herod.* 36 (= *Mor.* 869a–c) claims that Herodotus tried to shame the Naxians by giving all the credit for this turnabout to the trierarch Demokritos. Plutarch also quotes an epigram by Simonides of Keos in praise of Demokritos.

[169] Hdt. 8.82, commanded by Panaitios. Wallinga 1993, 113 says that from 5.85.1 onward Herodotus uses *trieres* as a generic term for 'warship' but Herodotus'

A viable question is whether these ship numbers reported in Herodotus accurately reflect the total number of warships active in these islands at the time. Assessments of such potential that rely on population estimates are methodologically unsound, since crewmen could have been hired from other communities.[170] It is possible that other Cycladic shipowners either remained neutral or even participated during Artemision and Salamis, but went unrecorded. Perhaps this is the origin of the story in Plutarch concerning objection to the inclusion of the Kythnians and the Melians on the Serpent Column,[171] although this has also been linked to the question of whether or not hoplites from the Cyclades fought at Plataia.[172]

The small numbers of warships provided by the Cyclades probably represented a combination of triremes, galleys and pentekonters.[173] However, warships of the older type would not have fought well either against triremes or alongside them, due to their smaller number of rowers.[174] They may have been relegated to reconnaissance and support roles. Why would Cycladic states have built small numbers of triremes, when it was impossible for any of them to mobilize the necessary resources to build enough to compete with the more powerful maritime states?[175] It is best explained as an extension of the phenomenon of competition seen in the later sixth century. Although none of the Cyclades could afford large fleets of such vessels, they would have needed them to assert any kind of control over local waters.

specificity in mentioning a few pentekonters alongside triremes shows that he is more exact than Wallinga allows.

[170] As exemplified by Ruschenbusch 1983*a*, 146, who uses his population estimates and the ship numbers in Herodotus to propose that Paros had 6 triremes and Andros had 5 triremes in 480.

[171] Plut. *Mor.* 873d–e; Constantakopoulou 2007, 110; Brun 1998, 657; Sheedy 2006, 52 proposes that the presence of only one Siphnian pentekonter represented an 'unwillingness to get involved' on the part of most of the Siphnians.

[172] Paus. 5.23.2 states that a bronze statue dedicated to Zeus at Olympia in thanks for the victory at Plataia listed the Keians, the Melians, and the Tenians, but that the Naxians and Kythnians had also been there and had been left out. Nicolet-Pierre 1997, 104 proposes that Diod. 5.52, which states that the Naxians were the first to turn away from Xerxes and also assisted the Greeks at Plataia, erroneously picked up this notion from their listing on the Serpent Column.

[173] Hdt. 5.30.4 may provide the clue that there were many additional Naxian warcraft than just their small number of triremes; Wallinga 1993, 139 n.28.

[174] Coates 1995, 136–8; Figueira (forthcoming *a*); *pace* Amit 1973, 24–36.

[175] Wallinga 1993, 143–4 states that the Persians would have wanted to eliminate even smaller forces of potentially-hostile triremes as a matter of policy.

At the Battle of Salamis, Demokritos of Naxos is described by Herodotus as 'their trierarch', and in command of several triremes. The distinction between private and public vessels may have been less rigid than admitted by some commentators.[176] It is true that pentekonters would have required a more substantial financial outlay, and as such could often be 'public' vessels.[177] But even triremes, specialized as they were in construction and operation, were sometimes in private hands. Philip of Kroton, who died *c.*510, was an Olympic victor who had his own trireme and paid crew.[178] We should also consider the private vessel of Kleinias who fought at Artemision.[179] Later in the fifth century, other examples of private owners of triremes include Perikles,[180] Alkibiades,[181] and Dorieos the Rhodian, who had more than one private warship.[182] Notice also the early fourth-century Athenian example of Makartatos, who operated his own trireme on Crete.[183] Such traditions died hard—witness the nature of the Rhodian trierarchy in the Hellenistic period, in which many warships were owned by the aristocracy.[184]

Although it can be hazardous to make close analogies between antiquity and other historical periods, it is intriguing to compare this situation with two others—that of the Greek revolutionary navy in the 1820s, and also the period of the Venetian maritime empire. The original warships of the Greek revolutionary navy hailed from three Aegean islands—Hydra and Spétses in the Saronic Gulf, and Psará in the northern Aegean—and were merchant vessels that had been converted into war craft, much like ancient pentekonters. The owners of these ships (such as Miaoúlis, Theophilos Kairis of Andros, or Emmanuil Xanthos of Patmos) had become wealthy from the grain trade, and on Hydra their dwellings were quite opulent, augmented by extensive fortifications. Miaoúlis and other officers sometimes commanded several ships (like Demokritos of Naxos in 480), but

176 Wallinga 1993, 19 proposes that pentekonters were generally state-owned, although at 47 n. 45 he states that pentekonters in Phokaia were private, though this is not clear from the context of Hdt. 1.163.2 and 164.3.

177 van Wees 2008, 137.

178 Hdt. 5.47.1.

179 Hdt. 8.17 (Kleinias).

180 Plut. *Vit.Per.* 35.2.

181 Thuc. 6.50.1 and 61.6.

182 Thuc. 8.35.1; Paus. 6.7.4; David 1984, 271.

183 Isaios 11.48; Wallinga 1993, 20 n.23; Gabrielsen 1997, 108–11; Casson 1995.

184 Gabrielsen 1997, 101.

there was no overall commandant and forces did not always act in unison. Eventually, despite disputes between several of the commanders, the fleet from the three aforementioned islands numbered ninety ships that were successfully employed near Samos in July 1821.[185]

A second analogy might be made with the commanders of Venetian galleys, who were generally noblemen. However, they sometimes proved difficult to control. Sources of the late sixteenth and early seventeenth centuries mention their frequent disobedience of orders from the central government, and that often they would 'hire out their galleys and trade with them'.[186] The 'desertion' of Demokritos from the Persian to the Greek side may reflect a similar situation.[187]

CONCLUSIONS

It may have been particular manifestations of some aspects of peer-polity interaction that pushed certain island states such as Naxos to concentrate their resources by the late sixth century on the minting of coins and the construction of monumental temples, and also on the maintenance of naval forces to control nearby sailing routes.[188] Many obscure events in the region earlier in the Archaic period, such as possible clashes stemming from allegiances in the Lelantine War, or other conflicts such as that between Naxos and Paros, may have been precursors of this interaction.[189] Yet the latter half of the sixth century saw major changes in naval organization in the Greek world and increasing involvement by outsiders, such as the Samians and Athenians, in the Cycladic region. Such involvement by outside powers, in addition to the advent of the trireme in Greek navies, could have intensified the level of competition among these islands. Athenian involvement would increase dramatically after the Persian Wars and create a hegemony which, even after its collapse, influenced the region through the end of the Classical period.

185 Brewer 2001, 89–99.

186 Tenenti 1967, 184 and n.18.

187 Note also the 'entrepreneurial' nature of sixteenth-century European war galley captains described in Guilmartin 2003, 36–46.

188 De Souza 1998, 272.

189 *SEG* XV.517; *IG* XII.5, 445 line 54; Berranger 1992, 205–7; Reger 2004, 764–5.

4

Under the Arkhē

The Cyclades in the Fifth Century (490–404)

The Persian Wars were a major turning point for the Cyclades. Some of the islands medized, others did not, and this allegiance may have influenced Athenian treatment of the islanders for many years after the creation of the Delian League. As members of this League, the Cyclades eventually turned over local hegemony to the greater Athenian *arkhē* and demobilized their warships. The payment of tribute brought financial aspects to Athenian hegemony, and at least two of the Cyclades saw the installation of klerouchies by mid-century. In effect, the Cyclades became the textbook example of Athenian subjects for historians like Thucydides.

Although commerce that traversed the Cyclades no doubt increased throughout the Pentekontaetia, it may be that Athens was able to redirect most of the excess wealth generated by such commerce, by the levying of tribute and later by the *eikostē* tax on harbour dues. Such wealth would have previously been appropriated by the local Cycladic *poleis* themselves during the late Archaic period. The replacement of tribute with the *eikostē* tax, in particular, may have generated more resentment in the region, leading to revolts after the failure of the Sicilian Expedition and the coup of the Four Hundred in Athens.

THE PERSIAN WARS AND THE FORMATION OF THE DELIAN LEAGUE

Herodotus states that all the islanders to whom the Persian heralds had come with a request for earth and water in 491 gave it, but mentions only the Aiginetans specifically.[1] In his play *Persians*, however, Aiskhylos says that Paros, Mykonos, Tenos, and Andros had submitted.[2] Herodotus further states that Naxos was attacked by the fleet under Datis in 490. Obviously the Fat Ones had not regained control of the island.[3] This time the Persians achieved greater success. Herodotus states that the Naxians fled to the hills, because 'they remembered what had happened before',[4] an odd statement considering that they had successfully withstood Megabates' siege of ten years earlier. But the Persian fleet in 490 was far more numerous; Herodotus gives a figure of 600 ships under Datis, as opposed to 200 under Megabates. Even if these figures are not exact, it is likely that the numbers reflect a substantial difference in scale between the two expeditions. It is also possible that the Naxians fled because they knew what had happened to Miletos at the end of the Ionian Revolt.[5] According to Herodotus, the Persians burned the Naxian temples and city centre and enslaved as many Naxians as they could capture (but see below on the possible exaggeration of the devastation).[6]

Fear of Persian attack then spread throughout the area. The Delians fled to Tenos at the approach of the Persian armada, but Datis gave his assurances that the sanctity of Delos would be respected, and made a 300-talent offering of frankincense to Apollo.[7] The Persians then sailed from Delos and 'put in at the islands, and from them they generated an army and also hostages—the sons of the islanders'.[8]

Submission to Datis was, in all likelihood, the only real recourse for the inhabitants of these islands. There was little hope that they could have put up a successful resistance to a fleet of this size, even if unified. Nevertheless, Cycladic *poleis* were not necessarily easy to subdue. Paros was able to survive an Athenian attack in the wake of the Battle of Marathon. Miltiades is said to have requested seventy ships from the Athenians and led the attack, promising them 'gold in abundance' in return. The pretext was that the Parians had provided a trireme for Datis, although Herodotus dismisses this idea and instead cites a personal enmity between Miltiades and a Parian citizen

[1] Hdt. 6.49.
[2] Aes. *Per.* 879–88; Nicolet-Pierre 1997, 100.
[3] Nicolet-Pierre 1997, 98–9.
[4] Hdt. 6.96: μεμνημένοι τῶν πρότερον.
[5] Nicolet-Pierre 1997, 99, who also speculates that the Naxians may have been caught working their fields.
[6] Hdt. 6.96. [7] Hdt. 6.97. [8] Hdt. 6.99.

named Lysagoras. Miltiades demanded 100 talents from the Parians, but after a siege of twenty-six days he was wounded and forced to return to Athens without success.[9]

Other traditions report that the Parians expected help from the Persians (who were technically still their allies).[10] Some modern commentators have proposed that the promised gold was going to come from Parian colonies in the north such as Thasos, the Thasian *peraia*, Eion, or even Mount Pangaion, places that could have fallen into Athenian hands after the capture of Paros.[11] Yet this is a very problematic theory. The idea that the colonies of Paros would have automatically submitted to Athens after the conquest of their metropolis is far-fetched at best.[12] Even though the Peisistratids may have already achieved some sort of Athenian foothold in the Strymon Valley region, this will not work as an explanation for Miltiades' expedition.

Could Miltiades in fact have been promising 'gold' from Paros and the rest of the Cyclades themselves? Again, modern opinion has differed,[13] but the use of the term 'gold' in Herodotus might have been more metaphorical than literal, and refer to any kind of wealth. And there are good reasons to propose that Paros was in fact wealthy at this time. One factor may have been the new artistic ascendancy of Parian marble. As mentioned in Chapter 2,[14] this trade grew by the late sixth century and early fifth, as Parian marble products were shipped to many locations. Examples from the eastern Aegean include the roof tiles of the Artemision at Ephesos, and the Kore of

[9] Hdt. 6.133; Nepos *Milt.* 7–8; Ephoros *FGrH* 70 F63; Develin 1977; Kinzl 1976; Lanzilotta 1987, 107–9; Garlan 1974, 129 and 132. Steph. Byz. *s.v. Miltiades* states that Miltiades brought siege machines to the island. This was also done against Melos in 416 (Ar. *Av.* 5.63) and Naxos in 377/6 (Diod. 15.34.4).

[10] Ephoros *FGrH* 70 F63 on the possibility of Persian assistance.

[11] Ehrenberg 1973, 141; Lavelle 1992, 14–15 and 20 n.50; Wallinga 1993, 145. The depth of connections between the Parians and Thasians at this time can be seen in Akeratos, who according to an inscription was archon of both *poleis* in the late sixth century: *IG* XII, Suppl. 412; Graham 1983, 74–6; Lanzilotta 1987, 106; Reger 2004, 767.

[12] Papalas 2000, 115 and n. 25 argues that Miltiades was planning to use the plunder from the expedition to build triremes and new harbour facilities in Athens.

[13] Those purporting Parian wealth include Beloch 1914 I, 407–9; French 1964, 75–6; Jackson 1969, 14 n.24. A more cautionary (though not entirely dismissive) view can be found in Develin 1977, 573 n.17.

[14] See Chapter 2, pp. 000–00.

Lindos on Rhodes.[15] This trade also extended into the Adriatic and sites such as Spina and Adria. The Parians may have established a colony at Anchiale (modern Brindisi) on the Adriatic coast early in the fifth century.[16] A parallel could perhaps be noted with the fifth-century colony established by the Aiginetans at Umbria.[17] It is also possible that connections between Paros and her colonists on Thasos may have comprised part of a greater trade network that also involved Khios and ultimately Egypt, due to finds of Thasian coins there.[18] If the Parians had such wealth available to them, given what has been said in Chapter 3 concerning peer-polity interaction we would expect them to have followed in the footsteps of Naxos and built warships. However, none of the accounts of Miltiades' attack on Paros mention naval combat, even though Herodotus attests to Parian warships sitting out the Battle of Salamis in 480.

What of the wealth of other islands in the region? Siphnos had enjoyed the benefits of her gold and silver mines throughout the sixth century, but had suffered since the attack by Samian exiles in 525 and at some point, the mines are said to have been flooded by the sea.[19]

Naxos supposedly fell on hard times after the Persian assaults of 500 and 490, which could have disrupted quarrying activity and trade in general.[20] But this does not necessarily mean that the Naxians fell victim to the 'eggs in one basket' economic scenario that has been observed in more modern studies of island economies.[21] Moreover, the damage to the island from the Persian attacks may have been exaggerated by Herodotus. For example, temple sites such as the one excavated at Iria near the ancient city show no evidence of damage.[22] A reference in Aristophanes' *Wasps*, performed in 422, indicates that

[15] Floren 1987; Sheedy 2006, 132.

[16] Steph. Byz. *s.v. Anchiale*; Berranger 1992, 162–4; Reger 2004, 767.

[17] For the colony: Strabo 8.6.16 C376; [Skylax] 16 (= Muller 1855, 1.24–25); [Skymnos] 367–9 (= Muller 1855, 1.211–12); Theopompos *FGrH* 115 F132; [Arist.] *Mir.Ausc.* 80; Steph. Byz. *s.v. Ombrikoi*; Figueira 1981, 268–9; Braccesi 1977, 153–4. For recent discussion of the Athenian and Aiginetan commercial presence at Adria throughout the fifth century, see Antonetti 2005.

[18] Roebuck 1950, 236; Pleket 1963, 71 and n. 7; Pouilloux 1954.

[19] Paus. 10. 11–12.

[20] Sheedy 2006, 125 posits this as a general phenomenon throughout the Cyclades in the years after the Persian wars, with the cessation of minting accompanied by a general downturn in trade.

[21] Royle 2001, 61–2, focusing on wine production in the Aiolian islands in the nineteenth century and its devastation at the hands of a parasite.

[22] Nicolet-Pierre 1997, 98, with references.

the *polis* of Naxos still had defensive walls when the Athenians suppressed its revolt in the 470s (see below), so presumably they had been rebuilt after the damage of 490.[23] Most tellingly, the Naxians would not have been able to field four to six triremes at Salamis (no matter what side they fought on) if they had become economically destitute.[24]

It is interesting that the more eastern Cyclades—Paros, Andros, and Tenos—medized in 480 while the more western ones—Keos, Kythnos, Seriphos, Siphnos—stayed loyal. It is possible that the medizing islands were under the control of oligarchs, who may have been more inclined to support the Persian side. It is also possible that the western islands were more aware of the sea power of nearby Greek states like Athens and Aigina and feared retaliation. But there is another possibility, and it brings us back to the question of just what Miltiades may have accomplished back in 490.

Ephoros and Nepos credit Miltiades with bringing some of the other islands in the region to heel even though Paros resisted him.[25] As was pointed out in Chapter 2, Ephoros was praised by none other than Polybios for his accuracy in naval matters.[26] Here may have been another motivation for Miltiades beyond the simple acquisition of financial spoils, and it underscores the central geographic location and strategic importance of the region, an importance that had just been demonstrated by Datis. Triremes required secure ports for longer journeys, and the position of the Cyclades on routes across the Aegean made them crucial for any state that wanted to project its naval power.[27] It is likely that Miltiades had these considerations in mind. Although its value as a source is questionable, it is worth noting that a scholion to Aelius Aristides' oration *Ὑπὲρ τῶν τεττάρων* mentions Naxos along with Paros as a target of Miltiades.[28]

While it may well be inaccurate to state that the Athenians gained control of some the Cyclades in 490, they may have still gained some

[23] Ar. *Vesp.* 354–5; Nicolet-Pierre 1997, 108.

[24] Rightly emphasized by Nicolet-Pierre 1997, 100.

[25] Nepos *Milt.* 7–8 and Ephoros *FGrH* 70 F63 both state that he attacked other nearby islands.

[26] See Chapter 2, pp. 46–7.

[27] Xen. *Hell.* 6.2.27–30 on this need for stopovers; Gomme 1933; Constantakopoulou 2007, 87; Morton 2001, 116–20; Develin 1977, 574; Hammond 1967, 219.

[28] Vol. III Dindorf, 531.8–532; Develin 1977, 575 and n.25; Kinzl 1976, 293, 295–6, and 302 n. 90; both warn, however, of the possibility of a corrupt tradition.

sort of political influence over them that was later reflected in which side each island took in 480. Although certainty is impossible, it is plausible that those Cyclades that took the Greek side in 480 did so as a result of Miltiades' expedition. It would be easy to say that they were cowed into submission—but Athens did not possess its Themistoklean fleet yet, and Paros had successfully resisted what Athens had been able to deploy at the time.

The consequences for medizing in this second Persian war were soon just as apparent as they had been to the Parians after Marathon.[29] The island of Andros was menaced by combined Greek forces soon after the Battle of Salamis. The ulterior motive given by Herodotus was the greed of their Athenian commander Themistokles. This anecdote contains the classic Andrian 'soundbite' in response to Themistokles' demand for cash: 'We have two useless gods who never leave our island, Poverty and Impotence.'[30] The siege of Andros ended unsuccessfully—however, Themistokles still exacted money from the Parians and Karystians, who paid out of fear.[31] For the Karystians, payment was not enough, for their land was devastated by Themistokles soon afterwards.[32]

The Andrian claim of poverty, even if it was actually made, should by no means be taken literally.[33] It is possible to see these events in the Cyclades as an early, if not the first, 'tribute' exaction by the Athenians, although limited to islands and states in the area that had medized. The example of Phaselis in southern Anatolia may be instructive, as that polis was attacked by Kimon and only joined the

[29] It is easy to overstate such 'consequences', however. Neer 2004, 73–4 has pointed out that despite Miltiades' assault, an Athenian state contract paid for the construction of the Athenian treasury at Delphi entirely out of Parian marble during the 480s; for the analysis of the marble in the Treasury see Palagia and Herz 2002. If Neer's thesis that Parian marble was chosen to discredit the memory of Miltiades while simultaneously celebrating the victory at Marathon is correct, then certain factors could outweigh the stain of medism.

[30] Hdt. 8.111.3: *καὶ Θεοὺς δύο ἀχρήστους οὐκ ἐκπλείπειν σφέων τὴν νῆσον ἀλλ' αἰεὶ φιλοχωρέειν, πενίην τε καὶ ἀμηχανίην*. Plut. *Vit.Them.* 21.2 tells the same story but changes the names of the gods: cf. Constantakopoulou 2007, 103.

[31] Hdt. 8.112.2, who admits his lack of knowledge regarding other islands hit with such exactions.

[32] Hdt. 8.121; Thuc. 1.98.3–4; Wallace and Figueira 2011, 239–41.

[33] It is perhaps best seen as a witty rejoinder of the same order as General McAuliffe's reply of 'Nuts!' during the Battle of Bastogne during the Second World War. Kurke 2002 characterizes the entire episode as a symbolic representation of Themistokles, although she does not deny the historicity of an attack on Andros.

League after arbitration and the payment of ten talents.[34] This sounds similar to the fate that befell the Andrians and Parians during Themistokles' activities in their area. One should keep in mind, however, that such a situation need not have led the Athenians to simply take a punitive stance. To continue the analogy with Phaselis, an Athenian decree (*IG* I^3 10) passed after its admission to the League, was not punitive. Among other provisions, it established the right of appeal in commercial cases to the Athenian polemarch.[35] Although the date of this document is disputed, the idea behind it is crucial. If more intransigent polities like the Phaselites eventually enjoyed these rights, presumably so did other members of the Delian League, even if they had also been reluctant members at the beginning.[36]

The victory at Mykale in 479 would have sent a clear message to any remaining medizers in the Cyclades that their position was no longer tenable. They perhaps could have united to resist their incorporation in the Delian League, but the enrolment of the major shipowning states of Samos, Lesbos, and Khios would have made such defiance futile.

Most scholars have followed Thucydides in describing the Delian League as an organization that changed over time from *hegemonia* to *arkhē*, from a voluntary alliance to an oppressive empire.[37] Recently it has been questioned whether or not the modern term 'empire' is truly appropriate for describing the Delian League. The term *arkhē* has become more common and is preferable, as its connotations of 'control' are more open-ended.[38]

The choice of Delos as the headquarters of the Delian League confirmed the idea of 'hegemony over all Ionians'.[39] Some have

[34] Plut. *Vit.Cim.* 12.3–4; Diod. 11.60.4. Sealey 1966, 246 suggests a Persian garrison had been at Phaselis, not something that would have been likely in the Cyclades in the early 480s.

[35] *IG* I^3 10 lines 4–6.

[36] McGregor 1987, 42. New proposals of an Arkhidamian War date for the decree include Jameson 2000–03 and Papazarkadas 2009, 70–1.

[37] Thuc. 1.95–99 details the supposed process; Diod. 11.70; for the view that this change was gradual and peaked after *c.*450 and the end of hostilities with Persia, see Meiggs 1972 and Rhodes 1992; for the opposing view that the change dates as far back as the suppression of the revolts of Naxos and Thasos in the 460s, see Fornara and Samons 1991.

[38] Kallet 2009, 56–8.

[39] Constantakopoulou 2007, 66–75; Morris 2009 has proposed that the Delian League was a supra-Ionian territorial state.

proposed that the Delian League was originally intended more to plunder Persians (and, by extension, medizers) than the traditional interpretation, which was to bring freedom to the Ionian Greeks.[40] The medism of certain Ionian states of the Aegean and Ionia itself may have given the people of Athens an additional justification for dominating them.[41] Thucydides gives a very negative assessment of the origins of the Delian League, stating that the Athenian *proschēma* or 'pretence' for establishing it was to retaliate against the Persians, but that it was actually done to increase the power of Athens.[42] It is true that Thucydides was writing long after these events, when Athens had in fact achieved hegemony, so he may have projected back to the early years of the League the situation familiar from his own day.[43] Thucydides also says nothing of the rate at which this change supposedly happened. Yet being an 'ally' of the Athenians could refer to vastly different circumstances, even at this early date.

Thus, the enrolment of the Cyclades in the Delian League may not have resulted in all of these islanders treated equally. Islands which had medized may have been forced to join and those who had fought on the Greek side may have joined voluntarily, although it is possible that some of the 'friendly' islands could have been recalcitrant as well. We have no tribute figures earlier than 454, but it is generally believed that ships and crews predominated over cash payments before that year.[44] It has been proposed that the actual levying of *phoros* may in the beginning have only been applied towards the islands that had medized—Paros, Andros, and Tenos—and resembled the *dasmos* previously owed to the Persians.[45] However, it is also possible that those islands that joined the League voluntarily contributed ships and thus had a chance at a share of plunder from successful raids, while the non-voluntary members either turned over their operational

[40] Thuc. 1.96.1. Petzold 1994, 29; Robertson 1980*a*, 70 n.31 and 1980*b*, 110; Sealey 1966, criticized by Jackson 1969. Constantakopoulou 2007, 77 cites Herodotus' statement at 9.101.3 that the islands and the Hellespont were 'prizes' for the victors as indicative of a growing equation of the Aegean islands with subjection to Athens. Moreover, the Council of Samos in 479 added islands such as Samos, Khios, and Lesbos to the League but no mainland Ionians (Hdt. 9.106.4; Sealey 1966, 248).

[41] Thuc. 6.82.3–4; Fornara and Samons 1991, 106–9.

[42] Thuc. 1.96.1, stressed by Rawlings 1977.

[43] For the latest discussion see Hornblower 2011, 12–13.

[44] Meritt, Wade-Gery, McGregor 1939, 250. As mentioned above, however, the Naxian revolt may have accelerated that process for the Cyclades.

[45] Smart 1977, 247 and n. 3; Murray 1966, 150; Wallace and Figueira 2010, 68.

warships to League control or paid cash (or both). States may also have rendered part of their obligation of *phoros* in the form of goods and services supplied to the fleet at their home harbours,[46] and the location of the Cyclades along key routes across the Aegean would have been ideally suited to this kind of system.[47]

Thucydides states that Aristeides and the Athenians decided at the foundation of the League which states would contribute money and which would contribute warships.[48] At this time most of the Cyclades probably would still have had small numbers of warships, judging from the numbers that appeared for battle in 480 (although as mentioned above, some craft may have stayed neutral). Moreover, we have no evidence for losses of warships that may have been sustained by Cycladic states in the engagements of 480. Compared to islands like Lesbos and Khios, their level of participation in post-480 League naval activity would have been minor.[49] Yet we should not discount their possible contributions entirely.[50]

The revolt of Naxos was, according to Thucydides, the first time that an ally in the League was 'subjugated in violation of the covenant'.[51] The precise date of the revolt is disputed, but it most likely began in the late 470s and was suppressed by 467/6.[52] We do not know what kind of factional disputes were occurring on Naxos, and if

[46] French 1972, 17–18, who uses it to explain many anomalies in the later *aparkhē* lists.

[47] For an interesting parallel with the need of the Carthaginian navy for bases provided by allies, see Rawlings 2010, 268–9 and 274–8.

[48] Thuc. 1.96.2; see also the statement at 6.76.3 that League members would not initiate hostilities with other League members on their own.

[49] Wallinga 1993, 167 n. 1 proposes that the original ship-contributing members of the Delian League were Samos, Khios, Lesbos, Thasos, and Naxos as the sole Cycladic contributor. But it is more likely that at least some of the triremes that survived the conflict in 480 would have served in the League navy for at least a few years. See West 1929, 272; Thuc. 1.96.1; Nicolet-Pierre 1997, 106.

[50] Wallace and Figueira 2010, propose that Naxos, Tenos, Kythnos, and Keos could have contributed ships during the early League years, but that Siphnos was unlikely to have because of only having one ship at Salamis. It should be remembered, however, that we do not know how many islander ships may have refrained from that battle for unknown reasons.

[51] Thuc. 1.98.4: παρὰ τὸ καθεστηκὸς ἐδουλώθη; Kagan 1969, 45–6 for the translation and discussion.

[52] For the revolt: Thuc. 1.98.4 and Polyain. *Strat.* 1.30.8. Various dates proposed include Rhodes 1985, 12–13 (475–470, followed by Reger 2004, 761); Strassler 1998, 53 (471/0); Meiggs 1972, 70–1 (468/7); Badian 1993, 100 (467/6); Steinbrecher 1985 (466). Milton 1979, 262 (466).

this revolt spread to other islands in the Cyclades, this fact was not recorded. Despite Thucydides' statement concerning 'subjection', he gives no other details regarding the settlement of Naxos after the revolt.[53] On analogy with Thasos, however, it is reasonable to assume that the ringleaders were exiled or forced to give over hostages, and there may have been demolition of fortifications along with the demobilization of warships.[54]

Why did the Naxians (or at least a powerful faction among them) feel that they had a chance of success, especially if other islands did not join them in the revolt?[55] Could they have hoped for Persian intervention?[56] If the Greek victory at the Battle of Eurymedon did indeed forestall a third invasion of Greece, could any of the Naxians have had advance intelligence of Persian plans?[57] Of course, even a hint of possible medism would have provided a ready pretext for League action against them.

For Thucydides, the Naxian revolt was obviously a watershed moment in the development of the Delian League. At this early date, plunder from League military action was still a viable source of income. The suppression of the Naxian revolt may have hastened the process of converting ship contributions in the Delian League to cash.[58] It might be seen as beneficial from a financial standpoint for states in the Delian League to have switched to contributions in cash, and Plutarch's biography of Kimon states that he encouraged it in an effort to help the allies while at the same time advancing the interests

[53] Pébarthe 2008, 138–9 on the symbolic nature of Thucydides' choice of words; Ostwald 1982, 38–9; Rhodes 1985, 28 n. 1; McGregor 1987, 39–40, also thinks that the allies had a hand in stopping the revolt.

[54] See Thuc. 1.101.3 for the settlement terms for the revolt of Thasos.

[55] Badian 1993, 77 proposes that the campaign to reduce Naxos took two seasons, but mainly to synchronize a problem in chronology and not on the basis of hard evidence; cf. Pritchett 1995, 83.

[56] Cawkwell 1970, 48 proposes that the Persians would have given more priority to regaining Ionia. Costa 1997, 185 considers their decision to secede from the League as indicating a desire to return to a position of neutrality, which he sees as the 'caratteristica più evidente della politica nassia post-ligdamea'. However, this does not explain just how the Naxians might have expected to preserve such neutrality in the face of a hostile Athens and its League.

[57] Robertson 1980*b*, 110 and n.88; Cawkwell 1970, 46–8; Meiggs 1972, 71; Harding 2008, 107. The date of Eurymedon is still hotly disputed, however, with some favoring an earlier date of 469/8 (cf. Rhodes 1993, 45).

[58] Meiggs 1972, 70–1.

of Athens.[59] Plutarch portrays this as a non-punitive response to widespread lethargy on the part of the allies and an unwillingness to render military service. The Naxians may not have agreed, however, and the revolt may have started as a withdrawal of their naval forces in protest because they wished to still operate their warships and share in the League's victories.[60] They may have underestimated the subsequent Athenian response, and/or underestimated the lack of support that they received from the other allies. Interestingly, while other allies of the League assisted in the suppression of the revolt on Naxos, an earlier attack on Karystos late in the 470s, which saw that city forced to join the League, appears to have been carried out solely by the Athenians.[61]

In any event, the Naxians had now seen their status in the Aegean reduced to something closer to those islands which had medized, such as Andros and Tenos. However, Herodotus chose to single out Demokritos and other Naxians for special praise for taking the Greek side at Salamis. This may reflect how much the view of the Naxians at Athens could have improved over the intervening decades.

THE CYCLADES DURING THE PENTEKONTAETIA

Oligarchy appears to have been common for Cycladic *poleis* in the Archaic period. It has been generally assumed that by a certain point in the history of the Delian League, however, many of the Cyclades had become democratic in their governmental structure.[62] In the case of Andros, there are few inscriptions from the fifth century, and it is not until Thucydides' account of the troubles of 411 (see below) that we get any indication that a democracy had been put in place sometime during the fifth century.[63] Epigraphic evidence for democracy on Ios, Naxos, and three Keian cities (Poiessa, Karthaia, and Koressos)

[59] Plut. *Vit.Cim.* 11; McGregor 1987, 49.

[60] This has been suggested by Nicolet-Pierre 1997, 109–10, who also dates the cessation of Naxian minting to the end of the revolt.

[61] Thuc. 1.98.3; Brock 1996, 359; Figueira 1991, 225; Brock 1996, 365–6; Salomon 1997, 209; Wallace and Figueira 2011, 241.

[62] See Meiggs 1972, 208–9; de Ste. Croix 1981, 294.

[63] Andros: Thuc. 8.64.1; Reger 2004, 736.

does not appear until the fourth century.[64] Only Ioulis on Keos and Siphnos show evidence of fifth-century democratic systems.[65] The exact nature of fifth-century government on Paros is unknown. An oligarchy was in place there in 410/9, but it may have been recently established at that time.[66] The governments of Mykonos and Seriphos remain obscure.[67]

We have no epigraphic evidence for the compulsory imposition of democracy (such as happened at Erythrai in Ionia[68]) for any Cycladic island during the period of the Delian League, although Naxos in the 460s remains a possibility. However, there is no clear evidence of a consistent policy on the part of Athens to establish 'democracies' in allied states in the fifth century.[69] Moreover, the very definition of the term encompasses more than one possible political arrangement or regime. Adherence to Athens was not an automatic corollary of democracy, nor adherence to Sparta an automatic corollary of oligarchy.[70] Thus it is not impossible that oligarchies in the Cyclades, perhaps at Paros or at Siphnos, continued to exist for some period of time in the fifth century. The oligarchs of Samos remained even after the suppression of their revolt, for example. It is probable, however, that the ascendancy of pro-Athenian factions would have been the most important characteristic of allied governments during the Delian League.

From the revolt of Naxos until the outbreak of Peloponnesian War in 431, we hear very little concerning the Cyclades. We are forced to speculate and make inferences based on events that took place around the region. All told, the impression is of an area that experienced a high level of economic integration with Athens. Although this

[64] Ios: *IG* XII.5, 1002 and 1004; Reger 2004, 743. Naxos: *SEG* XXXIII.676, 5–6; Reger 2004, 762. Poiessa: *IG* XII.5, 570; Reger 2004, 751; Karthaia: *IG* XII.5, 537; Reger 2004, 750; Koressos: *IG* II^2 1128; Reger 2004, 751.

[65] Ioulis: *IG* XII.5, 593 and Reger 2004, 749; Siphnos: Reger 2004, 773. Brun 1989, 121–38 proposes the existence of a Keian federation at some point in the fifth century, and this is tentatively supported by Reger 2004, 748.

[66] Reger 2004, 765.

[67] Reger 2004, 760 (Mykonos); 771–2 (Seriphos).

[68] *IG* I^3 14 (= Meiggs and Lewis 1989, #40) and I^3 15. However, see Hornblower 2011, 15 for some 'oligarchic' elements in this new arrangement for Erythrai.

[69] Brock 2009 points out that most references to such a policy are from the fourth century; Hornblower 2011, 15–16.

[70] Witness various democratic states that rebelled from Athens and kept their regimes: Akanthos and Amphipolis in the 420s, and Ephesos and Miletos later in the Peloponnesian War; cf. Brock 2009, 152–3.

Table 4.1. Some representative figures for island tribute

	450/49 (*IG* I^3 263)	441/0 (*IG* I^3 271)	433/2 (*IG* I^3 279)	425/4 (*IG* I^3 71)
Andros	6 T	6 T	6 T	15 T
Ios	840 dr.	—	3000 dr.	1 T (?)
Keos	4 T	4 T	3 T	10 T
Kythnos	3 T	3 T	3 T	6 T
Mykonos	—	1 T	—	2 T (?)
Naxos	—	6 T 4000 dr.	6 T 4000 dr.	15 T
Paros	16 T 1200 dr.	18 T	—	30 T
Seriphos	1 T (?)	1 T	1 T	9 T
Siphnos	3 T	3 T	3 T	1 T
Syros	—	—	1500 dr.	1 T
Tenos	3 T	2 T	2 T	10 T

integration would have potentially generated more wealth from a growth in commerce, the Athenians may have appropriated a good percentage of this increase in wealth, and the aristocracies of the islands might have been particularly affected. This situation may not have been entirely negative, however, since there were also possible benefits from maintaining a close relationship with the hegemon. Inter-island rivalries that had been so important during the Archaic period, such as that between Naxos and Paros, would now have been subsumed into the Athenian system.

The following Aegean islands were all eventually enrolled for tribute in the so-called Insular (*Nesiotikō phóro*) District: Andros, Astypalaia, Ikaria, Ios, Keos, Kythnos, Mykonos, Naxos, Paros, Pholegandros, Rheneia, Seriphos, Sikinos, Siphnos, Syros, and Tenos. Thus, the district included every island chosen for this study except for Amorgos (which was included in the Karian District). Table 4.1 displays totals from the *aparkhē* lists for all twelve of our chosen islands from a selection of years for which the amounts are well-preserved.

The division into specific tribute districts may in the beginning have simply reflected administrative convenience; given the state of our evidence, it is unclear whether it eventually created varying economic dynamics and led to different conditions in different regions of the *arkhē*. All of these islands appear in at least one *aparkhē* list from the 440s.[71] For those years in the 430s that tribute records

[71] Brun 1997, 185.

are extant, Andros, Naxos, and Paros all paid more than five talents; Keos,[72] Kythnos, Siphnos, and Tenos paid between one and five talents each; and only Mykonos, Seriphos, and Syros paid less than one talent.[73] The members of the Insular District during this period thus ranged from very affluent states to significantly smaller and poorer ones. It has been noted that given their reputations for wealth in the late sixth century, Siphnos and Naxos paid lower amounts of tribute than should be expected.[74] Nevertheless, they are respectable figures and cannot be said to indicate poverty.[75] Any consideration of these lists, however, must also address the problem of missing entries for many islands on the early lists. Does this mean that tribute was not paid in those years? The idea has been advanced that some of the islands defiantly refused to pay,[76] but the cases of Naxos and Thasos show that there could be serious repercussions from such a course of action. As suggested above, at least a few of the Cyclades could have escaped payments for at least a few years by contributing ships. Another recent hypothesis to explain the missing years is that the quota of one-sixtieth was sent to Delian Apollo rather than Athena for a transitional period.[77]

The requirement to pay tribute would have become the single greatest unifying economic force in the region.[78] Although certainty is lacking, the responsibility for the collection and payment of the tribute would most likely have been in the hands of local aristocrats.[79] Knowledge of the actual sources of funds for tribute payment remains outside of our reach. Some have stressed that it may have been based more on land, with elites rendering local versions of *eisphorai* in order

[72] The *polis* of Koressos paid separately in 451/50, although no figure for Keos as a whole is preserved for that year—*IG* I^3 262 col. I line 21; Meiggs 1972, 539.

[73] *IG* I^3 272 (440/39) through 281 (430/29); Brun 1996, 188; Meiggs 1972, 539.

[74] French 1972, 8.

[75] Brun 1996.

[76] Lewis 1994, 295–6, but rightly dismissed by Wallace and Figueira 2010, 65.

[77] Wallace and Figueira 2010, 65.

[78] Figueira 2005, 1 calls it 'the largest regular single transfer of output in the Aegean basin during the Pentakontaetia.'

[79] Pritchett and Pippin 1956, 100 and n. 26; Finley 1978, 125; Figueira 1981, 149 for Aigina; Pleket 1963, 72 is too 'Rostovtzeffian' in proposing Thasian 'merchant traders' as the main victims of Athenian exploitation, but his point on taxes from the wine trade as an important portion of the thirty-talent tribute assessment for this island is still valid. The responsibility of local elites to render taxes to hegemons continued during the Hellenistic and Roman periods on several of the Cyclades: Nigdelis 1990, 414–15.

to collect enough to make the payments.[80] Others have stressed indirect revenues such as harbour taxes as more probable sources.[81]

Athens remained focused on the Aegean after Naxos was reduced. In 460 the Athenians defeated the Aiginetan fleet and laid siege to the island, an operation that lasted until 457 and the forcible enrollment of Aigina in the Delian League. This was an expedition of not just Athens but also her allies, and due to their proximity, some of the Cyclades may have assisted, if not with ships than at least with crews or hoplites.[82]

At some point *c.*450, klerouchies were established on Andros and Naxos. Under his rubric for the year 453/2, Diodorus states that Tolmides divided a total of 1,000 settlers between Euboia and Naxos, and we know from epigraphic evidence that this individual did establish a klerouchy at Karystos in 453/2 or 452/1.[83] We do not have much information on these settlements, although Plutarch states that Naxos received 500 klerouchs and Andros 'half that number'.[84] The tribute of Andros was halved after the klerouchs settled on the island, dropping from twelve talents in the assessment of 451/0 to six talents in 450/9.[85] The first tribute amount for Naxos is recorded under the year 447/6, at 6 talents 4,000 drachmas.[86] Presumably the Naxian tribute was cut in half by its klerouchy as well, although this is conjecture.[87]

It has been proposed that the Egyptian disaster of 454 had created disaffection among the allies, and the establishment of klerouchies

[80] Samons 2000, 252.

[81] Figueira 2005, 11 and n.38.

[82] Thuc. 1.108.4; McGregor 1987, 51.

[83] Diod. 11.88.3; *IG* I[3] 259; Green 2006, 169 n. 364 feels that they need not have been established simultaneously; Moreno 2007, 96 and n. 91. Due to Diodorus' notoriously faulty fifth-century chronology, some have put the date of these klerouchies in 450 or even the early 440s: Green and Sinclair 1970, 519 and n.28; Meiggs 1972, 122 ('before 447').

[84] Plut. *Vit.Per.* 11.5; Paus. 1.27.5 implies that the klerouchs were actually settled there rather than exploiting the land *in absentia*. It is difficult to see why Zelnick-Abramovitz 2004, 327 thinks that the entire population of Naxos was expelled as it was on Aigina in 431, but this appears to be a misunderstanding of Thuc. 1.98 on the 'enslavement' of the Naxians after their revolt. If the Naxians had in fact been expelled from their island in the 460s, why would the Athenians have waited until fifteen years later to establish a klerouchy?

[85] For 451/0: *IG* I[3] 262 col. I line 19; for 450/49: *IG* I[3] 263 col. IV line 22; Meiggs 1972, 558.

[86] IG I[3] 265 col. II line 55; Meiggs 1972, 558.

[87] Green 2006, 169–70 n. 364 discounts the possibility.

was done in return for the lowering of tribute.[88] Tribute could have come from a variety of resources other than land (such as harbour dues or indirect taxation), but expropriated land could not have been withheld in the same way as tribute payments could have been.[89] Reductions of tribute could conceivably have been in granted in return for an exemption from harbour taxes for Athenian vessels or those vessels that were heading to Athens, as has been proposed for Karystos.[90]

Why klerouchies on Andros and Naxos and not others of the Cyclades?[91] The locations of these particular islands may have been important. Andros was on the grain route to the Bosporos, while Naxos was on the east-west route through the Aegean to Samos and Rhodes. The most common view of klerouchies is that they were poorer Athenians (often *thetes*) sent to garrison these locations.[92] One common suggestion is that klerouchies were meant to guard against revolts by the local inhabitants.[93] Thucydides describes the klerouchs of Mytilene in 428, however, as those Athenians who received allotments of confiscated land which the Lesbians then worked and paid rent to the new owners.[94] This interpretation of Athenian klerouchs as predominantly wealthy *rentiers* has gained momentum in recent scholarship.[95]

Perhaps klerouchs only took land from those who had actively resisted Athens,[96] but even local supporters of Athens probably considered them an encroachment on the sovereignty of their communities to some degree or another. The allotments would in all

[88] Brock 1996, 368–70.

[89] Nixon and Price 1990, 137–40.

[90] Brock 1996, 368.

[91] Chankowski 2008, 219 suggests that there may have been an Athenian klerouchy on Delos, which is hinted at in a few sources such as Diod. 12.73.1 (on the expulsion of the Delians in 422) and also Chankowski 2008, #50*A* line 13 (359/8) detailing possible burials of some of its former inhabitants.

[92] Meiggs 1972, 260–1; de Ste. Croix 1972, 43; Salomon 1997 for the idea that these were garrisons staffed by rotation.

[93] Meiggs 1972, 121–4: Kagan 1969, 119; Gomme, Andrewes, and Dover 1945, 373–6.

[94] Thuc. 3.50.2; Figueira 1991, 8–11.

[95] Plutarch's characterization of these settlements in *Vit.Per.* 11 may have been more reflective of Roman military colonies: Brunt 1966, 71–2; Jones 1957, 174–6; most recently Moreno 2007, 95–9 (main focus on settlements in Euboia) and 2009, 213–14.

[96] Figueira 1991, 197.

likelihood have taken some of the best land on the islands, and must have been greatly resented. The Naxian πελάτης or 'neighbour', who worked on Euthyphro's Naxian estate as a hired labourer but was later murdered, may have once owned the land that he had then been forced to work for pay.[97] Some statements in the fourth-century orators may lend some support to the idea that the klerouchs of Naxos were absentees.[98] Moreover, if the Andrian klerouchs were indeed absentee *rentiers* rather than thetic settlers, this would help explain why none of them are attested in 411 when Alkibiades attacked the island, which had recently revolted.[99]

Could they have been originally placed in *response* to revolts in the Cycladic region? A revolt on Keos has been advanced as an explanation for the separate entry of 'Koressioi' from the rest of the Keian cities in the tribute lists for 451/50, in which the Koressians paid 2.5 talents while the rest of the Keians collectively paid 1 talent 200 drachmai.[100] Following this line of reasoning, Koressos had remained loyal while the other cities had rebelled.[101] This is possible; however, it has also been noted that the Koressians, for whatever reason, may have had to delay their payment while the other communities of the Keian syntely did not.[102] Since their first appearance was in the rubric for 451/50 and they do not appear separately thereafter, it is also

[97] Pl. *Euthyph.* 4c4, 9a3, 15d5; Zelnick-Abramovitz 2004, 339–42; Schmitz 1988, 86 and Moreno 2009, 215 support the idea that Euthyphro was a wealthy *rentier*, but see the doubts of Figueira 1991, 60 n. 33. There is controversy over whether or not klerouchic lots were alienable, and if wealthy individual Athenians may have been able to acquire them *en masse*: for the affirmative see Erxleben 1975, 84–91; de Ste. Croix 1972, 245. For a negative view see Finley 1978. Recent support has been given by Moreno 2007, 89–93, citing examples such as Oionias of Atene and other Athenians whose overseas properties are listed on the stele of confiscations of the Hermokopidai (Pritchett 1953), and also Athenian lessees of sacred property at Histiaia (i.e. Panaitios in *IG* I^3 418, lines 6–7).

[98] Andok. 3.9 and Aiskh. 2.175 (possibly based on the former) mention Naxos, along with the Khersonese and Euboia, as having once been virtual prizes held by Athens (cf. Brock 1996, 366). However, the Andokian oration, *On the Peace*, which states that the Athenians held two-thirds of Euboia after the Peace of Nikias, has been soundly thrashed by a number of scholars due to its several egregious historical errors: de Ste. Croix 1972, 245; Finley 1978; Moreno 2007, 87 n. 42. One recent proposal has gone so far as to condemn the entire work as a Hellenistic forgery: Harris 2000.

[99] See below, pp. 134–5.

[100] *IG* I^3 262, I.21 and V.22.

[101] Lewis 1994, 296.

[102] Constantakopoulou 2005, 17, discusses more generally the phenomenon of payment by syntely by the islands and possible mechanisms of collection.

possible that they chose to pay separately in one year for some symbolic reason that we cannot reconstruct.[103]

There are, in addition, two possible literary references to trouble in the Cycladic region during mid-century. One is a line spoken by the character Philokleon in Aristophanes' *Wasps*, stating that he had once received two obols a day as payment for some sort of service on Paros.[104] A more telling reference is a line from a comedy recorded in Plutarch's *Life of Perikles*, where the Athenian *dēmos*, metaphorically portrayed as an unbridled and sexually excited horse, 'bit Euboia and leapt on the islands'.[105] This could refer to the establishment of settlers, or to the suppression of actual unrest in the region, or both.[106]

Eretria and Khalkis (and possibly Karystos[107]) participated in the Euboian revolt of 446. Perikles' suppression of the Euboian revolt resulted in the exile of the Histiaians, whose land was then settled with Athenian *apoikoi*.[108] The Thirty Years' Peace between Athens and Sparta was concluded soon after the Euboian revolt was suppressed.[109] It does appear that many times in the fifth and fourth centuries (see below, and also Chapter 5) the politics of Euboian cities (particularly Eretria) influenced the politics of several of the Cyclades, especially in the cities of Keos and also on Andros. The rebels may have hoped for support from outside Euboia, even if this was a false hope.[110] If revolts took place there is no way of telling under what terms the islands in question would have been readmitted to the Delian League, though it would not be outside the realm of possibility

[103] Cherry, Davis, and Mantzourani 1994 1*b*, 239; Anderson and Dix 2004, 11 n.28.

[104] Ar. *Vesp*. 1188–9.

[105] Plut. *Vit.Per*. 7.8: *ἀλλ ἐνδάκνειν τὴν Εὔβοιαν καὶ ταῖς νήσοις ἐπιπηδᾶν.*

[106] Meiggs 1972, 120–1 sees it as a reference to the settlement of klerouchs; Stadter 1989, 100 as military; Constantakopoulou 2007, 79 as more emblematic of general Athenian attitudes to islands as subjects.

[107] Reber, Hansen, and Ducrey 2004, 658 discount the possibility of a Karystian revolt at this time, despite Thuc. 1.114.2.

[108] Thuc. 1.114.3; Moreno 2007, 80–1. It is possible that there was an Athenian klerouchy at Eretria also: Hesychius *Eretriakòs katálogos* on sons of richest Eretrians sent as hostages in archonship of Diphilus 442/1; Photius *Paroem.gr.* ; Schol. Ar. *Vesp*. 715; Walker 2004, 278 and 288; Green and Sinclair 1970.

[109] Thuc. 1.115.1; Diod. 12.7.

[110] Witness Thuc. 8.24.5 on the revolt of Khios in 412: 'Nor was this revolt, in which they might seem to have erred on the side of rashness, ventured upon until they had numerous and gallant allies to share the danger with them' (Crawley translation).

to propose that something similar to the regulations for Khalkis in 446/5[111] could have been applied.[112]

There is another bit of evidence that has been used to support the idea of a revolt of some of the Cyclades around 450, but it may have a different explanation. Based on the list of contingents for the Sicilian Expedition in 413 recorded by Thucydides, it has been proposed that the Andrians, Keians, and Tenians had special troop obligations.[113] Thucydides states that some were forced to go as subjects, others as independent allies, and still others as mercenaries; but the Cycladic troops are characterized as 'subjects paying tribute'.[114] Thucydides appears to distinguish them from those allies that came to Sicily 'expecting to make money rather than to fight'.[115] Witness also the speech of Nikias before Syracuse, where he uses the term 'first of islanders', a somewhat problematic term since 'islanders' here may be synonymous with 'subject allies', and Nikias' motivation in employing it remains unclear.[116] As will be seen below, it is possible that the troop obligations were first imposed on several of the Cyclades in the wake of the Spartan expedition across the Aegean in 427 led by Alkidas.

The suggestion of mid-century Cycladic revolts is an intriguing one, but it must remain speculative, especially as a motivation for the establishment of klerouchies. The predilection of modern historians to explain all events in the *arkhē* as the result of allied revolts has been

[111] *IG* I[3] 40 (= Meiggs and Lewis 1989, #52); Balcer 1978. There is also a fragmentary decree from Eretria of similar nature (*IG* I[3] 39). The date given is the one proposed by Meiggs and Lewis 1989, #52, although like many other epigraphic documents from the fifth century it has been pushed closer to the 420s by Mattingly (in this case 424/3 in Mattingly 1992, 1996, and now 2002, tentatively followed by Papazarkadas 2009, 73–4). The silence of Thucydides makes this unlikely, although there is reference to trouble on Euboia in 424/3 (Philoch. *FGrH* 328 F130 = Schol. Ar. *Vesp.* 718).

[112] This decree, however, raises far more questions than it answers in regards to taxation and trading privileges, although the topic is too detailed to be dealt with here. See the discussion in Whitehead 1976; Smart 1977; Henry 1979; Ostwald 2002; Pébarthe 2005.

[113] Thuc. 7.20.2; Cawkwell 1997, 118–20. Hornblower 2008, 662 speculates that Keos was one of the islands where Argive hostages were sent by the Athenians in 416.

[114] Thuc. 7.57.5. After the failure of the expedition, these troops appear to have been offered freedom by Gylippos, and Thuc. 7.82.1 states that 'some few cities went over', but is not more specific.

[115] Thuc. 7.13.3; Hunt 2006, 28.

[116] Thuc. 6.68.2; Constantakopoulou 2007, 81 and n.79. This of course assumes that Thucydides did not place the term in Nikias' mouth.

recently (and rightly) questioned.[117] It can be assumed that some individuals from Cycladic islands were sent to Thourioi as colonists in the so-called Nesiotic tribe in 444/3, but as we have no other details on them or even names of their home islands, it would be speculative to attempt to connect them to events in the region at this time.[118]

The Cycladic region appears to have remained quiet during the Samian revolt of 440/39 as well. This revolt included Byzantion and potentially threatened the Delian League itself.[119] Plutarch states in his biography of Perikles that the aim of the Samians was not just to sever ties with Athens, but to take over their mastery of the sea.[120] For approximately fourteen days the Samians controlled the Aegean in their area, according to Thucydides.[121] The Persian satrap Pissouthnes tried to aid the rebels with warships.[122] The Samian rebels, however, already had substantial naval resources at their disposal, as the sea battle near Tragia saw them lose seventy triremes.[123]

There is no evidence that any of the Cyclades attempted to join in the rebellion. The proximity of the Cyclades to Athens may have been a factor here, and may have negated the possibility that Samian naval power could have enticed any of the islanders to defect from the League. Thucydides states that the Spartans did consider aiding the rebels, but by the terms of the Thirty Years' Peace, each side was 'to keep what it had', so the aid never materialized.[124]

TRADE ROUTES THROUGH THE CYCLADES DURING THE ARKHĒ

Although older studies stressed cessation of trade between states that were at war in the Classical period, it is clear that this was not the case. For example, some have proposed that trans-Aegean trade was

[117] Wallace and Figueira 2010.
[118] Diod. 12.11.3; Green 2006, 196 n. 61.
[119] Bolmarcich 2009; Green 2006, 217–18 n.127; Legon 1972, 151.
[120] Plut. *Vit.Per.* 25.3; Stadter 1989, 243.
[121] Thuc. 1.117.1, also referenced in 411 under Thuc. 8.76.4.
[122] Diod. 12.27.4.
[123] Thuc. 1.116.1.
[124] Thuc. 1.140.2 (words spoken by Perikles during a speech in 432/1 on the necessity of war with Sparta).

seriously compromised in the early fifth century by continued warfare between the Delian League and the Persians.[125] However, Attic imports to Ionia did not stop after the Persian Wars as previously conjectured; neither did Attic imports to Corinth during the Peloponnesian War.[126] There may have been disruption of trade at times due to warfare, but there appears to have been no true economic sanctions in place after the Persian Wars.[127] The so-called Elephantine Palimpsest, an Aramaic papyrus, gives details of shipping at that Egyptian port during the year 475. Greek imports included wine, oil, wood, wool, metal, and empty jars; these were exchanged for Egyptian natron, presumably destined for use in the manufacture of textiles.[128] This has been cited as an example of cabotage activity, since most of the vessels that visited the port at that time were of smaller size.[129]

Athens may have taken some steps to combat piracy during the Pentakontaetia, but all of our testimony is preserved in later sources. Kimon is said to have expelled pirates from the island of Skyros in 475.[130] The Congress Decree attributed to Perikles by Plutarch included a clause for protection of commerce; however, there is reason to consider this sentiment to be a century too early.[131] When the Athenians decided to assist the Egyptian rebels in the 450s, a large force of 200 warships was already in the waters around Cyprus and Phoenicia, the eastern terminus of the trade routes to Athens that passed through the Cyclades.[132] Stronger support comes from epigraphy. An example is *IG* I[3] 41, in which the *apoikoi* established at Histiaia after 446 could receive exemption from the *eisphora* if they captured pirates.[133] And Thucydides reports Athenian ships engaged in patrols at various times throughout the Peloponnesian War. They

[125] Cook 1961; Sheedy 2006, 125.

[126] Ionia: Miller 1997 and Carlson 2003, 597–8 (*pace* Cook 1961, 18). For Corinth: MacDonald 1982, 114–18 and Herbert 1977, 3 (*pace* Palmer 1964, 121).

[127] Miller 1997, 67–88.

[128] Porten and Yardeni 1993, 82–195 and excursus 3.

[129] As proposed by Horden and Purcell 2000, 149.

[130] Plut. *Vit.Cim.* 8.3; Thuc. 1.98; doubted by De Souza 1999, 30.

[131] Plut. *Vit.Per.* 17. For a discussion of the debate on the historicity of the Decree see Chapter 6, pp. 225–6. The only reference for anti-piratical expeditions under Perikles is Plut. *Vit.Per.* 19 on such activity in the Thracian Khersonese.

[132] Thuc. 1.104.2; Diod. 11.71.5 says 300 ships, but see Green 2006, 142 n.275; Meiggs and Lewis 1989, #33 for Athenian military action in the eastern Mediterranean. Plut. *Vit.Them.* 31.3 implies earlier Athenian interest in the region.

[133] McGregor 1982; Graham 1983; Wallace and Figueira 2011, 246; McDonald 1984, 83–4 proposes that these were exiles, not pirates.

were in the waters around Euboia on several occasions.[134] Cruises in the Saronic Gulf and near Attika, close to islands such as Keos and Kythnos, are also attested.[135]

While it is still an open question whether Athenian naval forces were truly able to keep the Aegean safe from piracy,[136] some of the treaties made between Athens and other states in the early years of the Peloponnesian War contained clauses that forbade the harbouring of pirates.[137] There are also several recorded instances of Athenian ships intercepting privateers in the eastern Aegean during the Peloponnesian War: near Karia and Lykia (in 430/29) to protect merchants from Phoinike and Phaselis in Lykia;[138] near Knidos (in 412/11) to protect ships coming from Egypt;[139] and also off Syme and Rhodes in that same year.[140] Even though the Athenian navy was weakened during the Dekeleian War,[141] the sea routes were still open enough for grain to be brought to Athens in 410.[142]

A passage in Thucydides set at the beginning of the conflict has a Corinthian ambassador to Sparta warn of the Athenian ability to control trade by sea.[143] This concept is also discussed in the pseudo-Xenophontic text entitled *The Constitution of the Athenians*, by the so-called 'Old Oligarch' who speaks of the nature of Athenian naval hegemony.[144] The Old Oligarch describes the Athenian control of the trade in vital shipbuilding materials:

[134] Thuc. 2.26.1 in 431; 8.74.4 in 411 (posted by the Four Hundred). In that same year a Spartan flotilla is said to have slipped past Athenian guards on its way from the Peloponnese to the Hellespont (Thuc. 8.80.1).

[135] Thuc. 2.93.4 for guard ships at Salamis; 2.94.2–3 for the Peiraeus.

[136] Meiggs 1972, 267; Cawkwell 1997, 93 n. 6. This practice may have begun as early as 482, if Nepos *Them.* 2.2 can be taken as reliable.

[137] Halieis in 424/3: *IG* I^3 75 lines 6–10; Mytilene *c.*427–424: *IG* I^3 67 lines 7–8.

[138] Thuc. 2.69.1; Diod. 12.47.1. Keen 1993, 153 thinks it unlikely that the 'Peloponnesians' mentioned by Thucydides were actual Spartan ships, as 'such forces would hardly have been able in 430 to cross the Aegean safely.' Yet, they are again attested as having done so in 427, so Keen's statement seems to me unjustified. Hornblower 1991, 355 is still sceptical, calling the protection of this region 'a tall order for a force of six ships'.

[139] Thuc. 8.35.

[140] Thuc. 8.41.4.

[141] Thuc. 8.1.2.

[142] Xen. *Hell.* 1.1.35; Conwell 2008, 100–5; de Ste. Croix 1972, 47–8 on the necessity of friendly bases in the Aegean to ensure the flow of grain to Athens.

[143] Thuc. 1.120.2.

[144] The text is undated. Most scholars opt for early in the Arkhidamian War, although some as far back as the 440s and one as late as the fourth century (see the

> If some city is rich in timber for shipbuilding, where will it dispose of it, if it does not have the consent of the ruler of the sea? What if a city is rich in iron or copper or flax? Where will it dispose of it, if it does not have the consent of the ruler of the sea?[145]

None of the Cyclades appear to have possessed any of the essential materials for shipbuilding to any great degree, with the possible exception of *miltos* from Keos and some iron sources on a few of the islands.[146] The warships that were constructed before 480 in the Cyclades would thus have been built with supplies brought in from other areas. Although we have no direct evidence, a probable example would be the Parians receiving timber from the Thasian *peraia*. However, the Thasian resources were eventually brought under Athenian control during the *arkhē*. We have epigraphic evidence that Perdikkas of Macedon agreed to export oars only to Athens at some point in the late fifth century.[147] The Cyclades may have been effectively rendered unable to build triremes, even if there had been desire to do so, due to Athenian control of the trade in shipbuilding materials.

It is important to keep in mind, however, that the statement that Athens would have blockaded those who did not comply could have been a rhetorical exaggeration. The assertion that only Athens had two or three of the necessary strategic materials available at home is another example of an exaggeration.[148] As discussed in Chapter 3, the ability of ancient navies to intercept merchant shipping or to maintain effective blockades has been questioned.[149] Nevertheless, Athens did attempt the latter on a few occasions during the Peloponnesian War.[150] The Athenians are attested as having blockaded Megara

various references collected in Marr and Rhodes 2008). Constantakopoulou 2007, 148 appears to favour the early fourth-century date, but Marr and Rhodes's dating of *c.*425–424, after the incident on Sphakteria but before Brasidas' march north, is preferable.

145 Marr and Rhodes translation of [Xen.] *Ath.Pol.* 2.11: *εἰ γάρ τις πόλις πλουτεῖ ξύλοις ναυπηγησίμοις, ποῖ διαθήσεται, ἐὰν μὴ πείσῃ τοὺς ἄρχοντας τῆς θαλάττης; τί δ'εἴ τις σιδήρῳ ἢ χαλκῷ ἢ λίνῳ πλουτεῖ πόλις, ποῖ διαθήσεται, ἐὰν μὴ πείσῃ τοὺς ἄρχοντας τῆς θαλάττης;*

146 See Chapter 3, pp. 63–4 for these issues in the Archaic period.

147 *IG* I[3] 89 line 31. This may have been a special wartime measure, however.

148 Marr and Rhodes 2008, 117–19.

149 See Chapter 3, pp. 70–1.

150 The most famous (and ultimately successful) blockade was that of Athens by Lysander in 404/3: Xen. *Hell.* 2.2.5–9; Diod. 13.107.2–4.

in 427[151] and Perdikkas of Macedon in 417/16.[152] We do not know if the Athenian blockade of Corinth in 430/29 was only for warships or also for commercial craft.[153] It has been tentatively proposed by Erickson that the near-cessation of all foreign imports to Crete in the fifth century may have been due to an Athenian policy of interfering with Peloponnesian trade with North Africa.[154] And decrees from the 420s for two states, Methone and Aphytis, demonstrate that Athens at least attempted to control how much grain certain allies could import directly.[155] Other than these few examples, however, there is little evidence that the sailing of 'enemy' merchant vessels was greatly restricted by Athens during the war.[156]

Above all other merchant shipping, those ships that brought grain to Athens would have been that city's chief concern. While the often-repeated dictum that Athens was dependent on regular grain imports from the late sixth century onwards (particularly from the Black Sea area) has come under criticism,[157] grain could and did come to Athens from various sources in the fifth century. The Egyptian disaster of 454/3 could have temporarily disrupted supplies from that direction,[158] but Psammetichos of Egypt gave wheat to Athens during a shortage in 445/4, possibly triggered by the Euboian revolt of 446.[159] The second expedition of Kimon to Cyprus in 450–448 shows that the route to the Levant and Egypt had become more important for

151 Thuc. 3.51 and 4.67.3; Marr and Rhodes 2008, 117.

152 Thuc. 5.83.4. Borza 1992, 157 proposes that Athenian control of several harbours in the north Aegean might have made this effective.

153 Thuc. 2.69.1; Marr and Rhodes 2008, 118–19; Pébarthe 2008, 148–9; Zimmermann Munn 2003.

154 Erickson 2010, 295–8.

155 Methone (in 423): *IG* I^3 61 lines 34–41; Aphytis (in 428): *IG* I^3 63.

156 The restrictions on vessels listed in Thuc. 4.118.5 probably applied only to warships: Gomme, Andrewes, and Dover 1956*b*, 601; Hornblower 1996, 367. On Spartan attacks on merchant vessels during wartime see Thuc. 2.67.4; 3.32.1.

157 For the standard view: Garnsey 1988 and 1999; Sallares 1991; Whitby 1998. For criticism: Tsetskhladze 2008*b* and 1998; Burstein 1999, 101. Most recently Moreno 2007 posits that Athens did require regular grain imports, and that these came mainly from Athenian klerouchies in the fifth century (especially on Euboia) and then the Spartokid Bosporan kingdom in the first half of the fourth.

158 Stadter 1989, 217 sees this as possible motivation for Perikles' expedition to the Black Sea.

159 Philoch. *FGrH* 328 F119 (30 000 *medimnoi*) and Plut. *Vit.Per.* 37 (40 000 *medimnoi*); Stadter 1989, 336 also mentions the undated fragment of *IG* I^3 30 describing a shortage.

Athens. Some credit this to an increasing need for imported grain and the harbours to ensure its flow.[160]

The route from Phaselis and Phoenicia to Athens was open during the winter months.[161] Several islands of the Cyclades studded this eastern route, most notably Naxos and Paros, but we do not know if they required grain imports at this time as no testimony has survived. We do have such evidence for the later fourth century, however, and it is reasonable to assume that from time to time the inhabitants of this region had need of imported grain just as the Athenians did.[162]

But did the level of trade in grain relate to the level of trade in other commodities? Although the evidence from most ancient shipwrecks points towards the practice of carrying mixed cargoes (representing a lessening of fiscal risk), as yet there is no direct evidence that ships carrying grain also moved other items on the same voyage, such as amphoras.[163] Of course, this may be an indication of nothing more than our small surviving archaeological sample of all the merchant vessels that plied the Mediterranean in antiquity. Grain cargoes, moreover, are close to invisible in an archaeological sense, and it is not even wholly certain whether grain was loaded aboard in sacks (*sitēgoi*), poured loosely into bins in the hold, or shipped by some other method.[164]

Many cargoes went directly to a destination, as sailing from port to port, trading on an ad hoc basis, could have resulted in an empty cargo hold and a less profitable venture.[165] Yet ships would still have needed to stop in various ports to take on water, food, and other supplies, which may have subjected them to taxation or fees other than customs dues.

It has been recently proposed that Euboia provided the majority of grain imports for Athens during the fifth century.[166] But the Cyclades themselves may have required grain, just as Aigina did at the

[160] Green 2006, 179–80 n.10.

[161] [Dem.] 56.30; Porten and Yardeni 1993 on the Persian harbour document which shows dues paid in winter months.

[162] See Chapter 6, pp. 212–14 for the inscription detailing grain distributions from Kyrene; Bissa 2009, 197 on the vulnerability of Aegean islands to grain shortages.

[163] See McCormick 2001, 90, however, on the possibility of other cargoes mixed with grain during Late Antiquity.

[164] Gibbins 2001, 277–8.

[165] Nieto 1997, 154.

[166] Moreno 2007, 117–43 and 323.

beginning of the fifth century.[167] This could have given further stimulation to grain shipments from Egypt and the Levant, regions from which vessels could follow well-defined routes in the Cyclades.

Another source of evidence is imports of pottery to the Cyclades. The site of the *polis* of Koressos on Keos has yielded a great deal of imported ceramics. Attic in particular is well represented from the Archaic through Hellenistic periods, as is Corinthian.[168] No Cycladic or east Greek ware of the Classical period has been identified from this site (although Archaic Melian, Siphnian, and Khian sherds have been found).[169] There is little evidence for local production (unless certain sherds have been misidentified as imports).[170] The sanctuary of Aghia Irini on Keos has also yielded Attic pottery finds from the mid-sixth to mid-fourth centuries. Siphnian ware, commonly used for votive deposits at this location in the sixth century, gives way to Attic and Corinthian in the fifth. Approximately 60 per cent of the Attic ware found on Siphnos is fifth century.[171] Paros and Naxos are also rich in Attic red-figure during this period, though early red-figure (*c.*525–490) is rare in the Cyclades except on Delos.[172] One site on Kythnos has yielded Classical finds both from Attica as well as eastern locales such as Ionia.[173] It is important to note, however, that these finds from Kythnos are votive deposits from a sanctuary and may not represent typical commercial links. Another example is the recently excavated temple site on the tiny island of Despotiko (not far from Paros and Siphnos), the finds from which illustrate not only the products of the neighbouring Cyclades but also Attic red-figure pottery, as well as pottery from eastern Mediterranean states such as Rhodes, Khios, Miletos, and Samos.[174]

Although we do not have good pottery deposits for all the islands,[175] there is no discernable gap or hiatus in imports in the

[167] Hdt. 7.147.2 on the destination of Aigina for the grain ships that Xerxes saw at the Hellespont; Figueira 1981, 285–6.

[168] Sutton 1991, 248–52.

[169] Sutton 1991, 253–4.

[170] Sutton 1991, 254 concedes the possibility.

[171] Butt 1977, 311–13, who cautions that these figures 'apply only to our small deposit' and cannot be extended to the island as a whole. Nevertheless, they are broadly similar to the other Keian ceramic evidence cited above.

[172] Bikakis 1985, 217–65; Paleothodoros 2009, 175 and n. 61.

[173] Mazarakis-Ainian 2005, esp.100–1.

[174] Kourayos 2005, esp.130–3.

[175] MacDonald 1979, 50–1.

Cyclades, as has been demonstrated by Erickson for Crete during the fifth century.[176] Several scholars have expressed doubts that finds of Athenian pottery can be used to track shifting Athenian political or economic policy.[177] For example, Bikakis has concluded from the study of Attic pottery finds on Naxos that Athenian policy towards the island (and by implication, the Cyclades in general) was not an important factor in its pottery trade.[178] Nevertheless, trade in pottery need not have been an end in itself. The intrinsic value (or lack thereof) of this material is not as crucial as its role as an indicator of larger trade patterns.[179] While the presence or absence of pottery in and of itself cannot be the only indicator of mercantile activity, it may still preserve an echo of changes in such activity.[180]

The importance of the east–west route from Athens is also shown by the extensive finds of Athenian pottery at sites in the Levant, such as Dor in Phoenicia.[181] These finds begin soon after 500, lessen in the second quarter of the century, and then steadily increase after *c.*449 to peak in the mid-fourth century.[182] In Syria and other sites in Palestine, Attic red-figure finds do show a decrease in the early fifth century but increase again after *c.*450. Egypt also sees an increase starting in mid-century, and Kyrenaica after *c.*420.[183] The Tektaş Burnu shipwreck, found off the coast of Turkey and dating to the mid-fifth century, was of a vessel carrying Khian, pseudo-Samian (from Erythrai), and Attic ceramics.[184] There have also been large numbers of amphoras from Knidos, Rhodes, and Khios found in the Athenian Agora, and also on Delos.[185]

[176] Erickson 2005 and 2010.

[177] MacDonald 1979, 120 and 1982; Arafat and Morgan 1994, 110; for caution on using pottery as an indication of volume of trade see Lawall 1998, 88–9; Osborne 1999, 329.

[178] Bikakis 1985, 302.

[179] Osborne 1996, 39; Miller 1997, 72; Erickson 2005, 644 rightly discounts attempts to see trade in pottery as a separate sphere from other trade.

[180] Erickson 2005, 642 on types of trade that would have left no 'ceramic footprint'; Tomber 1993, 144; Gill 1988, 102.

[181] Littman 2001, 161–2 (especially for the years 450–420).

[182] Stewart and Martin 2005, 87 and 89–90.

[183] MacDonald 1979, 116. Some areas in North Africa did see a decline in imports, however, such as at Tokra (cf. McPhee 1997, 76), showing that the overall picture requires nuance: Erickson 2005, 654.

[184] Carlson 2003.

[185] Sarikakis 1986, 122–3.

One possible example of a site outside the Cyclades that benefited from changing trade routes is Itanos on Crete. Attic and Cycladic ware dating to the late sixth century has been found at this location. After *c.*460, however, the flow of imports ceases, only to resume at some point in the late fifth century. This is one example of a general phenomenon at Cretan sites, where a sort of isolation appears during this period.[186] However, at some point in the 420s imports of Attic red-figure resume at Itanos.[187] This is much earlier than at several other Cretan cities where Attic imports do not appear again in the archaeological record until the beginning of the fourth century.[188] This may indicate renewed Athenian interest in trade routes with the Levant and Egypt. A fragment from the comedy *Phormophoroi* by Hermippos (performed *c.*425) mentions a 'Catalogue of Goods' that came to Athens from several locales, including sails and papyrus rope from Egypt, frankincense from Syria, and cypress wood from Crete.[189] Ships would have had to pass through the Cyclades to reach and return from these areas. While this passage must be interpreted cautiously (and may actually be parodic in nature),[190] other evidence of trade links with these regions shows that it would be foolish to discount it completely.

Another valuable material whose distribution may have been affected in this way was Parian marble. By the mid-fifth century, shipments of this marble to Etruria, which had been so extensive in the early fifth, began to dwindle (along with other Greek imports such as Athenian pottery[191]) and came to a complete halt by the start of the fourth century.[192] This coincides with the eclipse of Aiginetan trade. Imports of Parian marble continued to Sicily, however, which also

[186] Erickson 2010, 295–8; Greco 1999, 526.

[187] Erickson 2005, 640 and 653, where he proposes that local imitations of Attic ware 'often carried by Cycladic intermediares' may show Cycladic connections persisting even during this dark period of *c.*460–*c.*420. However, if they are local copies, they may have been produced in response to a continuing dearth of imports.

[188] For Eleutherna: Erickson 2005, 637 and 640; for Phalasarna: Gondicas 1988, 109–10; for Knossos: Coldstream 1973, 25–7; Callaghan 1992, 93–4.

[189] *PCG* V. fr.63–64, lines 12–14.

[190] Gilula 2000.

[191] This decline was part of a phenomenon across Tyrrhenian Italy: Cornell 1995, 225 and n.35. The one exception in Etruria was Spina, which continued to import Attic pots (albeit in unusual configurations such as stemmed plates) through the end of the Classical period: Boardman 1989, 235–6.

[192] Schilardi 2000*a*, 553.

saw decreased shipment of Attic pottery in the late fifth, although Corinthian continues to appear until the last quarter of the century.[193] Thus, under Athenian influence the trade in this lucrative resource may have been redirected during the height of the Delian League, and experienced a decline along with Athenian fortunes by the end of the Peloponnesian War. As we will see in Chapter 6, Parian marble began to be shipped in large amounts to Etruria again by the middle of the fourth century, which may indicate not only renewed exploitation of Parian resources but also renewed Athenian influence on its direction of export.[194]

The evidence of the movement of pottery in the Aegean in the fifth century indicates that traditional shipping routes through these islands continued to be used as they had been in earlier periods, with some possible modifications. This would offer qualification to the idea that inhabitants of the Cyclades were simply 'passive beneficiaries' of transit trade.[195] The export of local products, while taking advantage of maritime activity originating from outside the region, denotes much more than simple passivity. It is true that the Cyclades were no longer active in the sense of maintaining warships. If we examine the Cycladic region in general, we may see a process in which many aristocratic ship-owners in the Cyclades, as the fifth-century *arkhē* developed, were no longer able to engage in either local 'protection' of merchant shipping or privateering. Sometimes direct coercion from Athens was involved, as in the case of the suppression of the Naxian revolt. Other islands, to be sure, need not have been coerced. With cash beginning to replace ships for tribute, the counterparts of these Naxians in states such as Paros, Siphnos, and so forth that had not rebelled against Athens would have eventually have ended up in the same circumstances. If these *poleis* had been able to exercise some control over trade routes in their immediate vicinity in the late Archaic period (as proposed in Chapter 3), with increased wealth accruing from this practice, some of this wealth would have now been redirected into the hands of the Athenians through the

[193] Richter 1960, 146–7, listing statue finds from Leontinoi, Grammichele, and Megara Hyblaia. For Attic pottery to Sicily: MacDonald 1979, 141–8; for Corinthian: Munn 1983.

[194] For fourth-century exports of Parian marble see Chapter 6, p. 211.

[195] As proposed by Sherratt and Sherratt 1993, 366–7 for Cretan communities situated on Phoenician trade routes; Stampolidis 2003, 54; Prent 2005, 231. For criticism of these views see Erickson 2010, 279–81.

payment of tribute (and later during the Peloponnesian War, the *eikostē* tax on commerce—see below). However, given the high costs of operating triremes, members of the Delian League may have been purchasing protection from the Athenians inexpensively with their payments.[196] What has been called 'the loyalty of prudent self-interest,' along with occasional outright compulsion, kept the organization together.[197] A similar process has been proposed for the elites of the island of Aigina for the late Archaic period, in which they are seen as having led the way from piracy to entrepreneurship.[198]

Given recent attempts to apply the methodology of sociology to the ancient economy, we may draw upon a quote from Mark Granovetter better to understand this process. In a discussion of how trust and 'generalized morality' apply to economic relations, he states that:

> Malfeasance is here seen to be averted because clever institutional arrangements make it too costly to engage in . . . note, however, that they do not produce trust but instead are a functional substitute for it . . . concrete personal relations and the obligations inherent in them discourage malfeasance.[199]

How can we relate this to the situation in the Cyclades during the fifth century? The remarks on islanders by the 'Old Oligarch' are telling:

> Those who are subjects on land are able to unite their small cities and fight all together, but those who are subjects at sea, as many as are islanders, are unable to unite their cities into a single unit. For the sea lies between them, and their masters are rulers of the sea. Even if the islanders do manage, without being noticed, to join together on one single island, they will die of starvation.[200]

Compare this to the words that Thucydides placed in the mouths of the Mytilenian ambassadors to Olympia in 428, when they characterized the position of Delian League members as isolated and divided from each other:

196 Finley 1978, 113; McGregor 1987, 49.
197 Cawkwell 1997, 99.
198 Figueira 1981, 206 and 333.
199 Granovetter 1985, 488–9.
200 Marr and Rhodes translation of [Xen.] *Ath.Pol.* 2.2: *τοῖς μὲν κατὰ γὴν ἀρχομένοις οἷόν τ'ἐστιν ἐκ μικρῶν πόλεων συνοικισθέντας ἁθρόους μάχεσθαι· τοῖς δὲ κατὰ θάλατταν ἀρχομένοις, ὅσοι νησιῶταί εἰσιν, οὐχ οἷόν τε συνάρασθαι εἰς τὸ αὐτὸ τὰς πόλεις· ἡ γὰρ θάλαττα ἐν τῷ μέσῳ, οἱ δὲ κρατοῦντες θαλασσοκκράτορές εἰσιν. εἰ δ'οἷόν τε καὶ λαθεῖν συνελθοῦσιν εἰς ταὐτὸ τοῖς νησιώταις εἰς μίαν νῆσον, ἀπολοῦνται λιμῷ*; cf. Gabba 1997.

> Unable, however, to unite and defend themselves, on account of the number of confederates that had votes, all the allies were enslaved, except ourselves and the Khians, who continued to send our contingents as independent and nominally free.[201]

Ports in the Delian League could have been under some sort of Athenian supervision, perhaps from its inception but definitely by mid-century. There were large numbers of Athenian magistrates in allied cities, who could ascertain the provenance and destination of various cargoes.[202] The Megarian Decree of the 430s, for example, would probably have been enforced by such officials if it was in fact related to commerce. It may have been intended mainly to cut off Peloponnesian trade with the Black Sea region since Megara had ties with her colony Byzantion.[203]

Athens could have encouraged merchants to bring certain items to the Peiraeus, which would then have served as a redistributive market.[204] In a sense, the payment of tribute could have 'opened' local ports to economic participation in the *arkhē*.[205] Some smaller states may have even *voluntarily* become tribute-payers in the Delian League during the 430s.[206] A small Aegean island known as Kasos joined

[201] Crawley translation of Thuc. 3.10.5: *ἀδύνατοι δὲ ὄντες καθ' ἓν γενόμενοι διὰ πολυψηφίαν ἀμύνασθαι οἱ ξύμμαχοι ἐδουλώθησαν πλὴν ἡμῶν καὶ Χίων· ἡμεῖς δὲ αὐτόνομοι δὴ ὄντες καὶ ἐλεύθεροι τῷ ὀνόματι ξυνεστρατεύσαμεν.*

[202] Pébarthe 2000, 61–4 on documentation such as 'papiers de navires' (cf. Xen. *Anab.* 7.5.13–14); Balcer 1976 on imperial magistrates.

[203] For the Decree: Thuc. 1.67.4, 1.139.1, 1.144.2; Plut. *Vit.Per.* 29.4; Ar. *Ach.* 529–39; Legon 1981, 214–17 rightly argues against revisionist approaches such as that of de Ste. Croix 1972, 381–91, that see the Decree as more of a religious anathema than an economic policy. Legon's hypothesis is that the Decree was due to Megara selling shipbuilding timber to Corinth (this is followed by Pébarthe 2008, 150–1 who also mentions Megarian grain imports to the Peloponnese).

[204] Isok. 4.42, characterizing the Peiraeus as the 'market of Hellas' where smaller states disposed of their surplus and acquired what they could not produce themselves; Thuc. 2.38.2: 'the magnitude of our city draws the produce of the world into our harbor.' Pébarthe 2005, 91 proposes that no ships heading to Athens had to pay transit taxes in allied ports, based on his interpretation of the exemption for *xenoi* in the decree for Khalkis (*IG* I³ 40) as a grant of exemption from Khalkidian harbour taxes to those using their port while conveying their cargo to Athens. Yet, this inscription is quite controversial and many interpretations are possible.

[205] Pébarthe 2008, 136–7.

[206] The special rubric in question is *πόλες αὐται φόρον ταχσάμεναι*; Lepper 1962, who considers it to have been voluntary; Couch 1929 considers these cities to have been coerced by Athens.

in this manner.[207] The island of Syme near Rhodes was one of several states that joined the League through the initiative of private individuals, though it is a matter of debate whether these individuals were from the allied states or Athens.[208] If these *poleis* did join of their own accord, they may have actually envisioned benefits from membership in the League, including military protection and trading privileges.[209]

Under such a scenario, those who profited from Athenian protection for their ships and cargoes might have considered tribute payments a 'business expense.'[210] As almost all of the Cyclades were original 'founding members' (whether by choice or compulsion) they would not have come under these new categories of tribute. However, the motivation of these other states still makes this an important point for how tribute and commerce may have been inter-related.

COINAGE IN THE CYCLADES DURING THE ARKHĒ

It has long been assumed (at least since the mid-20th century) that the Standards Decree (also known as the 'Coinage Decree') effectively forbade the minting of silver by states in the Athenian empire and mandated the use of Athenian coins for all transactions.[211] Traditionally, this Decree has also been interpreted as a purely political act by the Athenians to extend their dominance over the allies, with no economic motivations whatsoever.[212] The Decree is known from several fragmentary epigraphic examples, with some of the most important parts heavily restored; as such, it is very problematic to interpret.[213] It has also been caught up in the decades-long debate

207 Steph. Byz. *s.v. Kasos* places this island in the Cyclades, but it was enrolled in the Ionian district—a similar situation to the syntely of cities on Amorgos.

208 Schuller 1981.

209 Lepper 1962, 48–51 favours the economic motive; Eddy 1968, 142 favours a defensive explanation—'most states . . . preferred Athenian rule as the least painful choice.' Meiggs 1972, 252 is sceptical of any special economic privileges resulting from these arrangements.

210 This is mentioned in a fourth-century source: Isok. 8.29 and 36 describe how Athens had compelled contributions 'from those who sail the sea'.

211 Figueira 1998, 4–9 and 431–63 for discussion of the history of the question.

212 This view is promoted especially vigorously by Finley 1999, 168–9 and 1978, 257 n. 46.

213 A new fragment (*SEG* LI.55, published in Hatzopoulos 2000/3) has now been attached to the Aphytis Fragment (*IG* I^3 1453C); Figueira 2006, 10–19.

over the dating of certain imperial inscriptions to either the 440s or the 420s (which involves not only the 'three-barred sigma' controversy, but also a fixation on which decade 'feels' more impressionistically imperialistic).[214] Nevertheless, there are now few who hold to the earlier date.[215]

A recent revisionist view, proposed by Figueira, states that the cessation of minting by the various states of the Athenian *arkhē* was not caused by the Standards Decree, nor did the decree in fact mandate such cessation. Instead, it simply mandated that the *phoros* be paid in Athenian coin, which was now also to be accepted in all the states of the *arkhē* as legal tender. This in turn prodded the allies into accepting Athenian coins as payment for indirect taxes, so that they could then render the tribute in the same coin.[216] Since many Greek states in the Aegean had already ceased minting silver by the mid-fifth century, the argument continues that it was not Athenian mandate but rather fiscal convenience that led to the greater use of Athenian coins throughout the *arkhē*. Thus, the increasing adoption of Attic currency was 'an organic development driven by the increasing integration of the Aegean economy'.[217] Although originally supporting a 440s date, Figueira has now proposed that there may have been several 'Standards Decrees', with the new Aphytis fragment possibly even hailing from the early fourth century.[218]

Figueira's approach to the Decree addresses several problems of interpretation, such as the lack of a definite watershed moment for the closing of allied mints. If local coinages were indeed banned by the Decree, it would have applied to silver coins only and not smaller bronze issues or even the electrum used to pay the *phoros* by certain

[214] Proponents of a mid-fifth century date include Schuller 1974; Meiggs 1966, 86–7 and 96; Walbank 1978, 31–42. For another recent overview of the controversy see Rhodes 2008.

[215] For many years H.B. Mattingly has kept up his assault, proposing a date in the 420s for the Standards Decree and many other inscriptions. Mattingly 1996 collects his papers on the subject, and the scholarly pendulum has now apparently swung his way. The papers from a conference on the Standards Decree at Oxford in 2004, including discussion of a newly discovered fragment from Aphytis, are forthcoming, but most favor a date in the 420s at the earliest (Papazarkadas 2009, 72); Kroll 2009, 201–2 would place it soon before 414, when it was parodied in Ar. *Av.* 1040.

[216] Figueira 1998, 263–73 and 2003, 86.

[217] Figueira 1998, 71.

[218] Figueira 2006, 23–7 and 38–9.

states such as Lampsakos and Mytilene.[219] Some states also paid their tribute in local coins or Persian silver.[220] While Figueira's reading of the Decree has not found favour among all scholars,[221] his proposal that Athenian coins had become ubiquitous in the Aegean by that same approximate date has seen more acceptance. While some criticism has been levelled that the hoard evidence does not show a predominance of Attic silver until at least 410,[222] studies of the so-called 'standardized tetradrachms' of the second half of the fifth century seem to indicate a massive amount of minting that literally placed millions of Athenian coins into circulation.[223] Only a few Aegean states continued to mint until the end of the fifth century, and all were special cases: they were peripheral states, or had exceptionally large economies, or predominantly used electrum coinage.[224]

What of the Cycladic mints? We have already examined the extensive Archaic coinage from the region in the last chapter.[225] Figueira's conclusions on early fifth-century coinage from these islands must now be modified by several recent and important die studies.[226] Andros and Naxos stopped minting before or around 478—but from 480–*c.*470 Siphnos, Paros, and the two Keian cities of Koressos and Ioulis continued to issue coins.[227] Whereas earlier Siphnian issues in the mid-late sixth century had shown Aiginetan influence,[228] these now show the influence of Athenian engravers. From *c.*470 to *c.*460 Siphnos continued to mint, and Seriphos issued its gorgoneion

[219] Martin 1985, 199; Figueira 1998, 88–90 and 395; Kallet 2001, 214 n.122.

[220] Eddy 1973, 47–70; Bodenstedt 1976, 71–3 and 83–4; Martin 1985, 201.

[221] Kallet 2001, 215–16; Mattingly 1999, who reaffirms his own dating of the 420s; Crawford 2001. Figueira continues to defend his position, however: Figueira 2003, esp. 81 n. 47, and 2006.

[222] Schönhammer 1993, 187–8; Sheedy 2006, 120–5, who also criticizes the notion that tribute or trade was facilitated by Attic coin since bullion or other coinage could be used for these purposes as well. See Thuc. 6.8 on Segesta contributing 60 talents of uncoined silver to pay for 60 Athenian triremes for a month in 415.

[223] Kroll 2009, 198–9, citing an unpublished 2004 paper by Andrew Meadows; Flament 2007, 57–120.

[224] Kroll 2009, 200.

[225] See Chapter 3, pp. 48–9 on Archaic Cycladic coinage.

[226] Sheedy 2006 on the mints of Keos, Paros, Naxos, Delos, Kythnos, Siphnos, Seriphos (and the Dorian islands of Melos and Thera); Nicolet-Pierre 1997 on Naxos.

[227] Sheedy 2006, 125 in general; 110 on Paros Class H; 49–50 on Siphnos Series II; 26 on Koressos Series IV;30 on Ioulis Series II.

[228] The hoard from Eirini on Paros (*c.*470) is predominantly of Aiginetan staters: *CH* 2.24; Sheedy 2006, 124–5.

tetrobols/drachms.[229] Siphnos and Karthaia on Keos held out until around 450.[230] After the middle of the century, only Melos continued to issue coinage in the Cyclades. These coins are different in all respects from others in the region, being on the Milesian standard and very distinct stylistically.[231]

Several islands struck coinage that could fit into more than one weight standard. The Siphnian Series II (*c.*475–460) was technically on the Aiginetan standard, but its fractions could work either as Aiginetan tetrobols or Attic drachms.[232] The same is true of the gorgoneion tetrobols made on Seriphos at this time. And although Kythnos appears to have stopped minting by 480, its own Series II coins from the 480s could also fit into both the Aiginetan and Attic–Euboic systems.[233] This may point to a realignment of trade routes following the conflict with Persia, most likely related to how Athens deployed its naval forces in the early decades of the League.

In his study of Cycladic coinage, Sheedy has proposed that the Standards Decree and the cessation of minting in the region by the mid-fifth century are unrelated, and that the continuation of some minting up to *c.*450 shows that not all the Cyclades would have joined the Delian League immediately after 478.[234] He connects the end of minting with a general level of poverty and decreased trade in the Cyclades in the wake of the Persian Wars, including Persian destruction on Naxos and the Athenian exactions placed on Paros and Andros.[235]

While the possible severity of destruction on Naxos could be a viable argument, we have seen that a depressed trade situation after the Persian Wars is not. It is true that several of the islands had exemplary coinages before the Persian Wars that were not minted after 480. The Naxian wreathed staters that began *c.*540–530, as well

[229] Sheedy 2006, 50–3.

[230] A case has been made by Erxleben 1970 and Figueira 1998, 477–8 that some of the Koressian examples can be dated as late as *c.*420, but this has been dismissed by Sheedy 2006, 31.

[231] The 1907 Melos Hoard (*c.*416) is of local silver on the Milesian standard (*IGCH* #27); cf. Sheedy 2006, 63–7, who nevertheless proposes at 34 that other islands of the Cyclades could have issued coins on the same standard, since we do not possess a full record of all minting activity and several specimens remain 'homeless'.

[232] Sheedy 2006, 49–50.

[233] Sheedy 2006, 39–40.

[234] Sheedy 2006, 120.

[235] Sheedy 2006, 125.

as the Parian staters of *c.*500–497/5 (referred to as Class C by Sheedy), may have been indicative of outstanding levels of wealth at a time when many islands of the Cycladic region had active mints.[236] Siphnos, Kythnos, Karthaia and Ioulis on Keos had also produced coins prior to 480.[237] Yet, Sheedy's reconstruction may only apply to a few of the islands of this region.

The availability of Athenian coins could have provided an incentive to stop minting activity in the Cyclades. Yet, many of the Cyclades had begun minting in the late sixth century, when Aiginetan coins had still been in wide and intensive circulation. If, however, we can accept the idea presented in Chapter 3 that late sixth-century minting in the Cyclades was mainly a function of peer-polity interaction, and meant for state expenditures to further such competition, such as monumental temple construction and (especially) the operation of warships, the end of such interaction could have provided yet another incentive for the cessation of minting in the Cyclades. Such interaction was no longer really possible, now that the Athenians held sway over the region.

The Decree also mandated that a re-minting fee was to be charged by the Athenians for conversion of allied silver into Athenian owls. This is strong evidence that the Athenians not only wanted to facilitate the accurate collection and tallying of tribute, but also envisaged making a profit from the promulgation of the Decree.[238] If the Athenians had simply wanted to make tribute collection easier, they could have required payments in Athenian coins without any mention of weights and measures, or of recoining.[239] Whether the Athenians actually did turn a profit or not from recoining is very uncertain, however.

There is additional reason to consider that the Standards Decree may have been economically motivated.[240] Some have proposed that

[236] Sheedy 2006, 90 (Naxos) and 103 (Parian Class C).

[237] Sheedy 2006, 48 (Siphnos Series I); 39 (Kythnos Series I); 26 (Karthaia Series I through III); 30 (Ioulis Series I). Sheedy dismisses the notion that the Karthaian coins cited here are actually Andrian, but see Figueira 1998, 577.

[238] Martin 1985, 200–1. The smallest restorable amount of the fee in the inscription is 2 per cent, but even this would have potentially yielded great profit if the Standards Decree was successful.

[239] Martin 1985, 203.

[240] Kallet 2001, 205–25, who suggests that discussion of the *eikostē* may have begun during the years immediately following the Peace of Nikias, when the level of trade in the *arkhē* may have increased. Figueira 2003, thinks that the Athenians could never

the aforementioned harbour tax (*eikostē*) of 414/13 and the Standards Decree were passed simultaneously, since it would have made the collection of said tax easier.[241] According to this argument, Athenian weights and measures would have been more easily enforced in allied cities because they would have been already familiar with these standards from trade.[242]

One potential objection is that Thucydides found the new tax worthy of mention but not the Standards Decree, and this would be surprising if the two were connected. However, he may have considered the Decree a sub-component of a larger policy, which he chose to describe in more general terms. Given Thucydides' other omissions, this is not out of the question.[243]

THE CYCLADES DURING THE PELOPONNESIAN WAR

Thucydides says that the only Aegean islands still outside the Athenian sphere of influence in 431 were Thera and Melos.[244] The significance of the exile of the Aiginetans and the resettlement of the island with Athenians in 431 would not have been lost on those who lived in the Cyclades.[245] Although there is little direct evidence for events in the Cycladic area during the Peloponnesian War until 411, there is indirect evidence that they remained vital throughout the conflict.

The Periklean strategy of turning Athens into a self-sufficient 'island' during the Arkhidamian War meant that the sea lanes had to be kept open for grain and other essentials to be shipped to Athens.[246] Several references in the comedies of Aristophanes tell us

have conceived of replacing the tribute with a harbour tax unless Attic coins already predominated in the *arkhē*.

241 Kallet 2001, 217. Kroll 2009, 201–2 is sympathetic.

242 Pébarthe 2000, 64 and 2008, 114–18; Giovannini 1968, 75–6 goes further by suggesting that stimulation of trade was the underlying motive for the whole Decree.

243 Kallet 2004, 479 n.59 on the issue of Thucydides' silence regarding the tax.

244 Thuc. 2.9.4; Diod. 12.42.

245 Thuc. 2.27.

246 Thuc. 1.143.4–144.1 for a general statement of the strategy; Thuc. 2.13.2 and 2.69.1. For modern discussion see Holladay 1978; Spence 1990; Ober 1996; Tritle 2010, 45–6 for criticism of the strategy, and Schubert and Laspe 2009 for the idea that the entire idea was a later Thucydidean construct. On the idea of the Athenians

that the urban population of Athens (now swollen with refugees from the countryside) was dependent on imports during this period.[247]

The routes taken by naval forces on both sides often passed through the Cyclades. Thucydides describes the voyage of a Spartan fleet of forty ships under Alkidas in 427 that used Delos, Mykonos, and Ikaros (Ikaria) as stopovers on its way east towards Lesbos.[248] Alkidas' original plan was to aid the rebellion at Mytilene, but he heard of its surrender to the Athenians while enroute and landed instead at Embaton near Erythrai, proceeding next to Myonnesos and Ephesos. Thucydides states that many Ephesians were captured because they mistakenly thought that Alkidas' ships were Athenian, and that no one would have expected Peloponnesian warships to cross the Aegean while the Athenians had naval hegemony.[249]

Alkidas' initial journey had progressed slowly through the region. Thucydides implies that this was due to fear of the Athenian fleet, and many modern scholars have agreed.[250] While the Cycladic *poleis* may not have actively assisted (or resisted) Alkidas and his men, they may have avoided future blame by shutting their gates and refusing supplies to this fleet.[251] Although he had tarried for a time in Ionia, Thucydides states that Alkidas' voyage home was done in haste because his ships had been spotted by the Athenians off Klaros, and Alkidas now 'made across the open sea, fully determined to touch nowhere, if he could help it, until he got to the Peloponnesos'.[252] His

engaging in naval imperialism to safeguard grain supplies, see de Ste. Croix 1972, 47–8 and 1981, 293; Pečirka 1982.

[247] Ar. *Ach.* 32–36; *Eq.* 792–794; *Pax* 550–604 and 632–640. For general discussion see Conwell 2008, 88–9.

[248] Thuc. 3.29–33; Prost 2001, 248–50. Melos may also have been used: Roisman 1987.

[249] Thuc. 3.32.3. Witness also the statement in the Melian Dialogue that the Spartans were not expected to 'cross over to an island while we [the Athenians] are masters of the sea' (Thuc. 5.109).

[250] Thuc. 3.29.1; Kagan 1974, 148; Wilson 1981, 160; Gomme, Andrewes, and Dover 1956*a*, 291 suggest that the Athenians could have been warned of such activity in the Cyclades by means of warning beacons. Roisman 1987, however, downplays this idea and instead proposes that Thucydides presented a picture of a timorous and overcautious Alkidas as a contrast with his picture of Brasidas.

[251] Roisman 1987, 394.

[252] Thuc. 3.33.1: *καὶ δεδιὼς τὴν δίωξιν ἔπλει διὰ τοῦ πελάγους ὡς γῇ ἑκούσιος οὐ σχήσων ἄλλῃ ἢ Πελοποννήσῳ.* Wilson 1981, 160 notes that Thucydides' statement strangely contrasts with Alkidas' delay in leaving Ionia once he learned of the fall of Mytilene.

return itinerary was more southern, since his force was scattered by a storm near Crete, although he may have had to make several detours to avoid interception.[253]

Why did Thucydides focus on these details of Alkidas' route? In contrast, when discussing Athenian naval expeditions that crossed the Aegean, Thucydides omits details of their itineraries. The real importance of Alkidas' expedition may have been the Athenian reaction to it, as they now exerted their authority over the southern Dorian Cyclades. The first appearance of several of these islands in the tribute lists is during the 420s. Anaphe first appears in 428/7, and a whole new contingent is listed for 425 (Melos, Kimolos, Sikinos, and Pholegandros).[254] Melos had been attacked in 426 by an Athenian force of 60 ships and 2,000 hoplites—Thucydides states that this was done because 'they were islanders and yet were unwilling to submit or join their alliance'. But the Athenian commander Nikias broke off the attack after ravaging some Melian territory.[255] Some scholars have surmised that the Melians (along with other Aegean states) had given money to Alkidas in 427 during his crossing.[256] However, this is not mentioned by Thucydides.[257]

Thera was also assessed for tribute at some point in this decade, although the lists are fragmentary and precision is impossible.[258] The decree of Kleonymos on the regulation of tribute collection lists both the Samians and the Theraians as owing *chrēmata* rather than *phoros*, and this has been recently interpreted as evidence that the Theraians had to be coerced into joining the Delian League and were treated as the defeated Samians had been.[259] Whether such monies were

[253] Thuc. 3.69.1; Lazenby 2004, 53–4; Prost 2001, 248 still calls his cruise 'un coup audacieux'.

[254] Anaphe: *IG* I³ 283; for the rest in 425: *IG* I³ 71; Piérart 1984, 165; Seaman 1997, 414; Ager 2008, 164 and n. 82.

[255] Thuc. 3.91.2–3; Diod. 12.65.1–3 also covers the event, but errs in the chronology (424); Seaman 1997, 407 n. 83. On the idea that the attack was actually meant as a feint to draw Spartan attention away from the west, see Gomme, Andrewes, and Dover 1970, 156; Tritle 2010, 132.

[256] Adcock 1932, 5; Hornblower 2011, 161–2; Loomis 1992, 81 and others have used this to date the so-called Spartan War Fund (*IG* V. 1.1) to the 420s.

[257] As emphasized by Seaman 1997, 398.

[258] The restoration of Thera in *IG* I³ 281 (430/29) is problematic: see Ager 2008, 164–5 for discussion.

[259] *IG* I³ 68 lines 21–5; Ager 2008, 165 suggests that the other small islands besides Thera and Melos may have joined more gracefully.

actually collected or not, it may be that Athens was attempting to deny the use of these islands as bases to the Spartans.[260]

There is also a strong possibility (though it has not been advanced to my knowledge by modern scholars) that the aforementioned troop obligations imposed on the Andrians, Tenians, and Keians were not a result of previous mid-century revolts, but could have first been levied on these islands by Athens soon after Alkidas' cruise. A possible parallel might be the decree concerning Miletos (*IG* I^3 21) that among other provisions stipulated the supplying of troops for the Athenian cause. Although traditionally dated to the 440s, it has recently been suggested that this decree might better fit the Arkhidamian War.[261] If so, these requirements might have been placed on the Milesians around the same time as on the Andrians, Keians, and Tenians. These requirements, like the new interest in the southern Cyclades, may have been motivated by new concerns for the loyalty of the islands after Alkidas had shown that the region was not off-limits to Sparta and her allies.

A similar situation is described by Thucydides in 412,[262] when twenty-seven ships under the Spartan commander Antisthenes departed Cape Malea in the Peloponnese for Miletos (with the aim of eventually reaching the Hellespont). After encountering Athenian ships near Melos, Antisthenes was concerned that they might warn the Athenian forces on Samos, so his flotilla took a more southern route and sailed via Crete, finally landing at Kaunos.[263] This underscores the importance of the routes through the region, whether northern or southern, for naval operations throughout the conflict.

Thucydides states that one of the reasons that Athens desired peace in 421 was because she feared that her recent defeats at Delion and Amphipolis would encourage revolts among the allies.[264]

260 Piérart 1984, 167.

261 Thuc. 4.42.1 mentions Milesians, along with Andrians and Karystians, with the Athenian forces at Corinth in 425; 4.53.1 on Milesians fighting at Kythera in 424; Papazarkadas 2009, 71 in support of the new date.

262 Earlier that year, Alkamenes had sailed to Khios with twenty-one warships to aid in their revolt from Athens. According to Thuc. 8.8.4, no attempt was made to hide these ship movements from the Athenians, who in the wake of the Sicilian disaster had no ready fleet to deploy. Yet these ships were bottled up by twenty-one Athenian vessels at Spiraion until later that summer, when they broke the blockade and sailed to Khios (Thuc. 8.23.1).

263 Thuc. 8.39.1–4, describing their fear of attack.

264 Thuc. 5.14.2.

According to Diodorus, many of the allies on both sides were suspicious that Athens and Sparta had designed the Peace to further their own interests.[265] A second Athenian assault on Melos occurred in 416. Thucydides states that there was allied assistance on this expedition.[266] Melos was technically neutral but suspected of aiding the Lakedaimonians,[267] and Thucydides' discussion of its fate in the Melian Dialogue is one of the most-discussed portions of his work.[268] It would seem that the Athenians were concerned about the possibility of island revolts and wanted to send a message.[269] It is also possible that they were concerned with restoring their prestige after the loss at Mantineia in 418.[270] Melos was now reduced and the island repopulated with 500 Athenian *apoikoi*. These settlers would most likely have been integrated into the trade routes of the Athenian *arkhē*, for after a gap in Attic ceramic imports after *c.*475, such imports now resume on Melos for the last decades of the century.[271] Lysander removed the settlers in 405 and restored the Melian exiles.[272] However, other details concerning the decade-long Athenian settlement on Melos are lacking.[273]

Did the Peloponnesian War have economic effects on the Cyclades? The reassessment of tribute in 425/4 brought dramatic increases, at least in theory. We are fortunate that the rubric for the

[265] Diod. 12.75.2–3. The allies were barely mentioned in the Athenian/Spartan treaty that followed soon after the Peace of Nikias (Thuc. 5.23) and this supports such claims.

[266] Thuc. 5.84.1; Lazenby 2004, 129–30; Hornblower 2011, 168.

[267] Seaman 1997, 391–402 gives references for the long-running debate as to whether or not the Melians were neutral at this time, concluding convincingly that they were.

[268] Thuc. 5.84.2 stresses the unwillingness of the Melians to the submit as other Aegean islanders had; cf. Bauslaugh 1991, 142–51. Meiggs 1972, 389 proposes that the Melians were enjoying Athenian sea protection without contributing financially in any way to it.

[269] An interpretation supported by Thuc. 5.97 and 99 from the Melian Dialogue; Seaman 1997, 390–1.

[270] Momigliano 1929, 377, followed by Seaman 1997, 415 and n. 109.

[271] Sparkes 1982, 235. The Melians had also adopted the Milesian weight standard for their coins in the fifth century, unlike the rest of the Cyclades. Green 1970, 92 suggests that the settlers helped open trade routes to Africa.

[272] Xen. *Hell.* 2.2.9; Plut. *Vit.Lys.* 14.3. Seaman 1997, 396–8 feels that some Melian adult males escaped or were spared, since Thuc. 5.116.4 states that they killed 'as many adult males as they captured'.

[273] It is not even known for certain if it was a true klerouchy: Graham 1983, 173–4; Jones 1957, 169–70.

Insular District is virtually complete (see Table 4.1).[274] The assessment of Siphnos increased from 3 talents to 9; Mykonos from 1 talent to 2; Syros from 1,500 drachmas to 1 talent; Andros from 6 talents to 15; Keos from 3 talents to 9; Kythnos from 3 talents to 6; Naxos from 6 talents 4,000 drachmas to 15 talents; Paros from 18 talents to 30, equalling Aigina's original assessment; and Tenos from 2 talents to 10.[275] Thus, many of the Cyclades, whether they had been assessed at low or high amounts initially, were reassessed at high levels in this year.

Whether or not such high amounts were ever actually collected is a matter of controversy.[276] How realistic were they to begin with, in terms of the potential of these islands to pay? One scholar has surmised that the tribute amounts are an indication of real economic potential and productivity, which had actually increased in the decades after Aristeides' original assessment in 478.[277] Another study has proposed that since the Cycladic region had not seen much devastation from the Arkhidamian War, the islanders were now expected to shoulder a greater financial burden than the rest of the allies.[278] But although the islands had not been a war theatre, islanders *had* participated and suffered casualties,[279] such as the Andrians who fought in the Corinthia in the summer of 425.[280] If there had been distinctions in tribute amounts early on between islands that had medized in 480 and those that had not, such distinctions appear to have vanished by this later date.[281]

The original editors of the tribute lists assumed that tribute was again reduced in 422/1, in the aftermath of the Peace of Nikias.[282]

[274] *IG* I[3] 71 lines 61–101; Wallace and Figueira 2010, 66–7.

[275] Siphnos: *IG* I[3] 71 line 66; Kythnos: line 72; Mykonos: line 75; Syros: line 80; Rheneia: line 82.

[276] Kallet-Marx 1993, 164–70, who points out that, given our lack of accounts for the early 420s, it is impossible to determine whether these increased amounts were arrived at incrementally or suddenly in 425/4.

[277] Brun 1996, 191–2.

[278] Brun 1996, 190; a *scholion* to Ar. *Ach.* 6 alleges that certain islanders bribed Kleon to get their tribute reduced.

[279] Although there is no direct evidence, it is possible that plague struck the nearby islands as well as Athens, since the disease had probably arrived aboard merchant shipping.

[280] Thuc. 4.42.1.

[281] Wallace and Figueira 2010, 68–9.

[282] *IG* I[3] 77 and Meritt, Wade-Gery, and McGregor 1939, 346–53, citing also the 'panhellenic warmth' attested in Aristophanes' *Peace*, performed at the Dionysia that same year; for a more critical view see Kallet 2004, 466–7.

Some of the islands may have seen their tribute reduced over the next several periods, if certain fragments of the remaining lists have been correctly dated. In the list currently assigned to 417/16, Paros returned to her original assessment of 18 talents and Naxos to 9 talents (partially restored).[283] Ios and Mykonos returned to their exact pre-425/4 levels.[284] Only Kythnos saw an increase, to 6 talents.[285] For the following year of 416/15, Andros reappears with a tribute of 7 talents.[286] It has even been proposed that the Insular District was assessed more lightly than the rest of the *arkhē* after the Peace of Nikias.[287] General remarks have also been made concerning Cycladic prosperity during the Peloponnesian War, based on these lists.[288]

One must be cautious with such statements, however. The lists from this later period are quite problematic and are extremely fragmentary. For example, the amounts for the Insular District for 418/7 are missing (except for Sikinos, which is restored).[289] The figures for Paros and Naxos in the list from 416/5 are restored, as well.[290] Moreover, it has been recently (and rightly) questioned whether these fragments even belong to these years (421/20–415/14) at all.[291] They may better fit the period between 425 and the Peace of Nikias.[292]

According to Thucydides, due to financial exhaustion the Athenians in 414/13 decided to replace the tribute with a 5 per cent harbour tax (*eikostē*) in the hope that it would increase revenue.[293] It was most likely implemented in the summer of 413, after tribute

[283] *IG* I^3 288, line 11 (Paros); line 4 (Naxos).

[284] Ibid., line 8 (Ios); line 9 (Mykonos).

[285] Ibid., line 5 (Kythnos). Brun 1996, 192 calls attention to the mineral resources of Kythnos as a possible source of wealth.

[286] *IG* I^3 289, line 21.

[287] Blamire 2001, 111.

[288] Brun 1996, 184–92, concluding that 'il est clair que la seconde moitié du Ve siècle est un temps de prospérité'.

[289] *IG* I^3 287, line 16.

[290] *IG* I^3 289, line 24 (Paros), line 27 (Naxos).

[291] Kallet 2004, 468 (questioning the reliability of the list assigned to 422/1) and 480–7 (for 417/16 and 416/15). Kallet goes so far as to question whether *IG* I^3 289 can even be definitely ascribed to a tribute quota list and not some other type of inscription.

[292] Kallet 2004, *passim*.

[293] Thuc. 7.28.4; Kallet 2001, 199–226; Figueira 2005; Finley 1978, 121 n. 51; Blamire 2001, 114 and n. 106.

had already been assessed but prior to the defeat of the Sicilian Expedition.[294] A number of possible advantages can be seen in the replacement, including what has been called the 'ease of transition' since commercial taxes were presumably already in place in almost all allied cities, and their annual yields would have been widely known.[295]

How long the new tax lasted is still disputed, since Thucydides does not mention if and when it expired. The general consensus is that the Athenians returned to tribute collection in 410, although the evidence is mainly circumstantial.[296] If the tribute was in fact reimposed, this could mean that the tax had been unsuccessful. However, line 363 of the *Frogs* of Aristophanes (produced in 405) mentions an *eikostologos* on Aigina, so it may have persisted for years on that island, whatever its effectiveness.[297] It has been pointed out, moreover, that references in literary sources to the raising of money by the Athenians during the Ionian War fit the pattern of exactions performed by *stratēgoi* in the field (*argyrologia* rather than *phoroi*).[298] As the situation continued to deteriorate in the Aegean from 412 onwards, conditions would not have been favourable for a reinstitution of tribute, although *argyrologia* were possible wherever Athenian naval power was successfully projected.[299] It has even been proposed that payment of the *eikostē* rather than the (more powerfully symbolic) tribute to Athens was a safer bet for allies who wished to remain 'on the fence' during the Ionian War.[300]

[294] Figueira 2005, 4.

[295] Ibid., 11.

[296] Samons 2000, 250–4; Kallet 2001, 223–5 and 2004, 294. The evidence for the restoration of tribute consists of fragments of *aparkhē* lists that *may* be post 414/13, and two cases where its collection may have been punitive and thus extraordinary: Khalkedon in 410 (Xen. *Hell.* 1.3.9) and Aigina in 405 (Ar. *Ran.* 363). Kallet 2001 proposes that Thucydides considered the tax irrational, but see Figueira 2005, 6 n. 17 for an opposing view.

[297] Rhodes 1985, 33; Blamire 2001, 114 thinks that losses from the Spartan occupation of Dekeleia could have negated its profits.

[298] Figueira 2005, 22–4, who reinterprets *IG* I^3 101 as detailing a loan to the Neopolitai of Thrace in 410/09 by Athenian *stratēgoi* from monies already collected from their harbour taxes. Examples of allies who were hit with similar exactions include Kyzikos (Thuc. 8.107.1 and Diod. 13.40.6) and, for our purposes, Paros (Diod. 13.47.7–8).

[299] Burke 2005, 28 says that collection of the harbour tax became unworkable due to the Spartan fleet, but wouldn't collection of tribute have been just as difficult?

[300] Figueira 2005, 25.

There is no direct evidence for taxation on commerce in the Cyclades until the Hellenistic period.[301] Moreover, we do not have figures for harbour revenues in the Aegean world in general for the fifth century, but a few amounts are attested for the fourth, and they are substantial.[302] Yet even in the absence of firm data, it is clear that this tax had as much potential for exploiting the wealth of the *arkhē* as did the *phoros*, if not greater potential.[303] In addition to allied communities, the reference in Aristophanes shows that Athenian klerouchs on Aigina and elsewhere may also have been liable to pay it.[304] It would have specifically targeted cities with major harbours (such as some of the Cyclades), and for the first time, the assets of metics in allied cities involved in commerce would have been included.[305] While it has been proposed that this put less pressure on the aristocracy than the payment of tribute, the upper classes benefited from trade, especially in the mineral products of the Cyclades, and may have been hit as hard as metics.[306] The *eikostē*, like the Standards Decree (see above), would have been easier to enforce on states that were closer in proximity to Athens and on established sea routes, and the Cyclades are generally put forward as prime candidates.[307] Could this even have been a factor in encouraging certain Cycladic oligarchs to support the Four Hundred in 411?

[301] The most complete discussion of the evidence for commercial taxes in the ancient Greek world is Vélissaropoulos 1980, 205–22. Delos levied the *pentēkostē* in the third century (*IG* XI.2, 161A, line 26), raising 14,200 drachmas in 279 and 17,900 the following year. There was also a transit tax or *paragōgion* at Delos in the third century (*IG* XI.2, 163A, line 24). Thasos had a group of officials in the early fourth century, the *karpologoi*, who regulated rights of navigation for Thasian citizens (*IG* XII Suppl.349; Vélissaropoulos 1980, 215–17).

[302] Ar. *Vesp.* 655–660 (from 422) gives a figure of 2,000 talents in total revenue (including tribute). For the fourth century: Dem. 23.110 on 30 talents from harbours in the Khersonese 'in peacetime', and 200 annually from harbours in Thrace. There exists the possibility that a *dekatē* tax was generally assessed in the fifth century: Finley 1978, 310 n. 51. It is also possible that Ar. *Vesp.* 658 refers to a 1 per cent harbour tax had already been levied in the empire at an earlier date.

[303] Kallet 2001, 199: 'a trend, culminating in the Peloponnesian War at the latest, in which the *arkhē* was becoming increasingly economic in nature and purpose.' Figueira 2005, 36 estimates that if the Athenians envisioned raising some 1,000 talents with the *eikostē*, then this would mean that annual commerce within the *arkhē* could have approached 20,000 talents.

[304] Ar. *Ran.* 363; Meiggs 1972, 369; Blamire 2001, 114 n. 106.

[305] Kallet 2001, 199–203.

[306] Samons 2000, 270–2 stresses Athenian oligarchic backlash against the tax.

[307] Figueira 1998, 66, with references.

CYCLADIC REVOLTS AFTER THE SICILIAN EXPEDITION

Several islands in the Cyclades revolted after the accession of the Four Hundred in Athens. Alkibiades had sent messages to Athens insinuating that the Persian satrap Tissaphernes might be induced to transfer his financial support from Sparta to Athens, as long as they set up an oligarchic system to 'gain the King's confidence'.[308] Alkibiades' idea was first broached to a small group of the Athenian commanders on Samos. One of the *stratēgoi*, Phrynichos, did not trust Alkibiades and thought him only interested in engineering his own recall. Moreover, Phrynichos was sceptical about allied reaction to an oligarchy in Athens, stating that local autonomy was more important to them than what type of system Athens would establish at home. Phrynichos also stated that the allies would be even less inclined to stay loyal because they would fear worse treatment from oligarchs.[309] Yet, Phrynichos was overruled, and Peisander was sent to Athens to propose the idea. Peisander's subsequent mission to Tissaphernes ended in failure, but he and the other envoys returned to Samos and decided to proceed with the *coup d'état* anyway, without the participation of Alkibiades. At this point, their stated goals were to 'best prevent the ruin of their cause, and meanwhile to sustain the war'.[310]

Next, during his voyage from Samos to Athens in the summer of 411, the oligarch Peisander abolished democracies wherever his ships put into port and took hoplites from these places as allies.[311] Thucydides states that armed groups of Andrians, Tenians, and Karystians, as well as Athenian settlers from Aigina, then assisted the Four Hundred in intimidating the population of Athens.[312] It may be

[308] Thuc. 8.53.3.

[309] Thuc. 8.48.5–6.

[310] Thuc. 8.63.4: *ὁρᾶν ὅτῳ τρόπῳ μὴ ἀνεθήσεται τὰ πράγματα καὶ τὰ τοῦ πολέμου ἅμα ἀντέχειν.*

[311] Thuc. 8.65; Gomme, Andrewes, and Dover 1981, 161; de Romilly 1966 proposes that these Athenian oligarchs knew that the oligarchic parties in allied cities would be stronger. Pl. *Leg.* 7.332c states that the Athenian empire lasted so long because of friends in the cities, which may (*pace* de Romilly) refer to oligarchic friends and not democratic ones.

[312] Thuc. 8.69.3; Gehrke 1985, 22 (Andros), 159 (Tenos); Heftner 2001, 90; Hornblower 2008, *loc. cit.*

that hoplites from these *poleis* were present simply because Peisander had stopped in Tenos, Andros, and Karystos on his return voyage, and reflect nothing more than his itinerary. However, for Thucydides to be so specific in this case warrants additional explanation.

The question arises as to what these islanders had in mind by assisting in the takeover of the Four Hundred. There has been very little scholarly discussion of this question.[313] As he made his cruise home to Athens, what kinds of promises would Peisander have made to these islanders? Would he have told them of the plans of the Four Hundred to try to come to an agreement with Sparta? While the original Athenian oligarchic conspirators on Samos had planned to continue the war effort, if Thucydides' testimony is accurate, they may have now decided that the best plan of action was to sue for peace.[314] One of the first acts of the Athenian oligarchs was to make an (albeit unsuccessful) overture for peace to Agis at Dekeleia.[315]

Were the Andrian and Tenian hoplites angered by the loss of a large number of their peers during the botched Sicilian Expedition? There may have been economic factors involved as well. If aristocratic resentment of levies of *eisphorai* helped trigger the *coup* of the Four Hundred in Athens, as has been suggested,[316] then it is possible that similar financial pressures had been brought to bear on their counterparts in the Cyclades. Perhaps the switch from *phoros* to the 5 per cent harbour tax was a catalyst, but we have no direct testimony.

There is no indication, however, that the Athenian oligarchs had any plans to abandon the *arkhē* completely. On the contrary, it seems that until this moment most late fifth-century Athenian oligarchs benefited from it to one degree or another.[317] Peisander would have given his islander supporters reason to think that they would enjoy a new level of power (or at least local power) in a newly oligarchic *arkhē*. Obviously, they would have required the loyalty of the fleet to achieve success. When the fleet at Samos declared itself as the rightful Athenian state, it would have become amply clear to anyone in the

[313] One of the few has been Figueira 1991, 99 n. 43, who simply proposes that they were motivated by greed or by the aspirations of their 'leaders' at home to achieve greater power.

[314] Thuc. 8.63.4.

[315] Thuc. 8.70.2.

[316] Christ 2006, 63–4; Balot 2001, 213; Gabrielsen 1994, 173.

[317] Thuc. 8.48.6 (see also below); Marr and Rhodes 2008, 20; Rhodes 2000, 126–31; Connor 1985. 1971.

Aegean that this force, combined with Samian ships, could have held the *arkhē* together independently from Athens. In fact, they prevented allied revenue from reaching Athens during the rule of the Four Hundred.[318] As the Four Hundred unravelled, there were obvious divisions in their ranks as to the proper course of action, with the most extreme of the oligarchs building fortifications at Eetioneia in the Peiraeus and making overtures for Spartan assistance.[319] Thucydides is clear on how their fortunes had changed:

> Their first wish was to have the oligarchy without giving up the empire; failing this to keep their ships and walls and be independent; while, if this also were to be denied them, sooner than be the first victims of the restored democracy, they were resolved to call in the enemy and make peace.[320]

The Cycladic supporters of the Four Hundred would most likely have not envisioned an end to the Athenian *arkhē* as a result of their revolt either, but the masses of citizens on their home islands probably did. Concurrent events on the island of Thasos may provide parallels. Peisander's associate Dieitrephes abolished the democracy on Thasos at around the same time. Yet, after two months the Thasians turned hostile to Athens and began to fortify the city, hoping for Spartan assistance:

> Things at Thasos thus turned out just the contrary to what the oligarchic conspirators at Athens expected; and the same in my opinion was the case in many of the other dependencies; as the cities no sooner got a moderate government and liberty of action, than they went on to absolute freedom without being at all seduced by the show of reform offered by the Athenians.[321]

[318] Thuc. 8.76.4–7.
[319] Thuc. 8.90.1.
[320] Thuc. 8.91.3: *ἐκεῖνοι γὰρ μάλιστα μὲν ἐβούλοντο ὀλιγαρχούμενοι ἄρχειν καὶ τῶν ξυμμάχων, εἰ δὲ μή, τάς γε ναῦς καὶ τὰ τείχη ἔχοντες αὐτονομεῖσθαι, ἐξειργόμενοι δὲ καὶ τούτου μὴ οὖν ὑπὸ δήμου γε αὖθις γενομένου αὐτοὶ πρὸ τῶν ἄλλων μάλιστα διαφθαρῆναι, ἀλλὰ καὶ τοὺς πολεμίους ἐσαγαγόμενοι ἄνευ τειχῶν καὶ νεῶν ξυμβῆναι καὶ ὁπωσοῦν τὰ τῆς πόλεως ἔχειν, εἰ τοῖς γε σώμασι σφῶν ἄδεια ἔσται.* Ceccarelli 1993, 469 points out that this passage supports the idea that the oligarchs did not make a direct connection between naval hegemony and democracy, since by keeping the fleet and walls they intended to maintain a similar military strategy to what had been implemented before.
[321] Thuc. 8.64.5: *περὶ μὲν οὖν τὴν Θάσον τἀναντία τοῖς τὴν ὀλιγαρχίαν καθιστᾶσι τῶν Ἀθηναίων ἐγένετο, δοκεῖν δέ μοι καὶ ἐν ἄλλοις πολλοῖς τῶν ὑπηκόων· σωφροσύνην*

The question of how popular or unpopular the Athenian *arkhē* was in the cities of the Delian League is a vexing one. Several passages in Thucydides would seem to indicate that the author himself thought that Athenian hegemony was unpopular.[322] The words placed by Thucydides in the mouths of various political figures paint a varying picture.[323] Some revolts (like that of Mende in 423) saw a small number of anti-Athenian partisans; that of Skione in the same year was an uprising of the majority of citizens.[324] The mass of citizens in many allied cities may have seen Athenian rule as preferable to that of their own oligarchs, but this need not have automatically meant that they had a true loyalty to Athens, and the Spartans could also have been viewed with suspicion since they potentially would have supported the local oligarchs.[325]

Thucydides says something very similar when he details the position of Phrynichos during the negotiations on Samos in 412/11: that the allies would have welcomed an oligarchic Athens even less than a democratic one, since the 'best people' in Athens were the ones who profited from the empire, and would be cruel in their treatment of allied populations.[326] One can see that several factions existed in many of the subject island cities. Spartan assistance at Thasos did eventually materialize, but not all Thasians favored it, any more than they had favored it from Athens. Xenophon records that the Spartan harmost Eteonikos and the *lakonistai* were driven out of Thasos by a revolution in 410.[327] The island did not return to Athenian control

γὰρ λαβοῦσαι αἱ πόλεις καὶ ἄδειαν τῶν πρασσομένων ἐχώρησαν ἐπὶ τὴν ἄντικρυς ἐλευθερίαν, τῆς ἀπὸ τῶν Ἀθηναίων ὑπούλου εὐνομίας οὐ προτιμήσαντες.

[322] Thuc. 2.8.5; 8.2.2.

[323] Unpopularity among the masses is stated or implied in Thuc. 2.63.1–2 (speech by Perikles); 3.37.2 (speech by Kleon); 8.48.5–6 (speech by Phrynichos). The reverse example would be Diodotos' speech at 3.47.2 on the *dēmos* of Mytilene. Modern accounts that support the popularity of Athens among the majority of allied populations include de Ste. Croix 1972 and Jones 1957, 67–8. In opposition see Quinn 1964.

[324] Thuc. 4.123.2 (Mende) and 4.132.1 (Skione) on the composition of these revolts; Quinn 1964, 262.

[325] Hornblower 2011, 186; Quinn 1964, 258–61 cites the examples of Akanthos and Amphipolis during the 420s, when rebels were suspicious of Sparta's intentions even when they requested aid from that city. Thuc. 4.81.2 states that the decision of many Athenian allies to revolt in 412/1 and seek Spartan assistance was due to Brasidas' policies.

[326] Thuc. 8.48.6.

[327] Xen. *Hell.* 1.1.32, who also states that a Spartan named Pasippidas and the satrap Tissaphernes were accused at Sparta of having abetted this event.

until 408, however.[328] This two-year interlude appears to have been one of the ascendancy of a faction that wanted *neither* side to interfere in Thasian affairs.[329] Once again, one must not fall into the oligarchy/democracy dichotomy too intensively. The Milesians also rebelled from Athens in 412, but the democracy there lasted until 405.[330]

Questions are also raised by the presence of Cycladic and other allied crewmen in an inscription that most likely dates to the latter part of the Peloponnesian War. An Athenian naval inventory lists foreigners (*xenoi*) who were citizens of the Cycladic islands of Naxos, Kythnos, Siphnos, Keos, and Kimolos; also included are men from other allied islands such as Khios, Rhodes, Peparethos, Euboia, Thasos, Samothrace, and Aphytos.[331] Several dates have been proposed for this inscription, and it has been variously interpreted as an honorary list or as a casualty list.[332] It would be incorrect to propose dates for the inscription on the basis of whether or not the home *poleis* of these islands were still loyal to Athens, since it would have been quite possible for individuals to serve in the Athenian navy even when their home islands were in a state of revolt against Athens (witness Phanosthenes of Andros below). Moreover, the Athenians would have been eager to list any such islanders in service in the fleet as symbols of loyalty to Athens, if Jordan's dating of 411 is correct.

The presence of Keians also brings to mind the possible aforementioned obligation for provision of conscripts from Keos during the earlier Sicilian Expedition. It may be, although this is purely

[328] Diod. 13.72.1. Events on Thasos at this time are, however, very unclear. For example, the relationship between the accounts of revolts on the island in 410 in *Hell.Oxy.* 10.3 and Thuc. 8.64: Bleckmann 1998, 216.

[329] Quinn 1964, 265 on the idea that normally pro-Athenian democrats on Thasos would have had no reason to stay loyal to the Athenians once Dieitrephes had put oligarchs in charge of their island.

[330] Thuc. 8.17.1–4 for 412; Diod. 13.104.5 and Plut. *Vit.Lys.* 8. Witness also the statement in [Xen.] *Ath.Pol.* 3.11 that the Athenians had once supported the Milesian oligarchs against their *demos.*

[331] *IG* I^3 1032 lines 229–60; Laing 1966; Jordan 1975, 210–40, who contends that those from allied states were free citizens of those states. However see Graham 1992 on the presence of slaves, esp. 266 n.40 for slaves owned by crew members Archedemos of Peparethos and Phanostratos of Kythnos.

[332] Jordan 1975, 72 for *c.*411; Laing 1966, 107–19 thinks that it dates to the aftermath of the Battle of Knidos in 394; Funke 1983, 164–9 proposes that it is a casualty list from Arginusai. Graham 1998 proposes that it was an honorary list from 412 for Strombichides' expedition of eight triremes to Samos and Ionia (citing Thuc. 8.15.1–16.1).

hypothetical, that this status had changed in some indeterminate way. Since few, if any, of those Cycladic conscripts would have escaped death or enslavement after the Sicilian debacle, these *nautai* would have been newer additions to the fleet, and the nature of the honors would seem to preclude the idea that they were conscripts. However, this must remain speculative as the evidence is simply insufficient. All that can be said with certainty is that Cycladic sailors were still serving in the Athenian fleet during the latter stages of the war, and that this inscription does not imply that they were of lower 'status' than their peers.

While the Four Hundred were still in power in Athens, the revolt of all the Euboian cities (except for Oreos) took place, accompanied by a Spartan/Eretrian victory over Athenian forces.[333] Diodorus states that the Euboian rebels were in great fear because 'living as they did on an island, they should be forced to surrender to the Athenians, who were masters of the sea'. Consequently these rebels joined forces with the Boiotians in order to build a causeway to link their island to the mainland.[334] Despite the importance of Euboia, it was not compelled to return to the Athenian fold for the remainder of the war. Any anti-Athenian factions in the Cyclades could not have failed to have been heartened by these events, and it is clear that at least a few of the islands became hostile to Athens at this time. With the account of Thucydides now ended, however, we are compelled to rely on other sources for Athenian operations in the Cyclades during this latter part of the war.

Diodorus states that in 410 the Athenian commander Theramenes, after failing to stop the construction of the aforementioned causeway to Euboia, took thirty ships and sailed towards the islands to attack the enemies of Athens and collect booty, and that 'when he put in at Paros and found an oligarchy in the city, he restored their freedom to the people and exacted a great sum of money of the men who had participated in the oligarchy.'[335]

This is a tantalizing passage that leaves many questions unanswered. Which islands at this time constituted the 'territory of the

[333] Thuc. 8.95.3–7. The revolt began in the harbour of Eretria.
[334] Diod. 13.47.3.
[335] Diod. 13.47.8: *καταπλεύσας δ'εἰς Πάρον καὶ καταλαβὼν ὀλιγαρχίαν ἐν τῇ πόλει, τῷ μὲν δήμῳ τὴν ἐλευθερίαν ἀποκατέστησε, παρὰ δὲ τῶν ἁψαμένων τῆς ὀλιγαρχίας χρημάτων πλῆθος εἰσεπράξατο.*

enemy?' If Peisander's voyage had resulted in the establishment of several island oligarchies, one would expect that Andros and Tenos would have been objects of Theramenes' expedition. But only Paros is mentioned.[336] It is probable that Andros had also broken away from Athens by this point, although it was not dealt with until 407 (see below), and if Theramenes did attack it at this time he was apparently unsuccessful. He may not have gone further to the east or south than Paros, since he next went northward to the Thracian area. He and his forces were later summoned to join the Athenian fleet that engaged Mindaros at the Battle of Kyzikos.[337]

The fate of Paros is described somewhat vaguely in Diodorus' account, and we have no other evidence of what actions were taken by Theramenes. There are only a few parallels of similar Athenian action at this time, such as Alkibiades' settlement of Selymbria in 408, which included a new treaty of alliance and the installation of a garrison.[338] The only real parallel of the Athenians replacing an island oligarchy with a democracy is the settlement of Thasos in 408. We can supplement Diodorus' testimony in that case with epigraphic evidence, a decree on the return of pro-Athenian exiles, apparently passed the following year in 407 at Athens.[339] One of these exiles, Apeimantos, is known from other inscriptions to have had his family property returned, and his sons received *proxenia* at Athens.[340] There also appears to be arrangements made for the payment of a *misthos*, perhaps for a garrison.[341] What is most interesting, however, is the section addressing the newly exiled oligarchs. They were to be sent to nearby Akanthos, yet they could be rehabilitated with grants of *ateleia* if they would make 'voluntary donations' to the new regime.[342] The

[336] Gomme, Andrewes, and Dover 1981, 180, propose that Naxos was also under an oligarchy, but only on the evidence of its proximity to Paros. Hornblower 2008, 943, thinks Naxos was also dealt with by Theramenes.

[337] Xen. *Hell.* 1.1.12 states that he arrived at Sestos from Macedonia with twenty ships; Diod. 13.49.3 states that he came from Thrace. Xenophon adds the detail that Theramenes had been collecting money, and that Thrasyboulos arrived from Thasos with his own ships and had also been collecting money, which may have happened while that island was under the control of a faction that was both anti-Athenian and anti-Spartan.

[338] *IG* I^3 118.

[339] *IG* XII.8, 262 and Grandjean and Salviat 1988 rule out other proposed dates for the decree.

[340] On the property: *IG* XII.8, 263; on the *proxenia*: *IG* II^2 26.

[341] Grandjean and Salviat 1988, 264.

[342] Ibid. 264–6.

editors of the inscription consider this to be more amicable than the situation on Paros in which money was simply taken from this same class of people, and as an example of a new policy of the Athenians trying to heal broken links with their allies.[343] Both cases sound quite different from the Athenian punishment of Khios in 412 as related by Thucydides. Thucydides describes his admiration for the Khians, and that their only real mistake at the time of their revolt was to believe prematurely that Athenian power was at an end. He then describes how the subsequent blockade and ravaging led some Khians to switch back to the Athenian side.[344] Nevertheless, the Khians were punished with devastation of their agricultural land by the Athenians,[345] with the result that amphora exports from Khios declined significantly until the end of the century.[346]

One could also note the effect of warfare and *stasis* on Thasos, as the island is said to have been suffering greatly when Thrasyboulos retook it for Athens in 407.[347] The lack of such severe consequences for the Parians may indicate that the Athenians still had a fair level of support on Paros. The oligarchy that Peisander found there may have been of very recent vintage, and so had attracted the attention of the Athenians.[348] The Athenian treatment of Paros, along with that of the Thasians, could be more indicative of a changed Athenian strategy for dealing with troubles among the allies. Unfortunately, if the Athenians passed a similar decree for the Parians at this time it has not survived.

Paros is not mentioned again in the sources until 407, when Alkibiades sailed from Samos after his re-election as *stratēgos* and stopped at Paros on his way home. No specific reason for this is given by Xenophon.[349] A recent monograph on Parian history proposes that it was done for fundraising purposes, since Xenophon mentions earlier in his account that soon after leaving Samos, Alkibiades had

[343] Ibid. 266 and 274; in general Smarczyk 1986 on the Athenian policy of reconciliation with rebellious allies during the Dekeleian War.

[344] Thuc. 8.24.4–6.

[345] Thuc. 8.14.2 on the revolt; 8.24.3 on its suppression, citing the previous prosperity of the Khians.

[346] Lawall 1998, 86–9 and 95 details the decline in finds of Khian amphoras at Athens and Gordion datable to this period.

[347] Xen. *Hell.* 1.4.9.

[348] Hornblower 2008, 943 *pace* Reger 2004, 765, who considers the Parian oligarchy to have been in place for some time.

[349] Xen. *Hell.* 1.4.11.

exacted a hundred talents from the Karians.[350] Yet the entire episode is unclear,[351] and the possibility that an anti-Athenian faction had taken over Paros again is unlikely.

Soon after his stopover at Paros and return to Athens in 407, Alkibiades led a force of a hundred ships against Andros.[352] He made a landing at the harbour of Gaurion where Alkibiades defeated the Andrians and their Spartan allies.[353] After killing some of the enemy and shutting them inside the city walls, Alkibiades left a garrison behind at Gaurion, set up a trophy and sailed for the east.[354]

The implication in both Xenophon and Diodorus (but especially the latter author) was that the majority of Andrians were in opposition to the Athenians. This may be the reason why the Athenians were forced to take and fortify Gaurion rather than the city itself. Neither Xenophon nor Diodorus say anything concerning any Athenian klerouchs that may have still remained on Andros.

Although there is no direct evidence for when these Spartan forces had established themselves on Andros, it is likely that it was around the same time as they had in Euboia.[355] A squadron of Spartan warships was still at Euboia later in 411 until it was summoned to Elaious in the Hellespont.[356] Thus nearly five years elapsed before the Athenians directed their attention to the recovery of Andros. The proximity of Andros to the Bosporan grain route could help explain both the Spartan decision to station forces there as well as the Athenian interest in regaining control of the island. The delay is more difficult to explain. It may be more important to note that Alkibiades made the expedition when it became possible to do so,

[350] Xen. *Hell.* 1.4.8 on Karia; Berranger-Auserve 2000, 94–5 on Paros.

[351] It has been suggested by Krentz 1989, 127 that Alkibiades would have had to spend the entire year of 408 in Karia in order to raise such a sum. But at p.128 the same author does not doubt Xenophon's testimony that Alkibiades stopped at Paros.

[352] Diod. 13.69.4 says it was one hundred ships.

[353] Diod. 13.69.4 says 'Peloponnesians', Xen. *Hell.* 1.4.22 uses the term 'Lakonians', and Plut. *Vit.Alc.* 35.2 says 'Lakedaimonians'; Krentz 1989, 133; Bloedow 1973, 72–4; Smarczyk 1986, 36–7.

[354] Xen. *Hell.* 1.4.23 says that he next sailed for Samos; Diod. 13.69.5 states that he next ravaged Kos and Rhodes. The passage in Diodorus also states that he left Thrasyboulos behind in command at Andros, but Krentz 1989, 133 thinks that 'Thrasyboulos' is an error for 'Thrasyllos'.

[355] Andrians were also among the allies who had assisted the Four Hundred in Athens; Lazenby 2004, 218–19.

[356] Thuc. 8.107.2.

and that it was considered important enough by Xenophon to record, showing the significance of control of Andros.

The existence of a variety of political factions on Andros is also implied by the career of Phanosthenes. After the defeat at Notion, the general Konon sailed from Andros to Samos with twenty ships, and was replaced at Andros by four ships under Phanosthenes.[357] This individual, a native Andrian, was honoured in an inscription (along with one Antiokhides, otherwise unknown) with an exemption to the 1 per cent tax at Athens in return for the provision of oar-spars (either at no cost or at a reduced price).[358] He appears to have been forced out of Andros after 411 (probably during the revolt against Athens), was later naturalized as an Athenian citizen, and was subsequently elected to a military office in 407/6.[359] It has been suggested that he was a *navarkhos* or *arkhōn tou nautikou*, one of the naval commanders subordinate to the *stratēgoi*.[360] Athenaios states that he had been promoted to his position by the people of Athens, and mentions him along with other prominent foreigners at Athens such as Herakleides of Klazomenai and Apollodoros of Kyzikos.[361] He was certainly exceptional, but may also have been somewhat exemplary of certain Cycladic islanders who actively worked to support Athens. Pro-Spartan Andrians, of course, were also active. An Andrian trireme crew had been captured and thrown overboard on the orders of the Athenian commander Philokles sometime before 404.[362] There is also the example of the Andrian exile Diomilos, who was killed at Epipolai leading 600 Syracusan troops.[363]

[357] Xen. *Hell.* 1.5.18–20. On his way to Andros, he captured two Thurian triremes and temporarily held hostage the well-known Rhodian 'outlaw' Dorieos.

[358] Engen 2010, #4 (= *IG* I^3 182) and #5 for further discussion. Dates from 425 to 414 have been proposed (Mattingly 1966, 200–1; Walbank 1978, 323–4) but a date after 411 appears most likely: MacDonald 1981, 144–6, followed by Engen 2010 above.

[359] Pl. *Ion* 541c–d; Ath. *Deip.* 11.506a; Xen. *Hell.* 1.5.18; Andok. 1.149; Osborne and Byrne 1996, 24; Reiter 1991, 286 and 292–4. The equation of the Phanosthenes in this inscription with the general detailed in Xenophon has been questioned by Figueira 2005, 20.

[360] Jordan 1975, 122; Krentz 1989, 144 doubts that he was ever one of the ten *stratēgoi*.

[361] Ath. *Deip.* 11.506a; Pl. *Ion* 541d.

[362] Xen. *Hell.* 2.1.31.

[363] Thuc. 6.96.3.

CONCLUSIONS

There has been much debate concerning economic motivations in Athenian imperial policy. Some have seen economic growth during the *arkhē* as a reality, but a phenomenon that was unintentional.[364] Others have credited the Athenians with more economic foresight.[365] Yet it seems clear that trade between Athens and the allies developed its own dynamic as time progressed,[366] binding the hegemon and her satellites economically.[367]

It is intriguing that the Athenians did not take steps to appropriate natural resources in the Cyclades directly (as they did with, for instance, the gold and silver mines operated by the Thasians at mainland sites such as Mount Pangaion).[368] We do not have definitive evidence on how the extraction of marble from quarries on Paros was organized, but there is nothing that indicates that Athens took over control of this activity in the fifth century or at any other time.[369] Similarly, we have no evidence that the Athenians took a particular interest in the Naxian quarries, or in mines on Siphnos or Seriphos. Given that productive lands on islands like Andros and Naxos would probably have been assigned to klerouchs, the lack of evidence for such a phenomenon is surprising.[370] The fourth-century decree that regulates the export of ruddle from Keos was a restoration of controls that had been in effect earlier—presumably, the period of the *arkhē*, although an exact date is lacking.[371] The usefulness of ruddle for painting trireme hulls may be the explanation; it may have been necessary for the Athenian navy to ensure its supply in the same

[364] Meiggs 1972, 272.

[365] Kallet-Marx 1993, 47.

[366] Schmitz 1988, 311.

[367] Schmitz 1988, 118: 'den Waren—und Geldkreislauf'; Schuller 1974, 187–92.

[368] Hdt. 6.46–7; Thuc. 1. 100.2 and 1.101.3; Plut. *Vit.Cim.* 14.2. The Athenians took over operation of the mines after the Thasian revolt ended in defeat by 462 (Thuc. 1.101.3), but may have restored them by the early 440s (Pébarthe 1999). Morris and Papadopoulos 2005, 195–200, however, do make comparisons between towers in Attika and Cycladic ones, and propose that the idea may have been 'imported' to allied states by Athenians during the fifth century.

[369] Berranger 1992, 295.

[370] There are no references in the Attic stelai, for example, to Cycladic properties owned by any of the Hermokopidai, although Adeimantos of the deme Skambonidai owned estates on Thasos (Pritchett and Pippin 1956, VI.55–6) and Nikides of Melite had lands in Euboia (Ibid., IV.20–21).

[371] Rhodes and Osborne 2003, #40 (= *IG* II^2 1128).

manner as shipbuilding timber from Macedon, and to deny such a strategic material to the Peloponnesian League.[372] The proximity of the Cyclades to Athens may have made such commercial control easier than for other states. It is of course possible that Athens *did* in fact take control of these resources, and the lack of surviving references to this is simply coincidental. However, it may have been logistically easier to leave the technical aspects of extraction in local hands that knew them well.

Only a handful of individuals of Cycladic origin are securely attested as residing in Attika in the fifth (and fourth) centuries.[373] Some, such as Phanosthenes or the comic poet Amphis (both from Andros), or the Delian Peisitheides, may have been political exiles who became naturalized in Athens.[374] The same may be true for the Keian individual found in a casualty list from the end of the fifth century.[375] Yet, as has been noted, even during the Hellenistic period when Rhodes was one of the most important maritime states in the Aegean, very few Rhodians are attested as having lived in Athens at that time.[376]

The Old Oligarch states that the *chrēstoi* ('best men') in Athens would protect the interests of their counterparts in allied cities.[377] The political 'behaviour' of a *polis* obscures much of the social machinations within that led it to that point of decision.[378] Those Cycladic aristocrats who did manage to adapt to the changed circumstances would have become important links in the *arkhē*, even under democratic regimes, a fact not often emphasized. It may have been the case that the large-scale defections of 411 were led by these families, groups with accumulated grievances against Athens that may have included increasing economic burdens. Those Athenians who established the short-lived oligarchy at home in 411 may have

[372] The fourth-century naval inventory *IG* II^2 1627, in a list of needed supplies, does not mention *miltos* (S.C. Lawrence, paper presented at the AIA annual meeting in January 2004), but this is not decisive evidence.

[373] Other than the *nautai* from the naval catalogue referred to above, and the special examples mentioned below, Osborne and Byrne 2001 list for the fifth century two Andrians (p. 24) and one Keian (p. 121); for the fourth century two Naxians (p. 243), two Kythnians (p. 134), one Tenian (p. 306), and three Andrians (p. 24).

[374] Osborne and Byrne 1996, 24 (for Amphis) and 63 (for Peisitheides).

[375] Ibid. 121.

[376] Reed 2003, 2 n. 4.

[377] [Xen.] *Ath.Pol.* 1.14.

[378] As elegantly described by de Romilly 1966.

been their natural allies. Thus, they first saw the possibility of a 'reformed' Athens as a desirable ally, until that possibility evaporated and they gravitated towards Sparta. Sparta's newly acquired sea power may in fact have given reason to envision a new economic unity based on her hegemony, one that would provide some of the same benefits as Athens but without some of the disadvantages of having large amounts of revenue drained away. As we will see in the discussion of the years immediately after the end of the Peloponnesian War, this vision, if it in fact existed, was shown to be false when Sparta attempted to levy tribute on the Athenian model. While speculative, this focus on elites in the Cyclades may help explain the nature of the Cycladic rebellions and who expected to benefit from them.

Thus we have seen that by the last quarter of the fifth century, the Cyclades had become a very different region, politically and economically, than in the Archaic period. Islanders, both as trireme crews and as hoplites, continued to serve in Delian League forces, although we do not know how many were compelled to do so.[379] All the islands gave up their local mints, either because of compulsion or because of convenience, and used Athenian silver. All gave up most of their warships (at least officially) and turned over such matters to the Athenian fleet, augmented by ships from larger allies such as Samos, Lesbos, and Khios. The type of 'thalassocracy' (as defined in Chapter 3 as local hegemony of territorial waters) that may have been exercised by Naxos and other Cycladic islands up to the time of the Persian Wars, would not have been tolerated by Athens. Local rivalries (such as that between Naxos and Paros) could no longer be played out in the same ways and had to be subsumed into the new relations within the Delian League.

It would seem that islands known to have medized—Andros, Naxos, Paros, and Tenos—had a tense relationship with Athens at various times in the history of the *arkhē*, and were not treated equally. Naxos rebelled in the 460s and lost its naval privileges. Andros and Naxos had klerouchies imposed on their territory. Andrians and Tenians assisted the Athenian oligarchs in their takeover in 411, and Andros and Paros saw oligarchic takeovers at home that were later dealt with by Athens.

[379] Andrian hoplites, along with those of Miletos and Karystos, participated in Nikias' campaign in the Corinthia and at the Battle of Solygeia in 425: Thuc. 4.42.2.

Though several of these islands were no longer proverbial for their wealth as they had been before the Persian Wars (particularly Siphnos and Naxos), they cannot be characterized as poor during the Pentekontaetia or Peloponnesian War either. It might be ventured that their prosperity was out of proportion to their smaller size and population, as compared to states in other areas within the *arkhē*. While certain islanders obviously suffered at Athenian hands, there would have been others who profited greatly from their Athenian connections.

5

Fluid Hegemonies

The Cyclades in the Early Fourth Century (403–355)

The Cyclades were among the prizes won by Sparta from her victory in the Peloponnesian War. However, there is little evidence that the victor took much interest in the spoils. The outcome of the Corinthian War left somewhat of a political vacuum in the region, and the *Aiginitikos* of Isokrates shows the effects of *stasis* in the region during this period. Most of the Cyclades joined the Second Athenian League either immediately after, or within a few years of, the Athenian victory at the Battle of Naxos in 376, and Athenian hegemony defined these islands to one degree or another for the next two decades. While Athens proved unable to protect the region during the troubles in the Aegean in the 360s, only one island, Keos, is known to have revolted from the League, and the entire region stayed loyal during the Social War of 357–355.

Many of the economic and fiscal issues already examined for the previous century remained important in the fourth: piracy, convoying, harbour revenues, and so forth. However, Athenian relations with the islands of the Aegean during the fourth century have drawn much less scholarly interest than relations during the fifth-century *arkhē*. One of the goals of the present study is to attempt to go beyond traditional value judgements of Athenian behaviour in the fourth century, which for years has been much too focused on the so-called 'failure' of the Second Athenian League, in order to more fully understand the experiences of communities such as the Cyclades.

FROM THE END OF THE PELOPONNESIAN WAR TO THE KING'S PEACE

There is little doubt that shock waves from the collapse of the Delian League in 404 would have affected the Cyclades in a variety of ways. What is unclear is how greatly the islands were affected economically, and whether the collapse of Athenian hegemony was perceived by inhabitants of these islands in a positive or negative light. The only reference we have to anyone associated with the Cyclades at this time is the re-publication in 403/2 of a previous honorary decree from 422 for Polypeithes of Siphnos, whose family had maintained ties with Athens since the Persian Wars.[1]

The replacement of the Athenian *arkhē* with a Spartan one was recorded in the sources with few details.[2] Throughout the Aegean, the Spartan commander Lysander removed the klerouchies so despised by Athens' former allies,[3] but in their place he installed garrisons, aristocratic governing councils known as dekarchies, and military governors known as *harmostai*.[4] The Spartans had become known late in the Peloponnesian War for engaging in *argyrologia*, or the exaction of contributions of money in order to support fleet operations.[5] Many sources allege that the Spartans levied tribute from the cities that came under their control, in blatant emulation of their defeated enemy.[6]

[1] *IG* I^3 227; *SEG* XXI.15 and XLI.9; Osborne and Byrne 1996, 294; Matthaiou 2000. This family remained important in Athens during the fourth century, with Kallaiskhros serving as trierarch in 366 (*IG* II^2 1609 line 27) and his son Stesileides holding multiple trierarchies in the 330s (*IG* II^2 1623 lines 203–19 and 268–70; *IG* II^2 1627 lines 194–9; and *IG* II^2 1631 lines 430 and 435); *pace* Whitehead 1977, 81 and n. 86. This family also held mining leases at Laurion: Lalonde, Langdon, and Walbank 1991, P18, 63; P29, 3 and 4–5.

[2] The classic discussion of the Spartan Aegean *arkhē* remains Parke 1930. For a discussion of how it was portrayed differently by various ancient sources, see Schepens 1993. Xenophon, for example, tends to downplay the maritime aspects of Spartan hegemony, while Theopompos stresses them.

[3] For the return of klerouchs see Xen. *Mem.* 2.8.1.; Pl. *Euthphr.* 4c (referring to Naxos); Strauss 1986, 77.

[4] For the dekarchies see Xen. *Hell.* 3.4.2, 7; Plut. *Vit.Ages.* 6.2 and *Vit.Lys.* 13.3–5; Nep. *Lys.* 3.1; Parke 1930; Bockisch 1965; Hamilton 1979, 56–61.

[5] See for example Thuc. 8.3.1 for the Malian Gulf in 413.

[6] Isok. 12.67–68, 4.131–132; Polyb. 6.49.10; [Arist.] *Ath.Pol.* 39.2; Diod. 13.106.8; Plut. *Vit.Lys.* 27.2.

The only numerical total given for such tribute is 1,000 talents, in Diodorus, generally considered to be an inflated figure.[7] However, the sums collected could still have been substantial. For example, Sparta had levied 32 talents from her ally Rhodes in 412.[8] One could also cite the demand that Elis pay for the expenses of the war against Athens,[9] as well as the order for island states to construct triremes for Agesilaos later in 395.[10] The Spartans may have chosen the term *synteleia* as a euphemism for tribute, similar to later Athenian usage of the alternative term *syntaxeis*.[11]

In addition to the logistical problems of collection that the Spartans would have had to face (not to mention the resentment that they might have experienced from the newly 'liberated' former members of the Delian League), there are other factors that could have worked against Sparta in assuming the mantle of naval hegemon of the Aegean. It is probable that Spartan ships did not patrol the Aegean with anything close to the regularity that Athens did before and during the Peloponnesian War. This is not surprising, since Sparta was neither dependent on grain convoys nor involved in interstate commerce to any great degree.[12] Sparta also did not possess a major *emporion* such as the Peiraeus to provide a centre for trade and redistribution. This is not to say that commerce was non-existent in Sparta. One could note Xenophon's statement that 4,000 non-Spartiates were mingling in the city's *agora* at the time of the conspiracy of Kinadon in 398.[13] Moreover, the merchant ships that ferried Spartan and Peloponnesian troops to Sicily were in all likelihood owned by *perioikoi*.[14] But to truly take the place of the Athenians at the nexus of the economic network that had been developed through the fifth century, the Spartans would have needed to implement a major overhaul of their economic apparatus, including the adoption of a

[7] Diod. 14.10.2; Parke 1930, 56–7 and n. 35 supports the figure.

[8] Thuc. 8.44.4.

[9] Diod. 14.17.5.

[10] Xen. *Hell.* 3.4.3.

[11] Lotze 1964, 63–4.

[12] Polyb. 6.49.6–10 on Spartan lack of resources. Xenophon does mention a Spartan presence for revenue collection at the Hellespont *c.*400, however: Xen. *Anab.* 7.1.20–25; Gabrielsen 2001, 233 and n. 60.

[13] Xen. *Hell.* 3.3.5.

[14] Thuc. 7.19.3.

viable currency standard.[15] Since many of Lysander's policies were short-lived, this is even more reason to doubt that the Spartans could have truly adopted the Athenian *phoros* system in all its aspects.[16]

Of course, Athens no longer provided the same 'services' to commerce as she had in the fifth century either. The status of the Peiraeus as a bustling *emporion* was seriously compromised after 404. From one of the speeches of Andokides it appears that the level of imports and exports in the harbour of Athens had dropped to 1,800 talents in that year, still a sizable sum but approximately 10 per cent of the level of 413.[17] The year after the surrender, the Thirty persecuted metics, who handled much of the trading activity in the Peiraeus.[18] The productivity of Attika was negatively affected as well. While agriculture may not have suffered to the extent previously thought, it is clear that the Laurion silver mines were neglected until the early 360s.[19]

Other aspects of Spartan control are equally obscure. It is unknown how many of the Cyclades may have 'hosted' garrisons, harmosts, and/or dekarchies. Most likely, the Spartans would have wanted to secure those islands situated on sailing routes to the east that they had used during the war. However, references to Spartan naval itineraries in the early fourth century are vague. During Agesilaos' crossing from Aulis in Boiotia to Ephesos, Xenophon only mentions a stop at Cape Geraistos to take on additional troops.[20] During the voyage of Ekdikos and Diphridas to Knidos in 391, it is also unclear as to what islands they used as ports of call.[21] Although the Ephors' Decree had supposedly removed the dekarchies, Xenophon reports the Boiotian

[15] Hamilton 1979, 57–8 speculates that the Gylippos affair triggered debate in Sparta about the assumption of Athens' naval empire. Hodkinson 2000 stresses pre-404 private use of coinage at Sparta at 170–6, and the possible usage of the Aiginetan standard by the Peloponnesian League during the fifth century at 168, to downplay the idea that Sparta was as economically underdeveloped as usually proposed. See however Figueira 2002*b*.

[16] Hodkinson 2000, 423–32 focuses mainly on how elites could have enriched themselves by means of military adventures abroad; David 1981, 50–77 on imperialism leading to supposed 'corruption' in Spartan society, esp. 66–77 on mortgaging of *klēroi*.

[17] Andok. 1.333; Thuc. 7.28; Strauss 1986, 48–50. Some Athenians had made fortunes during the war: Lys. 26.22.

[18] Isok. 7.66 claims that the Thirty destroyed dockyards in the Peiraeus.

[19] Strauss 1986, 46; Hopper 1953.

[20] Xen. *Hell.* 3.4.4. Thibron's crossing to Ephesos in 391 is also mentioned at 4.8.17 without any further details given.

[21] Xen. *Hell.* 4.8.21.

envoys to Athens in 395 as stating that some of them still remained in power in that year; even if the envoys were being mendacious, it is at least possible that a few remained in the Cyclades.[22]

Spartan hegemony over the Cyclades (whatever its exact nature) appears to have gone unchallenged until 394. Rhodes had revolted from Sparta in 396 and a democratic faction took control the following year, and soon afterwards the exiled Athenian commander Konon, commanding Persian warships, seized Egyptian grain vessels bringing supplies to Spartan forces in Asia Minor.[23] Then Konon and the Persian satrap Pharnabazos inflicted a major defeat on the Spartans at the Battle of Knidos. Only thirty out of eighty-five Spartan ships escaped.[24] Konon and Pharnabazos now took advantage of their victory.[25] They sailed throughout the Aegean in the months after the battle, expelling harmosts from cities that had been tributary to Sparta.[26] Diodorus states that after several islands and mainland cities in Ionia had changed sides, Konon and Pharnabazos brought the Cyclades into their camp, and then sailed for Kythera.[27] According to Xenophon, Konon told Pharnabazos that he would maintain their fleet by means of contributions from the islands.[28]

Xenophon also states that they made Melos their base on their way to ravage the coast of Lakonia and establish a garrison on Kythera.[29] Their exact route is unknown. Delos was a probable stop on their itinerary, since the temple of Delian Apollo had been removed from

[22] Xen. *Hell.* 3.5.13. Parke 1930, 53 considers the reference to the dekarchies in the present tense to be a 'rhetorical distortion', but see Smith 1948, 153, who thinks that the Ephors' Decree only removed those in Asia Minor. There was still a harmost at Aigina as late as 388, but his presence was not against the will of the Aiginetans: Xen. *Hell.* 2.2.3 and 5.15.10–12; Aiskhin. 2.78; Bockisch 1965, 183–4.

[23] Diod. 14.79.6; *Hell.Oxy.* 11.1; Paus. 6.7.6; Moreno 2007, 323 and 341.

[24] Xen. *Hell.* 4.3.10–12; Diod. 14.83.5–7; Polyain. *Strat.* 1.48.5; Hamilton 1979, 228–30.

[25] Isok. 4.154, 5.63, 9.56, 12.56; Diod. 14.84; Justin 6.4.1. As noted by Ager 2001, 114, however, and detailed further below, the Spartan navy remained a force to be reckoned with for another two decades.

[26] Xen. *Hell.* 4.8.1–2.

[27] Diod. 14.84.4 (during the spring of 393); cf. Xen. *Hell.* 4.8.7–8, who simply mentions Melos and Kythera.

[28] Xen. *Hell.* 4.8.9–10.

[29] Xen. *Hell.* 4.8.7. Chankowski 2008, 185 would place their Cycladic travels during the latter part of the summer of 394, and cites Erythrai as evidence that most of these cities welcomed them (*Syll.*^{3} 126). The statement in Pl. *Menex.* 245b on the defense of the Parians against the Spartans at this time is most likely a corruption for 'Persians': Urban 1991, 181.

Athenian control after the Peloponnesian War,[30] and there is a possible epigraphic reference to a Spartan harmost there.[31] Delos appears to have come under Athenian control again, documented in an account from 393/2, which also lists loans to Paros, Mykonos, and Syros in the Cyclades.[32] Another possibility for an island that changed hands is Keos, as a later speech of Demosthenes names Keos as having once been under the control of a Spartan garrison and governor.[33] While this may have been rhetorical exaggeration, Keos was located at the entrance to the Saronic Gulf and forces stationed there could have threatened Athenian grain supplies, as occurred in 376 (see below). Andros could also have still been in the Spartan camp since they had stationed troops there near the end of the Peloponnesian War, but this is also uncertain.[34]

It is possible, however, that most of the Cyclades had maintained a more or less 'neutral' stance towards both Athens and Sparta since 404.[35] A hint is preserved in Xenophon concerning Aigina, which by 389 had become a base for Spartan raids against shipping on the sea lanes around Attica. Xenophon implies that the Aiginetans were perhaps motivated more by Spartan pressures than by hostility towards the Athenians, with whom they had now spent a number of years 'in normal relations'.[36] It may be that the Cyclades also did not adhere to one power bloc or another unless forced to do so. Parallels to their situation might be seen in that of Megara. Although Megara was technically a Spartan ally during the Corinthian War, both Spartan and anti-Spartan forces might have moved freely through her territory.[37] It may be that the inhabitants of the Cyclades were not opposed to selling provisions to the fleets of either side.

[30] Rhodes and Osborne 2003, #3; Prost 2001.

[31] *Syll.*[3] 119a.

[32] Chankowski 2008, #11.

[33] Dem. 18.96, which also mentions Aigina; Parke 1930, 62.

[34] Xen. *Hell.* 1.4.9; Diod. 13.72; Bockisch 1965, 171.

[35] Laing 1966 has proposed that the Athenian naval catalogue *IG* I[3] 1032 dates to after the Battle of Knidos. The presence of Cycladic *nautai* in this list would make it significant for the present discussion, if he is correct, but this late date is very problematic. See Chapter 4, pp. 130–1 and n. 331 for discussion.

[36] Xen. *Hell.* 5.1.1; Bauslaugh 1991, 184–5.

[37] Bauslaugh 1991, 178 and n. 25, stressing Pl. *Tht.* 142c for Athenian forces. Xen. *Hell.* 4.3.15 states that Spartan troops had to sail back to the Peloponnese after the Battle of Koroneia, but is otherwise vague on whether or not Spartan forces could also traverse the region (*pace* Legon 1981, 264 n. 25).

It is important to remember that although he was an Athenian,[38] Konon's operations were essentially for Persian benefit.[39] Any benefit to Athens would have come as a corollary effect. Moreover, the victory at Knidos changed the equation of sea power in the Aegean only for the next few years. Yet, it did result in some advantages for Athens. In addition to Delos, the islands of Lemnos, Imbros, and Skyros were also retaken sometime before spring 392.[40] By 392/1, another Athenian commander, Thrasyboulos, had reinstated the *eikostē* or 5 per cent tax (that had temporarily replaced the *phoros* from 413–410) on many of Athens' former allies, including Thasos and Klazomenai.[41] Thrasyboulos also imposed (or perhaps took over from the Spartans) the levy of a *dekatē* (10 per cent tax) on shipping that passed through the straits of the Hellespont, resuscitating yet another fifth-century Athenian practice.[42] This tax was also collected by Iphikrates in the Hellespont in 389.[43] There are several reports in the sources of Thrasyboulos and others raising money by more coercive methods.[44] It is evident that some Athenians who had lost property abroad after the defeat of Athens were now members of a faction that wished to restore Athenian power in the Aegean.[45]

Xenophon admits to leaving out many details on the naval side of the Corinthian War and mentioning only those he considered to be most important.[46] But these naval operations led directly to the outbreak of war on the mainland by triggering the recall of Agesilaos.[47]

[38] Xen. *Hell.* 4.3.12.

[39] As rightly emphasized by Seager 1967, 102–3 and Funke 1980.

[40] On Delos: Chankowski 2008, #11; on Lemnos, Imbros, and Skyros: Xen. *Hell.* 4.8.15, Andok. 3.12,14; Seager 1967, 102 n. 66.

[41] Diod. 14.94.2; for Thasos: *IG* II^2 24a lines 3–6; for Klazomenai: *IG* II^2 28 lines 7–8. Figueira 2005, 30–5 sees the restoration of both the *eikostē* and the *dekatē* in the Hellespont (described below) as signs that the fifth-century *eikostē* had lasted down to Athens' defeat in 404, and that the *phoros* had not been re-imposed.

[42] Xen. *Hell.* 4.8.27; Dem. 20.60. For the levying of the tax in 410 see Xen. *Hell.* 1.1.22; Polyb. 4.44.3.

[43] Xen. *Hell.* 4.8.35; Rhodes and Osborne 2003, #18 (= Tod 1962, #114).

[44] Konon's arrest: Diod. 14.85.4. On the treasury: Ar. *Eccl.* 823–9. Lysias reports that after Konon's death some of his friends were prosecuted for these exactions; 28.5, 29.2. Thrasyboulos himself was killed in Aspendos in 389 during one of these fundraising excursions: Xen. *Hell.* 4.8.30.

[45] Cloché 1919, 156; Kagan 1961, 326; Strauss 1986 proposes a complex picture with numerous factions, which seems likely. Funke 1980, however, posits almost unanimous agreement among the Athenian citizenry for war with Sparta.

[46] Xen. *Hell.* 4.8.1; Perlman 1964, 71.

[47] Perlman 1964, 79.

When Agesilaos returned to the Greek mainland from Ionia soon afterward, he went by land through Thrace instead of retracing his sea route.[48] The temporary loss of Spartan control of the sea in 394 would no doubt have been the main reason for this, although Xenophon is silent on this issue.

One could also point, however, to turbulent political conditions in the Cyclades at the time that could have made such a journey problematic. At least a few of the Cyclades had now become chaotic sites of factional dispute. The events described in the *Aiginitikos* of Isokrates probably belong to this period.[49] The defendant, pleading his case before an Aiginetan court, was a Siphnian aristocrat who had been driven from his home island by civil strife. He had already placed some property in safekeeping with guest-friends on Paros, because he felt that that island was 'especially secure'.[50] However, Paros was soon attacked by one Pasinos (who is otherwise unknown to us), and an exile of oligarchs from Siphnos, including the defendant, subsequently occurred. It is possible that these two islands had now seen the removal of pro-Spartan factions, or even of Spartan garrisons. After risking his life to recover his property, the defendant stayed with guest-friends in other locales such as Melos, Troizen, and eventually Aigina. Some time later, he joined his fellow Siphnian exiles in a failed attempt to regain control of Siphnos with hired mercenaries, making it clear that the Cycladic region stayed tumultuous for an indeterminate period.[51]

We know of another (non-Cycladic) island that saw revolution and counterrevolution of this sort during this same period. The democratic uprising of 395 on Rhodes was a violent one, and the subsequent regime that lasted until 391 was very severe in its treatment of oligarchs, especially those who had performed trierarchies.[52] An oligarchic counterstroke began in 391 and the island appears to

48 Xen. *Hell.* 4.2.3–7; Diod. 14.83 is of no additional help.

49 Isok. 19, generally dated to 394–390: Mirhady and Lee Too 2000; Cloché 1963, 13–14; Brun 1996, 179–82; McKechnie 1989, 17–19; Rutishauser 2005.

50 Isok. 19.18.

51 Isok. 9.38–39; Rutishauser 2005.

52 Arist. *Pol.* 1302b21–25, 27–8, 32–3; 1304b20–25 and 27–31; *Hell. Oxy.* 10.3. The date accepted here is that supported by David 1984, though some have dated Aristotle's comments on the restoration of oligarchy to 355: Berthold 1980, 39 n. 30 and 43 n. 46.

have been secured by them by 389.[53] The bitter nature of this conflict may have been echoed in at least some of the Cyclades, if events were authentically related by the defendant in the *Aiginitikos*.

Spartan naval power was, of course, far from permanently finished after the Battle of Knidos. Some of their warships had escaped that engagement, and they were later joined by reinforcements.[54] Spartan vessels assisted the aforementioned oligarchic uprising on Rhodes in 391, although the force was comparatively small; Ekdikos' eight ships were joined by Teleutias with nineteen.[55] But this smaller flotilla was able to capture ten Athenian triremes that had been dispatched to aid Evagoras of Cyprus.[56] The routes taken through the Aegean by these Spartan forces are very unclear, although Aigina appears to have been important as a Spartan base.[57] Neither Xenophon nor Diodorus list stopovers for Thibron's voyage to Ephesos in 391.[58]

The waters near Attika also remained hazardous to the Athenians and their allies. Xenophon states that the Athenians had thirteen patrol ships in the area of Aigina during the Corinthian War.[59] However, Teleutias made a successful assault on the Peiraeus in 387/6, plundering merchant ships and taking captives. He then hit grain ships while they were rounding the cape of Sounion, selling the booty on Aigina.[60] The oration of Lysias dated to this year, *Against the Grain Dealers*, shows the effect that rumours of threats to the grain supply from the Hellespont could have on economic affairs in Athens.[61] By the end of 387/6, the Spartan navy had closed the Hellespont to grain traffic and forced Athens to sue for peace.[62]

The perception of these events by Cycladic islanders needs to be taken into account, even if specific evidence is lacking. Considering

[53] Diod. 14.97.1. Hierax was able to use Rhodes as a base in 389: Xen. *Hell.* 5.1.2–6; David 1984, 275–8.

[54] Diod. 14.83.7; Ager 2001, 114; Cawkwell 1963*c*, 153 and n. 22.

[55] Xen. *Hell.* 4.8.22–23.

[56] Xen. *Hell.* 4.8.24.

[57] Teleutias in 390/89 to Samos: Xen. *Hell.* 4.8.23–24; Hierax in 389/8 to Rhodes: Xen. *Hell.* 5.1.5; Antalkidas in 388/7 to Ephesos: Xen. *Hell.* 5.1.6; cf. Figueira 1993, 360.

[58] Xen. *Hell.* 4.8.17; Diod. 14.99.1.

[59] Xen. *Hell.* 5.1.5; Figueira 1993, 344.

[60] Xen. *Hell.* 5.1.18–23. Teleutias may even have collected tribute in the Cyclades in 389, as Xen. *Hell.* 5.1.2 mentions him taking away provisions from an unspecified island.

[61] Lys. 22; Descat 2004, 276–7.

[62] Xen. *Hell.* 5.1.30–1.

that the majority of Konon's fleet was comprised of Persian ships, would they have welcomed the prospect of Persian authority over their islands? Even when that possibility faded, they had now experienced a resurgent Athens after more than a decade when her power had been in abeyance. Would any of the islanders have welcomed the possibility of a return of the Athenian *arkhē*, perhaps because they could see it as potentially promoting trade?

Had commerce suffered in the Cyclades during the decade of 404–394 along with the decline of Athenian commerce? A decree that renewed a *symbolon* between Athens and Siphnos has been recently redated to the late fifth/early fourth centuries.[63] Although the date for this inscription could thus be potentially pushed as far back as the latest phase of the Peloponnesian War, another possible context is the late 390s, after the Battle of Knidos. This would coincide somewhat with the evidence of another recently published Siphnian inscription from roughly the same period, which indicates a democratic form of *polis* organization and, apparently, a grant of *proxenia* for an Athenian.[64] Other such agreements may have been renewed (or instituted for the first time) between Athens and other Cycladic islands, and have not survived.

There is also the question of coinage. One of the most important economic factors that we can reconstruct for this period is the increasing production of 'imitation' Attic silver coins in Egypt and the eastern Mediterranean, probably in response to a shortage in the supply of genuine Athenian currency.[65] Since most of the Cyclades had given up minting by the mid-fifth century,[66] Athenian silver had become legal tender in the *arkhē*. But at some point in the early fourth century, a few of the Cyclades began to mint again. Both Siphnos and Naxos issued silver coins on the Aiginetan standard (also known as 'Rhodian' because it was used by the Rhodians after their *synoikismos* of 408 and spread throughout the west coast of Asia Minor at this time).[67] The Siphnians struck staters and later tetrobols, while the

[63] Tracy 2003; Papazarkadas 2007, 144 and n. 16. I must now rescind my earlier hypothesis of a date in the 370s for this decree proposed in Rutishauser 2000.

[64] Papazarkadas 2007.

[65] Figueria 1998, 528–35; van Alfen 2005; Buttrey 1984.

[66] See Chapter 4, pp. 114–16.

[67] Nicolet-Pierre 1988, 160–2 for Naxos and Newell 1934 for Siphnos. Reger 2004, 763 and 773 simply gives 'C4' for both islands' issues without further comment. Ashton 2001 refers to the standard as 'Khian'.

Naxians minted in obol, trihemiobol, diobol, and tetrobol denominations (the last of which corresponds in weight to a Rhodian drachma). There is also evidence for Naxian tetradrachms, which appear in the accounts of Delian Apollo for 364/3.[68]

The publisher of the Siphnos hoard theorized that these coins were intended primarily for local use, as intermediaries between the Rhodian standard and the Attic.[69] The Naxian coins may have had a similar purpose, with the tetrobols of both islands able to fit into the systems used in Attika, the Peloponnese and Boiotia, and Ionia.[70] It seems that on both islands there was a single emission of tetrobols, followed by several issues of bronze coins, which have been found in greater abundance and display more stylistic development over time. The bronze issues probably continued to at least the mid-fourth century.[71]

It is interesting to speculate on where these islands acquired the silver to strike these coins. While Siphnos may still have had some local silver to exploit, Naxos did not have such resources at home.[72] The situation may have been similar to that of Kydonia on Crete, which struck 'pseudo-Aiginetan' coins starting around 460 even though silver was not locally available.[73] These coins might have provided additional revenue from money-changing fees if Cycladic *poleis* mandated their use for the payment of local customs dues.[74] It is possible that a sudden shortage of Athenian silver owls spurred these two temporary island issues.[75] While there could have also been some kind of assertion of political independence at work, considering the choice of standard it is more likely that the primary motivation came from the desire to promote trade in the new, unsettled conditions of the early fourth century.

[68] Chankowski 2008 #19, lines 66–7 and 105. Drachmas from Syros also appear in this list.

[69] Newell 1934, 19.

[70] Nicolet-Pierre 1988, 160–1, who discusses the stylistic parallels of these Naxian coins with other contemporary issues.

[71] Ibid. 161–2.

[72] Sheedy 2000, 118–19 discusses this fact in terms of Parian coinage early in the fifth century.

[73] Erickson 2005, 648 and n. 206; Figueira 1998, 122 considers these coins to be post-431.

[74] As seen in third-century Ptolemaic Egypt: Ashton 2001, 97 with references.

[75] Brun 1996, 157.

It is intriguing to compare minting practice on Siphnos and Naxos with another noteworthy numismatic phenomenon at this time, the minting of the so-called *ΣΥΝ* coinage by a combination of island and mainland states in Ionia: Byzantion, Ephesos, Iasos, Knidos, Kyzikos, Rhodes, Samos, and (possibly) Lampsakos. The date and political affiliation of this 'coinage alliance' is still debated. Some have dated it to 394–390 and thus seen the alliance as anti-Spartan.[76] It could even have been created after the Battle of Knidos as a statement of independence, not only from Sparta but also other states such as Athens and Persia.[77] However, a more likely date and context is *c.*405, as a series of pro-Spartan issues instituted by Lysander.[78] Accounts from the temple of Delian Apollo from the beginning of the fourth century distinguish between Attic and 'symmakhic' silver. These may have been *ΣΥΝ* coins, or they may have been coins struck by Peloponnesian League states on the Aiginetan standard.[79] Other former allies of Athens began to coin on the same Aiginetan standard as well.[80]

For our purposes, the political affiliation of this 'coinage alliance' does not matter as much as its possible economic ramifications. It could be indicative of a commercial agreement between these *poleis* in addition to a purely political one, as all specimens are on a common weight standard, in which one of these coins equalled 3 Rhodian drachms or 1 Aiginetan stater.[81]

It is interesting that no 'Cycladic Coinage Alliance' was formed at this time on the model of the Ionian one. Yet, if these Cycladic coins worked well with the 'symmakhic' coins, and others, in terms of exchange, it may not have been necessary for the Cyclades to either join the eastern Coinage Alliance or form one of their own. Although

[76] Buckler 2003, 181; Cawkwell 1963*c*, 152–4; Strauss 1986; Cahn 1970.

[77] Hamilton 1979, 230.

[78] Karwiese 1980; followed by Figueira 1998, 475–6 and 559, who proposes that it was an extensive but short-lived set of issues designed to pay the tribute to Sparta instituted by Lysander, and perished along with the dekarchies.

[79] Coupry 1959, 62–3 and Chankowski 2008, 180–1.

[80] Thuc. 8.101.1; Xen. *Hell.* 1.6.12; Figueira 1998, 158–61 and 2003, 90, who proposes that these standards were adopted to pay Peloponnesian forces. However, Spartan commanders also paid their forces in Athenian owls: Thuc. 8.5.5, 29.1–2 and Xen. *Hell.* 1.5–7; Kroll 2009, 199.

[81] This was recently proposed by Buckler 2003, 181–3, who hypothesizes that the later alliance of many of these states against Athens in the Social War of 357–355 can be seen in this earlier arrangement.

the Peiraeus apparently saw a lower volume of traffic, and the shipment of Egyptian grain to Athens may have abated,[82] the Cyclades could still have maintained their own commercial links with the east.

If at least two of the Cyclades had possessed enough wealth to issue their own coinage, could they have also begun to construct their own triremes again? We have no direct evidence of triremes in the hands of Cycladic *poleis* or individuals for the fourth century, any more than for the time of the Delian League the century before.[83] Yet, smaller islands could still have possessed them in the fourth century.

During the fighting between Alexander of Pherai and the Athenians at Peparethos in 362, Diodorus states that the tyrant's forces captured one Peparethian trireme along with five Athenian.[84] This could be an error in a late source, but it could also indicate that the phenomenon of smaller islands maintaining at least one or two warships (familiar from the time of the Persian Wars) may not have completely vanished.[85] To return to the beginning of the fourth century, it does not seem likely that the Spartans would have objected to the presence of Cycladic warships during their period of hegemony over the region, since it was common practice to require their allies to provide warships as far back as the Peloponnesian War.[86] Yet, if not compelled to do so there would have been little incentive for these islands to engage in that sort of financial outlay. With such large fleets still being deployed by the major powers it was simply not cost-effective for Cycladic *poleis* to try to compete by constructing and maintaining a few triremes, as they had done in the late Archaic period.

THE 'WRANGLE' OVER THE REGION (386–376)

The effect of the King's Peace (or Peace of Antalkidas) on affairs in the Cyclades is in many ways unclear. Athenian administration of the

[82] Figueira 1998, 535.

[83] Xen. *Hell.* 2.1.31 reports an Andrian trireme that had been captured by the Athenians and the crew thrown overboard sometime before 404, but it is not clear from the context whether the trireme itself had originated from Andros.

[84] Diod. 15.95.3. [85] Brun 1983, 113.

[86] Thuc. 2.7.2 for allies in Sicily and Italy in 431; 8.3.2 for the Peloponnesian League in 413.

Delian temple may or may not have lapsed again after 386.[87] Isokrates says that the Khians, Byzantians, and Mytilenians remained on the Athenian side after the Corinthian War, but lists no other Aegean states.[88] Isokrates apparently had little regard for the importance of the Cyclades, although he still found them worth mentioning when it suited his purposes.

In the *Panegyrikos*, written *c.*380, Isokrates speaks of a 'wrangle over the Cyclades' between Sparta and Athens (*τῶν Κυκλάδων ἀμφισβητοῦμεν*), whose inhabitants 'deserve pity' and are forced to till mountains because of scarcity of land.[89] He questions why Sparta and Athens were so distracted with fighting over this region when they could combine their forces and take lucrative lands from the Persians in Asia Minor.[90]

It is unclear, however, whether Isokrates' 'wrangle' refers to the time before or after the King's Peace.[91] Theoretically, the Spartans would have continued to hold sway over the region whether or not a 'wrangle' was truly occurring, since the Peace most likely included both the states that had actually fought in the Corinthian War as well as the noncombatants.[92] There is little evidence, however, that the Spartans were deeply concerned with events in the Aegean during the later 380s, even though they did become involved in disputes abroad such as with the Khalkidian Confederacy in the north.[93]

Scholars have also been divided as to whether or not the Spartans continued to receive tribute from the islands during this time,[94] but it would seem unlikely since there appear to have been no mobilizations of ships by the Spartans until 376.[95] Isokrates is very vague here in comparison to his criticism of Spartan actions on the mainland, and

[87] Coupry 1959, 56 and Sinclair 1978, 43–4 for a lapse in control; Chankowski 2008, 169–74 for a continuation of control. Chankowski also proposes that her inscription #13, detailing the prosecution of Delians for attacking Athenian amphiktyons, shows that the quadrennial cycle of the amphiktyonate persisted through the period 387/6–377/6, and thus so did Athenians on the panel.

[88] Isok. 14.28. [89] Isok. 4.132–6. [90] Urban 1991, 151.

[91] Chankowski 2008, 216–18.

[92] Buckler and Beck 2008, 74 n. 9, *pace* Badian 1991, 37.

[93] Sinclair 1978, 37.

[94] Smith 1954, 286 n. 5 accepts the possibility; Parke 1930, 73 considers the allegation to be no more than inflammatory rhetoric.

[95] Xen. *Hell.* 5.4.60–1; Diod. 15.34.5; Sinclair 1978, 45; Urban 1991, 118–19 on the lack of Spartan power in the Aegean at this time.

may simply be referring to the dispute over Delos.[96] This 'wrangle' could instead refer to the support of various factions on the islands. Naxos in particular may have hosted a Spartan presence, because Spartan forces are attested there in 376. It is possible that the Spartans were on the move in the Aegean again starting in 379. Diodorus' statement that Khabrias won over Peparethos, Skiathos, and 'other islands that had been subject to the Lakedaimonians'[97] comes after the author's report of Spartan interference at Histiaia.[98] Diodorus then follows with a list of Peloponnesian League allies from which troops were levied by the Spartans in 377/6, and no islands are among them, so Khabrias may in fact have been successful.[99]

It has been estimated that there were some sixty to seventy Athenian warships available in 387.[100] One scholar has proposed that Athens did not construct new triremes from 387–378 because she was forbidden to do so by the terms of the Peace of Antalkidas.[101] Yet there is evidence that Athens may have constructed some thirty-five warships during that period.[102] Whether or not any new ships were built during this time, however, it is unlikely that Athens was forced by the terms of the Peace of Antalkidas to demobilize all her warships. Athens was able to retain her klerouchies on Lemnos, Imbros, and Skyros according to the Peace, and this would seem to indicate negotiation from some position of naval strength. Moreover, these islands were vital links in the Athenian grain supply and Athens needed to protect shipping as well as safeguard her communications with the aforementioned klerouchies.[103]

The Athenians did make several bilateral agreements with various maritime states in the 380s. Khios was the first of these in 384,

[96] Sinclair 1978, 43 and n. 49 feels that the implication of the term ἀμφισβητοῦμεν is one of diplomacy rather than armed conflict, but diplomacy to what end?

[97] Diod. 15.30.5.

[98] Diod. 15.30.3–4. Sinclair 1978, 46 suggests that the commander responsible was the harmost for Thebes in 379, Herippidas (called 'Theripides' by Diodorus).

[99] Diod. 15.31.2.

[100] Sinclair 1978, 49 says 70 based on the evidence of Xen. *Hell.* 5.1.7, 10, 19–20, and 26–7; Robbins 1918, 366 suggests fifty; Amit 1965, 25 posits some 50–60 triremes.

[101] First stated by Cawkwell 1973, 52–4, and recently reiterated in Cawkwell 2005, 193–4 and n. 17. His argument hinges on retrojecting the terms of demobilization by land and sea contained in the Peace of 371 (Diod. 15.50.4 and Xen. *Hell.* 6.3.18).

[102] Clark 1990, 57–60; Sinclair 1978, 36 also dismisses Cawkwell.

[103] Dem. 18.301 on the need for naval bases; the Hebryzelmis Decree of 386/5 (*IG* II^2 31) implies that Athenian ships were escorting ships (presumably grain transports) heading to Athens from the Black Sea.

followed by Mytilene and Byzantion.[104] In 379 Thebes and Methymna were added to a 'stele of the allies' that in some ways constituted the prototype for the Second Athenian League that was formed nearly a decade later.[105] The most telling evidence against total Athenian demobilization is the treaty with the Khians. This was entered into on Khian initiative, and states that the Athenians will defend the Khians if they are attacked, while still honoring the provisions of the King's Peace.[106] Even if no new warships were constructed until the 370s, the Athenians were not absent from the Aegean.[107]

The statement of Isokrates in the *Panegyrikos* that 'pirates ruled the seas' thus requires some qualification.[108] It is possible that this is simply rhetorical exaggeration on his part.[109] It should also be stressed that whatever the strength of the Athenian navy and its ability to control piracy at this time, commerce would presumably still have been very active. Isokrates' villainous pirates must not have lacked prey. It has been pointed out that banking in Athens, which included bottomry loans for commercial shipping, began to prosper in this same decade.[110] Braudel's point on how commerce and piracy have always waxed and waned together in Mediterranean history is pertinent here.[111]

The turmoil on Paros described in the *Aiginitikos* may have eventually been a catalyst for the creation of a new Parian colony on the island of Pharos (modern Hvar) in the Adriatic. This was apparently done on the advice of an oracle, but no other motivation is attested.[112] Dionysios I of Syracuse provided military assistance to the colonists

[104] Khios: *IG* II^2 34 and 35; Mytilene: *IG* II^2 40; Byzantion: *IG* II^2 41; Urban 1991, 138–42.

[105] *IG* II^2 40 lines 15–16. See also Pritchett 1972, 164–9 (= *SEG* XXXII.50) for a *symmakhia* between Athens and another (unknown) state in 379/8.

[106] *IG* II^2 34 lines 24–9. Dušanić 2000 proposes that the treaty was established by the Khians to counter the threat posed by the Persian satrap Glos. Isok. 4.139 refers to Khian naval strength.

[107] Clark 1990, 60–1.

[108] Isok. 4.115.

[109] Sinclair 1978, 47; Clark 1990, 60 n. 72.

[110] Bogaert 1968, 61; Thompson 1979.

[111] Braudel 1972, 865–91.

[112] Diod. 15.13–14; [Skylax] 23; Strabo 7.5.5 C315; [Skymnos] 413–14, 426–7; Steph. Byz. *s.v. Pharos*; Pliny *NH* 3.140; Modern discussions include Wilkes and Fischer-Hansen 2004, 333–4; Kirigin 2006 and 1990, 296–302; Stylianou 1998, 193–6; Gaffney, Kirigin, Petrić, and Vujnović 1997, 217–38 collects all ancient literary and

against hostile Illyrians soon after settlement, probably with a squadron of vessels from Issa.[113] Obviously, the colonists could not have reached the island from Paros without ships, but it is unknown if they made the journey in their own vessels. The assistance of Syracusan triremes might imply that the Parians had few fighting craft themselves.

There has been little evidence found in excavations on Hvar to indicate strong contacts between Paros and her colony until the second century.[114] This would seem to bolster a case for the colony as a 'deduction', a case of forced emigration, perhaps of a political faction. It has been proposed that a pro-Spartan faction regained control of Paros after the promulgation of the King's Peace.[115] In an episode reported in Iamblichos' *Life of Pythagoras*, two Parians, Euephenos and Eukritos, intercede with Dionysios on behalf of some of their fellow Pythagoreans.[116] This has been seen as an indication of a strong oligarchic party on Paros, which would naturally lead to the conclusion that the colonists sent to Pharos might have been pro-Athenian democrats.

Although not entirely without foundation, such a view is speculative. To propose a Parian–Spartan–Syracusan political axis becomes problematic when it is remembered that alliances with Dionysios I could be tenuous at best. Before aiding the colonists, the Syracusan tyrant had made an alliance with the Illyrians and incited them to attack the Molossians, who were then aided by Sparta, Dionysios' supposed 'ally'.[117] Moreover, there is no reason to think that the presence of two Parian oligarchs in Syracuse is decisive evidence for oligarchy at home.

What *is* significant, however, is that the excavators on Hvar have proposed that the colony was small in population though large in

epigraphic testimony for Hvar, while pp. 151–215 provide a gazetteer of known archaeological sites from all periods.

113 Diod. 15.14.1–2; Woodhead 1971; Wilkes and Fischer-Hansen 2004, 334.

114 Robert 1960; Kirigin 2006, 101–6 gives an overview of possible economic activity on early Pharos, including the evidence for amphora production. A brief inscription (*CIG* 1837c) commemorating a victory over 'Iadisinoi and allies' might be dated to later in the fourth century: Gaffney et al. 1997, 236–7.

115 Lanzilotta 1987, 130–1.

116 Iambl. *VP*. 267; Lanzilotta 1987, 135.

117 Diod. 15.13–14; Braccesi 1977, 135–6; Beaumont 1936, 203 thinks that Dionysios' governor at Lissos may have helped the Parians on his own initiative.

territory, and many of the colonists probably wealthy, which may indicate that it was settled by a small oligarchic contingent, rather than by a large pro-democratic faction.[118] Diodorus states that the colony was located near the sea, implying a reliance on commerce.[119] The first silver and bronze coins were struck at Pharos soon after the colony was founded and were on the Syracusan weight standard, eventually circulating over a wide area including Sicily and Macedonia.[120] It is possible that the settlement may have later become a stopover for ships bringing Parian marble via the Tyrrhenian Sea and the Po river delta into Etruria, where its use, particularly for fine sarcophagi, began anew not long after the establishment of Pharos and increased throughout the second half of the fourth century.[121] It is also worth noting that Thasos, a Parian colony, also had ties in the Adriatic around this same time.[122]

Returning to the question concerning the identity of the Parian settlers on Pharos, the most likely explanation is that they were part of the exodus of a faction from their home island after *stasis*, though the exact nature of the faction is unclear. After some years had passed, the colonists may have reopened trading links with the mother city in order to profit more from the renewed trade in Parian marble to the west.

FROM THE SECOND ATHENIAN LEAGUE TO THE END OF THE SOCIAL WAR (378–355)

After the liberation of the Kadmeia of Thebes from Spartan rule in 379, the Athenians sent out ambassadors to various Aegean states in order to build an anti-Spartan coalition. Diodorus reports that first Khios and Byzantion, and then Rhodes, Mytilene, and 'certain other islands' (*τῶν ἄλλων τινὲς νησιωτῶν*) decided to throw in their lot with the Athenians, and a *synedrion* was established for the new allies.[123]

The inscription now properly called the 'prospectus' of the Second Athenian League[124] invites new allies to join the League and lists all

[118] Kirigin 1990, 299 and n. 42, which quotes a modern estimate of no more than fifty families for the colony.
[119] Diod. 15.14.
[120] Kirigin 1990, 301 and 2006, 108.
[121] See Chapter 6, pp. 108–9.
[122] Pouilloux 1954, 54–6.
[123] Diod. 15.28.3.
[124] Rhodes and Osborne 2003, #22(= *IG* II^2 43), also called the Stele of Aristoteles.

who had joined by the time the decree was passed in 377.[125] Group A on the front face of the stele includes the four states specifically mentioned by Diodorus (Khios, Byzantion, Rhodes, and Mytilene), and also Methymna on Lesbos.[126] The Parians appear on the front face also, among the second group of names to the left. This Group B includes Perinthos, Peparethos, Skiathos, Maroneia, Dion, and Athenai Diades on Euboia.[127] Others of the Cyclades are listed on the left side of the League prospectus.[128] These include Andros (line 112), Tenos (line 113), Mykonos (line 115), the three remaining *poleis* of Keos—Ioulis, Karthaia, and Koressos (lines 119–22), and Siphnos (line 126).[129] There are also Cycladic possibilities for the lost names on the lower right hand column of the front face. Syros, Naxos, Ios, Seriphos, and Kythnos are all likely candidates.[130]

The dating of the entrance of these various states into the League has not been satisfactorily resolved. Xenophon says virtually nothing of the formation of the League or its early operations, stating only that the Athenians built ships and assisted the Boiotians after the raid of the Spartan commander Sphodrias on the Peiraeus in 379.[131] Diodorus, however, states that after the raid of Sphodrias, the Athenian general Khabrias 'sailing to the Cyclades islands, won over Peparethos and Skiathos and some others which had been subject to the Lakedaimonians'.[132] In general, Diodorus gives substantially greater information concerning the League's activities.[133]

[125] Cargill 1981, 2.

[126] Badian 1995, 89 n. 34, has proposed that Diodorus' 'other islanders' reference may mean no more than this city, but Diodorus' later mention of the Cyclades could mean that perhaps the Parians can also be fit into this general framework.

[127] Cargill 1981, 38.

[128] Rhodes and Osborne 2003, #22, lines 112–27. Buckler 2003, 249 would fix the enrolment of the Parians, Poiessians, and Tenedians at this moment as well.

[129] Amorgos is also listed with the Cyclades at line 124.

[130] Cargill 1981, 37–8, as all except Kythnos are listed on the Sandwich Marble (Rhodes and Osborne 2003, #28 (= Chankowski 2008, #13*A*).); he also cites the crown awarded to Khabrias by soldiers on Syros: Burnett and Edmondson 1961, 81. Cargill does not accept the suggestion of Accame 1941, 82 that Melos was a member, on the evidence of [Dem.] 58.56, but see Chapter 6, p. 225 on the decree of Moirokles.

[131] Xen. *Hell.* 5.4.34; Baron 2006, 390 and n. 54.

[132] Diod. 15.30.5: *αὐτὸς δὲ ταῖς Κυκλάσι νήσοις ἐπιπλέων προσηγάγετο Πεπάρηθον καὶ Σκίαθον καί τινας ἄλλας τεταγμένας ὑπὸ Λακεδαιμονίοις*. Badian 1995, 89 n. 34, however, persists in disputing Diodorus' chronology and maintains that the League pre-dated the raid of Sphodrias.

[133] Diod. 15.28.1–4 refers to the establishment of the League, while 15.29.8 tells of the provisions of the decree moved by Aristoteles; cf. Baron 2006, 390 n. 54.

The Battle of Naxos in 376 was the most significant event for the entire Cycladic region since the Persian Wars.[134] A Spartan fleet of sixty-five triremes under Pollis had bottled up a grain convoy around Cape Geraistos on Euboia and provoked an Athenian response. Xenophon states that Pollis' ships were in the vicinity of Aigina, Keos, and Andros, implying that these islands were being used by him as bases.[135] However, he omits any details of the battle or any reference to a siege of Naxos, and only states that grain was delivered to Athens after the defeat of Pollis.[136] Xenophon's account is thus misleading—since the battle was fought in the area between Paros and Naxos rather than Euboia, the grain convoy may have been the catalyst for the engagement but not its focus.[137]

Diodorus proves to be the better source here.[138] Probably following Ephoros, he states that Khabrias and eighty-three triremes[139] first escorted the convoy to the Peiraius (apparently without trouble from Pollis), and then sailed to Naxos and attacked the city with siege engines,[140] drawing Pollis over to relieve the beleaguered island. On 16 Boedromion 376/5, Khabrias decisively defeated the Spartan force near the port of Naxos, destroying twenty-four of Pollis' craft and capturing eight.[141] According to Plutarch, Khabrias then sent Phokion to gather funds from nearby islands, and Demosthenes later

[134] And significant for the Athenians, as Plutarch *Mor.* 349 states that in his time its anniversary was commemorated at Athens along with those of other more famous engagements such as Marathon and Salamis.

[135] Xen. *Hell.* 5.4.61.

[136] Xen. *Hell.* 5.4.61–2.

[137] Tuplin 1993, 159 is rightly critical of Xenophon here, stating that he 'he totally failed to give a proper account of Athens' first genuine naval victory since 405'.

[138] Diod. 15.34.4–35.2.

[139] The figure is probably close to correct. *IG* II^2 1604 from 379/8 lists 100 (mostly older) vessels, and any Athenian triremes that were battle-ready were probably augmented by allied ships: Stylianou 1998, 308.

[140] The siege is only mentioned in Diodorus' account and Schol. Aristid. *Panath.* 173.16 (Dindorf); Stylianou 1998, 306. Burnett and Edmondson 1961, 81 n. 15 doubt that the siege of Naxos was successful, since its conquest is not mentioned by either Xenophon or Diodorus, but the former is a poor source for the battle of Naxos in general, and the latter probably assumed that his reader would understand that such a crushing defeat of the Spartans would have left little options for the Naxian defenders.

[141] In addition to Diodorus' account see Polyain. *Strat.* 3.11.2; Plut. *Vit.Phok.* 6.5–7; Aiskhin. 3.222, 243; Dem. 23.198 and 24.180; Din. 1.75.

claimed that Khabrias made several of these islands 'friends who had once been enemies'.[142]

We can now return to the matter of accessions to the League. Accame proposed that all the states listed on the front face of the prospectus joined the League prior to the Battle of Naxos in 376, and the states on the left side (including the Cyclades) joined after this battle. This has been followed by several scholars.[143] Recently, however, Christopher Baron has offered a new reconstruction that dates all the names of the left side to 373, after a fundraising expedition was carried out by Timotheos before embarking on his assigned mission to Kerkyra.[144] Xenophon is vague on this operation, but Diodorus states that Timotheos sailed through the Aegean and as far as Thrace in order to gather money and recruits.[145] The Athenians felt that he had wasted a campaigning season in this activity and subsequently removed him from his command. Nevertheless, according to Baron his labours bore fruit in the addition to the League of most of the Cyclades, as well as cities from the Khersonese, Propontis, Thrace, Lesbos, and Euboia.[146]

Baron also interprets a famous erasure at line 111 on the prospectus as a copyist's error of repetition. This erasure was formerly thought to have represented the secession of an ally from the League, the most common proposal being Jason of Pherai.[147] Baron, however, thinks that it was the Parians. Part of his argument is based on a long-known (but newly republished) inscription, which is also noteworthy for containing the only extant decree of the allied *synedrion*, coupled with an Athenian decree.[148]

The inscription involves the settlement of a dispute on Paros, but the exact circumstances are unclear. Most commentators have

[142] Dem. 20.77: καὶ φιλίας ἐποίησεν ἐχθρῶς ἐχούσας πρότερον. Later at 20.80 Demosthenes states that Khabrias had won over seventeen cities.

[143] Accame 1941, 99–104; Cargill 1981, 41–2 and 61–4; Cawkwell 1981, 45; Sealey 1993, 61.

[144] Baron 2006. For the expedition: Diod. 15.47.1–2; Xen. *Hell.* 6.2.12–13.

[145] Baron derives additional support from Apollodoros' prosecution of Timotheos later that year: [Dem.] 49.

[146] Baron 2006, 388.

[147] Mitchel 1984*b*, 48, who believes that it was a repetition from line 97 above, which he restores as 'Pheraion'. Cargill 1981, 44–9 does not accept his restoration.

[148] Oliver 1936 for the original publication; Wilhelm 1940, 3–12; Accame 1941, 229–44; Dreher 1995, 109–54. The most recent is Rhodes and Osborne 2003, #29, incorporating new readings by Charles Crowther, followed by Baron 2006, 392–4.

surmised that Paros had risen in revolt against the League and had been readmitted under certain conditions.[149] These conditions included the requirement that the Parians bring an ox and panoply to the Panathenaia, and an ox and phallos to the Dionysia. Similar provisions were normally decreed for Athenian colonists, and there is evidence that Paros was believed by some to have originally been a colony of Athens.[150]

However, it was most likely not a rebellion from the League, but rather an internal dispute on Paros which was settled by Athens and the *synedrion*.[151] Unlike most decrees promulgated by Athens against rebellious allies in both the fifth and fourth centuries, there is no provision for setting up a copy of the decree on Paros itself.[152] It has been noted also that the decree is of a comparatively non-imperialistic nature, as Parian possessions and land are guaranteed, and the sovereignty of Parian homicide courts is upheld.[153]

Baron is inclined to believe that the Parians seceded, and offers the following reconstruction: the Parians joined the League along with the other Cyclades after the cruise of Timotheos, but rebelled later in 373. He offers no explanation of how the matter was resolved on Paros (although the implication is that League forces were involved), but Paros was readmitted to the League in time to be inscribed on the left side. Baron proposes that the names were inscribed after Apollodoros' failed prosecution of Timotheos.[154] The erasure subsequently occurred when it was realized that the Parians had already been listed on line 89 of the front face.[155]

Baron's reconstruction is in some ways attractive. His proposal of the Parians for the erased name of line 111 is stronger epigraphically

[149] Oliver 1936, 462–4; Wilhelm 1940, 6–9; Accame 1941, 229–44; Cargill 1981, 121, 163–4.

[150] Thuc. 1.12.4; Isok. 12.43; Herakl. Pont. *FGrH* 2 F214. Other sources call Paros an Arkadian colony: Arist. fr. 611 Gigon and Steph. Byz. *s.v. Paros.* On some occasions these tokens of colonial status were brought to Athens voluntarily by delegates from a *polis*, such as Kolophon in 307/6 (*IG* II^2 456).

[151] Cawkwell 1981, 50; Dreher 1995, 110–41, followed now by Rhodes and Osborne 2003, #29 and Hornblower 2011, 244.

[152] Dreher 1995, 123. Lines 7–11, however, discuss the display of the decree in Athens.

[153] Sealey 1993, 63; Dillon 1997, 143–4 goes so far as to propose that the bringing of the ox and panoply could have been seen by the Parians as an honour.

[154] [Dem.] 49.

[155] Baron 2006, 393–4.

than others (such as Jason of Pherai). However, there are unresolved issues.

Baron does not attempt, for example, to explain why the Parians were listed the first time at an irregular location on the front face. Here we must turn to Diodorus. Baron rightly stresses the importance of Diodorus' testimony concerning Timotheos' cruise, which mentions that Thrace was part of his itinerary,[156] and this coincides with the appearance of a number of Thracian cities on the left side.[157] However, there is other testimony that Baron appears to ignore. On two occasions previous to the Timotheos passage, Diodorus describes Athenian naval activity in the Cyclades and the accession of new allies that followed. The first passage is the aforementioned report that Khabrias took 'Peparethos, Skiathos, and other islands subject to the Lakedaimonians' in 378, and the second passage states that the same commander brought new states into the Athenian camp after the Battle of Naxos in 376. The prospectus can be used to support some of Diodorus' testimony. As mentioned above, Group B on the front face includes Perinthos, Peparethos, Skiathos, Maroneia, Dion, and Athenai Diades on Euboia. Thus, Diodorus appears to be reliable on the matter of the early admission of Peparethos[158] and Skiathos to the League, and should be taken seriously.

When one looks at cities on the front face that were inscribed in irregular positions, it is reasonable to speculate that they may have joined the League at different times rather than in a bloc (the Tenedians and Poiessians of Keos are two examples). The variety of hands involved in entering these names on the stone would support the possibility of ad hoc additions to the roster. This may explain, for example, why Poiessa appears to have joined at a separate moment from the other Keian cities. The entry for the Parians is written in a different hand on the prospectus, 'the largest letters of any name

[156] Diod. 15.47.2–3.

[157] Baron 2006, 389–90, *pace* Stylianou 1998, 372. See also Woodhead 1962, 259. Xen. *Hell.* 6.2.12 does not mention Thrace, but that Timotheos simply sailed ἐπὶ νήσων.

[158] This is the first of two occasions when Diodorus mentions Peparethos as being part of the Cyclades (the second is during the sea raid of Alexander of Pherai in the late 360s: Diod. 15.95.1). But he may have been summarizing Ephoros: Accame 1941, 80. [Skylax] 58 also classifies the island as Cycladic. However, Strabo (at 2.5.21 C124 and 9.5.16 C436) does not (Reger 2004, 768).

anywhere on the stele,'[159] but greater precision in dating this addition is thought by some to be impossible.[160] Yet the placement of 'Parians' above 'Athenitai' would seem to rule out the possibility that the Parians were added much later, if at all, than the other allies in Group B. As mentioned above, Baron's view is that Paros was brought into the League as a result of Timotheos' cruise, then rebelled soon afterwards—'sometime in the second half of 373 and . . . [*its status*] resolved by the time that Timotheos' additions to the League were to be inscribed on the stele'.[161]

Although this is within the realm of possibility, there is something uncomfortable about the degree of time-compression involved. More tellingly, why would a pro-secessionist party on Paros feel that they had a chance of success in 373, especially immediately after a successful show of Athenian naval power in the region? Kallistratos' speech at Sparta in 371 includes the statement that, despite the adherence of *poleis* to one power bloc or another, 'in each city-state there are some who are pro-Lakonian and some who are pro-Athenian'.[162] At some point between 379 and 373, those factions on Paros that were opposed to Athens and to the League may have seen an opportunity to detach their island from the Athenian camp, probably in the hope of Spartan assistance. Yet this Spartan naval resurgence proved to be short-lived.[163]

Paros also had strong connections in the Aegean during the 380s, particularly with Khios. Proxeny decrees for Khians on Paros are extant,[164] as well as loans taken out by the *polis* of the Parians from unknown Khian individuals.[165] With these connections in mind, the bilateral defensive alliance of 384 between Athens and Khios takes on a new significance for Paros, and it is not unreasonable to suggest that there may have been a political shift by the Parians into the Athenian camp as the decade progressed.[166] Supporters of Athens were active

[159] Cargill 1981, 35.

[160] Cargill 1981, 38. Lanzilotta 1987, 135 suggests that Paros only joined the League because Khabrias had devastated Histiaia (Diod. 15.30.5).

[161] Baron 2006, 393–4.

[162] Xen. *Hell.* 6.3.4.

[163] Dreher 1995, 125; Gehrke 1985, 126.

[164] *IG* XII.5, 110 and 111.

[165] *IG* XII.5, 112; Migeotte 1984, 213–15.

[166] Rhodes and Osborne 2003, #20. There are other indicators of Athenian-Khian links. A recently-published inscription details the assistance Athens gave to some

on Paros, as we have reference to a certain Phanokrites honoured with *proxenia* and *euergesia* in 387/6 in return for military assistance.[167]

It is thus a speculative, but viable, interpretation of the available evidence that Paros joined the League before the Battle of Naxos in 376, probably at the same time or soon after the other cities that Khabrias enlisted in 379.[168] Khios may in fact be the 'missing link' between Paros and Athens, showing the pathway to a slow forging of political and economic connections that led to 'early adoption' of the new League by the Parians.

Paros, moreover, is close to Naxos. Khabrias' siege of Naxos would have been considerably more difficult if he had not secured at least one of the nearby islands.[169] The Naxians do not appear on the League prospectus, and the question of their membership remains unresolved.[170] It is unclear whether Naxos was hostile towards Athens in 376 because of a long-standing policy, or whether she had previously joined the Second Athenian League (perhaps at the same time as Paros?) and was now in revolt.[171] Naxos may in fact have been seized by a pro-Spartan element on the island that was heartened by Pollis' presence in the area.[172] If Paros had joined the League before the Battle of Naxos, it would not have been impossible for neighbouring Naxos to have done so as well, or at least seen the outbreak of *stasis* between various factions as events unfolded.

There is a fourth-century inscription that describes the restoration of legal arrangements between Naxians and Athenians after a time when they were in abeyance.[173] This inscription is in three fragments, and fragment C (lines 9 and 11) contain references to Thera as being

Khians in making a payment to the temple of Delian Apollo: Chankowski 2008, #8 (= *SEG* XXXIX.170); Lewis 1975, 717–19; Clark 1990, 54–5. Also, a Khian named Antimakhos is named in the naval inventory *IG* II^2 1604 (at line 79) as having returned the trireme *Aphrodisia*, which Clark 1990, 53 has linked to further negotiations with Khios leading up to the formation of the Second Athenian League. Jordan 1975, 90 considers Antimakhos to have been a metic trierarch at Athens.

[167] *IG* II^2 29.

[168] Berranger-Auserve 2000, 104 echoes the standard view that Paros joined with the rest of the Cyclades after the Battle of Naxos.

[169] Accame 1941, 85–6.

[170] Buckler 2003, 247–8 and Cargill 1981, 137 both doubt their membership.

[171] The latter is the position of Accame 1941, 81–2.

[172] Stylianou 1998, 306–7.

[173] *IG* II^2 179.

part of the negotiating process that led to the finalization of the agreement.[174] If other League members were involved, then the decree may not have been unilaterally ordained by Athens.

The dating of this inscription is problematic. One commentator prefers a date around 350 due to letter forms, and proposes that the restoration of normal judicial relations between Athens and Naxos was part of the aftermath of the Social War.[175] Another finds a date in the late 360s the most probable; that Naxos had its judicial autonomy limited after revolting from the League, in conjunction with the Keian cities.[176] Yet another scholar grouped the Naxos decree together with a similar resolution for Siphnos,[177] proposing that all of these inscriptions that refer to *symbolai* between Athens and Cycladic islands (Naxos, Siphnos, and Keos) would therefore be placed in more or less the same period, and all would have been of an oppressive character.

Woodhead argues in the same study, however, that other *symbolai* made by Athens with non-League states (probably in the early 360s): Stymphalos, Troizen, and an unknown Cretan *polis* (possibly Kydonia); are evidence of a supposed commercial policy regarding states that did not join the League, but still wished to create stronger economic links with Athens.[178] It is quite unlikely, however, that League members would not have been eligible for these same benefits. The notion that Athens, at the inauguration of a new League, would have excluded its new allies from commercial privileges that they instead extended to states that did *not* join the new alliance, is difficult to accept.[179]

[174] The grouping of the three fragments together, however, has not seen universal acceptance. See the doubts expressed by Dreher 1995, 138; Ager 2001, 110.

[175] Gauthier 1972, 168, followed by Buckler 2003, 378 n. 24.

[176] Cataldi 1979, 13. The presence of the *thesmothetai* at lines 10 and 17, he claims, show that the tribunal at Naxos had been suppressed. The decree for Keos: Rhodes and Osborne 2003, #39 (= *IG* II^2 111). For further discussion of the Keian revolts in the late 360s, see below.

[177] *SEG* XVII.19 (= Woodhead 1997, #50). See p. 50 above. This Siphnos decree, similar to the Naxian one, also speaks of an earlier *symbolai* with Athens that was now being renewed. A few scholars have dismissed the Siphnos and Naxos decrees as too fragmentary for discussion: Cargill 1981, 137; Buckler 1980, 173 n. 44 (Naxos only).

[178] For Stymphalos: *IG* II^2 144 (= Woodhead 1997, #47); cf. Walbank 1986. For Troizen: *IG* II^2 46 (= *SEG* XVII.17 = Woodhead 1997, #35). For the unknown Cretan city: *SEG* XVII.20 (= Woodhead 1997, #51).

[179] Athens granted even wider privileges to all merchants doing business in Athens sometime after 355 by instituting the *dikai emporikai* courts, which would mainly

Moreover, the idea of grouping the Cycladic examples around the late 360s might be another case of a modern scholarly tendency mentioned in Chapter 4, a tendency to see all relations between Athens and allied states as somehow the result of revolts and subsequent oppression.[180] Though troubles on Keos in the late 360s are well attested, and can account for the need to restore previous judicial conditions after the suppression of revolts, the same cannot be said for certain of Siphnos and Naxos. Moreover, the most telling point against Woodhead's thesis is that the Siphnos judicial decree can no longer be placed during this period. As mentioned above, it has now been redated to the late fifth/early fourth centuries due to the identification of the letter-cutter.[181]

A possible (and better) context for the judicial decree for Naxos could thus be the late 370s to early 360s, as part not only of the entry of the Naxians into the League but also of a wider phenomenon of renewed links between Athens and other states.[182] As such, although it remains an open question, it appears more likely that Naxos was in fact a member of the Second Athenian League, if at first one whose enlistment was more contingent on Athenian naval success.

As a sidenote to the economic implications of the various *symbolai* mentioned above, an interest on the part of the Athenians in promoting trade may also have been one of the motivations behind the law of Nikophon of 374/3. The aforementioned large number of imitations of Athenian coins in circulation during the early fourth century may have been one reason why the *dokimastēs* official would examine 'questionable' coins used in the Agora and the Peiraeus (see below).[183] Scholars have by no means reached a consensus on the exact purpose of the law of Nikophon, and while that topic is beyond the scope of this study, a few remarks may be made here. Several

have benefited those from states that did not yet have *symbolai* agreements with Athens: Moreno 2007, 288.

[180] See Chapter 4, p. 99–100 and n. 117.

[181] Tracy 2003; Papazarkadas 2007, 144 and n. 16.

[182] Perhaps there is some connection between a return of good relations and the crowns voted by the Siphnians in 370/69 (*IG* II^2 1425 line 125; Harris 1995, #454) and the Andrians in 368/7 (*IG* II^2 1425 lines 221–3; Harris 1995, #433) to Athena on the Acropolis. For a recurrence of this practice among other Cycladic states later in the century see Chapter 6, p. 192.

[183] Rhodes and Osborne 2003, #28; Stroud 1974 and 1998. The bibliography on this topic is also massive. See Engen 2005, 24 n. 13 for a comprehensive listing.

scholars have proposed that the main purpose of the law was to facilitate trade in the Peiraeus.[184] The law appears to be mainly concerned with transactions in the private sphere.[185] It is likely, moreover, that the law was directed not just towards commerce carried out in Athens, but also abroad; and was designed to ensure that not only good Athenian coins would be acceptable in commerce, but also the 'imitation' Athenian silver that was in wide circulation throughout the Aegean.[186]

As we did for the Corinthian War above, we must now try to hypothetically reconstruct attitudes of the inhabitants of the Cyclades to this new state of affairs. It had been almost twenty years since the Battle of Knidos, which had most likely brought chaos to the region, at least temporarily. And it had been nearly three decades since the collapse of the Delian League. There must have been some individuals still alive in the islands who remembered these earlier times and would have been wary of placing their *poleis* back into a dependent situation. Nevertheless, some fifty former members of the fifth-century Delian League eventually joined the new organization. The high number of island states in that total would support the idea that they were particularly willing to re-establish links with their old hegemon.[187]

How did membership in the Second Athenian League financially affect the Cyclades, especially compared to the earlier Delian League? One of the conditions of League membership was for the allies to pay 'contributions,' or *syntaxeis*, to provide for defense of League members.[188] The term itself was attributed by the historian Theopompos to the Athenian politician Kallistratos, as a deceptive euphemism to replace the hated fifth-century term *phoros*.[189] Many aspects of these contributions remain controversial. Although some scholars believe

[184] Placido 1980; Alessandri 1984; Engen 2005.

[185] Engen 2005, 16; Stumpf 1986, 30–5 proposes that the *dokimastēs* dates to 378/7 and the creation of the Second Athenian League, in order to make sure that *syntaxeis* and other payments were done in authentic Athenian silver.

[186] Stroud 1974, 179 and 185–6; Engen 2005, 17–18 and 20–1 on Nikophon's motivations. The collection of *syntaxeis* may have intensified the flow of imitations to the Athenian treasury (T.J. Figueira, pers.comm. 8/11).

[187] Cawkwell 1997, 103.

[188] Brun 1983; Cawkwell 1963*b*; Mitchell 1984*a*; Clark 1993.

[189] Theopomp. *FGrH* 115 F98; Harpocrat. *s.v. phoros*; Cargill 1981, 124.

that contributions were collected from the beginning of the League (or from 375),[190] they are not securely attested until 373.[191]

It would appear that early in the history of the League, contributions from each state were assessed by the allied council, or *synedrion*, and often collected by commanders in the field.[192] Exactly how the allies raised the funds to pay their obligations remains just as obscure as for the fifth-century tribute. Perhaps many of them had a system similar to the Athenian *eisphora*, but revenue from trade such as harbour taxes are another possibility.[193] By 346 the *syntaxeis* appears to have been fixed at an annual rate, and may have been brought to Athens rather than collected in the field by *stratēgoi*. Considering that most of the allies still remaining in the League at this point were relatively close to Athens (the Cyclades included), this would not have been particularly difficult from a logistical standpoint.

There is controversy over whether the Athenian *ekklēsia* or the allied *synedrion* determined this annual rate. Two speeches in the Demosthenic corpus imply that the *ekklēsia* did,[194] but there may be epigraphic evidence that the *synedrion* was still performing assessments in 340/39.[195] It is possible that the allies occasionally did levies on their own initiative.[196]

Only a few actual numbers for these contributions survive in the sources, and all are from this later period of standardization.[197] This has not prevented modern scholars from proposing various estimates for *syntaxeis* totals in earlier years of the League.[198] All are not much

[190] Marshall 1905, 38; Accame 1941, 132.

[191] [Dem.] 58.37–38; Cawkwell 1963*b*, 91; Brun 1983, 91–3 and 2004, 74.

[192] Plut. *Vit.Phok.* 11; [Dem.] 49.14; *IG* II^2 213 for the Mytilene garrison in 346; *IG* II^2 123 for the garrison on Andros; *IG* II^2 207 shows money from Lesbos assigned to Khares, Kharidemos, and Phokion.

[193] It appears that an *eisphora* was levied on Siphnos at some point in the 390s, but no details are known: Isok. 19.36 and Brun 1983, 108 and 116; Clark 1993, 365. See Dem. 23.110 for harbour revenues in general.

[194] Dem. 8.21 and [Dem.] 58.37–38.

[195] Rhodes and Osborne 2003, #72 (= *IG* II^2 233); Hornblower 2011, 243; Mitchell 1984*a*, 29 n. 16, Cawkwell 1981, 51 n. 45.

[196] Clark 1993, 366 n. 177. Marshall 1905, 39 proposed the existence of a separate allied chest, originally to hold the proceeds from fines and confiscations in allied territory as laid out in the League prospectus, lines 45–6.

[197] Aiskhin. 2.71 gives 60 talents for 346; Dem. 18.234 says 45 talents in 330; Aiskhin. 3.94, 100 states that Histiaia and Eretria each paid 5 talents annually from 357 to 349.

[198] Brun 1983, 138–42 posits 195 talents in 373–371 and just under 67 talents in 346; Clark 1993, 368–9 has devised a more elaborate scheme, calculating totals of

more than educated guesses, often based upon amounts preserved for these same *poleis* in the fifth-century tribute lists by circular reasoning. What is certain, however, is that Athenian naval operations in the fourth century were usually not able to subsist on the combined cash provided by the *syntaxeis* and the Athenian *eisphorai*. There are many accounts of the financial shortfalls experienced by fourth-century Athenian commanders in the course of conducting expeditions.[199] Demosthenes complains in a speech of 341 (*On the Khersonese*) that Diopeithes had been forced to exact money from other states to pay his fleet.[200] Demosthenes may have been exaggerating the difficulties of funding war at this time, but these problems were nonetheless real. Other references in speeches of Apollodoros also describe ad hoc measures.[201] Allied contributions during wartime in any case were probably not always directed towards the funding of naval operations; payment for garrisons also occurred from time to time.[202] Two sources state that the Peace of 375 was partially concluded because of Athenian financial exhaustion and the Athenian impression that the allies had in fact reaped all the benefits from the League.[203]

DELIAN APOLLO AND THE CYCLADES

There is another aspect of Cycladic finances in the first half of the fourth century that needs to be taken into account: namely, loan records for several of the islands from the accounts of the temple of

800–900 talents from 378 to 374, 700–800 talents from 374 to 370, 300–1020 talents from 370 to 362, 500–900 talents from 362 to 357, 480–1200 talents from 357 to 347, and 450–900 talents from 347 to 338.

199 A comprehensive list is given by Clark 1993, 375 n. 202.

200 Dem. 8.26.

201 [Dem.] 49.49 on Timotheos giving a Boiotian admiral money to pay his crews; [Dem.] 50.53.

202 Burnett and Edmondson 1961 for Syros. The presence of a garrison on Ios at some point in the fourth century is implied by *IG* XII.5, 1000; Cargill 1981, 156. According to Xen. *Hell.* 6.4.1, Athens 'withdrew garrisons from the cities' in 371; cf. Robbins 1918, 361–88. However, garrisons are again attested during the Social War on Andros and Amorgos (see below).

203 Xen. *Hell.* 6.2.1; Philoch. *FGrH* 328 F151. Clark 1993, 376 proposes that the Athenians more or less broke even during the period 378–375.

Table 5.1. Debts to Delian Apollo by Cycladic *poleis*

	Interest paid 393/2–389/8[a]	Interest paid 377/6–374/3[b]	Arrears in 374/3[c]
Andros	—	—	2 T
Ios	—	800 dr.	—
Keos	—	5,472 dr. 4.5 ob.	4,127 dr. 1.5 ob.
Mykonos	1000 dr.	1,260 dr.	420 dr.
Naxos	—	—	1 T 3,600 dr.
Paros	3000 dr.	2,970 dr.	4 T 1,830 dr.
Siphnos	—	—	2,089 dr. 2 ob.
Syros	1 T 103 dr. 1 ob.	2,300 dr.	4,900 dr.
Tenos	—	1 T	2,400 dr.

[a] Chankowski 2008, #11, lines 12–16.
[b]Chankowski 2008, #13A, lines 11–15.
[c]Chankkowski 2008, #13B, lines 3–10.

Delian Apollo (see Table 5.1).[204] Athenian amphiktyons are again attested epigraphically at the temple beginning at roughly the same time as the foundation of the League, in the temple accounts for 378/7–374/3 (also known as the Sandwich Marble).[205] Many cities and individuals from the Cycladic region had interest payments recorded during this cycle. Most of the named individuals are Delians, but from the Cyclades the greatest number of known individual debtors comes from Tenos.[206] Some very fragmentary accounts[207] survive from later in League history which record what appear to be new extensions of credit in 341/0 to Seriphos (4,000 drachmas) and to Paros (5 talents).[208]

Did the Delian loans and interest payments have any effect on League finances? It would seem sensible to modern minds that the Athenians would have made a conscious effort to gain control of the temple in the same year that their new alliance was created, not only to regain prestige, but also to help keep the finances of the allies solvent. Yet, the possibility of a connection between membership in

[204] After Migeotte 1984, 141–7.
[205] Rhodes and Osborne 2003, #28 (= Chankowski 2008, #13*A*).
[206] Chankowski 2008, 351–2 and 358.
[207] Two are from unknown years in the mid-fourth century: Chankowski 2008, #25 (355/4?), which states that the Siphnians paid 1,320 drachmas; and #28 (353/2 or 348/7), gives a total of over 3 talents of interest collected from all the cities, but of the Cyclades only Tenos is preserved on the stone.
[208] Chankowski 2008, #43*bA*, lines 19–21. Interest paid by cities in this same year are given in *aA*, lines 10–14, which preserve Paros, Keos, and Ios, but amounts cannot be matched to cities due to gaps in the text.

the Second Athenian League and the management of debts of states and individuals to Delian Apollo has not seen much favour among modern scholars.[209] There is no evidence, for example, that new credit was extended to allies either in or soon after 378/7, and thus the resources of the temple treasury may not have been utilized as an incentive to join the new League.[210] Moreover, it would seem likely that if temple funds *had* been directly allocated towards the financial well-being of the League, then the allies would have borrowed large sums each year. But the accounts show that the total amount of money invested by the temple in loans to various cities never passed a 'ceiling' of fifty talents, barely enough to cover the *syntaxeis* recorded by several orators for the mid-fourth, much less a year of the older fifth-century *phoros*.[211] As such, it seems clear that the temple treasury of Delian Apollo could never have provided a financial base for Athenian imperialism in either century.[212]

Yet potential connections still cannot be dismissed out of hand. Ptolemy II may have used the funds of Delian Apollo to enable tribute payments by the Cyclades under the aegis of the Ptolemaic Nesiotic League in 288, so it is still possible that the Athenians could have had similar goals in mind.[213] It does seem clear that no *one-to-one* correspondence can be established between *syntaxeis* payments and the Delian loans to Athens' allies. However, judging from the accounts over the next several decades after 378/7, the Athenian amphiktyons obviously did not insist on immediate repayment of debts to the temple. Some debtor communities, such as Naxos and Andros, appear to have never paid any interest on their debt throughout the fourth-century Athenian administration. There is no reason to think that the amphiktyons were suffering from selective blindness here. Part of the reason may have been that the main financial concern of the amphiktyons was to ensure that festivals such as the Delia were

[209] Coupry 1959, 65–6; Migeotte 1984, 142–5; Cargill 1981, 37; Brun 1996, 159; Chankowski 2008, 368–9.

[210] Dreher 1995, 255–9.

[211] Chankowski 2001, 89 and 2008, 368–9.

[212] Chankowski 2001, 91 proposes that the reserve from which the debts were drawn was from the *aparkhē* paid to Delian Apollo from 478/7 to 454/3. Dreher 1995, 244 and n. 251 accepts the idea that the debts may have originated in the fifth century, proposing that Paros was the highest debtor of the Cyclades because she had been assessed the greatest amount of tribute, but at 244 n. 251 he disagrees with Lanzilotta that Paros was impoverished during the League years.

[213] Delamarre 1904; an example is tribute paid by Keos in *IG* XII.5, 533.

able to be celebrated on a certain scale, with other considerations of 'cash flow' being secondary.[214]

It is possible that a few of these sums could have originally been lent to islanders as far back as the fifth century to assist them in paying tribute (or *eikostē*) to Athens, although in general their amounts represent less than one-year's worth of tribute.[215] One cannot assume, moreover, that the taking out of loans by a *polis* would necessarily indicate that it was in financial straits. The loans from Delian Apollo in the earlier part of the century may show not a lack of prosperity, but rather a need for liquid assets that the temple was willing to provide for those whose credit was good.[216] Many Cycladic communities may have been in need of liquid capital for various purposes. These could have included the payment of *syntaxeis* and other military expenses, but also for the support of civic festivals or the construction of fortifications. Many other possibilities exist, and it is currently impossible to know for certain what the precise needs of these cities were at all times.[217]

From 375/4–371/0, the Athenians appear to have allowed Andrians a share in the temple administration on Delos as well. The Andrian amphiktyons were equal in number to the Athenians (five), and are listed under the same rubric as the Athenian officials.[218] The account for 364/3 does not mention Andrians, yet the amphiktyons are specified as 'Athenians' in the inscription, which could indicate that non-Athenians were still involved in temple administration.[219] Non-Athenians are, however, definitely absent in 341/40, for the accounts of that year mention only five Athenians and a secretary.[220]

[214] Chankowski 2008, 365. [215] Coupry 1959, 65–6; Chankowski 2008, 369.
[216] Brun 1996, 158. [217] Brun 1996, 159; Chankowski 2008, 368–9.
[218] Chankowski 2008, #13 *Ab*, lines 63–4 and #15, lines 7–9 for the names of the Andrians, and Chankowski 2008, 241–5 for discussion. The Andrians appear to have been primarily responsible for musical and gymnastic contests, and received the same daily wage of a drachma a day as their Athenian colleagues (lines 74–6). There appear to have been other non-Athenian amphiktyons present in 393 (Chankowski 2008, #11, lines 1–5), but their place of origin is not preserved. Coupry 1972, #97 tentatively proposes that they were also Andrian, followed by Funke 1980, 132, who surmises that they may have been brought in to help conciliate the region because of the activities of Konon and Pharnabazos. However, this is doubted by Chankowski 2008, 192 and 241 (who proposes that they were actually Delians) and Dreher 1995, 217–18.
[219] Chankowski 2008, #19; Laidlaw 1939, 81.
[220] Chankowski 2008, #43.

It is unclear why the Andrians were chosen to share these duties. The loan accounts for the temple from these years do not give much indication of the status of Andros as compared to other islands. They list one Andrian individual as a debtor, and the *polis* of Andros did not pay any interest on its 2-talent debt during the period 377/6–374/3, but none of this is exceptional.[221] One of the earliest commentators on the Delian accounts theorizes that they were brought in by the Athenians as 'favoured helpers', and notes that the Andrians are listed before other Cycladic islands on the left face of the League prospectus.[222] The incorporation of the Andrian officials may have been an attempt by Athens to appease the allies, and promote the spirit of the King's Peace.[223]

If, as proposed above, the Parians had joined the Second Athenian League earlier than the other Cyclades, one might question why they were not chosen. However, they had no *oikos* on Delos. Moreover, if turmoil and contention had surrounded the enrolment of the Andrians in the League, then it may have been important to grant more concessions to them instead. The Andrians may in fact have become model allies after being given this privilege, as they bestowed a crown to the Athenian Boule in 368/7.[224]

It has also been proposed, however, that the office was an 'odium' shared between the Athenians and Andrians during these years.[225] The Andrians may have been brought in after the violence perpetrated against the Athenian amphiktyons in 376/5, perhaps even to mollify the Delians by demonstrating to them that the Athenians would not claim exclusive authority over the temple.[226] Their later departure may have allowed the inhabitants of Delos an opportunity to return to some position of authority in the temple after tensions had relaxed.[227] It is unclear, however, as to what duties the Andrians actually fulfilled. They may have been closely integrated into the operations of the temple and truly represented the other members of the League.[228] Conversely, they may have had minimal responsibilities, since they had no secretary or under-secretary as the Athenians did, and most aspects of the administration appear to have

[221] Chankowski 2008, #13.
[222] Homolle 1884, 290.
[223] Funke 1980, 132.
[224] See n. 182 above.
[225] Laidlaw 1939, 80.
[226] Chankowski 2008, #13*B* lines 24–30 and discussion on 249–53; Dreher 1995, 221–2; Osborne 1974.
[227] Dreher 1995, 226–7.
[228] Dreher 1995, 219–22.

remained in Athenian hands.[229] Given the state of our evidence, we are reduced to hypotheses, as Chankowski asserts.[230]

After the massive defeat of Sparta at Leuktra in 371, the original *raison d'être* of the Second Athenian League was gone. Through the first half of the 360s, Athens engaged in expansionistic policies vis-à-vis Samos, Amphipolis, and the Khersonese, culminating in the establishment of a klerouchy on Samos in 366.[231] It has been suggested that the Persian garrison removed from Samos because of this action had been a threat to Athenian trade routes, and to Athens' ability to protect the Aegean islands in general.[232]

Athens and Thebes also became increasingly hostile at this time. At the instigation of their leading general Epaminondas, and probably with the help of Persian funds, the Thebans began constructing a fleet of one hundred triremes in 366.[233] That this figure was reached is not accepted by all scholars, but no one doubts that a Theban fleet of some size did eventually sail.[234] The bases used by the fleet are unknown, although Aulis has been proposed.[235] In 364 this force made a cruise through the Aegean, attempting to lure states like Byzantion, Khios, and Rhodes into a new alliance.[236] An Athenian squadron under Laches sailed out to intercept, but withdrew without engaging Epaminondas' vessels, further support for the idea that the Theban ships were numerous.[237] It is possible that the expedition included a stop at Crete, and may even have temporarily brought Kyrene over to the Theban side.[238] Epaminondas also courted the

[229] Chankowski 2008, 243–5, who calls their tenure 'une amphictionie imaginaire'.

[230] Chankowski 2008, 245.

[231] Sources for the klerouchy: Diod. 18.18.9; Strabo 14.1.18 C638; Herakl. Pont. *FGrH* 2 F216. On allied suspicions and fears: Isok. 15.111; Din. 1.14. Modern discussion: Habicht 1957; Cargill 1983.

[232] Hornblower 2011, 261, who nevertheless criticizes the Athenian action. For the strategic positioning of Samos for control of the Ionian coast, see Isok. 15.108.

[233] Diod. 15.79.1.

[234] Stylianou 1998, 494 scoffs at the idea of Persian subsidies and also Diodorus' number, stating that it was beyond the resources not only of Thebes, but also 'those of Athens at the time, and no better argument can be advanced than that'. Buckler 2008*a*, 181 defends the figure and asserts that the fleet was not mentioned further because supplies of Persian money were no longer available. Cawkwell 1972, 271 proposes that it may have been closer to forty triremes. The true number is probably somewhere in between, but closer to that of Diodorus.

[235] Buckler 2008*a*, summarizing previous opinions on the matter.

[236] Buckler 1980, 172–3; Hornblower 2011, 262–3.

[237] Diod. 15.78.4–79.1; Justin 16.4.3–4; Buckler 2008*a*, 182–3.

[238] Dušanic 1980, 25 n. 119 and 27 n. 134 (on Crete) and 19 n. 81 (on Kyrene).

major island states off the coast of Asia Minor such as Rhodes and Khios. If all of these overtures had been successful, Thebes could have controlled the termini of major trade routes that traversed the Cyclades.

However, nothing more is known of Epaminondas' possible naval accomplishments, although a recently published inscription indicates that Epaminondas received *proxenia* at Knidos, including the right to sail in and out of the harbour.[239] If he had been able to bring states that he visited such as Khios and Rhodes into a true *symmakhia*, then their triremes could have created a serious challenge to Athenian hegemony.[240] But did Epaminondas really gain much traction with these Aegean states? Diodorus reports that 'he made the cities Thebes' own,' and this has been taken to refer to a true *symmakhia* or military alliance.[241] A recent study claims, however, that this sentence is too vague and cannot be used as strong evidence that any real alliance was created.[242] No matter what the meaning of Diodorus' words, whatever was accomplished by Epaminondas' cruise appears to have been temporary, with the exception of the secession of Byzantion.[243] Nevertheless, the revolt of the Keian cities, followed by a second revolt of the *polis* of Ioulis, may have been triggered or at least inspired by the brief naval ascendancy of Thebes. We are fortunate to have several inscriptions relating to the revolts and how Athens arranged affairs on the island afterward.

Although there is still some controversy, it is generally agreed that Koressos, Karthaia, and Ioulis were federated at the time that Keos became a member of the Second Athenian League. The roots of the

[239] First published in Blümel 1994, 157–8; *SEG* XLIV.901; Buckler 2008*b*, 202–4.

[240] During the Social War of 357–355, Khios, Rhodes, and Byzantion were able to launch a total of 100 triremes against Athens (Diod. 16.21.2). Stylianou 1998, 495 proposes however that Diodorus may have garbled his information and that Epaminondas' 100 triremes were simply his goal for an allied fleet.

[241] Diod. 15.79.1: ἰδίας τὰς πόλεις τοῖς Θηβαίοις ἐποίησεν; Ruzicka 1998, 60; Hornblower 1982, 200 n. 37. Ruzicka goes so far as to posit the defection of not only Byzantion (accepted by most) but also Khios and Rhodes, and that they all briefly rejoined the League right before the outbreak of the Social War. Yet, at the same time he states at 62–4 that Epaminondas' objective was 'not naval hegemony itself but rather the demonstration that Athens held no such hegemony.'

[242] Buckler 2008*b*, 174–5.

[243] Hornblower 2011, 262; Isok. 5.53 states that the Thebans sent triremes to Byzantion to 'attempt' to dominate the Aegean.

federation may date back to some point in the fifth century.[244] In 450/49, the first appearance of any Keians on an Athenian tribute list, Koressos was inscribed separately from the rubric of *Κειοι*, although the reasons for this distinction are obscure.[245] All subsequent tribute lists simply contain 'Keians.' When the Keian cities were inscribed on the League prospectus, they were listed separately instead of as 'Keians', probably in (at least symbolic) observance of the prohibition in the King's Peace against federations.[246] The fourth city, Poiessa, joined the League separately and is conspicuously absent from most of the evidence linking Keos to Athens during the Classical period.[247]

An inscription securely dated to the archonship of Khariklides in 363/2, and proposed on the motion of Aristophon, refers to the re-integration of Keos into the League. The first revolt (which may have broken out in 364 and was perhaps related to the growth of Theban sea power)[248] included all three cities of the federation, while the second was an uprising apparently limited to Ioulis, the federation's capital.[249] According to this decree, the first revolt had included the murder of the Athenian *proxenos* on the island by a certain Antipatros, as well as the deaths of other supporters of the Athenians.[250] Two treaties of *isopoliteia* with the Euboian cities Histiaia and Eretria are extant,[251] concluded at some point after Euboia fell away from the

[244] Lewis 1962, 2 considers this to have been a *synteleia* designed only to facilitate the payment of tribute, with no political ramifications.

[245] *IG* I^3 263 col.2, line 21.

[246] Lewis 1962; Moggi 1976, 334–9; Cargill 1981, 134–5; Brun 2004, 74; Constantakopoulou 2005, 14.

[247] Poiessa is listed on the front face of the League prospectus, in the middle column between the Rhodians and Arethousians. The other three are on the left side of the stone (Cargill 1981, 34). There is also a reference to 'Keians' on the Sandwich Marble (Chankowski 2008, #13*A*, line 113). Other clues as to the existence of a federation of the Koressians, Karthaians, and Ioulietans may be an inscription listing Keian athletic victors at the Isthmian and Nemean Games (*IG* XII.5, 608; Brun 1989, 135) and some bronze coins known as Koinon Series I (Sheedy 1998).

[248] Dreher 1989, 267 and n. 21 suggests 363 for the first revolt.

[249] Rhodes and Osborne 2003 #39 (= *IG* II^2 111). Buckler 1980, 169 has proposed that the establishment of the Samian klerouchy may also have influenced these revolts.

[250] Rhodes and Osborne 2003 #39, lines 38–9.

[251] Treaty with Histiaia: *IG* XII.5, 594 (= Tod 1962 #141); treaty with Eretria: Bengtson 1975, #232; Dunant and Thomopoulos 1954, who place it earlier than the revolt; *SEG* XIV.530–1. Both decrees were discovered at Ioulis. Lewis 1962 alone would date the isopolity with Eretria and the formation of the federation itself after the revolt of Eretria from the Delian League in 411. However, the 360s have been favored by most commentators and seems more likely: Brun 1989, 134; Reger 1998, 637 n. 19; Cooper 2008*a*, 33.

Second Athenian League and sided with Thebes in 370.[252] The isopolity agreement with Histiaia, moreover, specifically mentions the rights of citizens to import and export in all the involved *poleis*.[253] This may have been an attempt by the Keian federation to strengthen economic as well as political contacts, which could also have been part of the underlying motivation behind the formation of such a federation in the first place.[254] It may also indicate support for the pro-Theban stance of the two Euboian cities.[255]

The leading modern study of *isopoliteia* states that economic considerations were not predominant in such treaties. The rights of import and export were meant for the private needs of those who decided to activate their citizenship in both *poleis*.[256] Yet this does not preclude the possibility of economic benefits, whether or not such concerns were the *primary* ones when negotiating such agreements. In their gravitation towards Euboia and the Theban sphere, many Keians may have seen Epaminondas' naval activity as paving the way towards the replacement of Athens by Thebes as the main Aegean hegemon. The subsequent raids in the Cyclades by Alexander of Pherai might have hardened such attitudes.[257] Though evidence is lacking for decisive political realignments among Aegean states due to Epaminondas' naval expedition, one must not use too much hindsight in evaluating how it may have been perceived at the time on Keos and elsewhere in the region.

The Athenian general Khabrias put down this first insurrection, executed Antipatros, and made a new treaty with the Keians.[258] The anti-Athenian faction, however, took power again in Ioulis soon afterward and killed some Athenian sympathizers and confiscated

[252] Xen. *Hell.* 6.5.23 and 7.5.4; Guagliumi 2005.

[253] *IG* XII.5, 594, lines 11–14.

[254] Lätsch 2005, 174–6; for a discussion of possible economic motives behind the synoikism on Kos in 366/5, see Sherwin-White 1978, 65–8; for a dissenting view that emphasizes external threats more than economic concerns, with particular concern paid to the Rhodian synoikism of 408/7, see Demand 1990, 91 and 167–9.

[255] Guagliumi 2005.

[256] Gawantka 1975, 46–91.

[257] Buckler 2003, 371 links the Keian revolts more to the activities of Alexander of Pherai. It is true that this tyrant had become an (inferior) ally of the Thebans in 364 after a defeat: Diod. 15.80.6 and Plut. *Vit.Pelop.* 35.2; Cargill 1981, 170. As Alexander focused more on the Cyclades than Epaminondas appears to have done, this possibility must be considered.

[258] Rhodes and Osborne 2003 #39, line 8.

their property, and cast down the stele on which Khabrias' settlement had been inscribed.[259] Subsequently, the *stratēgos* Aristophon led another Athenian force to the island and banished the perpetrators from Athenian and Keian territory, confiscating their property on behalf of the *dēmos* of Ioulis. The Ioulietan *stratēgoi* were also ordered to help recover other property confiscated by the anti-Athenian faction during the first revolt.[260] The *polis* of Karthaia is expressly thanked for having remained loyal, while Koressos is unmentioned. It may be that the Koressians stayed inactive or neutral while the Karthaians assisted the Athenians in the suppression of Ioulis.

The regulations end with oaths to protect the Keians (rebels or non-rebels, or both?) from unjust retribution by Athens or any of her allies, and that those Keians who wished to emigrate to allied states could do so.[261] Apparently this second revolt was instigated by a single faction, if a fairly numerous and powerful one. This faction may have counted on Theban intervention and/or protection that never materialized.[262]

A second inscription, of uncertain date, appears to reaffirm the breakup of the Keian federation by stating that the Keians were now to govern themselves 'city by city', but it also allows for the repair of the fortifications of the 'coastal' Keian cities.[263] The decree mentions the requests of prominent Keian citizens for assistance, the nature of which is unclear. One reconstruction dates the decree to 363, after the first revolt but *before* the second revolt of Ioulis, and assumes that Khabrias had destroyed the original fortifications. According to this argument, Ioulis and the other cities could only have been referred to singly in *IG* II^2 111 if the federation had already been dissolved; thus,

[259] Ibid., lines 27–41. [260] Ibid., lines 11–17.

[261] Ibid., lines 57–69.

[262] Buckler 1980, 173 speculates that Epaminondas would have seen no advantage in helping out the Keians: 'isolated and scattered uprisings, especially by small and helpless islands, would only have led to the dissipation of his strength.'

[263] *IG* II^2 404 (= SEG XIX. 50); Schweigert 1939; Maier 1959–61, 157–9; Lewis 1962, 4; Brun 2004. The beginning of the inscription is badly damaged, and neither the archon date nor the tribe in prytany have been preserved. For the walls, portions of which are still visible at Koressos, see general discussion in Reger 2004, 749–51; for Koressos see also Maier 1959–61, #37 and Cherry, Davis and Mantzourani 1991*b*, 236; for Ioulis see also *SEG* XIV.532 and Migeotte 1992, #56. It is unclear whether the coastal fortifications mentioned in the document would have included the *harbour* of Ioulis, the location of which is disputed: Merker 1968; Whitelaw 1998, 233.

IG II^2 404 predates *IG* II^2 111.[264] Repairs for fortifications could then have been designed to ward off Theban intervention on the island. Another possibility is that the Athenians allowed them to be rebuilt later in 362, perhaps due to the new threat posed by Alexander of Pherai (see below).[265]

Other scholars, however, have compared this decree to the Andros decree from the time of the Social War (*IG* II^2 123), with which it shares some epigraphic similarities. A date during the Social War, when general requests for assistance from Athens to rebuild coastal fortifications would be more likely, can thus be proposed instead.[266] This view raises a strong objection to dating the decree to the period right after the Keian revolts. Would the coastal Keian cities have been allowed the right to perform fortification repairs so soon after instigating a revolt?

But there is still another factor that would support a date in the late 360s for *IG* II^2 404, and this was the continued hostility of Eretria and Histiaia, both gone from the Second Athenian League in 370 and neither of which rejoined until 357.[267] If the Keian federation was allowed to stand until that year, then the Keian cities could have been allowed to maintain *isopoliteia* with enemies of Athens for some five more years after the suppression of *two* revolts on their island, an unlikely scenario.[268] While isopolity agreements did not always affect foreign policy and alliances,[269] the proximity of Keos to Athens and the role of the previous revolts could have made them more dangerous from an Athenian perspective. A third possibility is that the federation was indeed broken up at some point during the rebellions of 362, and that *IG* II^2 404 simply reaffirms the breakup of the Keian federation after the outbreak of the Social War.[270]

[264] Dreher 1989, who also argues that an Athenian *stratēgos* would not have had the authority to negotiate such a settlement with Ioulis unless ambassadors had already been sent from Keos to Athens. Such ambassadors *are* mentioned in *IG* II^2 404.

[265] Maier 1959, followed now by Cooper 2008*a*, 39–40, who feels that the inscription preserves at least some of the provisions of Khabrias' original settlement with the Keians after the first revolt.

[266] Brun 2004; Buckler 2003, 377 n. 24; Schweigert 1939; Lewis 1962.

[267] *IG* II^2 124, line 16 on their readmittance.

[268] Cargill 1981, 136 feels that there is no reason to assume that Athens did not allow isopolities between League members. However, isopolities between League members and enemies of Athens are more difficult to accept.

[269] Gawantka 1975, 87–91.

[270] Reger 1998, 637 n. 19.

Although a date in the late 360s seems most likely, there is simply not enough evidence to be certain. However, the general significance of the situation still prevails whichever date is correct. Despite one general island-wide uprising, followed by a second from Ioulis, the Athenians trusted the Keian *poleis* with new fortification walls. Obviously the Athenians felt that they could count on the loyalty of the factions that were now in control of these cities, and shared their concerns about protecting the cities from attack by sea. Despite the second revolt, there was still a somewhat conciliatory tone for the regulations for Ioulis, with punishment only being directed towards the guilty parties. It does seem clear, however, that the Athenians were uncomfortable with the concept of the Keian federation. Nevertheless, it would be hasty to consider that the Athenians were actually seeking to create disunity among their own allies, as has been proposed for *IG* II^2 111.[271]

The Keian revolts must also be understood in light of evidence that general maritime safety in the Aegean began to be seriously compromised in the late 360s. Although there are several references to piracy from 378 onward,[272] there is also evidence that Athens had made at least some attempt to keep the sea lanes secure.[273] By the late 360s, however, Athenian resources were becoming increasingly strained and the city experienced a serious naval crisis in the year 362.[274] Warships from Byzantion, Kyzikos, and Khalkedon commandeered grain ships heading for Athens because of shortages in their own cities.[275] In addition, the allied island of Prokonnesos was attacked by the Kyzikenes. Worst of all from the standpoint of those who lived in the Cyclades was the piratical expedition of Alexander of Pherai in

[271] Claire Taylor's review of Cooper 2008*b* in *BMCR* 2009.05.23.

[272] Dem. 52.5, where pirate vessels captured Lykon of Herakleia *c.*369 in the Argolic Gulf while he was enroute from Athens to Libya; Dem. 53.6, where Nikostratos was captured and sold on Aigina while in pursuit of escaped slaves; Hornblower 1982, 204.

[273] Xenophon records eight warships cruising in the neighbourhood of Attika in 372 (Xen. *Hell.* 6.2.14), as well as a squadron that had taken 'guard stations' near Corinth in 366 (ibid. 7.4.4). This practice was eventually regularized, since a late fourth-century source mentions 20 ships in the fleet as being earmarked for coast guard duty ([Arist.] *Ath.Pol.* 24.3).

[274] Cawkwell 1984, 10.

[275] [Dem.] 50.4–9, 17–20. The *sitopompia* or escorting of grain ships by triremes during the autumn sailing season apparently became necessary throughout the second half of the 360s: Hornblower 1982, 203.

that same year.[276] He attacked several of the Cyclades and seized Tenos, reducing its inhabitants to slavery, as well as making a raid on the Peiraeus in which money was taken from the merchants' tables in the *Deigma*.[277] Soon afterward (possibly in 361/60) Alexander besieged Peparethos and defeated an Athenian naval contingent under Leosthenes near that island, capturing one Peparethian trireme and five Athenian triremes.[278] The question was raised above whether any Cycladic triremes were operating during the fourth century, and this statement of Diodorus could perhaps indicate that such a situation was possible. However, if Polyainos is correct in saying that Leosthenes summoned warships from Samos for assistance, this implies that no other ready reinforcements were close at hand.[279]

These naval activities came near the end of Alexander's power, after he had lost the title of *tagos* of Thessaly, and were directed against his former allies the Athenians.[280] Some have even tried to link Alexander's activities with those of the Thebans, and that Alexander's fleet may have used the same ports as their ships.[281] Trade from Pherai's port of Pagasai, which may have included grain from Larissa in Thessaly and other commodities,[282] probably provided Alexander with much of his income. But what kinds of trade ties might Pagasai have already had with Cycladic islands? Alexander's predecessor Jason had built triremes, but beyond that fact we do not hear more about he may have used them.[283]

It is intriguing that most discussions of this expedition do not try to delve more into his possible motivation. Was it purely meant to

[276] Xen. *Hell.* 6.4.35 calls him an 'unjust robber by land and sea' and Diod. 15.95.1 refers to his 'pirate ships' (ληστρίδας ναῦς).

[277] [Dem.] 50.4–6, generally attributed to Apollodoros, states that the Athenian assembly discussed the attack on Tenos on 23–4 Metageitnion in the archon year of Molon: Ballin 1978; Bers 2003. Diod. 15.95 places the event during the archonship of Nikophemos in 361/0, but states only that Alexander 'sent pirate ships to the Cyclades' without specifying any islands. For the Peiraeus raid see Dem. 51.8, in which Aristophon prosecuted the subcontractors of the triremes after the event.

[278] Diod. 15.95.3 states that Leosthenes was condemned to death for treason; Aiskhin. 2.71 states that he fled to Macedonia; Polyain. *Strat.* 6.2.1–2 for the Peiraeus.

[279] Polyain. *Strat.* 6.2.1. Brun 1983, 113 proposes that smaller Aegean islands could still have maintained a few warships each during the fourth century.

[280] Sprawski 2006, 145.

[281] Sordi 1958, 223–4; Stylianou 1998, 549.

[282] Xen. *Hell.* 5.4.56; Sprawski 2006, 140 and 144.

[283] Xen. *Hell.* 6.4.21.

plunder,[284] or did Alexander aim at conquests within the Cycladic region? The Tenian captives taken by Alexander's forces may have found a ready market in Pagasai. Tenos was no doubt the most hard-hit of all the Cyclades and thus received special mention in the Demosthenic corpus. Was Tenos wealthier than the other islands, or perhaps less well fortified or defended? Or were the Pheraians well known to the Tenians and thus able to ravage their *polis* after some sort of subterfuge? What is most intriguing about this sad event for the Tenians was that it appears to have been the catalyst for a relocation of their community, as we will see in Chapter 6.[285]

In 357, Khios, Rhodes, and Kos, with the assistance of Byzantion and the Karian satrap Mausolos, seceded from the League and inaugurated the Social War.[286] Whether or not the Athenians had been truly attempting to rebuild their fifth-century empire, it is generally agreed that widespread allied disaffection with Athenian military ambitions in the north Aegean and on Samos had caused this conflict.[287] The war did not go well for Athens. Khabrias was killed in an attack on the harbour of Khios,[288] and in 356 the rebels, with a fleet of a hundred ships, attacked the Athenian possessions of Lemnos, Imbros, and Samos, as well as several (unnamed) islands of the Cyclades.[289] The implication is that the rebels did not expect any of these islands to join their cause.

The rebel fleet defeated the Athenian general Khares at Embata in that same year, and because of lack of funds for the campaign he decided to hire out his forces to the rebellious satrap of Phrygia, Artabazos. This led King Artaxerxes Ochos of Persia to threaten intervention on the side of Athens' former allies unless Khares broke off his support for Artabazos. Faced with such a prospect, the Athenians had no choice but to agree to peace terms by 355.[290] In addition to the aforementioned states of Khios, Rhodes, and Kos,

[284] Stylianou 1998, 549 thinks that it was mainly done to raise money.

[285] See Chapter 6, pp. 218–24.

[286] Hornblower 2011, 271–4; Buckler 2003, 377–84 challenges the notion that the main Athenian objective during the Social War was the retention of Rhodes; Hornblower 1982, 212; Sherwin-White 1978, 73 n. 224.

[287] Diod. 16.7.3 on the naval help given to them by the satrap Mausolos. Athenian ships were known to attack merchant shipping during this period; Dem. 24.11–12 on property held by two Athenian officials from a ship from Naukratis.

[288] Diod. 16.7.

[289] Diod. 16.21.

[290] Diod. 16.21–2; Dem. 4.23–4; Isok. 7.8, 10, 81; Polyain. *Strat.* 3.9.29.

the League also lost the membership of smaller states such as Selymbria and Perinthos.[291]

Significantly, all evidence indicates that the Cycladic states remained loyal both during and after the war.[292] As we have seen for the late fifth century, anti-Athenian activity on Euboia, particularly involving Eretria, could spread quickly to the Cyclades, and a general Euboian revolt did take place in 357.[293] But those in the Cyclades who wished to shake off the Athenian yoke and who might have expected help from that quarter were soon to be disappointed, as Theban forces withdrew and the cities of Karystos, Eretria, Khalkis, and Histiaia realigned with Athens, although they apparently were not formally readmitted into the Second Athenian League.[294] To be fair, there are records of garrisons and governors on some islands that probably date to this time, at Andros and at Arkesine on Amorgos.[295] But the inscription concerning the garrison on Andros, securely dated to the archonship of Agathokles in 356,[296] contains a *dogma* of the allied *synedrion*, which states that the cost of the garrison is to be paid for by *syntaxeis* contributions from all the allies.[297] Such circumstances do not support the idea that the installation of a garrison on Andros was a repressive act per se on the part of Athens, although this is not to say that Athenians could not have taken advantage of the situation. Aiskhines implicated the Athenian politician Timarkhos in

[291] Dem. 18.234; 15.26; Plut. *Vit.Dem.* 17; Brun 1983, 134.

[292] The one possible exception is Thera, suggested by Ager 2001, but the civil strife on the island hinted at in several fourth century inscriptions remains difficult to date, and could just as easily have occurred in the 370s.

[293] Dem. 8.74 and 21.174; Aiskhin. 3.85; Diod. 16.7.2; Polyain. *Strat.* 5.29.

[294] *IG* II^2 124 for all four cities, 125 for Athenian/Eretrian relations; *Syll.*^{3} 172; Buckler 2003, 379–80.

[295] Andros: *IG* II^2 123 (= Tod 1962, #156); Arkesine on Amorgos: Rhodes and Osborne 2003, #51 (= *IG* XII.7,5). Buckler 2003, 381 would place both the Andrian and Arkesinian garrisons in 356, as part of an Athenian reaction to losses in Ionia. Hornblower 2011, 248 (following Cawkwell 1981, 51) prefers the 360s for the garrison on Amorgos, citing a brief installation of a garrison at Kephallenia in 372 (Bengtson 1975, #267 lines 16–18) as evidence of earlier Athenian breaches of the League agreement.

[296] It is possible that an Athenian garrison had also been present on Andros at some time in the 360s. Aiskhin. 1.107 accuses Timarchos of paying thirty *minai* to become governor on Andros, and this reference could be placed around 363/2, perhaps linking it to troubles on Keos at that time (Reger 1994*b*). Reger's article also shows convincingly that *IG* XII.5, 714, formerly thought to refer to this garrison of the 350s, should instead be placed in the third quarter of the third century.

[297] *IG* II^2 123, lines 11, 16–21.

corrupt practices while the latter held an (unspecified) magistracy on Andros.[298] We do not know if the notice in Aristotle's *Politics* (*c*.350) that refers to officials on Andros being bribed and bringing 'the whole state to ruin' is any way related to this affair.[299] For the Athenians to have taken steps to secure an island in close proximity to the Bosporan grain route is not surprising.[300]

The cost of the Arkesine garrison (usually dated no later than 357/6) was paid for by the Athenian general Androtion, who also gave the city an interest-free loan and ransomed Arkesinian captives.[301] The last few lines of the inscription are damaged, but appear to refer to yet another decree of the allied *synedrion*.[302] This would seem to show that the allies approved of this garrison also, even if they did not provide funds for it. The garrison may have even been requested by the inhabitants of Arkesine.[303] While it has been proposed that the fate of Arkesine was not as important to the allies,[304] it should be pointed out that the island of Amorgos was located on the eastern/southern grain route. We do not know how long the garrisons at Andros and Amorgos put in place during the Social War lasted.[305] To be sure, the potential was there to forfeit the loyalty of some of the Cyclades as had occurred after the raid of Alexander of Pherai in 362.[306] This may have given the Athenians additional reason to take steps to safeguard the islands during this conflict. The lesson of Keos must have been foremost in their minds.

[298] Aiskhin. 1.107.

[299] Arist. *Pol.* 1270b.

[300] Cargill 1981, 155–6; Dreher 1995, 43 speculates that the safety of Andros may have concerned all of the allies.

[301] Rhodes and Osborne 2003 #51, lines 10–15; Accame 1941, 185–7; Cargill 1981, 158–9. The captives were presumably victims of the Social War, although Rhodes and Osborne theorize that the garrison was in place before the Social War broke out, and thus may have been of a more coercive nature. It is intriguing that Androtion *may* have been involved in a land lease from Amorgos around this time as well (Jameson 1987).

[302] Rhodes and Osborne 2003 #51, line 25: συμμάχοις ἔδοξε.

[303] Cargill 1981, 158 n. 29; Brun 1983, 125.

[304] Cargill 1981, 155.

[305] Zelnick-Abramovitz 2004, 343 n. 50 proposes that the Athenians pulled the Arkesine garrison after Androtion's return, since he had paid for its support and received unusual honors at Arkesine.

[306] Hornblower 1982, 204 and n. 175 for instances of piracy in the 370s and 360s, where he notes 'it was still not possible to sail . . . without risk to personal liberty . . . it is arguable that Athens was not doing quite all she could.'

It may be instructive here to contrast the situation of the cities of Keos in the 360s with the cities of Amorgos in this following decade. In many respects, the three *poleis* of Amorgos, Arkesine, Minoa, and Aigiale, took on many aspects of a federation during the Classical period. They had appeared as a syntely of 'Amorgians' in the fifth-century tribute lists,[307] and were similarly designated in the prospectus of the Second Athenian League.[308] Moreover, they issued a common bronze coinage with the legend 'AMO' during the fourth century.[309] But they do not appear to have actually been federated, at least during the periods of Athenian ascendancy.[310] It may be that attempts at forming a federation at this time would have been opposed by the Athenians as they were on Keos. The need of smaller states for Athenian protection, however haphazard such protection may have been, probably tipped the balance in favor of remaining in the Athenian sphere. As one scholar has put it: 'there was a real advantage for a Tenos, a Prokonnesos, or a Maroneia in being able to seek the aid of the Athenian navy.'[311]

CONCLUSIONS

In contrast to the fifth-century Athenian *arkhē*, the first half of the fourth century saw a certain 'fluidity' of hegemony in the Aegean. The Spartans, the Thebans, and the Athenians all made their presence known in the Cycladic region at various moments during this period. The first two decades of the century, in particular, seem to have been times of turmoil in the area. However, we have some indication that the inhabitants of the Cyclades took steps to adapt to the new conditions and to gain economic benefits. While the new issues of coinage on Siphnos and Naxos may be interpreted as expressions of political independence, they may also have promoted trade with the

[307] See Table 4.1.

[308] Rhodes and Osborne 2003, #22, line 124; Constantakopoulou 2005, 6 for more epigraphic references to 'Amorgians.'

[309] Head 1991, 481; Liampi 1998, 215–16; Constantakopoulou 2005, 11 and n. 61.

[310] Migeotte 1984, 191 thinks that *IG* XII.7, 68 may indicate some sort of federation on the island in the late fourth/early third centuries, disputed by Constantakopoulou 2005, 19.

[311] Cawkwell 1981, 48.

east. In the next chapter, we will see other Cycladic coinages begin from the mid-fourth century. The membership of most of the Cycladic communities in the Second Athenian League could have also had economic ramifications. This can be seen in the regulation of interest payments by the Athenian administrators of the temple of Delian Apollo (with apparently lax enforcement and even occasional grants of new credit), the payment of *syntaxeis* for League military operations, and the establishment (or re-establishment) of treaties of *symbolai* between Athens and several Cycladic states. The continued loyalty of most of the islands in the Cyclades, even during the chaotic period of the late 360s and the Social War, may have been due as much to perceptions of economic benefit as to compulsion on the part of the Athenians. It is to the period after the Social War that we must now turn, a period that in many ways is one of the most intriguing from an economic standpoint.

6

A (Nearly) Perfect Symbiosis?

The Cyclades in the Later Fourth Century (355–314)

The period after the Social War up through the final loss of Athenian control of Delos is the most intriguing, yet in many ways ignored, period of Classical Cycladic history. Until 338 the islands remained members of the (now attenuated) Second Athenian League, but received scant mention in Athenian sources, other than some passing (and sometimes scornful) mention in a few contemporary speeches by the Attic orators. Yet, there are several indicators of increased connectivity and economic activity in the Cyclades during this period. A number of inscriptions show good relations between several of the islands and Athens. The inhabitants of Tenos rebuilt their *polis* at a new coastal location and appear to have prospered. Parian marble is once again attested in sculpture and architecture in Sicily and Italy. Survey evidence gives a broad picture of high population and exploitation of the countryside on several Cycladic islands. And two phenomena of the late sixth century—local coinage and monumental temple construction—reappear in the region and continue to the end of the century and into the early third.

From the Athenian standpoint, during the ascendancies of Euboulos and Lykourgos there appears to have been an increasing interest in the grain trade, control of piracy, and the promotion of commerce. Moreover, the Athenian preoccupation with the grain trade not only affected islands and states along the northern route to the Bosporos, but also along the 'southern' route to Egypt and the Levant, which included routes that returned through the Cyclades from eastern states such as Samos and Rhodes. Although not involved in major overseas adventures in the Aegean, the Athenian navy was stronger numerically during this period than any time since the Peloponnesian War.

These factors may indicate that the economies of the Cyclades and of Athens were closely linked after mid-century, and that for several decades the Cyclades could have enjoyed the benefits of Athenian naval hegemony without having to endure the kinds of abuses perpetrated by that hegemon during the days of the Delian League in the fifth century. As such, they may have found the 'perfect fit' of political and economic circumstances.

FROM THE SOCIAL WAR TO CHAIRONEIA (355–338)

By the end of the Social War in 355, Athens was in a depressed economic state. In several of his orations, Demosthenes gives ample testimony to a reduction in public revenues, as well as arrears in the collection of *eisphorai*.[1] Other contemporary sources paint a similar picture: Isokrates' *On the Peace* describes a decline in trade, the poor condition of the docks in the Peiraeus, and the desertion of Athens by traders and metics.[2]

The Athenian politician Euboulos, influential during the years 355–342, implemented many financial reforms while serving as theoric commissioner.[3] Some of the recommendations for the revitalization of Athens detailed by Xenophon in his contemporary work *Poroi* (*On the Revenues*)[4] seem to have been adopted in the programme of Euboulos.[5] The resumption of mining activity at Laureion was one of these initiatives, which eventually led to a renewal of minting of Athenian silver.[6] Another method was to speed up the trials of

[1] On revenues (down to 130 talents in 355): Dem. 10.37; 20.24 and 115; 23.209; on *eisphorai*: Dem. 20.42–48; 24.8–11 and 160–75; on festivals: Dem. 24.11.

[2] Isok. 8.19, 21, 69.

[3] For Euboulos generally see Cawkwell 1963*a*; Burke 1984; Hintzen-Böhlen 1997, 90–105; Engen 2010, 60–5.

[4] Giglioni 1970; Gauthier 1976; Schütrumpf 1982; Doty 2003; Lewis 2009. The treatise has been dated by most to approximately 355/4, although 346 has also found support. For a recent discussion see Bloch 2004.

[5] Cawkwell 1963*a*, 47–67, who proposes however that much of the *Poroi* is 'fantastic'; for a differing view see Burke 1984.

[6] Hopper 1953, 251.

commercial suits at Athens by the creation of special courts for this purpose, the *dikai emporikai*.[7] Xenophon had seen the revenue potential contained in the Peiraeus, and proposed various ways of enticing non-citizens to the port.[8] Facilities in the Peiraeus were also improved under Euboulos' direction,[9] and grants of *enktēsis*, or the right of non-citizens to own property in Attika, began to increase. Although primarily honorific, many of these awards were made to merchants who provided grain to Athens in time of shortages.[10]

The Athenian fleet was another of Euboulos' major preoccupations. At the outbreak of the Social War in 357/6, Athens had 283 triremes, and this number had increased to 349 triremes by 353/2.[11] Ship sheds and an arsenal for the fleet were also constructed.[12] Athens took some steps to secure the seas during this period. The klerouchy on Samos appears to have been reinforced in 351/0.[13] This action could be interpreted as renewed protection of the grain route from the south and east, just as the klerouchy established in 353/2 in the Khersonese was designed to help guard the grain route from the Bosporos.[14] Other foreign adventurism was avoided during this period, however—for example, the Athenians did not follow Demosthenes' recommendation that they intervene to help Rhodian democrats against that island's oligarchy.[15]

[7] Orations that record such cases (all but one involving non-citizens) are Dem. 32, [Dem.] 33, 34, 35, and 56; Burke 1984, 115 n. 23; Vélissaropoulos 1980, 241–5; Moreno 2007, 285–99; Länni 2006, 160–2.

[8] Xen. *Por.* 3.1–5.

[9] Din. 1.96–8; *Syll.*[3] 1216.

[10] Engen 2010, *passim*; Peĉirka 1966, 122–30, 152–6; Burke 1992, 209.

[11] In 357/6: *IG* II[2] 1611 lines 5–9; in 353/2: *IG* II[2] 1613 line 302; Burke 1984, 116 and n. 25; Cawkwell 1963, 65.

[12] Aiskhin. 3.25–6; Din. 1.96.

[13] Schol. Aiskhin. 1.53; Philoch. *FGrH* 328 F154.

[14] Dem. 8.14–16; 9.34–5; 10.68; 18.241 and 301, this last passage emphasizing the need for friendly coasts to keep Athens supplied with grain.

[15] On the oligarchy see Diod. 16.7.3 and 22.2; the speech is Dem. 15, who says at 9–13 that it was unlikely that the Persians would oppose the Athenians, as they had not when the Samian klerouchy was founded: Badian 2000, 31–3; Ryder 2000, 52–3. For an important cautionary note as to how much Athenian foreign policy at this time was due to Euboulos, however, see Harding 1995, 123–4. Harris 2006, 133–4 uses these military expenditures to question the idea that Euboulos represented a 'pacifist' faction in the city, as put forward by de Romilly 1954, 327–32 and Mossé 1973, 55–7. However, it should be kept in mind that preparations for defense do not automatically imply a belligerent policy (see the later policies of Lykourgos below).

Many of Euboulos' efforts appear to have borne fruit. Athenian revenues increased from the low point of 130 talents in 355 mentioned above, to the figure of 400 talents by 341.[16] The Cycladic *poleis*, all of which appear to have remained in the League as allies of Athens, could have shared in this prosperity. While it could be misleading to assume that the Athenians were overly concerned for the economic well-being of anyone but themselves, a secondary effect of their self-interested policies may have been an increase in commerce through the Cyclades, and subsequent benefits for the inhabitants of those islands.

Many of these islands maintained strong political ties with Athens throughout this period. The islands continued to pay *syntaxeis* until the League was dissolved in 338, and during the 340s two of them—Paros and Naxos—reaffirmed their loyalty to Athens through the dedication of crowns.[17] This was a renewal of a Cycladic tradition last seen in 368/7, when Andros and Siphnos made similar dedications.[18] The practice could also work in reverse, as the Tenians were granted a gold crown by Athens in the mid-fourth century, albeit for unknown reasons.[19] Proxenies and honours were also voted to individual Athenians by Cycladic *poleis*—although precise dating is impossible, they appear *c.*350 and include a crown and exemption on import/export taxes to a new Athenian *proxenos* (name unknown) on Ios,[20] and grants of proxeny from the Parians to the *stratēgos* Kephisophon[21] and also to two other Athenians.[22]

There is one item of epigraphic evidence that must be addressed, although its economic implications are unclear. The Athenian decree regulating the export of *miltos* (ruddle) from Keos is undated, but has

[16] Dem. 10.37–9; Theopomp. *FGrH* 115 F166.

[17] Paros and Naxos in 348/7: *IG* II^2 1441 lines 5–17; Naxos again with various non-Cycladic states in 345/4: *IG* II^2 1443 lines 108–22; Harris 1995, #446–448; Brun 1983, 115 n. 7.

[18] See Chapter 5, p. 167 n. 182. This practice is also seen in states from other regions of the Aegean. Mytilene and Samos, for example, are also known from 349/8. For Mytilene: *IG* II^2 1438 line 19 and Harris 1995, #445. For Samos: *IG* II^2 1438 lines 23–4 and Harris 1995, #449.

[19] *IG* II^2 660. It is possible that military assistance may have been involved, as it was in the case of Aratos of Tenedos, who received a gold crown in 340/39 for assistance rendered to Byzantion during Philip II's siege: *IG* II^2 233; Pečirka 1966, 94–5.

[20] *IG* XII.5, 1000 (= Brun 2005, #71.A).

[21] *IG* XII.5, 114 (= Brun 2005, #71.D).

[22] Brun 2005, #71F.

been placed by most scholars in the mid-fourth century.[23] Three of the Keian cities, Ioulis, Karthaia, and Koressos, are mentioned in the inscription, although the section concerning Karthaia (lines 1–8) is badly preserved.

The section on Koressos is a reaffirmation of a previous agreement (date also unknown) between this city and Athens on the export of this commodity (line 11: *κ]αθάπερ πρότερον*). The producers of ruddle are to pay a transport fee of 1 obol on the talent to those who will ship the product (lines 12–14, partially restored). It is not, strictly speaking, *Athenian* ships that are mentioned in the Koressos section of the inscription, but if the restoration is correct it is rather ships designated *by* them.[24] This could refer, therefore, to *any* ships or merchants that the Athenians decided to bestow this favour upon. The producers must also pay the 2 per cent export duty or *pentēkostē*.

The Ioulis section is somewhat different. The ruddle is to be shipped to a certain destination ('Athens' has been restored in line 27) and to no other. In this case, however, there is no mention of a transport charge paid to merchants. Moreover, the Ioulietan producers are to be exempt from taxation, starting from a certain month. A lacuna prevents exact identification of the tax in question,[25] but it has usually been assumed that it refers to the *pentēkostē* mentioned in the decree for Koressos.

If the proposed dating is correct, these decrees were passed at some point after the troubles on Keos in the late 360s. This inscription is generally used to bolster arguments for Athenian political and/or economic oppression of her League allies.[26] In particular, the provision for freedom for slave informers who help ensnare those who break the regulations in either Koressos or Ioulis has received recent attention.[27] Yet, a close examination of the decrees hints at unknown factors at work at the time. One would expect that Ioulis, the city that had twice risen in revolt, would have been given harsher terms. Yet it is Ioulis that receives the exemption from taxes and transport charges, while Koressos, which had remained loyal during the second revolt of

[23] Rhodes and Osborne 2003, #40 (= *IG* II^2 1128); Velissaropoulos 1980, 185–9 and 210–11; Wallinga 1964, 8–10.

[24] Rhodes and Osborne 2003, #40 line 13—*ἐξάγειν ἐμ πλοίωι ὧι [ἂν Ἀθηναῖοι ἀποδείξωσιν, ἐν ἄλλωι]*.

[25] Rhodes and Osborne 2003, #40 line 32.

[26] Emphasized again by Rhodes and Osborne 2003, 209.

[27] Osborne 2000*b*, 86–9.

Ioulis, is subject to both. Clearly, we are lacking some important details concerning the politics of Athenian–Keian relations at this time. Perhaps privileges were granted to the Ioulietans in order to secure their loyalty; or, one city or faction was favoured over another in order to forestall the re-creation of the Keian federation. The real motivation, in other words, may lie in factional machinations for which no other evidence has survived.[28] Moreover, as 'high-handed' as some of the provisions may be, the lack of uniformity in the sections applying to different cities shows that Athens did not completely dictate all the specific terms.[29]

Although there are several ancient literary references to uses for *miltos*,[30] scholars have been unable to agree on why Athens would have been so interested in securing supplies of this material.[31] Its use in the painting of trireme hulls has been posited as the most likely reason. Considering the program of Athenian shipbuilding inaugurated by Euboulos, this would fit well with the supposed date of the decree. It is possible that the earlier Koressos decree that is renewed in this inscription actually dated back to the fifth century, when the need for securing supplies of shipbuilding materials had also been paramount.[32] *Miltos* was also available from Lemnos (an Athenian possession) and Sinope, but the proximity of Keos to Athens probably aided in the speedy transportation of this commodity. Also, it might have been important to Athens to deny shipbuilding materials to potential rivals in the fourth century, such as Thebes in the 360s and Philip II in the following decades.

[28] Brun 1989, 126 has speculated that the proxenies bestowed on two Athenians, Kleomelos and Khaireias, for assisting two Karthaians around the mid-fourth century (*IG* XII.5, 528, line 8 and 538, line 6) may have been connected to violations of the *miltos* decree.

[29] Admitted by Rhodes and Osborne 2003, p. 206 as 'the degree of flexibility that was allowed in allies' responses'.

[30] Theophr. *De Lap.* 8.52; Pliny *N.H.* 33.111, 35.30; Strabo 12.2.10 C540 on *miltos* from Sinope; *Syll.*^{3} 972 line 155; *IG* II^2 1672 lines 12, 69, and 184 (this last inscription records the price of Sinopic *miltos* in 329/8). Wallinga 1964, 9–10 uses this figure to estimate profits accruing from the Keian product, but his analogies to volumes of mineral shipments in Roman times seem to yield inflated totals (i.e. 5,000 talents of *miltos* shipped to Athens annually, or just under 15 talents worth).

[31] Photos-Jones et al. 1997; Osborne 2000*b*, 88 discounts possible economic motivations completely.

[32] [Xen.] *Ath.Pol.* 2.2 speaks of Athens forcing its allies to bring shipbuilding materials to the Peiraeus. Meiggs 1972, 195, however, notes that there is little evidence for specific Athenian interest in *miltos* in the fifth century.

By mid-century, tensions between Athens and Philip II began to build, although the Cycladic region was not a central concern. All known Aegean operations directed by Philip against Athenian interests targeted the Bosporan grain route. Philip's fleet in all likelihood did not number more than twenty triremes,[33] but his flotilla could still wreak some havoc in wartime. In 352/1 it struck Lemnos and Imbros as well as a group of merchant ships near Cape Geraistos on Euboia, and seized the 'sacred trireme' at Marathon.[34] There is no evidence, however, that any of the Cyclades or any shipping along the eastern/southern routes were attacked in this manner.[35] Consequently, the Athenian orators of the time, particularly Demosthenes, paid very little attention to the Cyclades. When Demosthenes does mention Aegean islands in military terms, they are located on the Bosporan route. For example, in 351 he praised Skiathos and other nearby islands for provisioning the Athenian fleet.[36] He also boasted that he had helped Athens regain the alliance of the Euboians and made that island a stronghold for the Athenians against naval threats.[37] Again, the threat was from the north and the Cyclades were not involved (only Andros and Keos could have been said to have been close enough to those sea routes to matter to Demosthenes, and we hear of no trouble on those islands). But if Euboia had fallen to Philip, the Cyclades and the coast of Attika itself would have become vulnerable, and the Peiraeus gravely threatened.[38]

The secession of Eretria from the Athenian sphere during 348–343[39] does *not* seem to have inspired similar activity in the Cyclades. The situation was the same during the period of brief rule in Eretria by a pro-Macedonian faction in 342–341,[40] and also during the possible formation of a short-lived Euboian League, led by Khalkis

[33] Hammond and Griffith 1979, 311–12.

[34] Dem. 4.34; Androtion *FGrH* 324 F24; Philoch. *FGrH* 328 F47.

[35] In fact, the only contemporary reference we have to the seizure of a ship on this route was one perpetrated by an *Athenian* crew on a ship from Naukratis in 355 (Dem. 24. 11–12).

[36] Dem. 4.32.

[37] Dem. 18. 237 and 301.

[38] Dem. 18.141; Burke 1984, 119.

[39] Secession under the tyrant Ploutarkhos: Plut. *Vit.Phok.* 12–13. Readmittance to the League in 343: Aiskhin. 3.92, 94, 100 and *IG* II^2 125.

[40] Dem. 9.57, 10.8; new Athenian/Eretrian alliance in 341: *IG* II^2 230; Philoch. *FGrH* 328 F160.

and also comprised of Eretria and Histiaia/Oreos, by 340.[41] This passivity represents a major break from the pattern seen in the fifth century in which trouble in Euboia tended to equate to trouble in the Cyclades (from the Athenian point of view).[42]

The Delian loan accounts for 341/40, the latest that have been preserved, list new credit granted to Seriphos (4,000 drachmas), Ios (amount unpreserved), and Paros (5 talents).[43] It should be noted that the Parians also voted honours to four of the Athenian amphiktyons on Delos in 341/40, perhaps in gratitude for this new credit.[44] This is in sharp contrast to continuing anti-Athenian feeling on Delos itself, seen in the appeal by the Delians to an unknown third party (most likely the Delphic Amphiktyony) to remove the temple from Athenian control at some point *c.*345–343.[45] This was countered from the Athenian side in a lost oration by Hypereides, and the appeal was rejected, although virtually nothing else is known concerning this event.[46] During the 330s, a pro-Athenian Delian was forced to flee to Athens.[47]

[41] Aiskhin. 3.89 and 94. This is controversial. The possibility of a Euboian League having been established as far back as 411 has been raised by many commentators: Brunt 1966; Cawkwell 1978; Picard 1979 . Other than the testimony of Aiskhines, this is primarily based on coinage, although there is also a fragment of a treaty between Athens and 'the Euboians' (*IG* II^2 149 = Bengtson 1975, #342) that probably dates to the late 340s. However, several scholars are dismissive that there was any true Euboian federation until the second century: Larsen 1968, 97–103; Beck 1997, 28; Reber, Hansen, and Ducrey 2004, 643.

[42] See Chapter 4, pp. 98–9. The Parians were able to renew certain diplomatic links with the Thasians *c.*340, as indicated in *IG* XII. 5, 114, although there is no reason to assume (*pace* Rubensohn 1902, 199) that this should be taken as a *sympoliteia* between the two communities: Pouilloux 1954, 341–2; Lanzilotta 1987, 148–50; Berranger-Auserve 2000, 108.

[43] Migeotte 1984, 146–7.

[44] *IG* XII.5, 113; Chankowski 2008, 366; Berranger-Auserve 2000, 105. Note, however, that this inscription appears to have vanished from the Paros Museum. I thank Grégory Bonnin of the University of Bordeaux for this information (pers. comm. 7/28/10).

[45] Osborne 1974, 176 n.19; Wankel 1976, 727–30; the suggestion that the Delphic amphiktyons heard the case has been questioned by Sanchez 2001, 247–50 and Chankowski 2008, 256–7.

[46] Hyp. 13 frag. 67–75 Jensen; Dem. 18.134–6.

[47] *IG* II^2 222, dated by Osborne 1974, 175–84 to 334; Gehrke 1985, 49; Reger 2004, 739. For a new fragment of amphiktyonic accounts discovered during the construction of the Athens Metro that also refers to this event, see Parlama and Stampolidis 2001, 139–40.

The reasons for the new extension of borrowing privileges are unknown. Although preparations for war with Philip II may have been a contributing factor, Philip had made no known aggressive moves in the Cycladic region.[48] The alliance brokered by Demosthenes that eventually faced Philip at Khaironeia included Thebes, which was granted co-command of the naval side of the conflict, implying that combat at sea with the small Macedonian fleet was expected.[49] Yet we do not hear of any warships lent to the Cyclades in the manner of those sent to Khalkis in 340.[50]

There is no reason to automatically assume that Cycladic poverty was a reason for these loans, since islanders could and did contribute to the Athenian cause in the dark days after Khaironeia. In his oration against Leokrates, Lykourgos states that after their defeat Athens sought the aid of several communities, including Andros and Keos in the Cyclades.[51] Two Andrians, Drakontides and Hegesias, appear to have answered the call and later received honours at Athens. We do not know the nature of the services they rendered to Athens, although it has been conjectured that they assisted in some way with the grain supply.[52] It also appears that the Keian federation may have emerged again in some form after 338, although there is no evidence of it displaying any enmity towards Athens.[53]

There is no direct evidence that any of the Cyclades were members of the League of Corinth,[54] but it is likely that they were enrolled at

[48] Although Philip may not have posed much of a naval threat, there are references in later authors to money collected from 'the allies' before Khaironeia, which may have included islanders: [Plut.] *Mor.* 846a and Plut. *Vit.Dem.* 17.

[49] Aiskhin. 2.132–45.

[50] *IG* II^2 1629 lines 516–18.

[51] Lycurg. *Leoc.* 1. 42. Lykourgos is not more specific which Keian *poleis* he is referring to in this speech. For a recent discussion of this oration see Ober 2008, 183–4.

[52] *IG* II^2 238 (= Schwenk 1985, #2).

[53] *IG* XII.5, 609 for a *sympoliteia* of Koressos and Ioulis; see Ruschenbusch 1982; Reger 1998, 637–8. Reger's statement, however, that the use of 'Keioi' could simply be an ossification in bookkeeping practices obscures the matter, since it is not just 'unpaid debt' that is carried over from previous years, but new interest payments that are recorded for that year, 341/0.

[54] Dem. 18.201; Polyb. 9.33.7. For general discussion of the League of Corinth see Ellis 1976, 204–9; Hammond and Griffith 1979, 623–46; Worthington 2008, 158–63. Raue 1937 attempts to restore the presence of the Andrians, Parians, and Naxians on line 5 of Fragment B of *IG* II^2 236. Worthington 2009, 219 proposes that the the two fragments have been incorrectly joined and that Fragment A is not a copy of Philip's Common Peace but instead a bilateral peace between Philip and Athens.

the same time as other island states such as Khios in 336.[55] Argos, acting on behalf of the *synedrion* of this League, intervened in a dispute between two of the Cyclades, Kimolos and Melos, at some indeterminate time soon after 338.[56]

Soon after the formation of the League of Corinth, Lykourgos son of Lykophron began his twelve-year tenure as financial administrator at Athens, and he set the tone for Athenian policy until the Lamian War of 323/2.[57] This period was even more extraordinary for the economy of Athens than the time of Euboulos. Athenian state revenues are attested to have risen from the 400 talents recorded in 346 to 1,200 talents a year, without the benefit of any sort of outside tribute.[58] All of the available evidence points to commerce and extractive industry as the main sources of this increased wealth. Indirect taxes (such as the harbour tax) and the renewed exploitation of the silver mines were responsible.[59] There are also several indications of Lykourgan policies that benefited metics and merchants. On his proposal, the Athenian *ekklēsia* decreed in 333/2 that traders from Kition on Cyprus would be granted permission to acquire land (*enktēsis*) in order to build a temple to Aphrodite.[60] The inscription that records this decree also mentions that Egyptian merchants had previously been granted the same right for construction of a temple to Isis, although no date for this earlier grant is given. It is quite likely that Lykourgos was trying to encourage trade along the eastern/southern Aegean route, in grain and in other products, with such legislation.[61]

Metics who rendered assistance to Athens during this period received extensive honours, an example being Heraklides of Salamis on Cyprus, who in 325/4 was honoured for selling grain at a

[55] Diod. 16.91.2–4; Khios: Rhodes and Osborne 2003 #84.

[56] Rhodes and Osborne 2003 #82 (= Tod 1962 #179 = Ager 1996 #3); Ellis 1976, 299 n. 137.

[57] Diod. 16.88.1; [Plut.] *Mor.* 841b-843f; Mitchel 1970, 163–214; Burke 1985 and 1992; Hintzen-Böhlen 1997, 105–35.The enumeration and scope of Lykourgos' official titles are still obscure, but he appears to have had control over public finances in Athens.

[58] [Plut.] *Mor.* 842f.

[59] Faraguna 1992, 397–9; Burke 1985, 251–2. Engen 2010, 65–6 and 171.

[60] Rhodes and Osborne 2003 #91 (= *IG* II^2 337). It is noteworthy that Egyptian worshippers of Isis are also attested in Eretria in roughly this same period: *IG* XII Suppl. 562; Fraser 1972, 260.

[61] Simms 1989, 220.

reasonable price during a shortage in 330/29, and for contributing cash for the city's food supply in 328/7.[62] Although there is no way to tell how much the metic population of Athens may have increased during these years, there are multiple references to their presence in orations delivered from the late 350s through the 330s, and one must assume that such policies of encouragement had an effect.[63]

As in the period of Euboulos' ascendancy, the Athenian fleet was not neglected under Lykourgos. The naval inventory for 330/29 lists 392 triremes and 18 quadriremes.[64] It has been theorized that this Lykourgan-era fleet was built chiefly as a deterrent against Macedon.[65] However, the naval inventories for years such as 330/29, 326/5 and 325/4 all show between forty and sixty ships at sea at certain times.[66] It is unlikely that Lykourgos would have expended such resources simply on a show of strength, since the suppression of piracy was a major concern during these years (see below).[67] Moreover, Athens refrained from military adventurism during this period.

The establishment of what might be called a 'peaceful hegemony' of Athens was seen as possible by at least a few fourth-century Athenians,[68] and the decades after the end of the Social War may in fact have seen this concept realized.[69] In the *Poroi* Xenophon speaks of how in Athens' past, times of war had always drained the treasury, while times of peace had always enabled it to grow.[70] He proposes a

[62] Rhodes and Osborne 2003 #95 (= *IG* II^2 360); Tracy 1995, 31.

[63] Dem. 23.23, 21.163, 57.48, 22.68, 24.166, and [Dem] 25.57 for evidence of metics. However, the figure of 10,00 metics in Athens by the end of the fourth century, preserved in Ath. *Deip.* 6.272c, should be viewed cautiously.

[64] *IG* II^2 1627, lines 266–9, 275–8. The decree of Stratokles, *IG* II^2 457, also attests to the readiness of 400 triremes; cf. [Plut.] *Mor.* 852c.

[65] Bosworth 1988, 208–9.

[66] *IG* II^2 1628 lines 481 ff. (326/5) and 1629 lines 783 ff. (325/4); Burke 1985, 258 and n.40.

[67] Burke 1985, 257.

[68] There are also fifth-century sources that equate peace with wealth: Thuc. 6.26 on the accumulation of wealth during the Peace of Nikias; Thuc. 5.28.2 and Ar. *Pax* 475–7 on the neutrality of Argos; Hunt 2010, 31–3 and Hornblower 2011, 87 for discussion.

[69] Habicht 1997, 22–3; Mitchel 1973; Burke 2005, 33–4, and Engen 2010, 66, *pace* the comments of Humphreys 1985, 219–20 on a supposed 'absence of any constructive foreign policy' under Lykourgos.

[70] Xen. *Por.* 5.11; cf. Isok. 8, *passim*. This provides an important corrective to Finley 1985, 74–6, who states that ancient wars were 'the basic factor of economic growth' in antiquity, and that the ancients were aware of this—despite his multiple assertions that the ancients had no true understanding of their economy.

new type of dominance, one that would be primarily economic.[71] A powerful fleet, a cash reserve, and a restrained attitude that kept Athens out of wasteful attempts at territorial expansion would be aspects of such a policy.[72] Xenophon also recalls the fifth-century Periklean imagery of Athens as an island and the centrality of the Peiraeus for imports and exports.[73] In speaking of hegemony, he refers to the role Aegean islanders played in helping the Athenians create the Second League, but only with assurances that Athens would refrain from acts of injustice.[74]

It is interesting that conditions at this time corresponded in some aspects to what had been advocated many decades earlier by Andokides in his speech *On the Peace*, traditionally dated to 392. A recent case has been made to dismiss this speech as a Hellenistic forgery;[75] even if this is true, it may have been influenced by the same historical context and outlook that spurred Xenophon to compose the *Poroi*.[76] In his attempt to persuade the Athenian assembly to accept the peace deal that had been recently brokered with Sparta, Andokides speaks of what Athens needs to maintain hegemony: fortification walls, a cash reserve, and a strong fleet.[77] Throughout the speech, he proposes that strong military power that is not squandered in wasteful wars is the key to Athenian success: 'Peace means safety and power for the democracy, whereas war means its downfall.'[78]

THE AEGEAN AND LAMIAN WARS

The so-called Aegean War did see the Cyclades again becoming a battleground, albeit briefly. At the beginning of the sailing season in

[71] Xen. *Por.* 5.5; Dillery 1993, 6.

[72] For further discussion see Brun 1983, 179–81. Ober 2008, 215 n. 7 states that Athenian imperialism in the fourth century 'was unlikely to have produced net revenue gains'. This is correct, insofar as it was imperialism in the style of the fifth century that was unlikely to achieve such gains.

[73] Xen. *Por.* 1.7; Dillery 1993, 4.

[74] Xen. *Por.* 5.6.

[75] Harris 2000, rejected by Hunt 2010, 274.

[76] Witness the same concept expressed in Kephisodotos' sculptural group of Eirene carrying Ploutos, cited by Lattimore 1997, 257 (and n. 36 with references) as 'Peace fostering Wealth'; Hunt 2010, 241.

[77] Andok. 3.5, which appears to have been followed by Aiskhin. 2.173–7 in discussing Athens' power before the Peloponnesian War.

[78] Andok. 3.12; Hunt 2010, 245 proposes that Andokides meant that the Athenians should conserve their resources for a 'necessary' war instead of squandering them on a 'wasteful' one.

333, Memnon of Rhodes, on the orders of Darius III of Persia, began a naval campaign in the Aegean. Boasting a fleet of some 300–400 ships,[79] Memnon captured Khios and several Lesbian towns (Antissa, Methymna, Pyrrha, and Eresos), then began a siege of Mytilene.[80] As rumours of a coming attack on Euboia began to circulate, Diodorus claims that several Cycladic communities sent embassies to Memnon at this point, and that some (unnamed) cities were bribed by him to offer their submission.[81] Memnon may also have either engaged in privateering himself or used pirates as his allies.[82] At this news, Alexander ordered the reformation of the Aegean fleet which he had sent into retirement after taking Miletos in 334.[83] Soon afterwards, Memnon died, leaving as his successor his nephew Pharnabazos.[84] Pharnabazos sent ten ships under Datames into the Cyclades while himself taking the main part of the fleet northward to seize Tenedos at the entrance to the Hellespont.[85] Datames may have been dispatched to the Cyclades to force the submission of the remaining Cycladic *poleis* as well as to harass shipping on the eastern/southern route.[86] The Persians may have also hoped to force the Athenians to resume warfare with Macedon.

The Macedonian reprisal was swift and decisive. Proteas attacked Datames and his force off of Siphnos and sank or captured eight of his ten ships.[87] Hegelochos and Amphoteros recovered Tenedos some time afterward. An anonymous oration preserved in the Demosthenic corpus, tentatively dated to 332/1, states that Macedonian warships had forced ships sailing from the Hellespont to wait in the harbour at Tenedos until the Athenians sent one hundred triremes as reinforcements.[88]

[79] Ruzicka 1988, 133 n. 5 attempts to reconcile the differing figures of 400 in Arr. *Anab.* 1.18.5 and 300 in Diod. 17.29.2 by theorizing that 100 ships had been left to support Halikarnassos.

[80] Arr. *Anab.* 2.1.1–2; Diod. 17.29.1–2.

[81] Diod. 17.29.3.

[82] Bosworth 1980, 180; Tod 1962, #191 lines 11 ff. and 51 ff.

[83] Arr. *Anab.* 2.2.3; Curt. 3.1.19–20. Some twenty Athenian ships had been retained by Alexander (Diod. 17.22.5).

[84] Arr. *Anab.* 2.1.3–4, Diod. 17.29.4, Curt. 3.2–3.

[85] Arr. *Anab.* 2.2.2–3.

[86] Ruzicka 1988, 134.

[87] Arr. *Anab.* 2.2.4–5. Antipater had charged Proteas with gathering a force of fifteen ships from Euboia and the Peloponnese.

[88] [Dem.] 17.19–20, which unfortunately does not specify when this event took place. Ruzicka 1988, 139 n. 21 points out that the bulk of the Persian fleet was gone by late summer of 332, and makes a strong case for 333 as both the year of the demand for escorts and also the year of Macedonian reconquest of the island. Thomassen

In late 333 Pharnabazos sailed with one hundred ships to Siphnos.[89] Although Arrian says nothing concerning this, according to Curtius he garrisoned Andros before putting into port at Siphnos, exacting funds from the inhabitants of both islands.[90] While his main objective was to cut off communications between Alexander and the Greek mainland,[91] it is also possible that he continued to threaten merchant shipping passing through the Cyclades.[92] It was on Siphnos that Pharnabazos received news of the Persian defeat at Issos, and upon hearing this he took twelve ships back to Khios.[93] Alexander's conquest of Phoenicia early in 332 triggered the defection of over 200 ships from the Persian fleet.[94] Crete now became the centre of the naval war, with Agis stepping into the role of Persian commander. It is possible that Agis tried to recruit Athenian assistance to his cause in 332, although there is no strong evidence that he succeeded in this endeavour.[95]

We have already mentioned the incident at Tenedos where the Macedonians detained the grain fleet until Athenian assistance was forthcoming. It seems that the Athenians had repeatedly ignored Macedonian requests for warships, and that compelling the grain ships to dock at Tenedos was a way to force the issue.[96] If one combines Plutarch's testimony that in 332/1 some Athenians wanted to send out triremes to help 'those who were revolting from Alexander'[97] with other similar evidence in the sources such as anti-Alexander demonstrations at Athens,[98] and with embassies sent by

1984, 102 thinks that the internment of the ships (presumably grain transports) at Tenedos was in retaliation for an Athenian refusal to send the 100 ships in the first place.

[89] Arr. *Anab.* 2.13.4. [90] Curt. 4.1.37.

[91] Burn 1952, 82–3. [92] Ruzicka 1988, 142.

[93] Arr. *Anab.* 2.13.5–6. Ruzicka 1988, 143 surmises that the remainder of the ships at Siphnos went to Halikarnassos.

[94] Arr. *Anab.* 2.20.1–3. Pirate vessels in service with Pharnabazos and his ally Aristonikos of Methymna were captured at this time (see also *IG* II^2 284 = Tod 1962 #170), so it would appear that Pharnabazos had continued his predecessor's encouragement of privateering; Bosworth 1975, 33; Thomassen 1984, 89–91.

[95] Plut. *Mor.* 818e–f relates the story of Demades' persuasion of the Athenians not to divert public money to the support of Agis. Ruzicka 1988, 147–9 dates this story to late 332/early 331 as many Athenian ships may have been sent back by Hegelochos for the winter. Potter 1984 sees the titulary inscription of his article as testimony that some Athenians did aid Agis and were later ransomed.

[96] Thomassen 1984, 52, 60, 102–3.

[97] Plut. *Mor.* 818e–f; Ruzicka 1988, 147.

[98] Aiskhin. 3.164.

Athens to the Persian King before Issos,[99] one does see a pattern of Athenian disaffection from Alexander. However, they appear to have been careful to avoid open revolt.

It is unfortunate that the surviving naval inventories do not cover the years 333–331, when conflict in the Aegean was actually underway, so we do not know if the same numbers of ships were out on patrol as in later years, such as 330/29 or 325/4, where the numbers have been preserved. As mentioned above, it seems that during the Lykourgan era it was common for Athens to have some thirty to forty of its triremes out at sea. We have already noted the apparently increasing importance of the southern trade route to Egypt and Libya during the 330s, and the possibility that Datames intended to attack shipping on this route by entering the Cyclades. Why, then, do we have no record in the sources of Athenian ships responding to this threat? Perhaps Datames did not directly threaten those ships heading for Athens, in the hope that the Athenians would join the Persian side. It is evident that the Athenians refused to support the Macedonians either, while at the same time avoiding any outright action against them for fear of reprisal. Their apparent neglect of the southern grain route (and the Cyclades) by not sending ships against Datames is thus best explained from a political standpoint. It would have suited their purposes to withhold military support from the Macedonian cause, hoping for the eventual defeat and death of Alexander. They may have even hoped for a return to their old hegemony in the Aegean upon his death, if not perhaps on a pre-Social War level but at least on that of the 340s. As several of the Cyclades had already submitted to the Persians, this may have led many in Athens to feel that they had no obligation to protect these islands at this time.

How did Cycladic *poleis* handle this situation? The embassies that some of them sent to Memnon (no specific names of islands being preserved by Diodorus) can be seen as expressions of a concern with simple self-preservation.[100] They had no (or perhaps few) warships of their own, and they may have been fully aware of a lack of Athenian interest in engaging the Persian fleet. We hear of no later Macedonian reprisals against any of the islands for such latter-day medizing, and the Athenians would have had no authority to punish them either.

[99] Arr. *Anab.* 2.15.2–4; Curt. 3.13.5.

[100] Jehne 1994, 21.

The extent to which trade was disrupted by the Aegean War is difficult to determine and conflicting interpretations have been put forward.[101]

It was not until the so-called Lamian War that naval combat was once again seen in the Aegean. Our only literary source for this conflict is Diodorus, and as usual there has been controversy as to how to interpret this author's testimony, particularly in the area of Athenian fleet strength and deployment.[102] It is not clear if all available Athenian ships were placed in a single squadron, or if some ships would still have been deployed for guard duty around the coasts of Attika.[103] There is evidence of Athenian troops being based on Samos earlier in the 320s,[104] but Alexander had ruled that the island be returned to the Samian exiles, and Perdikkas had reaffirmed this decision.[105]

Unlike the Aegean War of a decade earlier, there is no evidence that any of the Cycladic communities were garrisoned or exploited for supplies by either Macedonian or Athenian forces. In Diodorus' list of Athens' allies during this conflict, the only *polis* that could be

[101] Burke 1985, 261 and n.59 minimizes the disruption; De Souza 1999, 40–1 emphasizes it. It should be noted that there is evidence in the sources for food shortages at Athens in 335 and in 330/29, but not during the years of the war itself ([Dem.] 34). Garnsey 1988, 154 n. 13 links the expedition of Diotimos in 335/4 with the earlier of the two shortages. It has been theorized that the Kyrene grain distribution dates to this period (see below).

[102] Walek 1924. Much of the controversy hinges on Diod. 18.10.1–3 which details the numbers of warships that the Athenians resolved to dispatch at the beginning of the war (40 triremes and 200 quadriremes). Some scholars, unable to accept that the newer quadriremes would have been so highly represented in the overall fleet strength, have proposed emending the text by transposing these numbers. Ashton 1977, 7–9 accepts the emendation, and by comparison with the fragmentary naval inventory for 323/2 (*IG* II^2 1631 lines 167–74) restores 184 triremes at sea + 50 quadriremes = 233 ships. This has been challenged by Morrison 1987, who proposes that quadriremes were becoming increasingly important at this time and that Diodorus' text requires no emendation.

[103] Ashton 1977, 8–9; Morrison 1987, 90 and 97 disagrees. Walek 1924, 24 n.1 and 25 proposes that part of the Athenian fleet blocked the 110 triremes under Antipater's command in the Malian Gulf, while the remainder went to challenge Kleitos. He rejects, however, the idea that the coast of Attika required guarding at this time. The Hellespont was the scene of a clash between the forces of Euetion and the Macedonian admiral Kleitos (*IG* II^2 398 [an honorary decree from 320/19] and II^2 493 lines 19–21 [one from 303/2] are our sole evidence for this battle (Ashton 1977, 7).

[104] Shipley 1987, 160. Diphilos was sent with a force to Samos in 326/5, as reported in an inscription from Priene (von Gaertringen 1906, #5, line 8).

[105] Diod. 18.8.7, 18.18.9; *Syll.*^{3} 312; O'Sullivan 2009, 259.

considered as actually in the 'Cycladic sphere' is Karystos, and this list may simply reflect those who assisted during the land campaign at Krannon.[106] The waters off Amorgos, however, were the scene of the decisive engagement. While Euetion may have happened to have been caught off Amorgos on his way home,[107] the central location of Amorgos on trade routes through the Aegean is important.[108]

Although the Battle of Amorgos has generally been considered the swan-song of the Athenian navy, there is some evidence that Athens did not completely abandon all naval activity afterwards.[109] However, the key difference is that Athens did not have control over its own foreign policy after 322. Rather, its forces were called upon by one or another of the Diadochi in their struggles.[110] It has been theorized that a flotilla of ten Athenian ships helped Antigonos Monophthalmos win a victory over Perdikkas off Cyprus in 321.[111] In 319, Polyperkhon 'returned' Samos to Athens.[112] Although it would seem that nothing much came of this gesture, there are fragments of two Samian decrees, both undated, that mention attacks on Samos, and Athenians are mentioned in one of them.[113] Although most commentators have refrained from inferring too much from these texts, it is assumed that they refer to events sometime between 319 and 307.[114]

It has been recently proposed that the regime of Demetrios of Phaleron from 317 to 307 was yet another time of prosperity for Athens, and as in the Lykourgan period, the lack of warfare helped

[106] Diod. 18.11.2; Paus. 1.25.4.

[107] Morrison 1987, 97.

[108] Bosworth 2003, 20.

[109] Green 2003, 2; Hypereides' *Funeral Oration* for the dead at Lamia later that year makes no mention of the naval defeat at Amorgos, but at 6.5 states that Athens gives the Greeks 'a common safety.'

[110] Diod. 18.74.1–3 on Kassander's establishment of Demetrios of Phaleron as ruler of Athens: 'the Athenians were to retain their city and territory, their revenues, their fleet, and everything else, and to be friends and allies of Kassander.' However, see O'Sullivan 2009, 278–87 for a new emphasis on how Athens often derived benefits from operations ordered by Kassander.

[111] Hauben 1974, 64 n. 23.

[112] Diod. 18.56.7; Shipley 1987, 171.

[113] Habicht 1957, #18, lines 5–6 and #19, lines 4 and 8.

[114] Shipley 1987, 172 tentatively proposes the year 313 for the attack of Myrmidon, who is attested as leading 10,000 mercenaries in the service of Kassander: Diod. 19.62; *Syll.*^{3} 320. Habicht 1997, 52 n. 41 considers two different periods to be plausible: one between spring 318 and summer 317, due to Polyperkhon's edict; the other 315/14 and connected to Thymochares' operations on Kythnos.

create those conditions.[115] In addition, lessened state expenditure on ships and monumental construction in Athens (in contrast to the time of Lykourgos' administration) may have kept more accumulated revenue in reserve.[116] Nevertheless, the Athenian navy did not refrain completely from military action. In addition to supporting the cause of Kassander, they also attempted to stop Antigonos Monopthalmos from usurping their traditional role in the Aegean.[117] In 315/14, an Athenian naval force under Thymochares captured the 'pirate' Glauketes. This individual had established a base on the Cycladic island of Kythnos. According to the epigraphic testimony, Thymochares had been assisted by the Kythnians themselves in his operation.[118] The island of Kythnos is at the entrance to the Saronic Gulf, and could have posed a threat to shipping near Athens.[119] Antigonos appears to have used piracy as an instrument of policy at this time, so it is possible that Glauketes may have been part of this policy.[120]

In 314, Kassander demanded that Athens send twenty warships to attack Lemnos, which was still under the control of Antigonos. This squadron was routed by Antigonos' admiral Dioskourides.[121] Dioskourides then made his way to Delos and emancipated the island from Athenian control.[122] He appears to have handed over temple administration to local *hieropoioi*, as well as cancelling leases on sacred estates and offering new leases only to Delians.[123]

Dioskourides also, according to Diodorus, made 'a circuit of the sea, guaranteeing the safety of the allies and winning the support of the islands that had not yet joined the alliance'.[124] The parallel to the actions of Khabrias after the battle of Naxos is evident. At some point

[115] Diod. 18.74.3; O'Sullivan 2009, 189–95 for an overview of the Athenian economy in this period; Oliver 2007, 52 for continued prosperity in the Peiraeus.

[116] Ath. *Deip.* 12.542c; O'Sullivan 2009, 191–2.

[117] O'Sullivan 2009, 280–1.

[118] *IG* II^2 682 (= *Syll.*^{3} 409) lines 9–13 and II^2 549 (= *IG* XII.5 testimonia 1297).

[119] Sheedy, 1996, 443–4, who also mentions a similar Athenian operation on Kythnos in the first century.

[120] O'Sullivan 2009, 189.

[121] Diod. 19.68.3–4. The chronology of these events is still disputed, see Habicht 1997, 63 n. 75 for discussion. The majority consensus is followed here in assigning such events to 314 rather than 313.

[122] Diod. 19.62.7; *IG* XI.2, 138 for the liberation of Delos; Buraselis 1982, 41–2; Billows 1990, 118 n. 45.

[123] Reger 1994*a*, 161–2. Tréheux 1948 suggests that the Oikos of the Andrians was also confiscated at this time.

[124] Diod. 19.62.9 (Oldfather translation).

before 306 (and quite possibly in 313 during a second expedition under the same commander) a new Nesiotic League was formed, centred on Delos.[125] The same factors that had made the Cyclades so militarily important to Athens, such as the positioning of harbours for the support of warships on vital shipping routes, probably motivated Antigonos.[126]

THE NESIOTIC LEAGUES AS COMPARANDA

The creation of the Antigonid version of the Nesiotic League (which is presumed to have lasted from 314 until 287, with brief interruptions) was another watershed in the history of the Cyclades, and marks the (approximate) end point of our historical survey of the Cycladic region. Similar leagues also appear later in a Ptolemaic (285–260, and again 246–245) and also a Rhodian incarnation (199–167). The Antigonid version remains fairly obscure in its structure, although it is generally assumed that one can project the Ptolemaic evidence backwards to some degree.[127]

The Antigonid version had a *synedrion*, and it could levy *syntaxeis* contributions from its members and punish members who did not comply.[128] This league differed from both the Delian League and the Second Athenian League, however, in that it was an actual federal state, in which the *synedrion* could most likely confer citizenship in all member states at once.[129] Individual *poleis* within the League, however, could still demonstrate civic independence. The *polis* of Ios, for example, awarded a crown to Antigonos at an indeterminate date.[130]

[125] *IG* XI.4, 1036 is a decree of the islanders dated to shortly after the victory of Demetrios Poliorketes at Cypriote Salamis in 306; Merker 1970; Billows 1990, 220.

[126] Buraselis 1982, 43.

[127] Billows 1990, 221; Bagnall 1976, 136–58 covers the Ptolemaic League.

[128] *IG* XI.4, 1036 lines 7, 36, 45. This is also seen under the Ptolemies, when their admiral Philokles collected tribute: *IG* XII.7, 506 (the Nikouria Decree), and also pressured those who delayed in paying back loans to Delian Apollo: *IG* XI.4, 559; Merker 1970, 148–51.

[129] This is known from multiple examples in the Ptolemaic period (*IG* XI.4, 1039, 1040, 1042, 1046) and most likely can be pushed back to this earlier period as well: Billows 1990, 222.

[130] *IG* XII Suppl. 168; Billows 1990, 224. For crowns bestowed collectively by the third-century League to the Ptolemies, see *IG* XII.7, 13 and *Syll.*^{3} 390. For Siphnos: *IG* XII.5, 481; for a possible crown from Arkesine on Amorgos: *IG* XII.7, 13.

Some of the Cyclades provided soldiers to the Antigonids. Keos, Kythnos, and Mykonos all had troops campaigning for Antigonos in the Peloponnese in 312/11, and later epigraphic evidence points to warship contributions, although the circumstances are very unclear.[131] Under the Antigonids, a garrison was stationed on Andros that was later driven out in 308 by Ptolemaic forces.[132] This could be taken as evidence that Antigonid garrisons in the Cyclades were common at this time. It has been suggested, however, that Antigonos' nephew Polemaios, who had passed through the islands on his way to Kos in 309, had in fact established the garrison, presumably without authorization.[133] The Andrian garrison may very well have been unique and thus a target for the Ptolemies.

Neither the Antigonid nor the Ptolemaic Leagues were fully integrated into the administration of their respective kingdoms, as were most cities in such areas as Syria and Asia Minor.[134] It has been stated (with particular reference to the Ptolemaic League) that it would have not been profitable for these monarchs to have taken direct administrative control, and that the repayment of loans extended by them (or by the temple on Delos) to the islanders appear to have been the main financial concerns.[135] It has been suggested that the Cyclades first became a true regional unit after 314 and the creation of this Antigonid Nesiotic League,[136] but that they also became financially burdened under this organization.[137] On face value, the Cyclades could thus be seen as having returned to some aspects of their fifth-century situation, albeit with the Antigonids rather than the Athenians as their hegemon.

However, it is important not to place too much emphasis on the impact of the League at its beginning. The loss of Andros to the Ptolemies in 308 may show that the new organization was operating in a fairly fluid situation with regard to naval hegemony. Antigonid

[131] Billows 1990, 222; Geagan 1968, 381–4 for the land forces; *OGIS* 773 for the naval. Reger 1992, 366–8 has suggested that Tenian forces participated in Demetrios' expedition in 307 (*pace* Habicht 1997, 69 n. 7).

[132] Diod. 20.37.1.

[133] Billows 1990, 225, citing Diod. 20.27.3.

[134] Reger 1994*a*, 33–4 and n. 47.

[135] Bagnall 1976, 156.

[136] Reger 1994*a*, 165. Lätsch 2005, 185.

[137] Reger 1994*a*, 38. An inscription of the time of Ptolemy I (*IG* XII.7, 506 line 16) draws attention to the exactions of Demetrios.

control of the Cyclades may have even briefly lapsed because of that event.[138] When Demetrios Poliorketes entered Athens in triumph in 307, a number of cities sent embassies and awarded crowns to the Athenians. Most were in Asia Minor, but a few were island states—Tenedos, Peparethos, and Tenos in the Cyclades. The Tenians saw either the establishment (or possibly the renewal) of a *symbola* agreement with Athens at this time; it has also been suggested that an undated inscription detailing a block grant of *isoteleia*, the right to pay taxes at the same rate as Athenian citizens and also the right to own property, belongs to this same period.[139] As the *symbola* inscription names Tenians who 'fight with' the Athenians, there were presumably Tenians helping Demetrios to liberate Athens from Demetrios of Phaleron and Kassander.[140]

While Tenos is the only Cycladic island known to have sent an embassy to Athens at this time, it is possible that others did as well. Although some caution is in order, the events of 307 may show that the Athenian loss of Delos in 314 had more of an immediate effect on Delos than it did in the Cycladic region in general. Although the Battle of Amorgos had dealt a severe blow to Athenian sea power, Athens was still important enough in the Aegean to be the object of diplomacy (trade-related and otherwise) from many states. As described above, Athens' navy was still somewhat viable (although Demetrios' promise of enough timber for 100 warships may have been empty posturing[141]). Perhaps more importantly, Athens was still a viable trading partner.

TRADE ROUTES THROUGH THE CYCLADES DURING THE LATER FOURTH CENTURY

The discussion of the fifth-century *arkhē* in Chapter 4 addressed the possibility of trade routes changing under Athenian influence.[142]

[138] Buraselis 1982, 45–6, followed by Reger 1992, 367.

[139] *IG* II^2 466 for the *symbola*; *IG* II^2 660 for *isoteleia* and Reger 1992, 368 for the link.

[140] Reger 1992, 367–8, noting the strategic location of Tenos for naval operations.

[141] Plut. *Vit.Demetr.* 10.1.

[142] See Chapter 4, pp. 100–12.

After the middle of the fourth century, Athenian exports of ceramics to the Bosporos region taper off.[143] This is at the same time that they increase at sites such as Dor in Phoenicia on the eastern/southern route.[144] Another indication may be the return of Attic and other imports to Cretan cities during the fourth century. Phalasarna, Eleutherna, and Knossos all have yielded increased finds of Attic pottery for this period.[145] Unfortunately we do not have the amount of evidence of fourth-century Attic pottery in the Cyclades as we do for the fifth. Paros and Naxos have yielded, however, fairly numerous finds of red-figure dating up through the third quarter of the fourth century, including the deposit at Kaukara Fragiskaki on Naxos.[146] Fourth-century Attic has also been found at Koressos and Ayia Irini on Keos.[147]

Wine was exported in amphoras from both Paros and Naxos beginning in this period. The earliest Type I Parian amphoras appear to have had a production run from the late fourth through early third centuries.[148] Amphora workshops on Paros and Naxos have been excavated, with one of the Parian and two of the Naxian production sites dated to the late fourth century.[149] These workshop sites are all located close to the sea, implying that they were primarily directed towards production for export.[150] Some of the Parian amphoras are included in finds from the famous Kyrenia shipwreck discovered near Cyprus. This wreck has yielded a large number of amphoras that may indicate trade patterns in the eastern Aegean.[151] Some eleven different amphora types were identified, the most common being Rhodian but also specimens from Samos and Paros. There were also grinding stones that could have come from islands such as Kos, Melos, or Thera.[152] While the presence of these goods does not guarantee that

143 Tsetskhladze 2008*b*, 52.

144 Stewart and Martin 2005, 87 and 89–90.

145 For general discussion of this pattern (with references) see Erickson 2005, 637–8.

146 Bikakis 1985, 227–44 and 254–6 on Kaukara Fragiskaki, identified by inscriptions as the location of a *hieron* to Demeter.

147 Sutton 1991, 250–2; Butt 1977, 311–13.

148 Whitbread 1995, 224–9 (quote on 224). Whitbread does not discuss Naxian amphoras in his study.

149 Empereur and Picon 1986, 504 and 508–9.

150 Garlan 1999, 380.

151 Whitbread 1995, 23 and 224–33; Swiny and Katzev 1973.

152 Swiny and Katzev 1973, 353.

this particular ship had stopped at all of these islands, it does indicate a level of demand for the products of different locales such as Paros.[153] The wreck has been dated to the late fourth/early third century, as two Antigonid coins were found and give the wreck a *terminus post quem* of *c.*306.

Parian marble continued to be a viable export product in the second half of the fourth century. Several quarries on the island were apparently still being exploited during this period, and may have been state-owned due to the finds of *horoi* similar to those attested for the Penteli quarry in Attica.[154] Sarcophagi of Parian marble become common again in Etruria and Carthage during the second half of the fourth century.[155] There are also possible late fourth-century objects crafted from Parian marble at Olympia[156] and Epidauros.[157] It should also be noted that many other Cycladic islands had marble quarries, even if only on a small scale, and these could have provided additional sources of income.[158] We have seen that trade in *miltos* from Keos continued in the fourth century, albeit with restrictions. And while it is probable that some former mineral resources, such as gold and silver on Siphnos and iron from Keos, were not as abundant at this time, they may still have been exploited to a lesser degree.[159] It has also been theorized that islands such as Amorgos and Keos were centres for the reweaving of silk imported from the east.[160]

153 Swiny and Katzev 1973, 357–8.

154 Schilardi 2000*b*, 53.

155 Berranger-Auserve 2000, 103.

156 Herrmann 2000, 389. A memorial fashioned from Parian marble to Ptolemy II and Arsinoe was placed there *c.*270, but the identification of the material used for the Philippeion and the Echo Colonnade (both from the third quarter of the fourth century) remains controversial.

157 Peppa-Papaioannou 2000, 372. Inscriptions relating to the temple and the tholos (*c.*360–320) mention two Parian sculptors, Thrasymedes (who among other objects was responsible for the cult statue to Asklepios, and was paid 9,800 drachmae, more than any other craftsman at the sanctuary) and Sannion. The accounts of the Hieromnamones also mention supplies from Paros.

158 Renfrew and Peacey 1968, 65–6 list three quarries on Antiparos (at Soros, Marmora, and Despotikon); two on Keros; one on Syros; two on Siphnos (at Kamares and Aspropyrgos); two on Keos (at Kephala and A. Joannis); and one on Skyros. The fame of the Parian sculptors Skopas and Satyros at this time is also noteworthy (Lattimore 1997, 260–2).

159 Reger 1994*a*, 20 gives a bleak assessment, but then on p. 42 mentions possible residual silver on Siphnos in the Hellenistic period.

160 Miller 1997, 77 and n.100. For Amorgos and the famous 'Amorgian chitons' see Richter 1929. For silk from Keos see Gansiniec 1973.

In the discussion of trade routes during the fifth century, the Athenian need for grain as a potential driving force for all commerce was advanced,[161] and this topic should now be addressed for the mid-fourth century. An important inscription (which has been variously dated to the late 330s to early 320s) lists substantial grain distributions from Kyrene in North Africa to several Aegean and mainland cities.[162] From the Cyclades, the list includes Kythnos (line 25), Paros (line 29), and Ioulis, Karthaia, and Koressos on Keos (lines 45, 51, and 55 respectively). Tenos has been tentatively restored for line 15.[163]

The distributions might have occurred during the Aegean War itself, motivated by the desire of Alexander to ensure the loyalty of the said communities.[164] Yet the presence of the Persian fleet in the Aegean during that war could have made such shipments difficult.[165] Whatever the date of the inscription, it is important potential documentation for trading routes through the Cyclades. While the recipient cities do not appear to be listed on the stone in geographic order, if they are plotted on a map we see a familiar network emerge, leading from the eastern Aegean to Attika (see Figure 6.1). This hypothetical route passed from Rhodes to Kos, Astypalaia, Thera, Paros, Tenos, Kythnos, Keos, Aigina, and finally Athens.[166]

The presence of Rhodes as one of the termini of this route indicates that this island was taking on a more pivotal role in these years in the

[161] See Chapter 4, pp. 104–5.

[162] Rhodes and Osborne 2003 #96 (= Tod 1962, #196); Bresson 2000, 135–7, who considers it not an actual distribution but a grant of 'export rights' to these cities; Brun 1993*b*; Engen 2010, 302–3.

[163] All line numbers are from Rhodes and Osborne #96. The reading of Tenos on the inscription is controversial: Reger 2004, 777 for discussion. Interestingly, there is an entry for 'Keians' (line 53) that is separate from the listings for Karthaia (line 51), Koressos (line 55), and Ioulis (line 45) on that island.

[164] Kingsley 1986, 169–75, followed by Engen 2010, 302.

[165] Brun 1993*b*, 190. Isager and Hansen 1975, 204–5. Although Brun's argument is persuasive, there is reason to doubt that the inscription is later than 330. Perhaps the distributions began after Pharnabazos left Siphnos in 332? Yet the absence of Siphnos on the stele would then be harder to explain, since it might have required a grain shipment after being fined and garrisoned.

[166] See the routes detailed in Chapter 2 for similarities. Horden and Purcell 2000, 59–74 see this text as indicative of the normal pattern of grain distribution from Kyrene to these locales. Previous ties between Kyrene and Athens are indicated by *IG* II^2 176 (mid-fourth century) which shows a grant of proxeny to certain Kyrenians who rendered assistance to Athenians in their city. It is possible, though by no means certain, that grain could have been part of this assistance: Rhodes and Osborne 2003 #96, p. 491.

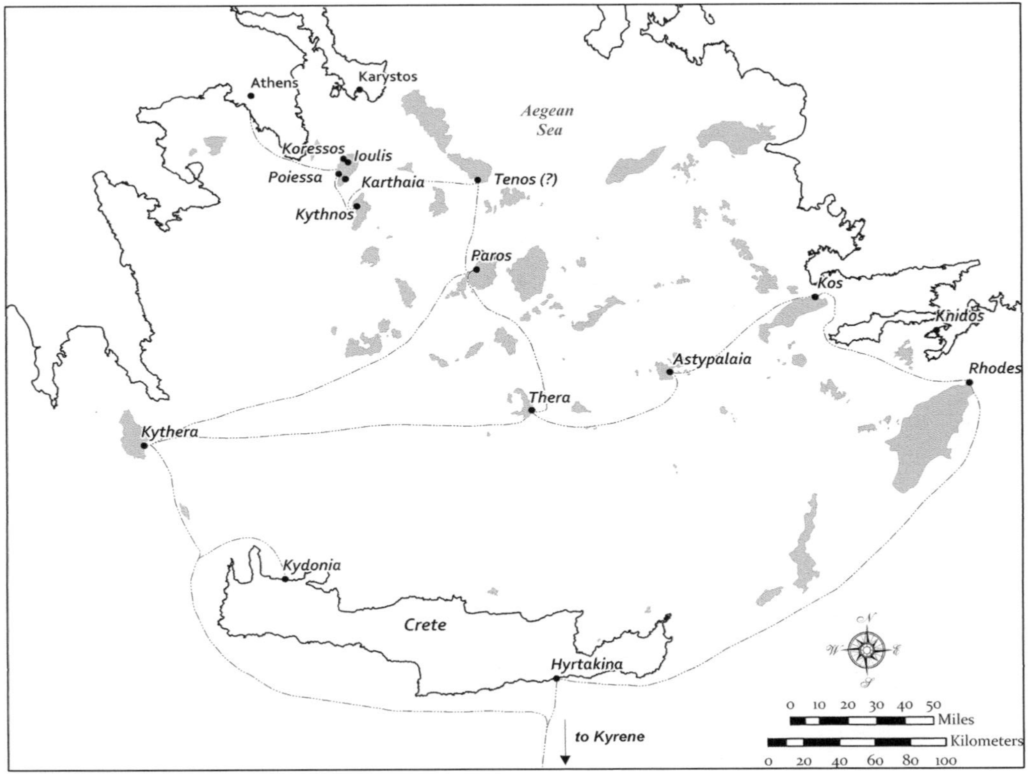

Fig. 6.1. Possible Trade Routes Based On Cities Listed in the Kyrene Grain Inscription.

grain trade, and this inscription is not our only evidence for this phenomenon.[167] In 338, grain merchants intending to sail to Athens were blocked by the Rhodians from leaving port.[168] At some point in the 320s, Demosthenes prosecuted merchants who had put in at Rhodes after contracting to bring Egyptian grain to Athens.[169] As we move into the 320s, the epigraphic evidence continues to grow for the increasing dependence of Athens on grain shipments from the south and east,[170] which would have put the Cyclades in an increasingly important position for shipping. Most of the inscriptions in question cannot be precisely dated but can be placed with some confidence in this decade.[171] One honours a merchant from Kos who, with the assistance of Athenian klerouchs and merchants from Samos, assisted the city during a shortage.[172] Similar honours were given to a Sidonian merchant.[173] A Milesian merchant appears to have been instrumental in bringing grain ships from Cyprus.[174] As mentioned above, in 325/4 one Heraklides of Salamis on Cyprus was honoured in the inscription *IG* II^2 360 for bringing in grain and selling it at a reasonable price in 330/29 (lines 8–10, 29–31) and for contributing money for the food supply in 328/7 (lines 11–12 and 70).[175] A Kyzikene was similarly honoured in 321/0,[176] and late in the 320s an unknown individual supplied wheat from Asia Minor.[177] It seems to have become more and more important for Athens to diversify its supply portfolio to ensure that its population would be fed.[178] It is curious, however, that more than one important study of the grain trade downplays the significance of the southern grain route

[167] Brun 1993*b*, 190–1.

[168] Lycurg. *Leoc.* 1.18–19.

[169] [Dem.] 56.9. An honorary decree for five Rhodians who assisted Athens during a grain shortage (*SEG* XXX.65), at first dated to the years 330–326, may actually date to the early third century: Tracy 1995, 35.

[170] Moreno 2007, 302 and 340–1.

[171] Descat 2004, however, downplays the idea that the decade of the 320s was marked by major shortages, instead proposing that grain prices had risen gradually higher after 335, as a 'conjuncture' of the grain market in the Aegean.

[172] *IG* II^2 416b.

[173] Schwenk 1985, #84 (= Tod 1962, #196).

[174] *IG* II^2 407.

[175] Tracy 1995, 31.

[176] *IG* II^2 401.

[177] Engen 2010, #29 (= *IG* II^2 398a + 438 = *SEG* XL.78); Walbank 1987, 10–11.

[178] Hunt 2010, 38–9, however, stresses that Athens was facing more severe limitations in what she could do militarily in the fourth century to ensure grain supplies.

to Athens.[179] A merchant from Cyprian Salamis in the late 340s/early 330s brought both Egyptian grain as well as some ransomed Athenian captives from Sicily,[180] and in 332/1 grain was indeed brought from Sicily to Athens, but by two merchants from Tyre.[181] Presumably those who dealt in grain could have operated in more than one region. It is perhaps best to interpret the evidence as indicating that the southern/eastern route was just one of several that Athens was beginning to seriously depend on by the 320s, but one that is as well documented as any other.[182]

It is interesting to note that, despite the evidence of the Sidonian merchant mentioned above, there may have been a shift in trade routes away from the Phoenician cities of the Levant at this time (in contrast to the situation in the first half of the fourth century). A recent study of Classical Phoenicia has noted that after experiencing major economic growth in the first half of the fourth century, many of its communities began to see a decline in the second half.[183] While it is beyond the scope of this work to address the validity of this thesis, it may require some qualification, considering the aforementioned rise in Attic pottery imports in the late fourth to Dor.

For the Cyclades themselves, we have epigraphic evidence (other than the Kyrene inscription) of their own dependence on grain imports, at least periodically. Andros apparently offered incentives to merchants bringing grain to their polis, and Arkesine on Amorgos also honoured traders for this activity.[184] It is interesting to speculate whether any of the Cycladic *poleis* took more strenuous steps to ensure supplies, perhaps methods such as those seen in the Teian grain law from the fifth century, which shows the type of situation that could be faced by smaller states in the Aegean during the

[179] Garnsey 1988, 152–3; Moreno 2007, 322–3 stresses the continuing importance of the klerouchies on Lemnos, Imbros, and Skyros, as well as the new level of imports from the Bosporan kingdom, and states that no 'systematic' method of importation from other locales was implemented. This may be true, but a lack of systematization does not necessarily mean a lack of activity.

[180] Engen 2010, #15 (= *IG* II^2 283); Reed 2003, #50; Garnsey 1988, 151 uses it to underscore the grain trade with Sicily but not Egypt!

[181] Engen 2010, #25 (= *IG* II^2 342 = *SEG* XXIV.104); Pečirka 1966, #2.

[182] The statement in Garnsey 1988, 152–3 that deliveries from Sicily, as opposed to Egypt, were regular and expected is based only on [Dem.] 56.7–8, a source that he describes earlier in the same paragraph as 'tendentious'(!)

[183] Jigoulov 2010, 105–10, focusing primarily on issues of coinage as an indicator.

[184] Andros: *IG* XII.5, 714; Arkesine: *IG* XII.7, 11; Bissa 2009, 197.

Classical period.[185] Yet, the very location of the Cyclades on well-travelled routes for grain ships might have made conditions easier.

A *proxenos* was recognized as the representative of a foreign *polis* to the people of his own community. Many discussions of this institution have emphasized the political and elite nature of these grants, while downplaying any possible economic motivations on the part of the awarding cities.[186] Nevertheless, while economic factors may not have been primary in all cases, it would be misleading to discount them completely.[187] In the case of Athens, awards of proxeny to coastal and island states began to increase in the fourth century,[188] and both Athens and other *poleis* gave these awards to *emporoi* and *nauklēroi* in the second half of this century.[189] It would appear that by the mid-fourth century the institution had some relation to the promotion of commerce.[190] Merchants and metics who received them were particularly instrumental in helping with the grain supply of Athens.[191]

A list from the Keian *polis* of Karthaia of individuals in foreign states who had received grants of *proxenia*, generally dated to *c.*350,[192] lists several other Cycladic communities: Tenos (line 45), Syros (line 46), Seriphos (line 48), Delos (line 49), and Andros (line 4, right side). Eretria (line 8) is the only extant Euboian city, although the text is fragmentary and others are certainly possible. States from the coastal area of Asia Minor are also represented, namely Kyzikos (line 54), Tenedos (lines 50 and 52), and Knidos (line 26). Aristophon,

185 Meiggs and Lewis 1989, #30, lines 6–12. The exact purpose of this law is still conjectural, with most scholars seeing it as a response to a particular crisis: Bravo 1983; Jameson 1983. However, Bissa 2009, 199–202 argues that the city 'legislated negatively' over its citizens and metics to avoid shortfalls.

186 Marek 1984, 332–85; Reger 1994*a*, 65–75; Herman 1987, 137–42; Gerolymatos 1986.

187 Culasso Gastaldi 2004 and 2005 discuss the increasingly economic nature of such decrees into the fourth century, especially those bestowed by Athens on individuals from eastern Aegean states; Engen 2010, 146–55 also emphasizes the practical benefits to those awarded with *proxenia* by Athens.

188 Out of 54 grants datable to the fourth century, island/coastal cities predominate over mainland ones in a ratio of 2 to 1; Marek 1984, 9; Burke 1992, 206 n. 31; Culasso Gastaldi 2004.

189 There are five known instances of this practice: Marek 1984, 359–61; Burke 1992, 206–7.

190 Burke 1992, 207; Hopper 1979, 113–17.

191 Engen 2010, *passim*; Culasso-Gastaldi 2004 and 2005.

192 *IG* XII.5, 542; Brun 1989, 125–6.

the Athenian *stratēgos* who suppressed the second revolt on Keos and proposed the regulations for Ioulis, also appears on line 43. Aristophon was prosecuted (unsuccessfully) by Hypereides in connection with misdeeds on Keos after the rebellions of the late 360s, which apparently included profiteering.[193]

Two Thracian cities are mentioned, Ainos (line 23) and Maroneia (line 60). Moving westward from Keos, Aigina (line 24), Sparta (line 18), Pellana (line 20) and Kyphanta (line 21) in Lakonia, Thebes (line 27) and Lebadeia (line 25) in Boiotia, and Corinth (line 14) are included. There are strong similarities between this inscription and a list of proxenies from the small island of Anaphe in the Sporades, dated to the later fourth century, although the more specific honours restored for the Karthaian decree (see below) are missing from this latter list.[194]

Considering the location of the foreign states listed in the Karthaian inscription, such as Knidos on the east–west route through the Aegean and Tenedos on the northern grain route to the Bosporos, this decree may indicate that Karthaia participated in commercial activity along these shipping lanes. Many fourth-century proxeny decrees from Knidos, for example, give *proxenoi* the rights of sailing in and out of the harbour (*espleo* and *ekpleo*) without paying tolls (*asyli*),[195] and this same grant of rights has been restored on the Karthaian decree.[196] The main problem is that we have little evidence for cabotage among the Cyclades, or between Cycladic islands and the Peiraeus. There are some scattered references to ferries, or *porthmeia*, on Rheneia and Mykonos, probably connected to the Delian sanctuary in some capacity.[197] A recent discussion of cabotage has distinguished between direct routes as opposed to routes of redistribution, so that finding goods in a certain archaeological location whose place of origin can be determined does not automatically indicate a direct

[193] Hyp. 3.28 and Schol. Aiskhin. 1.64; Cooper 2008*a*, 44–7, who proposes that Aristophon's award of *proxenia* from Karthaia (*IG* XII.5, 542, line 43) may have been connected to such profiteering.

[194] *IG* XII.3, 251; Berranger-Auserve 2000, 109–10; Reger 2004, 735; Lanzilotta 1987, 150. This Anaphaian document mentions connections in the Cyclades with Paros (Kallignetos and Lysagoras at line 15) and Mykonos (line 9).

[195] Blümel 1994, 157–8 (lines 6–8: *καὶ ὑπάρχεν α[ὐτοῖ]ς ἔσπ[λο]υν ἐ[ς Κνίδον καὶ ἔκπλουν]*; Blümel 1992, 1–9; Buckler 2008*b*, 202–5.

[196] *IG* XII.5, 542, line 4: *[λειαν πάντων καὶ ἐσπλέοσι καὶ ἐκπλέο]σι.*

[197] Constantakopoulou 2002, 225 and n. 9; 2007, 176–227, with references.

trade connection between these two points.[198] Since the Peiraeus could be a destination in and of itself (as for grain convoys that supplied Athens), as well as a central hub of redistribution, it could perhaps be characterized as both types of port.

Another type of grant to citizens of foreign states that was used increasingly in Athens during the fourth century was the award of *enktēsis*, which allowed such individuals to own property in the Athenian *polis*. Of the approximately forty awards of *enktēsis* in the fifth through fourth centuries, approximately half were awarded between 355 and 322.[199] Moreover, many of these later Athenian awards were to individuals connected with the grain trade, including citizens of communities on the aforementioned southern/eastern grain route such as Tyre, Sidon, Salamis on Cyprus, and Naukratis.[200] It is significant that the term *enktēsis* has also been restored within the text of the Karthaian proxeny decree.[201]

The increasing connectivity and economic integration of the Cyclades with both Athens as well as the eastern and southern Aegean sailing routes can be seen most dramatically in the case of Tenos. As described in Chapter 5, the *polis* of Tenos had suffered considerably when Alexander of Pherai seized the island and reduced its inhabitants to slavery during the archonship of Molon in 362/1.[202] Archaeological and epigraphic evidence indicates that by the middle of the fourth century the *polis* had been re-established on a new site on the island and soon developed into a fairly prosperous settlement, augmented by the turn of the century by the nearby temple of Poseidon and Amphitrite.[203] The refounded city centre was near the southern coast of the island at the modern-day bay of San Nicolo,

[198] Nieto 1997, 153–5.

[199] Engen 2010, 192–7; Burke 1992, 209; Pečirka 1966, 122–30, 152–6.

[200] Tyre: see n. 181 above; Sidon: *IG* II^2 34; Salamis: *IG* II^2 360; Naukratis: *IG* II^2 206; Burke 1992, 209; Engen 2010, 65–6. Earlier connections between Sidon and Athens are indicated by Rhodes and Osborne 2003, #21 (= *IG* II^2 141) which is undated but probably falls in the early 370s. This honorary decree specifically mentions privileges for Sidonian merchants who visit Athens, including exemption from the tax on metics and from the *eisphora* (lines 29–36).

[201] *IG* XII.5, 542 line 5: [πολέμωι καὶ γῆς ἔγκτησιν καὶ πρόσοδο]ν.

[202] See Chapter 5, pp. 181–2.

[203] Etienne 1990, 11–30 for a general discussion of the topography of Tenos and the foundation of the new city. There may have been some smaller settlement near the southern coast during the Archaic period, but on a different site than the later *astu* (cf. 20 n. 27).

while the older settlement had been located further inland at Xombourgo (See Figure 6.2).

An inscription from the late fourth century clearly differentiates between the newer town (*astu*) and the older one (*polis*).[204] The tribes of the Tenians may have been reorganized in accordance with the new settlement as well.[205] The defensive walls erected around the *astu* appear to have been built during the mid-fourth century, since the construction style shows no influence of late fourth-century siege techniques.[206] The older Geometric and Archaic site at Xombourgo does not show any remains past the fourth century, so it appears to have fallen out of habitation some time after the creation of the *astu*.[207] However, the *chōra* continued to be exploited heavily after the creation of the new city.[208]

Another strong indicator of the dynamic recovery of Tenos later in the fourth century is a list of property transactions from the end of the century which shows extensive exploitation of the countryside. This registry of land sales and dowry gifts details forty-five individuals making some forty-seven transactions, with over 70,000 drachmas changing hands, and twenty-three toponyms are listed, although various locations have been proposed for them.[209] Most of the holdings mentioned in the inscription have the appearance not of residences, but of farms outside the villages of residence of the owners.[210] A similar situation may have existed at Karthaia on Keos around the same period, where a stele listing private land leases has yielded some ninety individuals involved in 181 transactions, with over two talents worth of land involved.[211]

Although the harbour of Tenos is generally considered to be inferior to others in the Cyclades,[212] it has been suggested that the decision to move the city centre closer to the sea may have been

[204] *IG* XII.5, 872, line 90.

[205] Etienne 1990, 45–7; Reger 2004, 777.

[206] Garlan 1974, 183–200 and 244–69; Etienne 1990, 21 n. 29; Brun 1996, 147 dates them to no earlier than the beginning of the fourth. Earlier studies dated the wall to the sixth century: Graindor 1910, Fiehn *RE* s.v. *Tenos* col.509.

[207] Etienne 1990, 22.

[208] Etienne 1990, 24.

[209] *IG* XII.5 872; Brun 1996, 153–4; Etienne 1990, 51–75 notes that the price of houses on Tenos equaled those in Athens during the same period; Psarras 1994.

[210] *IG* XII.5 872; Osborne 1987, 72–3; Chankowski 2008, 361–2 and 369.

[211] *IG* XII.5, 544, 1075, 1076; Osborne 1988, 319–22.

[212] Etienne 1990, 15–24.

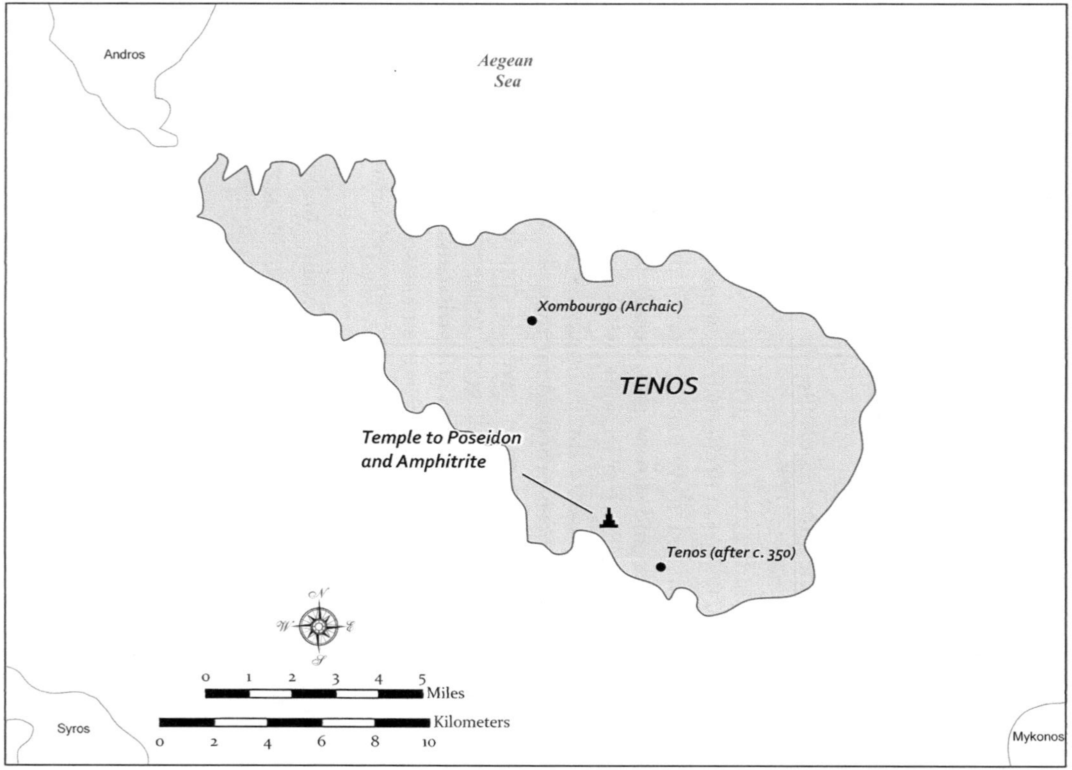

Fig. 6.2. Map of Tenos.

motivated by the possibilities of greater engagement in maritime commerce.[213] Although the northern bay at Panormos is superior in many respects, the southern coast is preferable to the northern due to the intensity of the north winds during the prime sailing season.[214] The placement of the new port on the southern coast put it squarely on the route from the east that also passes close to Paros and Naxos. The subsequent growth of the new *astu* would seem to indicate that the Tenians had made the correct decision. In addition, the new sanctuary of Poseidon and Amphitrite was established a few kilometers from the *astu* around the same time, and prospered into the early Hellenistic period.[215]

It is intriguing to note that this same phenomenon of coastal resettlement also appears at several other eastern Mediterranean locales during both the Classical and the Hellenistic periods. The *metoikion* between the two pre-existing *poleis* of Astypalaia and Kos Meropis on the island of Kos in 366/5, though of course not an exact parallel, can still provide an important comparison with the relocation on Tenos.[216] Although there has been debate on the issue, it seems clear that the two Koan communities were separate *poleis* before this event, which was a true political unification.[217] The older site continued to be used for ritual purposes.[218] Diodorus states that the population of Kos moved to the new centre and constructed walls and a harbour, and thus prospered economically. Pseudo-Skylax mentions an artificial harbour as well.[219] Excavation of the site of Kos Meropis shows that the fourth-century *agora* was also situated near the coast.[220] Export of Koan wine to the Black Sea region is first mentioned in the late fourth century in a speech in the Demosthenic corpus, but later during the Hellenistic and Roman periods it is mentioned in several literary sources, and the extent of its trade is evident from archaeological finds of stamped amphora handles.[221]

213 Etienne 1990, 21. 214 Etienne 1990, 14–15.

215 Etienne and Braun 1986; Strabo 10.5.11 C487.

216 Diod. 15.76.2; Strabo 14.2.19 C657.

217 Sherwin-White 1978, 63–7; Demand 1990, 127–32; Reger 2004, 753; Constantakopoulou 2005, 13. For a contrary view see Stylianou 1998, 484–5. Thuc. 8.41.2 mentions Kos Meropis in the context of events in 411.

218 Sherwin-White 1978, 62.

219 Diod. 15.76.2; [Skylax] 99 (*c*.350).

220 Morricone 1950, 54–75; Sherwin-White 1978, 24–5.

221 [Dem.] 35. 32, 35 for the fourth century; Sherwin-White 1978, 236–41 lists references for the Hellenistic and Roman periods.

We can also find parallels on Crete. Several new foundations on the southern coast of Crete *c.*400 (Hierapytna, Lisos, Biennos, Lasaia, and Ampelos) may have been done to take advantage of shifting trade patterns after the collapse of the Athenian *arkhē*.[222] This phenomenon can be seen during the Hellenistic period as well.[223] The absorption of inland Oleros by coastal Hierapytna in the late second century led to the near-disappearance of the former in the epigraphic record, although archaeological evidence indicates that it continued as a settlement.[224] The creation of a second coastal enclave by the inhabitants of Lato during the third century, known as Lato at Kamara, resulted for the most part in the eclipse of the older community although it continued to exist.[225] A similar economic interpretation has been advanced for the creation of this new harbour, which may have generated sufficient wealth for the citizens of Lato to begin the minting of coinage.[226] Another example is the *sympoliteia* of Lyktos and Chersonasos in the early second century, leading the latter to be designated as 'Lyktos by the Sea.'[227] The former settlement, now known as Upper Lyktos, continued as an active centre and both communities appear in agreements with foreign states, although the new harbour town never appeared in such documents on its own.[228]

Comparison with the situation of the *poleis* of Lesbos during the Classical and Hellenistic periods might also prove instructive. The cities of Hiera, Pyrrha, and Arisbe, all situated in the interior of the island and all possessing good agricultural territory, were nevertheless eclipsed politically and economically by Methymna and Mytilene, coastal *poleis* that were well poised to take advantage of shipping routes down the length of Ionia. These commercial axes were apparently so crucial, especially in terms of harbours that were protected from adverse winds, that communities on the opposite coast like Antissa and Eresos did not prosper.[229]

[222] Perlman 2000, 120; for some notes of caution, see Erickson 2005, 651 and n. 228.

[223] Brulé 1978, 148–56.

[224] Perlman 2004, 1166 and 1995, 134 and 139.

[225] Perlman 2004, 1173 and 1995, 133; Chaniotis 1996, 104–8.

[226] Brulé 1978, 154.

[227] Perlman 2004, 1176 with references; van Effenterre 1948, 97 and nn. 10–11.

[228] Perlman 1995, 132–3.

[229] Bresson 2000, 101–8. Similar motivations have been adduced for the foundation of the *astu* of Thasos at the extreme north end of that island. Brunet 2000, 187–8 suggests that it was done mainly to promote the export of local wine.

This phenomenon is important for an overall understanding of the ancient economy, since here we have evidence of activity that was in direct opposition to certain statements from famous Athenian philosophers. In the *Laws*, Plato puts into the mouth of the Stranger a view that considered sea access as detrimental to the well-being of a community, since a port 'infects a place with commerce and the money-making that comes with trade'.[230] Aristotle considered ports a necessary evil so that a *polis* could import necessities that it could not produce from its own territory. Yet he feels that safeguards should be put in place to stop the port from becoming a centre of *entrepôt* trade, which could harm the morals of the citizenry.[231] Judging from the many examples cited above, however, perhaps these philosophers have been taken as too representative of general Greek attitudes by modern historians.

No ancient source mentions the relocation of the Tenian *polis* or its eventual prosperity, but this is also true of the Hellenistic Cretan cities. The extraordinary set of circumstances on Tenos in the later fourth century remains largely ignored in modern scholarship.[232] The leading study in English of the phenomenon of urban relocation in Greek history, for example, describes several island *synoikismoi* but fails to mention the relocation on Tenos.[233] That study proposes that movement of a *polis* centre was generally done in response to external threats or pressure. Mausolos exerted such pressure on Kos in 366/5.[234] But it should be kept in mind that the Tenians, after a seaborne attack by Alexander of Pherai, responded by moving their city *closer* to danger.[235] However, they were also moving closer to economic integration with the rest of the Aegean. And there may be another Cycladic example from roughly the same period—the

[230] Pl. *Leg.* 4.705a.

[231] Arist. *Pol.* 1327a 25–31; Meikle 1995, 100.

[232] Brun 1996, 147 is one of the few commentators to draw attention to it.

[233] Demand 1990.

[234] Demand 1990, 129; Hornblower 1982, 104. Strabo 14.2.19 C657 states that it was due to *stasis*. Demand 1990, 167–9 stresses the possible negative effects of such relocation, such as disruption of food supplies.

[235] Brun 1996, 147. This is also applicable to Kos Meropis, vulnerable to attacks from the coast of Asia Minor. Sherwin-White 1978, 65–8 and 71–2 sees the relocation as essentially democratic and designed to increase prosperity; Constantakopoulou 2005, 13 rightly stresses that such a relocation could only have succeeded with support from a majority of the island's population.

so-called Long Walls of Bryocastro on Kythnos, which connected the older acropolis with the sea, and that were built some time after the mid-fourth century.[236]

We do not know how many of the original inhabitants of Tenos were available to found the new settlement, or if they accepted settlers from other locales.[237] If prominent Athenians on occasion ransomed allied prisoners, as Androtion did while governor of Arkesine on Amorgos during the Social War,[238] then it is not unreasonable to speculate that the Tenians may have been assisted in this way, and this may have been the reason for Apollodoros' reference[239] to this otherwise-ignored event. We also know that certain Tenians who were resident in Attika received *isoteleia* during the second quarter of the fourth century, but we do not know if this is connected to the devastation and relocation.[240] One prominent Tenian, Bion, served as a dignitary for the Second Athenian League in mid-century.[241]

While it is not impossible that the Tenians could have rebuilt their prosperity without relocation of their city centre, the evidence of prosperity resulting from proximity to the coast cannot be dismissed. As such, it provides some of the best support for commercial prosperity in the Cyclades during the later fourth century. Perhaps the Tenians were one of the examples that the fourth-century author Ainias Taktikos had in mind in the *prooemia* of his work on urban defense. He states that sometimes when disaster befalls a community, 'the survivors may after some time restore their affairs to their former condition, like certain Greek peoples who, after being reduced to extremes, have re-established themselves'.[242]

[236] Mazarakis-Ainian 1993; see Brun 1996, 148–50 on other examples of settlement relocation in the Cyclades through the Ottoman period and their connections to commerce.

[237] Although caution is appropriate, a stray reference in Plutarch's *Life* of Timoleon may indicate that the Cycladic region could attract settlers. He is said to have returned during the 330s a large number of exiles to Akragas and Gela on Sicily, who had fled to Keos previously (Plut. *Vit.Tim.* 35).

[238] Rhodes and Osborne 2003, #51.

[239] [Dem.] 50.5.

[240] *IG* II^2 660; Pečirka 1966, 93–5.

[241] *IG* II^2 279; Lewis 1954.

[242] Aen. Tac. *Polior. prooemia* 4: *ἀλλ' οἵ γε λοιποὶ τὰ ὑπάρχοντα εἰς ταὐτό ποτε καταστήσαιεν ἄν, καθάπερ τινὲς τῶν Ἑλλήνων εἰς τὸ ἔσχατον ἀφικόμενοι πάλιν ἀνέλαβον ἑαυτούς.*

Piracy and Convoying

One of the clauses of the Peace of Philokrates of 346 involved a mutual agreement by Athens and Philip II of Macedon to suppress piracy.[243] Diodorus states that Philip II called for a general peace to be enforced by the members of the League of Corinth according to their military and naval capabilities.[244] There is evidence that Athens and other members of the League contributed warships at certain times.[245] Other provisions of the League have been preserved in the pseudo-Demosthenic oration *On the Treaty with Alexander*, delivered in 331/30, including the stipulation that members should sail the seas in freedom from any hindrance or from any compulsion to put into a harbour.[246] Some scholars have noted these maritime aspects of the idea of a 'Common Peace' and proposed that the Congress Decree, attributed by Plutarch to Perikles in the mid-fifth century, may actually be a fourth-century forgery which would more precisely fit this context.[247] The problem of the date of the Congress Decree may be unsolvable, but it must be admitted that its statements on security of shipping lanes do find more parallels in the mid-fourth century. In addition, a decree of Moirokles at Athens (undated, but mentioned in a speech of the 340s) fined the Melians for harbouring pirates.[248] Yet piracy, whether 'official' or not, could be used by both sides to damage the economy of their enemies, and denouncing piracy was useful for

[243] [Dem.] 12.2.

[244] Diod. 16.89.2.

[245] Plut. *Vit.Phok.* 16.5 on triremes from Athens; Tod 1962, #192, line 9 on triremes from Khios.

[246] [Dem.] 17. 8, 19; Ellis 1976, 299 n.136.

[247] First broached by Seager 1969, who proposes the time of the Peace of Philokrates. Bosworth 1971 retains some agnosticism but proposes that the time after the formation of the League of Corinth is a strong possibility. De Souza 1999, 30 is sympathetic. Those who continue to advocate for a Periklean date include Griffith 1978*b*; MacDonald 1982; Stadter 1989, 202–3.

[248] [Dem.] 58. 53, 56. It is not certain that this fine was ever actually collected, however. De Souza 1999, 39 and n. 61 downplays the significance of the decree; Gabrielsen 2001, 226. The Thasians are said to have broken the treaty in 341/0: [Dem.] 12.2. Two Athenian naval commanders who had kept booty from a captured ship in 355 had been investigated under the terms of a decree moved by Aristophon which authorized inquests into the affairs of anyone who held sacred or public funds: Dem. 24.11–12. Meidias, it has been pointed out, held an official position and thus cannot be categorized as a privateer during the Social War period: Dem. 21.173; McKechnie 1989, 107; Gabrielsen 2001, 226; Jackson 1973, 333 n.29.

purposes of propaganda. The speech of Demosthenes' ally Hegesippos *c.*342 concerning the dispute over the island of Halonnesos brings out the importance of political claims to control piracy.[249] It also raises some interesting issues of how the concept of Aegean islands as being under Athenian hegemony was still current in Athens.

Philip had seized the small island of Halonnesos after clearing it of pirates, probably in 342.[250] Halonnesos was not the only small Aegean island to have earned a reputation as a den of pirates at this time, as Myonnesos is another example.[251] Hegesippos spoke in response to a letter from Philip that included an offer to 'give' (*dounai*) Halonnesos to Athens.[252] Philip also made an offer to join forces with Athens to suppress piracy.[253] Hegesippos tells the Athenians to reject Philip's offer as the island had belonged to Athens in the first place, and Philip should in fact 'give it back' (*apodounai*).[254] In this speech Hegesippos explicitly compares Halonnesos to Athenian possessions such as Lemnos and Imbros. He also underscores the importance of perceptions of Athenian sea power, stating that if they could not preserve their island possessions without going into arbitration with a third party (as proposed by Philip), then they would also be forced to give up any pretensions as a land power. He portrays Philip's appeals to the Athenians to assist him in suppressing piracy as nothing more than a veiled attempt 'to corrupt the islanders and raise them in revolt against you'.[255]

Philip supposedly answered the charges of Hegesippos in a letter sent to the Athenians in 340.[256] This document states that the Peparethians had seized Halonnesos from Philip after the Athenians rejected his requests for arbitration, taking some members of the Macedonian garrison hostage. Philip also took the opportunity to complain about other provisions of the Peace of Philokrates broken

[249] [Dem.] 7; translation and commentary in Phillips 2004, 140–8; MacDowell 2009, 343–6; Hammond and Griffith 1979, 510–16. De Souza 1999, 38–9 feels that Athenian interests revolved more around the concept of *posing* as suppressors of piracy rather than actually achieving such goals.

[250] [Dem.] 12. 12–15. It is unclear which island was Halonnesos, and whether it was actually a *polis* or not: Ath. *Deip.* 6.223d–224b; Strabo 9.5.16 C436; Reger 2004, 733; MacDowell 2009, 343 n. 1 on three possible modern identifications.

[251] Aiskhin. 2.72. [252] [Dem.] 7. 2–8.

[253] [Dem.] 7. 14–16. [254] [Dem.] 7.6. [255] [Dem.] 7.14–15.

[256] [Dem.] 12; authenticity cautiously accepted by MacDowell 2009, 363–6, citing earlier debates; Phillips 2004, 181–6, who notes that despite questions of authenticity, it still preserves the Macedonian outlook of the time.

by the Athenians, including pirates based on Thasos that he claimed the Athenians had not suppressed.[257] In 340, Philip attacked Peparethos itself, and it was finally brought under Macedonian control in 338.[258] Philip may have been attempting to 'isolate and encircle' Athens through these activities.[259]

In contrast to the fifth century, we see more evidence of Athenian naval efforts to maintain maritime security in the fourth. The term for convoying of ships (παραπέμπω) appears in several contexts.[260] Warships were sent out to protect grain shipments from the Bosporos during the crises of 362.[261] In 335/4 a certain Diotimos was sent on an anti-piratical expedition,[262] and in 325/4 a colony was apparently established in the Adriatic to combat pirates there and secure commerce.[263] The continuing importance of protecting the food supply is shown by the reference to four Athenian quadriremes under the command of one Thrasyboulos, acting as grain escorts according to the naval inventory for 326/5.[264] Athenian commanders were sometimes open to prosecution for levying εὐνοῖαι, or 'benevolences,' the charging of merchants for fees for protection.[265] On such occasions the costs of escort could be considered a 'shakedown'.[266]

[257] [Dem.] 12.2–5.

[258] Dem. 18.70 with schol.; Strabo 9.5.16 C436.

[259] Brunt 1969, 262.

[260] Dem. 21.167–8, where Meidias is accused of leaving a convoy of grain ships from Styra to attend to personal business during his service as trierarch; Pritchett 1991, 331.

[261] [Dem.] 50.17–21; Dem. 18.77 on Leodamas' vessels, ostensibly sent as escorts for grain ships from the Hellespont; and 17.20–2 on Menestheos sent with a hundred triremes to Tenedos.

[262] *IG* II^2 1623 (= Tod 1962, #288), lines 276–80. The success or failure of his mission is still disputed: see De Souza 1999, 41. See also *IG* II^2 408 (*c*.330); Pritchett 1991, 331.

[263] Rhodes and Osborne 2003, #100 (= *IG* II^2 1629), lines 217–32; Cargill 1995, 31–4; Ober 2008, 124–33, who points out that the discrepancy in ship numbers shows that the expedition did in fact sail. No trace has been found of this colony archaeologically, however, and it is not known how long it lasted. It was the subject of two lost orations, one by Hypereides (F8 Loeb) and one by Demades (F6 Loeb); cf. Pritchett 1991, 339.

[264] *IG* II^2 1628 lines 37–42; Pritchett 1991, 338–9.

[265] Dem. 8.24–26, defending Diopeithes in 342 for ravaging Philip's territory, stating that Athenian generals had routinely taken such 'protection money' to provide escorts for shipping near the states of Asia Minor; MacDowell 2009, 346–9; Cawkwell 1981, 48; Burke 1984, 117 and n. 29.

[266] Lys. 19.50 on the extra 10 talents 'pocketed' by the commander Diotimos from merchants; Dem. 51.13–15 on corrupt trierarchs; Dem. 24 on the seizure of a ship from Naukratis; Aiskh. 2.71–2 on the seizure of a merchant ship by Khares.

While we do not have specific testimony on the convoying of grain ships through the Cyclades, given the aforementioned examples of grain ships coming from the eastern Mediterranean and Levant, it may simply be the case that no orations concerning problems on these routes have survived. As Demosthenes was mainly concerned with the threat posed by Philip to the Bosporan route, his focus on that source of supply is understandable. Moreover, Cycladic communities could have benefited from the usage of their harbours for grain convoys, without being liable for the aforementioned 'benevolences', which would have most likely been paid by merchants from outside the Cycladic region.

If convoying of grain ships became a fairly regular and repetitive practice, then it is likely that the use of certain routes and sailing times would have become ossified practice, further unifying cooperative commercial activity.[267] It is important to note that even if merchant vessels did not require frequent 'supply stops', the same cannot be said of the triremes that would have escorted them, and this would inevitably have led to logistical problems in convoying.[268]

How would such 'convoys' have been organized?[269] Again, an analogy with a different historical period may prove instructive here. In the late sixteenth century, the republic of Venice attempted to implement a system of regular patrols by naval galleys in their maritime empire. A total of twenty-nine galleys were employed in five 'zones' of patrol: the Gulf of Venice and Istria (two galleys along with three *fuste* or support vessels); the north Adriatic down to Ancona and Zara (four galleys); from Ancona to Brindisi (seven galleys of the so-called 'Gulf Squadron'); the Ionian Sea (twelve galleys using Corfu as their base); and from the Ionian Sea to eastern Crete (four galleys). On paper the Venetian navy also had over a hundred other warships in reserve, but there was no way to put this entire force to sea.[270]

[267] Dem. 21.167–8 implies regularity.

[268] [Dem.] 50.20–2 gives details on the towing of grain ships by triremes from Sestos in the Hellespont to Stryme in Thrace; Gomme 1933, 16–24; Casson 1971, 281–96; Wallinga 1993, 33–65; Stroud 1998, 49.

[269] For the Roman period, we have one reference in a letter of Seneca to the arrival of an Egyptian grain fleet at Puteoli, as well as the formation of an escort fleet for grain ships from Africa during the reign of Commodus (Rickman 1980, 129–30).

[270] Mallett and Hale 1984, 444–5; Tenenti 1967, 121; Crouzet-Pavan 2002, 84–5.

There was also a Venetian naval base on Tenos, which made use of the local inhabitants for guard duty and other labour.[271]

Aegean *poleis* probably expected that whoever claimed hegemony over the region had to at least *attempt* to control piracy. There is no reason to assume that total protection was required or even possible. What counted was that a naval power could protect some merchant ships under some circumstances, that a *reasonable* level of security could be provided, and that the psychological perception of a state as an effective *prostatēs* played an important role.[272]

COINAGE AND MONUMENTAL CONSTRUCTION IN THE LATER FOURTH CENTURY

There are two important economic factors that are once again apparent in the Cycladic region after the mid-fourth century, and both represent new manifestations of economic phenomena last seen in the region on a wide scale during the late sixth century. These are: (*a*) a broad pattern of a return of minting by Cycladic poleis; and (*b*) public monumental construction, particularly of temples but also of fortification walls, on several of the Cyclades, indicating a higher level of public investment in infrastructure.

As mentioned in Chapter 5,[273] Siphnos and Naxos (and perhaps Syros) had apparently struck coinage at some point in the early fourth century, and Naxian silver and bronze on the Rhodian standard continued to be minted throughout the century.[274] By the mid-to-late fourth century, local minting in the Cyclades appears on a wide scale for the first time since the late Archaic period. It must be emphasized that any conclusions drawn from these issues must remain tentative. All have been found in small numbers, and with the exception of the Keian issues these late Classical coinages of the Cyclades have not been subjected to extensive die studies.[275] But the

[271] Mallett and Hale 1984, 455.

[272] De Souza 1999, 40 takes the view that both the Athenians as well as Philip understood that island bases were necessary for attacking enemy shipping, and that this was of far more concern than any kind of protection. This is supported by Bresson 2000, 140.

[273] See Chapter 5, pp. 150–3.

[274] Nicolet-Pierre 1988.

[275] Brun 1996, 157.

similarity of phenomena here is striking, even if it may have occurred on different islands in different phases through the second half of the century.

The Parians began to mint their own silver again after 357, also on the Rhodian standard.[276] Ios also minted silver in the late fourth century.[277] Andros may have minted during the fourth century, but it is also possible that the surviving examples are Hellenistic.[278] The case of Keos is more complicated, as a die study has been undertaken but many aspects of the chronology remain unclear.[279] For the individual cities, it is clear that during the fourth century Ioulis and Karthaia minted both silver and bronze on the Attic standard,[280] but there are also several series of coinages by a Keian federation, of which the so-called Series I may belong to the early fourth-century federation (dissolved by the Athenians in the 360s), or a possible late fourth-century incarnation.[281]

Tenos minted silver much later, beginning about 315, and on the Attic standard.[282] Mykonos produced bronze coinage that either dates to the late fourth century or the Hellenistic period.[283] Yet there are also several Cyclades for which no fourth century coinage is known, including Seriphos and Kythnos, both of which minted in the late Archaic period.[284]

The return of large-scale production of Athenian coins in the second half of the fourth century (the so-called *pi* style) was mainly

[276] Reger 2004, 767, although Berranger-Auserve 2000, 109–10 would date this activity to post-338.

[277] Head 1991, 486; Reger 2004, 743.

[278] Reger 2004, 737. Nevertheless, a Tenian made a donation at the sanctuary of Trophonios in Lebadeia around 350 in 'Andrian silver' (*IG* VII, 3055 line 20); cf. Brun 1996, 157.

[279] Papageorgiadou-Banis 1997 is the study; but see the qualifications of Sheedy 1998 and Reger 2004, 748–51.

[280] For Ioulis: Head 1991, 484; Papageorgiadou-Banis 1997, 25–7; Reger 2004, 749. For Karthaia: Head 1991, 483; Papageorgiadou-Banis 1997, 34–9; Reger 2004, 750. The issues of Koressos may not have begun until the end of the fourth century: Head 1991, 483–4; Papageorgiadou-Banis 1997, 19–21; Reger 2004, 751.

[281] Papageorgiadou-Banis 1997, 43 would place Koinon Series I in the late fourth century. This is disputed by Sheedy 1998, 253–5, who would place them in the first half of the century. Reger 1998 collects other evidence for a possible late-fourth century federation, but this is not stressed in Reger 2004, 748.

[282] Head 1991, 493; Sippel 1986, 42; Etienne 1990, 225–38; Reger 2004, 778, reversing his earlier position in Reger 1994*a*, 42 n. 70.

[283] Head 1991, 487; Reger 2004, 760.

[284] See Chapter 3, p. 62 and n. 77.

due to a revival of the Laureion mines, although a new article proposes that there was also a program of recalling and reminting Athenian silver in the 350s.[285] As all these Cycladic coins have been found in small numbers, it may be that Attic silver (still found in large quantities at Delos and Delphi at this time) was more plentiful from the middle of the century onwards.[286] As an example, a recently excavated site of a marble workshop at Paroikia on Paros, tentatively dated to the late fourth/early third centuries, yielded eleven Athenian silver and fourteen Parian bronze coins.[287] Another is the small hoard found at Philoti on Naxos in 1963, a mixture of Naxian bronzes and Attic hemidrachms that appears to date from the end of the fourth century.[288]

However, to our knowledge Athens did not attempt to compel anyone to use its coins in the fourth century, even its own allies in the Second League.[289] Nothing is said of coins, weights, or measures in the League prospectus, and fourth-century authors such as Isokrates did not even mention the earlier fifth-century Standards Decree in their discussions of the old Athenian *arkhē*.[290] It is unknown whether coins or other monetary instruments such as bullion were used to pay *syntaxeis*.[291] The League of Corinth probably did not exercise any control over allied coinage either.[292]

The only published[293] Athenian decree concerning coinage from the fourth century is the famous law of Nikophon from 375/4, and whatever its exact nature and purpose, it arguably did not forbid the

[285] Kroll 2006 and 2011; van Alfen 2005.

[286] Brun 1996, 157. While other scholars have proposed that Attic silver circulated much less extensively in the fourth century than the fifth (Gauthier 1976, 79; Pečirka 1982, 122; Schonert-Geiss 1974), the proximity of the Cyclades to Athens and their location on trade routes probably negated that phenomenon.

[287] Efstratiou 2000, 107–8.

[288] *ADelt* 1964, Chronika, 10–11; Nicolet-Pierre 1988, 162.

[289] This is unsurprising, since during the Ptolemaic version of the Nesiotic League the Cyclades minted on the Rhodian standard, not the Ptolemaic (Reger 1994*a*, 12).

[290] Martin 1985, 206–7.

[291] Figueira 1998, 559–60; Sheedy 2006 thinks Xen. *Por.* 3.2 is unclear on whether or not merchants should acquire Athenian silver owls, or simply Athenian silver bullion.

[292] Martin 1985, 166–95 (*pace* Ellis 1976); Picard 1979, 252–3 on continuation of local coinages on Euboia after Chaironeia. The Euboian Confederacy had switched to the Attic standard after 357, however (ibid. 174–5).

[293] It will be intriguing to see what the forthcoming publication of an Athenian decree on coinage from 354/3 (*Agora* inv. 7495) by Richardson and Camp will add to this discussion.

use of non-Athenian coins for transactions in Athens.[294] It also would have driven up transaction costs for merchants if the Athenian state had mandated that imitations be exchanged for Athenian silver.[295]

The weight standards used for these fourth-century coinages in the Cyclades could also have facilitated transactions among merchants from both sides of the Aegean. Cycladic communities may have selected their minting standards at this time mainly to promote trade, as Histiaia may have done earlier in the fourth century.[296] It is interesting that during the later fourth century and early third centuries (*c*.330–280), several Cretan cities (Kydonia, Phalasarna, Rhithymna, Khersonasos, Olous, Hierapytna, Allaria, and Aptera) minted coins on the Rhodian standard as well.[297] It is unlikely that the choice of a standard other than the Attic in the Cyclades at this time was indicative of any kind of political break with Athens.

It is also intriguing to note yet another (later) period in Cycladic history that shares this economic characteristic. After minting nothing but local bronzes during most of the third century, starting *c*.230–220 several of these same Cycladic islands (Paros, Tenos, Naxos, and Andros) struck well-fashioned silver coins on the Rhodian standard,[298] and this activity has been proposed as a marker of increased prosperity.[299] Whether this is correct or not, what is more important is that it represents an economic phenomenon that was repeated at several times in antiquity in the Cyclades.

Monumental construction of temples and fortification walls had been other hallmarks of the late sixth century, and they also reap-

[294] Rhodes and Osborne 2003, #25. The literature on this decree is extensive. Stroud 1974 for first publication and the idea that it mandated the acceptance of good non-Athenian silver; Buttrey 1981 for a rebuttal; Martin 1985, 207; Engen 2005 and Ober 2008, 220–45 see the decree as mainly intended to promote trade. Ober proposes at 220 that the decree presents an example of economic rationalization prior to the end of the Social War.

[295] Ober 2008, 235.

[296] Wallace 1984, 25 and #28 and #29.

[297] Le Rider 1966.

[298] Bauslaugh 1979; Sheedy and Papageorgiadou 1998 propose that civic expenses such as fortifications spurred the need for such coins. There was also coinage from a revitalized Keian federation at this time: Head 1991, 482; Constantakopoulou 2005, 14 and n.94 and 95. Reger and Risser 1991, 305–15 propose that this incarnation of the Keian organization was modeled on the Aitolian federation.

[299] Reger 1994*a*, 42 and 262–3, who proposes that evidence of increased piracy in the area during this same period is also indicative of a high level of commerce.

pear.[300] Although precise dating is problematic, the temples include the Stoa of Palaiopolis on Andros, and a number of structures on Paros: the Asklepieion, the Marmara temple and temple of Apollo Pythios (actually begun earlier in the century but completed by 350), the Tholos, and the Archilocheion and 'Hestia' complex.[301] On Tenos, the first stage (E1) of the temple of Poseidon and Amphitrite dates from *c.*320–280, along with associated structures such as Building B and Hestiatorion Q.[302]

There had been no comparable temple building attested for the fifth century in the Cycladic region. It may be that Athenian tribute exactions made such ostentation impossible. The Naxian klerouchy has also been proposed as a hindrance to fifth-century construction there.[303] Yet the Naxians did not build during this later fourth century period either, so the presence or absence of a klerouchy apparently was not crucial.

Moreover, it should be noted that with the exception of Attika, temple construction all across the Greek world had come to a virtual halt in the fifth century, not just in the Cyclades. While a lack of temple construction cannot in itself indicate a lack of economic prosperity, one scholar has reversed this point, stating that a building program cannot in and of itself serve as an indicator of economic prosperity either.[304] Nevertheless, as has been conclusively shown for several instances of temple construction in ancient Greece, a large amount of funding was needed to pay for building materials and skilled workmen needed for such projects.[305] As has been proposed for Cycladic temple construction in the late sixth century, the need for coinage to make such payments might have spurred *poleis* like Paros and Tenos to mint coinage in various denominations, thereby leading to more monetized local economies. If it is correct that the Cyclades had been in need of liquid assets in the first half of the fourth century,

[300] Lodwick 1996, 242–5.

[301] Ohnesorg 2005, 149–50; Berranger-Auserve 2000, 101 refers to this as 'la reprise d'une grande activité de construction', and at 110 also cites the renewal of minting, calling both markers of increased prosperity on Paros.

[302] Etienne and Braun 1986, 188–92. There is also a late fourth-century gymnasion known from Amorgos.

[303] Lodwick 1996, 214–15.

[304] Osborne 1999, 323–7.

[305] Shipton 2000, 8–9; For the Parthenon and Propylaia in Athens: Meiggs and Lewis 1989, #59 and #165, yielding approximately 2000 talents; for wages: *IG* II^2 1672 and 1673. For Delphi in 360: Homolle 1902, 23, 105–15; Burford 1969.

this need may have abated by the second half as seen in the renewal of minting.

There is another type of monumental construction that had been active in the late sixth century in some of the Cyclades, which now appears on several more islands from the mid-to-late fourth century: the construction of *polis* fortification walls.[306] Andros, Kythnos, the new coastal centre on Tenos, and (possibly) Arkesine on Amorgos all had such structures either built or rebuilt during this period.[307] As mentioned in Chapter 5 there were fortifications built by Ioulis, Poiessa, Karthaia, and Koresia on Keos after the demolition of earlier walls by the Athenians in the late 360s.[308] It should be noted as well that other islands may have built walls that are unattested either in written sources or still undiscovered archaeologically.[309]

The (possible) beginning of construction of some rural towers on at least a few of the Cyclades in the late fourth century may indicate that many of these islands by this time had highly-populated country-sides that were being intensively exploited.[310] Although the exact dating and function of the towers remains controversial (they may have had more than one function), it is clear that their construction required a major outlay of capital.[311]

It must be kept in mind that the dating of monumental architecture is imprecise and that Lodwick's dates, though currently accepted by some,[312] must remain tentative. Such building activity, moreover, did not stop after the formation of the Antigonid Nesiotic League, It

306 On their economic significance see Brun 1996, 150–1.

307 For Andros: Sauciuc 1914, 10–16 and Reger 2004, 736 (though walls are mentioned in sources for the fifth century: Hdt. 8.112 and Diod. 13.69.4). For Kythnos and the so-called 'Long Walls' at Bryokastro: Mazarakis-Ainian 1996, 256–70 and 1998, 368–70; Gounaris 1998; Reger 2004, 756. For Tenos: Graindor 1910, 236–42; Etienne 1990, 15–18; Reger 2004, 778. For Arkesine: Brun 1996, 151 and Reger 2004, 735, though the visible remains are probably Hellenistic.

308 See Chapter 5, pp. 179–80.

309 The modern towns of Seriphos and Syros cover their remains (Reger 2004, 772 and 775); a small but undated section is known on Ios (Brun 1996, 149–50 and Reger 2004, 743).

310 Brun 1996, 116–17; Korres 2005, esp.192–4. Most appear to date from the Hellenistic period but several may have been constructed in the fourth century. Morris and Papadopoulos 2005, 171–4 describe a tower on Seriphos located near an iron mine with evidence of fifth-century workings. The tower at Drios on Paros was situated near a marble quarry (Rubensohn 1901).

311 Tausend 2006 for similar towers in the Argolid that may date to the fourth century.

312 Osborne 1999, 324.

continued on Delos and Tenos (and finally resumed on Naxos) into the early third century.[313] Further research on such construction in the Cyclades may help shed more light on island conditions during this period, as further die studies would for the coinage of the period.

One might object that such evidence as the temples, the coins, and the amphora workshops of Naxos and Paros are being compressed into a too narrow chronological framework. Yet, we are speaking of general economic trends over the course of several decades. None of these economic factors began or ended at the same time on all the islands of the Cyclades.

CONCLUSIONS

We have outlined several different testimonia for economic conditions in the Cyclades during the second half of the fourth century. In some ways (the production of local coinage and temple construction) the situation appears to resemble that in the late sixth century. Other aspects of that earlier period, however, are not necessarily evident, most notably warships in the Cyclades. What was mentioned above for decades after the end of the Peloponnesian War, however, would perhaps still have applied in this period, that it was simply not necessary or effective to build warships in the small numbers that Cycladic *poleis* could have, in an attempt to compete with greater naval hegemons such as Sparta, Athens, Thebes, or Persia. Once again, their central position offered the inhabitants of the Cyclades unique advantages (if also disadvantages).

Although dismissed by Aiskhines in 343 as a few 'wretched islanders',[314] a sentiment followed by some modern historians,[315] there are more intriguing economic possibilities for these communities during this period than at almost any other in antiquity. For the period 355–338, for example, Athens and the remnants of her League are often assumed to have limped along between the end of the Social

[313] Lodwick 1996, 216.

[314] Aiskhin. 2.71, 'ταλαιπώρους νησιώτας' speaking of events in 346 when sixty talents of *syntaxeis* came to Athens annually from these states. Although he does not use the term 'Cyclades' specifically, it is clear from the context.

[315] See e.g. Ceccarelli 1989, 935.

War and Chaironeia, the *synedrion* now a kind of 'Rump Parliament' bereft of its strongest and most influential members.[316] While this assessment is not completely false, it does not necessarily follow from it that the remaining islands of the League (of whom many were Cycladic) now amounted to nonentities, orators like Aiskhines notwithstanding.

A good parallel of a smaller Greek state that achieved economic prosperity in the fourth century despite its lack of political influence could be Megara. Megara is described by Isokrates in his oration *On the Peace* (355) as having followed a policy of *sophrosynē* or political moderation, with the result that the community had become wealthy from commerce.[317] He explicitly states that this success was achieved despite a lack of good agricultural resources in Megarian territory, which echoes his statement on the lack of productivity in the Cyclades during the 380s. Some of the best-known Megarian local products were woollen garments called *exōmides* or *chlamiskia,*[318] and this would provide a rough parallel to local Cycladic mineral products that could be exported at profit. The fourth century also saw the beginning of Megarian local silver coinage, despite their lack of precious metals.[319] Moreover, like the Cycladic states Megara did not build warships in the fourth century, even though she had once contributed twenty triremes to the battles of Artemision and Salamis.[320] Apart from a brief border dispute with Athens in 350/49,[321] the Megarians successfully stayed aloof from the political turmoil around them until the late 340s, when an attempted *coup* by supporters of Philip II led the Athenians under Phokion to reconstruct the Megarian Long Walls to the port of Nisaia.[322] Such a neutral political stance may have been more possible under the conditions of the mid-to-late fourth century than under those of the fifth.[323]

[316] 'Parlement Croupion' is the term used for this viewpoint in Brun 1983, 137, who also casts doubt on this interpretation.

[317] Isok. 8.117; Legon 1981, 264–5 and 278.

[318] Legon 1981, 87.

[319] Legon 1981, 282; Head 1991, 329–30.

[320] Artemision: Hdt. 8.1.1; Salamis: Hdt. 8.45.

[321] Philoch. *FGrH* 328 F155; Dem. 13.32; *Syll.*^{3} 204.

[322] Dem. 19.204, 326–34; Plut. *Vit.Phok.* 15.

[323] Bauslaugh 1991, 240–1.

At first glance, there is less of an effect traceable in Athenian relations with the Cyclades in the later fourth century. There were no klerouchies or Athenian officials stationed in the region (although we do not know when the garrisons on Andros and Amorgos were removed). The islands contributed to Athenian naval efforts through *syntaxeis* payments, but only until 338. There was no known Athenian attempt to control what types of coinage were used by the allies before 338 either. Nevertheless, there were some strong unifying factors. These islands and their harbours remained just as important for the Athenian fleet as they had been in earlier times, in order to maintain trade routes and safeguard especially the shipment of grain to Athens. The Athenian fleet had a presence until 322, although as the events of the late 360s and late 330s show it could not always guarantee safety. Many of the islands began to mint their own coins again, especially after 355. While they did not all follow the same standard, they were all compatible with the various trade standards on each side of the east–west route across the Aegean. When combined with the increasing need by Athens (and sometimes the Cyclades themselves) for grain from the Levant and Egypt, these would have been great stimuli to commerce. After 355 the steps taken by Athens to promote trade could have drawn more and more shipping through the Cyclades. The spate of new temple construction on several of the islands might indicate a new level of disposable income. Local products from the Cyclades were still in high demand, especially the Keian *miltos* that had its trade monitored by Athens or the marble of Paros that was once again shipped on a large scale to Italy and Sicily. Islands that had been on bad terms with Athens even in the early fourth century, such as Andros, Naxos, and Paros, were her firm allies after 355.

Raymond Descat has recently proposed that an economic 'conjuncture' of sorts occurred in the Aegean world in the second half of the fourth century, characterized by several factors such as increased monetization and a growth in the grain trade, along with an increased population and exploitation of landscapes.[324] The evidence of land use attested on Tenos and at Karthaia on Keos would also dovetail with what was seen in Attika at this time.[325] Increased monetization, of course, can be seen in the new Cycladic coinages. From 338 to 314

[324] Descat 2006, 357 (and 2004 on the grain trade).
[325] Descat 1987, 248.

the Aegean was a mainly peaceful area (with two brief exceptions in the Aegean War and the naval theatre of the Lamian War), but also an area that saw the presence of a numerically strong Athenian navy. This navy carried out anti-piracy expeditions while staying out of major conflicts until 322.

It could be tentatively proposed that the minting of coinage and the construction of temples and fortification walls could point to a growth in the public economies of Cycladic *poleis*. In the late sixth century, oligarchic shipowners may have been the main engines driving the public economies by controlling the shipping lanes in the region. In the fifth century, whether democratic or oligarchic, these cities may have seen revenues from commerce that they formerly controlled locally now redirected to Athens by means of tribute, the *eikostē*, or ad hoc exactions by military commanders. While it had been necessary to pay *syntaxeis* in the early fourth century and the heyday of the Second League, this would have also loosened in the second half of the fourth century. The period from 355 to 314 may have seen similar levels of commerce and economic integration between the Cyclades and Athens as in the decades of the fifth century prior to the outbreak of the Peloponnesian War, but without the same drain of resources to Athens. Hence, while the level of 'imperial' control of trade would have been less, the inducements of the Peiraeus and the benefits of payment for naval protection would have stayed at the same level. Thus, this situation may have come about by a more 'organic' process than in the fifth century.

In some ways it appears that certain aspects of an environment of peer-polity interaction, similar to that of the late Archaic period, could have returned to the region in the late fourth century. These aspects were not seen under the fifth-century Athenian *arkhē*, and (with the exception of coinage) also did not appear in the time of 'fluid hegemonies' of the early fourth century. All told, it may be that a specific combination of factors converged to create a 'good fit' between the interests of Athens and those of the Cycladic states at this time.

Conclusion

Throughout this study, we have examined evidence for economic conditions in the Cyclades islands at key periods in Greek antiquity. The aim has been to call into question the standard wisdom that after an apex of wealth and power in the late Archaic period, the islands fell under the oppressive hand of Athens in the fifth century Delian League, and then again in the fourth century under the Second Athenian League, subsequently sliding into irrelevance until the creation of the first Nesiotic League by the Antigonids. Although it is clear that Athens exerted a major influence on the region during her periods of hegemony, such hegemony need not have had a negative impact at all times, or in all circumstances.

Beginning *c.*540, we see signs in the Cycladic region of the minting of silver coinage, monumental construction of temples and fortifications, and the building and operation of warships. Such phenomena are attested on enough islands to be counted as signs of what has been termed 'peer-polity interaction'. The *poleis* of the region used wealth generated from commerce that plied trade routes through the region (and in some cases generated by the export of local resources) and displayed this wealth in various forms of ostentation. While such interaction may have had roots earlier in the Archaic period, it intensified due to changes in Greek naval warfare and the increasing involvement of outside powers such as the Samians. In the case of warships, it is likely that aristocrats on the islands played a major role by funding pentekonters (and later triremes) directly, although the possibility exists that on some islands such as Naxos there was eventually a greater level of state involvement in local navies. It has been proposed here that Cycladic islanders created local 'hegemonies' by using these warships to patrol local waters and even compel merchant ships to use their harbours in order to collect customs dues. The Naxians, however, were the only inhabitants of the Cyclades who had sufficient naval power to be enshrined in the tradition of Aegean thalassocrats. The Naxians may have been able to exploit a particular geographical advantage in that most routes through the Cyclades passed by their location. A possible parallel for Naxos can be seen in Thucydides' description of Kerkyra in the later fifth century, in which the inhabitants of that island may have had some control over shipping at the key crossing between the Greek mainland and Italy. Thucydides implies that Kerkyraian naval strength, coupled with a non-aligned political stance, represents a more ancient practice. The rest of the Cyclades would have exercised such local control on a much smaller scale, and this might be seen in the small numbers of Cycladic warships attested during naval operations in the Second Persian War in 480.

With the enrolment of the Cyclades in the Delian League, conditions changed dramatically. Local operation of warships in the Cyclades came to an end as the Athenian fleet grew in power in the Aegean. Local Cycladic minting also ceased, although it is unclear whether this was due to Athenian compulsion, or to a more organic process whereby Athenian silver owls came to dominate exchange. Trade routes through the Cyclades appear to have grown in importance, but the new reality was that the Athenians were in a position to appropriate some of the increased wealth generated by their hegemony through tribute payments and later, harbor taxation. As long as they remained loyal to Athens, the islanders received protection in return, and a tradition of the region being under outside hegemony was now firmly established into the Hellenistic period.

It is possible that islands that had medized, or that had resisted incorporation into the Delian League in one way or another, were treated in a more negative fashion for many decades later. It is also possible that some of the Cyclades revolted (along with Euboia) in the 440s, and this may have given the Athenians a pretext for the klerouchies on Andros and Naxos. Several defections in the region definitely occurred late in the Peloponnesian War. While modern scholarship has often implied that these revolts represent some sort of natural reaction to the Athenian disaster in Sicily, this may have been just one of the catalysts. There may have also been resentment among the aristocracies on the islands at financial burdens placed on them under the *arkhē*. The actions of the Four Hundred in Athens provided a trigger. Islanders would have been concerned as to whether or not Athenian hegemony would continue, and whether it would continue to maintain the same character.

The nature of the Spartan hegemony during the years after the end of the Peloponnesian War is extremely difficult to reconstruct. However, conditions in the Cyclades may have become increasingly turbulent during the 390s, if the *stasis* on Siphnos described in Isokrates' *Aiginitikos* can be taken as at all representative. The lack of a strong hegemon in the region throughout the 380s does not appear to have led to local economic benefits (although the renewal of minting by Siphnos and Naxos, which most likely dates to the early fourth century, might be a response to the changed conditions).

Many of the Cycladic *poleis* may have thus foreseen benefits accruing from enrollment in the Second Athenian League when it was established. Although most of them may have joined only after the Athenian victory at the Battle of Naxos in 376, when Athenian hegemony over the region was much more assured, it is possible that a few such as Paros had joined earlier. However, Athens was not able to protect the region during the crisis years of the late 360s, leading to severe devastation on Tenos and multiple revolts on Keos. Despite these troubles, there are no recorded defections of any of the Cyclades during the Social War of 357–355.

Relations between the Cyclades and Athens appear to have been positive after 355. The *synedrion* continued to meet until 338, and several of the islands voted honorary crowns to Athens during these years. The *polis* of Tenos was re-founded in a coastal location poised to take advantage of commerce through the Cyclades, and it prospered as a community through the second half of the century. Several islands renewed economic practices last seen in the late Archaic period that we have associated with certain aspects of peer-polity interaction, namely the minting of silver and bronze and also the construction of temples and fortification walls. The use of Parian marble is again attested, especially in western Greek contexts. And if the evidence of certain inscriptions and island surveys can be taken as valid, several of the islands saw heavy agricultural exploitation, and perhaps their highest populations in antiquity, in the late Classical period.

Athens also appears to have achieved a certain level of prosperity by implementing a mixture of policies designed to promote commerce, while at the same time keeping a navy powerful enough to police the seas but steering clear of warfare until 322. Athens became increasingly reliant on grain imports from a number of sources after mid-century, including Egypt and the Levant, ensuring the continued importance of routes through the Cyclades. Though our sources are mostly silent concerning the Cyclades during the second half of the century, there is reason to think that these islands shared in some of this Athenian prosperity, and that commercial ties with Athens remained important even after the Athenians ceased to be a naval power in the Aegean and hegemony shifted to the Antigonids. The interests of the Athenians and the interests of the islanders could thus have worked synergistically for many decades.

While many studies have operated from the assumption that the lack of a hegemon over the Cyclades was the only context in which the islands could prosper, the reality may have been more complex. What may have really changed (more or less permanently) economic conditions in the region was the Athenian *arkhē*, in that from the fifth century onwards the islanders more or less came to expect the presence of a hegemon as an inevitability. The Spartans, Persians, Athenians, Thebans, Pheraians, and Macedonians all projected naval power in the Aegean at different moments in the fourth century. It was no longer possible for islands like the Cyclades to control local trade routes with their own warships, as they might have in the sixth century, as small flotillas had little chance of competing against the large and prohibitively expensive fleets deployed by the superpowers.

Hostility to Athens in the region during the fourth century seems to have been manifested only when Athens was perceived as unable to maintain its position in the Aegean. Nevertheless, threats to Athenian power after the formation of the Second Athenian League did not often result in defections among the Cyclades, even when trouble materialized on nearby Euboia (Keos was the exception here).

Economic strategies employed by the Cycladic islanders from the fifth century to the end of the Classical period had to take into account their geographic position, as well as the policies of the current hegemon. Although their lack of naval power might make them appear passive, there were methods of economic adaptation used by these communities that were quite active in their own way. Thus, while there were certain constants in the nature of insularity for the Cyclades, they were more than just victims of outside influence.

Bibliography

Abulafia, D. (1990), *A Mediterranean emporium: the Catalan kingdom of Majorca*. Cambridge.

Accame, S. (1941), *La lega ateniese del sec.IV. a.c.* Rome.

Acheson, P. (1997), 'Does the "economic explanation" work? Settlement, agriculture, and erosion in the territory of Halieis in the late Classical-early Hellenistic period.' *JMA* 10.2, 165–90.

Adcock, F.E. (1932), 'Alcidas ἀργυρολόγος.' *Mélanges Gustave Glotz*, vol.1. Paris.

Adornato, G. (ed.) (2010), *Scolpire il marmo: artisti itineranti, scuole artistiche nel Mediterraneo antico. Atti del convegno di studio tenuto a Pisa, Scuola Normale Superiore, 9–11 novembre 2009. Archeologia e arte antica.* Milan.

Ager, S.L. (1996), *Interstate arbitrations in the Greek world, 337–90 B.C.* Berkeley.

——(2001), '4th century Thera and the second Athenian sea league.' *Ancient World* 32.1, 99–119.

——(2008), 'Rescuing local history: epigraphy and the island of Thera.' In Cooper 2008*b*, 150–76.

Agouridis, C. (1997), 'Sea routes and navigation in the third millennium Aegean.' *Oxford Journal of Archaeology* 16, 1–24.

Alcock, S., and Cherry, J.F. (eds.) (2004), *Side-by-side survey: comparative regional studies in the Mediterranean*. Oxford.

Alessandri, S. (1984), 'Il significato storico della legge di Nicofonte sul dokimastes monetario.' *ASNSP* 14, 369–93.

Alston, R. (2008), 'Introduction.' In Alston and van Nijf 2008, 1–15.

——and van Nijf, O.M. (eds.) (2008), *Feeding the ancient Greek city*. Leuven.

Amandry, P. (1953), *Le Colonne des Naxiens et la portique des Athéniens*. Paris.

Ambaglio, D. (ed.) (2008), *Diodoro Siculo: Biblioteca storia: libro XIII: commento storico*. Milan.

Amit, M. (1965), *Athens and the sea: a study in Athenian sea power*. Brussels.

——(1973), *Great and small poleis*. Brussels.

Ammermann, A.J., Matessi, C., and Cavalli-Sforza, L.L. (1978), 'Some new approaches to the study of obsidian trade in the Mediterranean and adjacent areas.' In Hodder 1978, 179–96.

Anderson, C.A., and Dix, T.K. (2004), 'Small states in the Athenian empire: the case of the Eteokarpathioi.' *Syllecta Classica* 15, 1–31.

Anderson, J.K. (1974), *Xenophon*. New York.

Andrewes, A. (1966), *The Greek tyrants*. London.

Angeli Bertinelli, M.G., and Donati, A. (eds.) (2005), *Il cittadino, lo straniero, il barbaro, fra integrazione ed emarginazione nell'antichita: Atti del I Incontro Internazionale di Storia antica, Genova, 22–24 maggio 2003*. Rome.

Antonetti, C. (2005), 'I Greci ad Adria fra il VI e il V secolo a.C.' In Angeli Bertinelli and Donati 2005, 115–41.

Arafat, K., and Morgan, C. (1994), 'Athens, Etruria, and the Heuneburg: mutual misconceptions in the study of Greek-barbarian relations.' In Morris 1994, 108–34.

Archibald, Z.H. (ed.) (2001), *Hellenistic economies*. New York.

——Davies, J.K., and Gabrielsen, V. (2005), *Making, moving, and managing: the new world of ancient economies, 323–31 BC*. Oxford.

Aron, R. (1973), *Peace and war: a theory of international relations*. New York.

Ashton, N.G. (1977), 'The *naumachia* near Amorgos in 322 B.C.' *BSA* 72, 1–11.

Ashton, R.H.J. (2001), 'The coinage of Rhodes 408-c.190 BC.' In Meadows and Shipton 2001, 79–116.

Austin, M.M., and Vidal-Naquet, P. (1977), *Economic and social history of ancient Greece: an introduction*. Berkeley.

Baba, K. (1984), 'On Kerameikos Inv. I 388 (*SEG* XXII, 79): a note on the formation of the Athenian metic-status.' *BSA* 79, 1–5.

Babelon, E. (1901–33), *Traité des monnaies grecques et romaines 1–4*. Paris.

Badian, E. (ed.) (1966), *Ancient society and institutions: studies presented to Victor Ehrenberg on his 75th birthday*. Oxford.

——(1991), 'The King's Peace.' In Flower and Toher 1991, 25–48.

——(1993), *From Plataea to Potidaea: studies in the history and historiography of the Pentecontaetia*. Baltimore.

——(1995), 'The ghost of empire: reflections on Athenian foreign policy in the fourth century BC.' In Eder 1995, 77–106.

——(2000), 'The road to prominence.' In Worthington 2000, 9–44.

Bagnall, R.S. (1976), *The administration of the Ptolemaic possessions outside Egypt*. Leiden.

Bakewell, G.W., and Sickinger, J.P. (eds.) (2003), *Gestures. Essays in ancient history, literature, and philosophy presented to Alan L. Boegehold*. Oxford.

Bakker, E.J., de Jong, I.J.F., and van Wees, H. (eds.) (2002), *Brill's companion to Herodotus*. Leiden.

Balard, M. (1974), 'Escales génoises sur les routes de l'Orient Méditerréen au XIVe siècles.' *Les grand escales. Recueils de la societé Jean Bodin*. Brussels.

Balcer, J.M. (1976), 'Imperial magistrates in the Athenian empire.' *Historia* 25.3, 257–87.

——(1978), *The Athenian regulations for Chalkis: studies in Athenian imperial law.* Wiesbaden.

Ballin, N. (1978), *A commentary on [Demosthenes] 50 'Against Polykles'.* PhD Diss. Washington, DC.

Balot, R.K. (2001), *Greed and injustice in classical Athens.* Princeton.

Bang, P.F., Ikeguchi, M., and Ziche, H.G. (eds.) (2006), *Ancient economies, modern methodologies: archaeology, comparative history, models and institutions.* Bari.

Barber, G.L. (1935), *The historian Ephorus.* Cambridge.

Barber, R.L.N. (1987), *The Cyclades in the Bronze Age.* London.

Baron, C.A. (2006), 'The Aristoteles Decree and the expansion of the Second Athenian League.' *Hesperia* 75, 379–95.

Bauslaugh, R.A. (1979), 'The posthumous Alexander coinage of Chios.' *ANS Museum Notes* 24, 1–45.

——(1991), *The concept of neutrality in classical Greece.* Berkeley.

Beaumont, R.L. (1936), 'Greek influence in the Adriatic Sea before the fourth century B.C.' *JHS* 56, 159–204.

Beck, H. (1997), *Polis und Koinon: Untersuchungen zur Geschichte und Struktur der griechischen Bundesstaaten im 4. Jahrhundert v. Chr.* Stuttgart.

Bedermann, E. (2001), *International law in antiquity.* Oxford.

Belli Pasqua, R. (2010), 'Scultura architettonica e officine itineranti. Il caso dell'*Heraion* a Capo Lacinio.' In Adornato 2010, 171–84.

Beloch, K.J. (1914), *Griechische Geschichte I.* Strasbourg.

Bengtson, H. (1975), *Die Staatsverträge des Altertums II^2.* Munich.

Benson, C. (2000), '"Paros and Athens: a stylistic message on the Parthenon frieze.' In Schilardi and Katsonopoulou 2000, 179–85.

Bent, J.T. (1885), *The Cyclades, or life among the insular Greeks.* London.

Berranger, D. (1992), *Recherches sur l'histoire et la prosopographie de Paros à l'époque archaïque.* Clermont-Ferrand.

Berranger-Auserve, D. (2000), *Paros II: prosopographie générale et étude historique du début de la période classique jusqu'à la fin de la période romaine.* Paris.

Bers, V. (2003), *Demosthenes. Speeches 50–59.* Austin.

Berthold, R.M. (1980), 'Fourth-century Rhodes.' *Historia* 29, 32–49.

Bevan, A., Frederick, C., and Krahtopoulou, N. (2003), 'A digital Mediterranean countryside: GIS approaches to the spatial structure of the post-medieval landscape on Kythera (Greece).' *Archeologia e Calcolatori* 14, 217–36.

Biagini, E., and Hoyle, B. (eds.) (1999), *Insularity and development: insular perspectives on islands.* London.

Bikakis, M.H. (1985), *Archaic and classical imported pottery in the museums of Paros and Naxos.* PhD Diss. University of Cincinnati.

Billows, R.A. (1990), *Antigonos the One-Eyed and the creation of the Hellenistic state*. Berkeley.

Bintliff, J. (2005), 'Human impact, land use history and the surface archaeological record: a case study from Greece.' *Geoarchaeology* 20, 135–47.

Birgalias, N. (ed.) (forthcoming), *Great is the power of the sea: the power of sea and sea power in the Greek world of the archaic and classical periods*. Athens.

Bissa, E.M.A. (2009), *Governmental intervention in foreign trade in archaic and classical Greece*. Leiden.

Blackman, D.J. (ed.) (1973), *Marine archaeology*. London.

Blamire, A. (2001), 'Athenian finance, 454–404 B.C.' *Hesperia* 70, 99–126.

Bleckmann, B. (1998), *Athens Weg in die Niederlage. Die letzten Jahre des peloponnesischen Krieges*. Stuttgart.

Blegen, C., Palmer, H., and Young, R.S. (eds.) (1964), *Corinth. Vol.13, the north cemetery*. Princeton.

Bloch, D. (2004), 'The date of Xenophon's *Poroi*.' *Classica et mediaevalia* 55, 5–16.

Bloedow, E.F. (1973), *Alcibiades reexamined*. Wiesbaden.

Blümel, W. (1992), *Die Inschriften von Knidos. Vol.1*. Bonn.

——(1994), 'Two new inscriptions from the Cnidian peninsula.' *EA* 23, 157–9.

Boardman, J. (1980), *The Greeks overseas*. 3rd edn. London.

——(1989), *Athenian red-figure vases: the classical period*. London.

——and Vaphopoulou-Richardson, C.E. (eds.) (1986), *Chios: a conference at the Homereion in Chios*. Oxford.

Bockisch, G. (1965), 'Ἁρμοσταί.' *Klio* 46, 129–239.

Bodenstedt, F. (1976), *Phokäisches Elektron-Geld von 600–326 v. Chr. Studien zur Bedeutung und zu den Wandlungen einer antiken Goldwährung*. Mainz.

Bogaert, R. (1968), *Banques et banquiers dans les cités grecques*. Leiden.

Bolmarcich, S. (2009), 'The Athenian regulations for Samos (*IG* I^3 48) again.' *Chiron* 39, 45–64.

Bommelaer, J.-F. (1991), *Guide de Delphes: le site*. Paris.

Bommeljé, S., and Doorn, P.K. (1987), *Aetolia and the Aetolians: towards the interdisciplinary study of a Greek region*. Utrecht.

Bookidis, N., and Williams, Ch.K. (eds.) (2003), *Corinth Vol.20: the Centenary*. Athens.

Borza, E.N. (1992), *In the shadow of Olympus: the emergence of Macedon*. Princeton.

Bosworth, A.B. (1971), 'The Congress Decree: another hypothesis.' *Historia* 20 (5/6), 600–16.

——(1975), 'The mission of Amphoterus and the outbreak of Agis' war.' *Phoenix* 29, 27–43.

——(1980), *A historical commentary on Arrian's 'History of Alexander' Books I–III*. Oxford.
——(1988), *Conquest and empire: the reign of Alexander the Great*. Cambridge.
——(2003), 'Why did Athens lose the Lamian War?' In Palagia and Tracy 2003, 14–22.
Braccesi, L. (1977), *Grecità adriatica: un capitolo della colonizzazione greca in Occidente*. Bologna.
Braudel, F. (1972), *The Mediterranean and the Mediterranean world in the age of Philip II*. London.
Bravo, B. (1977), 'Remarques sur les assises sociales, les formes d'organisation et la terminologie du commerce maritimes grec à l'époque archaïque.' *DHA* 3, 1–59.
——(1983), 'Le commerce de céréales chez les Grecs de l'époque archaïque.' In Garnsey and Whittaker 1983, 17–29.
——(1984), 'Commerce et noblesse en Grèce archaïque.' *DHA* 10, 99–160.
Bresson, A. (1980), 'Rhodes: une famille camiréenne de commerçants en blé.' *Index* 9, 144–9.
——(2000), *La cité marchande*. Paris.
——(2007), *L'économie de la Grèce des cites (fin VIe-Ier siècle a.C.). I. Les structures et la production*. Paris.
——(2008), *L'économie de la Grèce des cites (fin VIe-Ier siècle a.C.). II. Les espaces de l'échange*. Paris.
Brewer, D. (2001), *The Greek war of independence: the struggle for freedom from Ottoman oppression and the birth of the modern Greek nation*. New York.
Briant, P., and Joannès, F. (eds.) (2006), *La transition entre l'empire achéménide et les royaumes hellénistiques (vers 35–300 av. J.-C.)*. Paris.
Brock, J.K., and Mackworth Young, G. (1949), 'Excavations in Siphnos.' *BSA* 44, 1–92.
Brock, R. (1996), 'The Tribute of Karystos.' *EMC* 40 n.s.15, 357–70.
——(2009), 'Did the Athenian empire promote democracy?' In Ma, Papazarkadas, and Parker 2009, 149–66.
——and Hodkinson, S. (2000), *Alternatives to Athens: varieties of political organization and community in ancient Greece*. Oxford.
Broodbank, C. (2000), *An island archaeology of the early Cyclades*. Cambridge.
Brotherston, G. (1992), *Book of the fourth world: reading the Native Americans through their literature*. Cambridge.
Brown, C.L., and Morgan, P.D. (eds.) (2006), *Arming slaves: from classical times to the modern age*. New Haven and London.
Brulé, P. (1978), *La piraterie crétoise hellénistique*. Paris.
Brun, P. (1983), *Eisphora-Syntaxeis-Stratiotika*. Paris.

Brun, P. (1989), 'L'île de Kéos et ses cités au IVe siècle av. J.C.' *ZPE* 76, 121–38.

——(1993*a*), 'La faiblesse insulaire: histoire d'un topos,' *ZPE* 99, 165–96.

——(1993*b*), 'La stèle des céréales de Cyrène et le commerce du grain en Egée au IVe s. av. J.-C.' *ZPE* 99, 185–96.

——(1996), *Les archipels égéens dans l'antiquité grecque (V^{e}-IIe siècles av. notre ère.* Paris.

——(1997), 'Du fromage de Kythnos au marbre de Paros: la question des appellations contrôlées (?) dans l'antiquité grecque.' *REA* 99, 401–9.

——(1998), 'Pauvreté et impuissance de Kythnos: essai pour un jugement équilibré.' In Mendoni and Mazarakis-Ainian 1998, 657–68.

——(2000), 'La prospérité après la richesse: Siphnos classique et hellénistique (V^{e} –IIe av. J.-C.).' In Zervoudakis 2000, 227–38.

——(2004), 'La datation de *IG* II^{2} 404, décret athénien concernant les cités de Kéos.' *ZPE* 147, 72–80.

——(2005), *Impérialisme et démocratie à Athènes: inscriptions de l'époque classique.* Paris.

Bruneau, P., and Ducat, J. (1983), *Guide de Délos.* 3rd edn. Paris.

Brunet, M. (1990), 'Contribution à l'histoire rurale de Délos aux époques classique et hellénistique.' *BCH* 114, 669–82.

——(ed.) (1999), *Territoires des cités grecques: actes de la table ronde internationale organisée par l'École Française d'Athènes, 31 octobre-3 novembre 1991.* Athens.

——(2000), 'Thasos. Structure du territoire et fonctionnement économique de la cité.' In Domaradzki 2000, 183–90.

Brunt, P.A. (1966), 'Athenian settlements abroad in the fifth century B.C.' In Badian 1966, 71–92.

——(1969), 'Euboea in the time of Philip II', *CQ* 2nd series 19, 245-65.

Bücher, K. (1912), *Industrial evolution.* 3rd edn. Trans. S.M. Wickett. New York.

Buckler, J. (1980), *The Theban hegemony, 371–362 B.C.* Cambridge, Mass.

——(2003), *Aegean Greece in the fourth century BC.* Leiden.

——(2008*a*), 'Boiotian Aulis and Greek naval bases.' In Buckler and Beck 2008, 180–98.

——(2008*b*), 'Epaminondas and the new inscription from Cnidus.' In Buckler and Beck 2008, 199–210.

——and Beck, H. (2008), *Central Greece and the politics of power in the fourth century B.C.* Cambridge.

Bunbury, E.H. (1883), *A history of Ancient Geography* 2. London.

Buraselis, K. (1982), *Das hellenistische Makedonien und die Ägäis: Forschungen zur Politik des Kassandros und der drei ersten Antigoniden (Antigonos Monophthalmos, Demetrios Poliorketes und Antigonos Gonatas im Ägäischen Meer und in Westleinasien.* Munich.

Bürchner, L. (1923), 'Seriphos.' *RE* II: V, col. 1729–34.

Burford, A. (1969), *The Greek temple-builders at Epidauros.* Toronto.
Burke, E.M. (1984), 'Eubulus, Olynthus, and Euboea.' *TAPA* 114, 111–20.
——(1985), 'Lycurgan finances.' *GRBS* 26, 251–64.
——(1992), 'The economy of Athens in the Classical era: some adjustments to the primitivist model.' *TAPA* 122, 199–226.
——(2005), 'The habit of subsidization in classical Athens: toward a thetic ideology.' *Classica et mediaevalia* 56, 5–47.
Burn, A.R. (1929), 'The so-called "trade leagues" in early Greek history and the Lelantine War.' *JHS* 49 (1), 14–37.
——(1952), 'Notes on Alexander's campaigns 332–330.' *JHS* 72, 81–91.
——(1962), *Persia and the Greeks: the defence of the West 546–478 B.C.* London: Arnold.
Burnett, A.P., and Edmondson, C. (1961), 'The Chabrias monument in the Athenian Agora.' *Hesperia* 30, 74–91.
Burrer, F., and Müller, H. (2008), *Kriegskosten und Kriegsfinanzierung in der Antike.* Chapel Hill.
Burstein, S.M. (1999), '*IG* I^3 61 and the Black Sea grain trade.' In Mellor and Tritle 1999, 93–104.
Butt, K. (1977), 'A deposit of Archaic and Classical Greek pottery at Ayia Irini, Keos.' *Hesperia* 46, 299–314.
Buttrey, T.V. (1981), 'More on the Athenian coinage law of 375/4 B.C.' *NAC* 10, 71–94.
——(1984), 'Seldom what they seem—the case of the Athenian tetradrachm.' In Heckel and Sullivan 1984, 292–4.
Cahn, H.A. (1970), *Knidos. Die Münzen des sechsten und des fünften Jahrhunderts v. Chr.*
——(1973), 'Skione-Stagira-Akanthos.' *Zur Griechischen Kunst. Antike Kunst* 9, 7–13.
Cairns, F. (1991), 'The "Laws of Eretria" (*IG* XII.9 1273 and 1274): epigraphic, legal, historical, and political aspects.' *Phoenix* 45, 296–313.
Callaghan, P.J. (1992), 'Archaic to Hellenistic pottery.' In Sackett 1992, 89–136.
Cargill, J. (1981), *The second Athenian league: empire or free alliance?* Berkeley.
——(1982), 'Hegemony not empire: the second Athenian league.' *Ancient World* 5.3–4, 91–102.
——(1983), '*IG* II^2 1 and the Athenian kleruchy on Samos.' *GRBS* 24, 321–32.
——(1995), *Athenian settlements of the fourth century B.C.* Leiden.
Carlson, D.N. (1996), 'The decree of Aristoteles: some epigraphical details.' *Ancient World* 27, 39–51.
——(2003), '"The Classical Greek shipwreck at Tektaş Burnu, Turkey.' *AJA* 107, 581–600.

Carradice, I. (ed.) (1987), *Coinage and administration in the Athenian and Persian empires.* Oxford.
Cartledge, P. (1982), 'Sparta and Samos: a special relationship?' *CQ* 32.2, 243–65.
——(1987), *Agesilaus and the crisis of Sparta.* Baltimore.
——(1998), 'The economy (economies) of ancient Greece'. *Dialogos* 5 (1998) 4–24.
——Cohen, E.E., and Foxhall, L. (2002), *Money, labour, and land: approaches to the economies of ancient Greece.* London and New York.
Casson, L (1971), *Ships and seamanship in the ancient world.* Princeton.
——(1995), 'A trireme for hire.' *CQ* 45, 241–5.
Cataldi, N. (1979), 'Atene "polis ekkletos".' *ASNP* 9, 1–37.
Cavanagh, W., Mee, C., and James, P. (2005), *The Laconian rural sites project. BSA supplementary volume 36.* London.
Cawkwell, G. (1963*a*), 'Eubulus.' *JHS* 83, 47–67.
——(1963*b*), 'Notes on the Peace of 375/4.' *Historia* 12, 84–95.
——(1963*c*), 'The *ΣYN* coins again.' *JHS* 83, 152–4.
——(1970), 'The Fall of Themistocles.' In Harris 1970, 39–58.
——(1972), 'Epaminondas and Thebes', *CQ* n.s. 22 (2), 254-78.
——(1973), 'The foundation of the second Athenian confederacy.' *CQ* 23, 47–60.
——(1978), 'Euboea in the late 340s', *Phoenix* 32.1, 42-67.
——(1981), 'Notes on the failure of the second Athenian confederacy.' *JHS* 101, 40–55.
——(1984), 'Athenian naval power in the fourth century B.C.' *CQ* 34, 334–45.
——(1997), *Thucydides and the Peloponnesian War.* New York.
——(2005), *The Greek wars: the failure of Persia.* Oxford.
Ceccarelli, P. (1989), 'Nesiotika.' *Annali della Scuola Superiore di Pisa* 29, 903–35.
——(1993), 'Sans thalassocratie, pas de démocratie? Le rapport entre thalassocratie et démocratie à Athènes dans la discussion du Ve et IVe siècle av. J-C.' *Historia* 42, 444–70.
Chaniotis, A. (1996), *Die Verträge zwischen kretischen Poleis in der hellenistichen Zeit, Heidelberger Althistorische Beiträge und Epigraphische Studien 24.* Stuttgart.
Chankowski, V. (2001), 'Athènes, Délos, et les Cyclades à l'époque classique: un réseau économique?' *REA* 103, 83–102.
——(2008), *Athènes et Délos à l'époque classique. Recherches sur l'administration du sanctuaire d'Apollon délien.* Athens.
Charre, R., and Le Dinahet, M.Th. (1999), 'Sites de fermes à Rhénée." In Brunet 1999, 135–58.

Chatzanastasiou, O. (1998), '*Σεμείοσεις απὸ τήν Κύθνο.*' In Mendoni and Mazarakis-Ainian 1998, 259–63.

Cherry, J.F. (1986), 'Polities and palaces.' In Cherry and Renfrew 1986, 19–45.

——and Davis, J.F. (1998), 'Northern Keos in context.' In Mendoni and Mazarakis-Ainian (1998, 217–26.

——Davis, J.L., and Mantzourani, E. (eds.) (1991*a*), *Landscape archaeology as long-term history: northern Keos in the Cycladic islands from earliest settlement until modern times.* Los Angeles.

——Davis, and Mantzourani (1991*b*), 'Introduction to the historical and epigraphical evidence.' In Cherry, Davis, and Mantzourani 1991*a*, 235–43.

——and Renfrew, C, (eds.) (1986), *Peer-polity interaction and socio-political change.* Cambridge.

Christ, M.R. (2006), *The bad citizen in classical Athens.* Cambridge.

Christesen, P. (2003), 'Economic rationality in fourth century BCE Athens', *Greece and Rome* 2nd series 50, 31–56.

Christiansen, J., and Melander, T. (eds.) (1988), *Proceedings of the 3rd Symposium on ancient Greek and Related Pottery, Copenhagen, August 31–September 4, (1987).* Copenhagen.

Clark, M. (1990), 'The date of *IG* II^2 1604.' *BSA* 85, 47–67.

——(1993), *The economy of the Athenian navy in the fourth century B.C.* PhD diss. Oxford.

Clay, D. (2004), *Archilochus Heros: the cult of poets in the Greek polis.* Washington, DC.

Cloché, P. (1919), 'Les conflits politiques et sociaux à Athènes pendant la guerre Corinthienne (395–387 avant J.-C.).' *REA* 21, 151–92.

——(1963), *Isokrates et son temps.* Paris.

Coates, J. (1995), 'The naval architecture and oar systems of ancient galleys.' In Gardiner 1995, 127–41.

Cohen, E.E. (1992), *Athenian economy and society: a banking perspective.* Princeton.

Coldstream, J.N. (1973), *Knossos; the sanctuary of Demeter. BSA Suppl. 8.* London.

——(1990), 'Cycladic and Euboean imports in the North Cemetery at Knossos.' In Descoeudres 1990b, 25–30.

Connor, W.R. (1971), *The new politicians of fifth-century Athens.* Princeton.

Consolo Langher, S.N. (1996), 'Naxos nell'Egeo arcaico e nella colonizzazione "calcidese" dell'Occidente.' In Lanzilotta and Schilardi 1996, 120–54.

Constantakopoulou, C. (2002), 'Connectivity in the Aegean: the practice of *porthmeutice* and its importance for small-scale interaction.' *Journal of Mediterranean Studies* 12 (1), 223–6.

——(2005), 'Proud to be an islander: island identity in multi-polis islands in the Classical and Hellenistic Aegean.' *MHR* 20, 1–34.

Constantakopoulou, C. (2007), *The dance of the islands: insularity, networks, the Athenian empire, and the Aegean world*. Oxford.

Conwell, D.H. (2008), *Connecting a city to the sea: a history of the Athenian Long Walls*. Leiden.

Cook, J.M. (1961), 'The problem of Classical Ionia.' *PCPS* 187, 9–18.

Cooper, C. (2008*a*), 'Hypereides, Aristophon, and the settlement of Keos.' In Cooper 2008*b*, 31–56.

——(ed.) (2008*b*), *Epigraphy and the Greek historian*. Toronto.

Cornell, T.J. (1995), *The beginnings of Rome*. Oxford.

Costa, V. (1996), 'Ligdami, Pisistrato e la fondazione della tirannide nassia.' In Lanzilotta and Schilardi 1996, 155–70.

——(1997), *Nasso: dale origini al V sec. a.C.* Rome.

Couch, E.B. (1929), 'An interpretation of the prescript πόλεις αὔται φόρον ταχσάμεναι in the Athenian tribute lists.' *AJA* 33, 502–14.

Counillon, P. (2001), 'Les Cyclades chez les géographes grecs.' *RÉA* 103, 11–23.

Coupry, J. (1959), 'Inscriptions de Délos.' *Atti del terzio congresso internazionale di epigrafia greca e latina*. Rome, 55–69.

——(1972), *Inscriptions de Délos: La période de l'amphictyonie Attico-Délienne*. Paris.

Courtils, J., Moretti, J.-C., and Planet, F. (eds.) (1991), *De Anatolia Antiqua I*. Paris.

Craddock, P.T. (ed.) (1980), *Scientific studies in early mining and extractive metallurgy*. London.

Crane, G. (1998), *Thucydides and the ancient simplicity*. Berkeley.

Crawford, M.H. (2001), Review of T. Figueira, *The power of money*. *JHS* 121, 199–201.

Crouzet-Pavan, E. (2002), *Venice triumphant: the horizons of a myth*. Baltimore and London.

Culasso Gastaldi, E. (2004), *Le prossenie ateniesi del IV secolo a.C. Gli onorati asiatici*. Rome.

——(2005), 'Per un bilancio comparative sulle prossenie ateniesi del IV secolo a.C.' In Angeli Bertinelli and Donati 2005, 45–75.

Cunliffe, B., and Osborne, R. (eds.) (2005), *Mediterranean urbanisation*. London.

Dalongeville, R., and Rougemont, G. (eds.) (1983), *Les Cyclades: matériaux pour une etude de géographie historique*. Paris.

————(1993), *Recherches dans les Cyclades: résultats des travaux de la RCP 583*. Paris.

Daux, G., and Hansen, E. (1987), *Le Trésor de Siphnos*. Paris.

David, E. (1981), *Sparta between empire and revolution (404–243 BC): internal problems and their impact on contemporary Greek consciousness*. Salem.

——(1984), 'The oligarchic revolution at Rhodes, 391–89 B.C.' *CP* 79(4), 271–84.

Davies, J.K. (1998), 'Ancient economies, models and muddles.' in Parkins and Smith (1998, 225–56.

——(2005), 'Linear and nonlinear flow models for ancient economies.' In Morris and Manning 2005, 127–56.

——(2007), 'Classical Greece: production.' In Scheidel, Morris, and Saller 2007, 333–61.

Davies, O. (1935), *Roman mines in Europe*. Oxford.

De La Genière, J. (ed.) (2006), *Les clients de la céramique grecque. Actes du colloque de l'Academie d'Inscriptions et Belles Lettres, Paris, 30–31 janvier 2004*. Paris.

de Libero, L. (1996), *Die archaische Tyrannen*. Stuttgart.

De Ligt, L., and de Neeve, P.W. (1988), 'Ancient periodic markets: festivals and fairs.' *Athenaeum* 66, 391–416.

de Romilly, J. (1954), 'Les modérés Athéniens vers le milieu du IVe siècle: échos et concordances.' *REG* 67, 327–54.

——(1963), *Thucydides and Athenian imperialism*. Oxford.

——(1966), 'Thucydides and cities of the Athenian empire.' *Bulletin of the Institute of Classical Studies* 13, 1–12. Reprinted in Low 2008, 277–93.

de Souza, P. (1998), 'Towards thalassocracy? Greek naval developments.' In Fisher and van Wees 1998, 271–98.

——(1999), *Piracy in the Greco-Roman world*. Cambridge.

de Ste. Croix, G.E.M. (1954), 'The character of the Athenian empire.' *Historia* 3, 1–41.

——(1972), *The origins of the Peloponnesian War*. London.

——(1981), *The class struggle in the ancient Greek world*. London.

——(2004), *Athenian democratic origins and other essays*. Oxford.

Delamarre, J. (1904), 'Les contrats de prêt d'Amorgos.' *RPh* 28, 81–102.

Demand, N. (1990), *Urban relocation in archaic and classical Greece*. University of Oklahoma Press.

Descat, R. (1987), 'L'économie d'une cité grecque au IVe siècle avant J.-C.: l'exemple athénien.' *REA* 89, 239–57.

——(2004), Les années 330–325 av. J.-C. et la politique athénienne du blé." *Pallas* 64, 267–80.

——(2006), 'Aspects d'une transition: l'économie du monde égéen (350–300).' In Briant and Joannès 2006, 353–73.

Descoeudres, J.-P. (1973), 'Zagora auf der Insel Andros- eine eretrische Kolonie?' *AK* 16, 87–8.

——(ed.) (1990*a*), *Greek colonists and Native Populations*. Oxford.

——(ed.) (1990*b*), *ΕΥΜΟΥΣΙΑ: Ceramic and iconographic studies in honour of Alexander Cambitoglou (MeditArch Suppl.1)*. Sydney.

Develin, R. (1977), 'Miltiades and the Parian expedition.' *L'Antiquité classique* (1977), 571–7.
Di Napoli, V. (2005), 'The silver coinage of Siphnos during the archaic and classical period.' In Zervoudakis 2005, 197–206.
Dillery, J. (1993), 'Xenophon's *Poroi* and Athenian imperialism.' *Historia* 42 (1), 1–11.
——(1995), *Xenophon and the history of his times.* London and New York.
Dillon, M. (1997), *Pilgrims and pilgrimages in ancient Greece.* New York.
Domaradzki, M. (ed.) (2000), *Pistiros et Thasos. Structures économiques dans la péninsule balkanique aux VIIe-IIe siècles avant J.-C.* Opole.
Doty, R. (2003), *Xenophon. Poroi.* Lewiston.
Dougherty, C., and Kurke, L. (2003), *The cultures within ancient Greek culture: contact, conflict, collaboration.* Cambridge.
Doukellis, P.N., and Mendoni, L.G. (eds.) (1994), *Structures rurales et sociétés antiques: actes du colloque de Corfou (14–16 mai (1992).* Paris.
Dreher, M. (1989), 'Zu *IG* II^2 404, dem athenischen Volksbeschluss uber die Eigenstaatlichkeit der keischen Poleis.' *Symposion 1985.* Vienna, 263–81.
——(1995), *Hegemon und Symmachoi: Untersuchungen zum zweiten athenischen Seebund.* Berlin.
Drews, R. (1962), 'Diodorus and his sources.' *AJP* 83, 383–92.
——(1963), 'Ephorus and history written *κατὰ γένος*.' *AJP* 84, 244–55.
——(1976), 'Ephorus' *κατὰ γένος* revisited.' *Hermes* 104, 497–8.
Ducrey, P. (1983), 'Les Cyclades à l'époque hellenistique: la piraterie, symptôme d'un malaise économique et social.' In Dalongeville and Rougemont 1983, 143–8.
Dunant, C., and Thomopoulos, J. (1954), 'Inscriptions de Céos.' *BCH* 78, 316–48.
Dunbabin, T.J. (1979), *The western Greeks.* Chicago.
Dušanić, S. (1980), 'Athens, Crete, and the Aegean after 366/5 B.C.' *Talanta* 12/13 (1980), 7–29.
——(2000), 'The Attic-Chian alliance (*IG* II^2 34) and the 'troubles in Greece' of the late 380's BC.' *ZPE* 133, 21–30.
Eadie, J., and Ober, J. (eds.) (1985), *The craft of the ancient historian.* New York and London.
Earle, T.K., and Erickson, J.E. (1977), *Exchange systems in prehistory.* New York.
Eckstein, A. (2006), *Mediterranean anarchy, interstate war, and the rise of Rome.* Berkeley.
Eddy, S.K. (1968), '*Epiphora* in the tribute quota lists.' *AJP* 89, 129–43.
——(1973), 'Some irregular amounts of Athenian tribute.' *AJP* 94, 47–70.
Eder, W. (ed.) (1995), *Die athenische Demokratie im 4. Jahrhundert v. Chr.* Stuttgart.

Efstratiou, K. (2000), 'Εργαστερία Γλυπτίκες στην Παροικια Παρου.' In Schilardi and Katsanopoulou 2000, 105–11.
Ehrenberg, V. (1973), *Aspects of the ancient world: essays and reviews.* New York.
Ekshmitt, W. (1993), *Die Kykladen: Bronzezeit, geometrische und archaische Zeit.* Mainz.
Ellis, J.R. (1976), *Philip II and Macedonian imperialism.* London.
Empereur, J.-V., and Picon, M. (1986), 'Des ateliers d'amphores à Paros et à Naxos.' *BCH* 110, 495–511.
Engen, D. (2001), 'Trade, traders, and the economy of Athens in the fourth century B.C.' In Tandy 2001, 179–202.
——(2004), 'Seeing the forest and the trees of the ancient economy.' *AHB* 18, 150–65.
——(2005), 'Ancient greenbacks: Athenian owls, the law of Nikophon, and the Greek economy.' *Historia* 30, 1–23.
——(2010), *Honor and profit: Athenian trade policy and the economy and society of Greece, 415–307 B.C.E.* Ann Arbor.
Érard-Cerceau, I., Fotou, V., Psychoyos, O., and Treuil, R. (1993), 'Prospection archéologique à Naxos (région nord-ouest).' In Dalongeville and Rougemont 1993, 59–96.
Erdkamp, P. (2005), *The grain market in the Roman empire: a social, political, and economic study.* Cambridge.
Erickson, B.L. (2005), 'Archaeology of empire: Athens and Crete in the fifth century B.C.' *AJA* 109.4, 619–63.
——(2010), *Crete in transition: pottery styles and island history in the archaic and classical periods. Hesperia Suppl. 45.* Athens.
Errington, R.M. (1975), 'Samos and the Lamian War.' *Chiron* 5, 51–7.
Erxleben, E. (1969–71), 'Das Münzgeset——des delisch-attischen Seebundes.' *Archiv für Papyrus Forschung* 19: 91–139; 20: 66–162: 21: 145–62.
——(1975), 'Die Kleruchien auf Euböa und Lesbos und die Methoden der attischen Herrschaft im 5 Jh.' *Klio* 57, 83–100.
Etienne, R. (1990), *Ténos II: Ténos et les Cyclades.* Paris.
——and Braun, J.-P. (1986), *Ténos I: le sanctuaire de Poséidon et d'Amphitrite.* Paris.
Evans, J.D. (1977), 'Island archaeology in the Mediterranean: problems and opportunities.' *World Archaeology* 9, 12–26.
Fagan, G., and Trundle, M. (2010), *New perspectives on ancient warfare.* Leiden, Boston.
Faraguna, M. (1992), *Atene nell-età di Alessandro: problemi politici, economici, finanziari.* Rome.
Figueira, T.J. (1981), *Aegina: society and politics.* New York.
——(1991), *Athens and Aigina in the age of imperial colonization.* Baltimore.

Figueira, T.J. (1993), *Excursions in epichoric history: Aiginetan essays*. Lanham, Maryland.
——(1998), *The power of money: coinage and politics in the Athenian empire*. Philadelphia.
——(2002*a*), 'Typology in archaic Greek maritime states.' *Ancient West and East* 1(1), 24–7.
——(2002*b*), 'Iron money and the ideology of consumption in Laconia.' In Powell and Hodkinson 2002, 137–70.
——(2003), 'Economic integration and monetary consolidation in the Athenian *arkhē*.' In Urso 2003, 71–92.
——(2005), 'The imperial commercial tax and the finances of the Athenian hegemony.' *Incidenza dell' Antico* 3, 1–51.
——(2006), 'Reconsidering the Athenian Coinage Decree.' *Annali Instituto Italiano di Numismatica* 52, 9–44.
——(forthcoming *a*)), 'Patterns in archaic Greek naval warfare.' In Birgalias (forthcoming).
——(forthcoming *b*), 'Aigina as paradigm.' In Powell and Meidani (forthcoming).
Finley, M.I. (1978), 'The fifth-century Athenian empire: a balance-sheet.' In Garnsey and Whittaker 1978, 103–26. Reprinted in Low 2008, 14–37.
——(1985), *Ancient history: evidence and models*. London.
——(1999), *The ancient economy*. Updated edition. Berkeley.
Fisher, A.R. (1985), 'The early state module: a critical assessment.' *Oxford Journal of Archaeology* 4 (1), 1–8.
Fisher, N., and van Wees, H. (eds.) (1998), *Archaic Greece: new approaches and new evidence*. London.
Flament, C. (2007), *Le monnayage en argent d'Athènes de l'époque archaïque à l'époque hellenistique*. Louvain-le-Neuve.
Flensted-Jensen, P., and Hansen, M.H. (1996), 'Pseudo-Skylax' use of the term *polis*.' In Hansen and Raaflaub (1996, 137–68.
——Nielsen, T.H., and Rubinstein, L. (eds.) (2000), *Polis and politics. Studies in ancient Greek history presented to Mogens Herman Hansen*. Copenhagen.
Floren, J. (1987), *Die geometrische und archaische Plastik*. Munich.
Flower, M.A., and Toher, M. (eds.) (1991), *Georgica. Greek studies in honour of George Cawkwell*. London.
Foley, A. (1988), *The Argolid 800–600 BC. An archaeological survey*. Gothenburg.
Foot, M.R.D. (ed.) (1973), *War and society: historical essays in honour and memory of J.R. Western*. London.
Fornara, C.W. and Samons, L.J. II (1991), *Athens from Cleisthenes to Pericles*. Berkeley.

Forrest, W.G. (1969), 'Two Chronological Notes.' *Classical Quarterly* 19, 95–110.

——(1982), 'Euboea and the islands.' *Calif.H* III.3, 249–60.

Fossey, J.M. (1989), *Topography and population of ancient Boiotia*. Chicago.

Fox, R.L. (2008), *Travelling heroes: Greeks and their myths in the epic age of Homer*. London.

Foxhall, L. (2005), 'Village to city: staples and luxuries? Exchange networks and urbanization.' In Cunliffe and Osborne 2005, 233–48.

——(2007), *Olive cultivation in ancient Greece: seeking the ancient economy*. Oxford.

Fraser, P.M. (1972), *Ptolemaic Alexandria*. Oxford.

——and Bean, G.E. (1954), *The Rhodian peraea and islands*. Oxford.

Freeman, K. (1963), *Greek city-states*. New York.

French, A. (1964), *The growth of the Athenian economy*. London.

——(1972), 'The tribute of the allies.' *Historia* 21, 1–20.

French, C.A.I., and Whitelaw, T. (1999), 'Soil erosion, agricultural terracing and site formation processes of Markiani, Amorgos, Greece: the micro-morphological perspective.' *Geoarchaeology* 14 (2), 151–89.

Fried, S. (1987), 'The Decadrachm Hoard: an introduction.' In Carradice 1987, 1–9.

Fuchs, W., and Floren, J. (1987), *Die Griechische Plastik 1: die geometrische und archaische Plastik*. Munich.

Fulford, M.G. (1989), 'To east and west: the Mediterranean trade of Cyrenaica and Tripolitania in antiquity.' *Libyan Studies* 20, 169–91.

Funke, P. (1980), *Homonoia und Arche: Athen und die griechische Staatenwelt vom Ende des peloponnesischen Krieges bis zum Königsfrieden (404/3–387/6 v. Chr.). Historia Einzelschriften 37*. Wiesbaden.

——(1983), 'Konons Rückkehr nach Athen im Spiegel epigraphischer Zeugnisse.' *ZPE* 53, 149–89.

Furobotn, E.G., and Richter, R. (2005), *Institutions and economic theory: the contribution of the New Institutional Economics*. Ann Arbor.

Gabba, E. (1997), 'Gli argomenti economici nell'*Athenaion Politeia* Pseudosenofontea.' In Gigante and Maddoli 1997, 71–7.

Gabrielsen, V. (1985), 'The naukrariai and the Athenian navy.' *Classica et Mediaevalia* 36, 21–51.

——(1994), *Financing the Athenian fleet: public taxation and social relations*. Baltimore and London.

——(1997), *The naval aristocracy of Hellenistic Rhodes*. Aarhus.

——(2001), 'Economic activity, maritime trade and piracy in the Hellenistic Aegean.' *REA* 103, 219–40.

Gaffney, V., Kirigin, B., Petrić, M., and Vujnović, N. (1997), *The Adriatic Islands Project: contact, commerce, and colonialism 6000 BC- AD 600*. Vol. I: *The archaeological heritage of Hvar, Croatia*. Oxford.

Gale, N.H. (1979), 'Some aspects of lead and silver mining in the Aegean.' *Miscellanea Graeca* 2, 9–60.

——and Stos-Gale, Z.H. (1981), 'Cycladic lead and silver metallurgy.' *BSA* 76, 169–224.

Gallant, T.W. (1991), *Risk and survival in ancient Greece.* Cambridge.

Gallet de Santerre, H. (1958), *Délos primitive et archaïque.* Paris.

Gansiniec, Z. (1973), 'Note on silk in Greece.' *Archaeologia Polona* 14, 87–8.

Gardiner, R. (ed.) (1995), *The age of the galley: Mediterranean oared vessels since pre-classical times.* London.

Garlan, Y. (1974), *Recherches de poliorcétique grecque.* Paris.

——(1989), *Guerre et économie en Grèce ancienne.* Paris.

——(1999), 'Production et commerce des amphores: contribution à l'étude du territoire des cités grecques.' *BCH Supplément 34*, 371–85.

Garnsey, P. (1988), *Famine and food supply in the Graeco-Roman world: responses to risk and crisis.* Cambridge.

——(1999), *Food and society in classical antiquity.* Cambridge.

——and Saller, R. (1987), *The Roman empire. Economy, society, and culture.* London.

——and Whittaker, C.R. (eds.) (1978), *Imperialism in the ancient world.* Cambridge.

————(1983), *Trade and famine in classical antiquity.* Cambridge.

Gauthier, P. (1972), *Symbola: les étrangers et la justice dans les cités grecques.* Nancy.

——(1976), *Un commentaire historique des 'Poroi' de Xénophon.* Paris.

Gautier, J. (1993), 'Les cyclades antiques: caractérisation de centres de productions céramiques par microscopie optique.' In Dalongeville and Rougemont 1993, 167–204.

Gawantka, W. (1975), *Isopolitie: ein Beitrag zur Geschichte der zwischenstaatlichen Beziehungen in der griechischen Antike.* Munich.

Geagan, D.J. (1968), 'Inscriptions from Nemea.' *Hesperia* 37, 381–5.

Gehrke, H.-J. (1985), *Stasis: Untersuchungen zu den inneren Kriegen in den griechischen Staaten des 5. und 4. Jahrhunderts v. Chr.* Munich.

Georgiou, H., and Faraklas, N. (1985), 'Ancient habitation patterns of Keos. Locations and nature of sites on the northwest part of the island.' *Ariadne* 3, 207–66.

————(1993), '*Αρχαία κατοίκηση στην Κέα. Το Βόρειο τμήμα της ανατολικής πλευράς του νήσιου.*' *Ariadne* 6, 7–57.

Gerolymatos, A. (1986), *Espionage and treason. A study of the proxenia in political and military intelligence gathering in classical Greece.* Amsterdam.

Getz-Preziosi, P. (1987), *Sculptors of the Cyclades: individual and tradition in the third millennium BC.* Ann Arbor.

Gibbins, G. (2001), 'Shipwrecks and Hellenistic trade.' In Archibald 2001, 273–312.

Gigante, M., and Maddoli, G. (1997), *L'Athenaion Politeia dello Pseudo-Senofonte*. Perugia.

Giglioni, G.B. (ed.) (1970), *Xenophontis De vectigalibus*. Florence.

Gill, D. (1988), 'The distribution of Greek vases and long distance trade.' In Christiansen and Melander 1988, 175–81.

Gilula, D. (2000), 'Hermippus and his catalogue of goods (fr.63).' In Harvey and Wilkins 2000, 75–90.

Giovannini, A. (1968), *Rome et la circulation monétaire en Grèce au IIe siècle avant Jesus-Christ*. Basel.

Gish, D., and Ambler, W. (eds.) (2009), *The political thought of Xenophon. Polis. The journal for ancient Greek political thought*. Vol. 26, No. 2. Exeter.

Gofas, D.C. (1993), *Études d'histoire du droit grec des* affaires. Athens.

Gomme, A.W. (1933), 'A forgotten factor of Greek naval strategy.' *JHS* 53, 16–24.

——Andrewes, A., and Dover, K.J. (1945), *An historical commentary on Thucydides*. Vol.1. Oxford.

——————(1956*a*), Vol. 2. Oxford.

——————(1956*b*), Vol. 3. Oxford.

——————(1970), Vol. 4. Oxford.

————(1981), Vol. 5. Oxford.

Gorgoni, C., and Pallante, P. (2000), 'On Cycladic marbles used in the Greek and Phoenician colonies of Sicily.' In Schilardi and Katsanopoulou 2000, 497–506.

Gorman, V.B. (2001), *Miletos the ornament of Ionia: a history of the city to 400 BCE*. Ann Arbor.

Gould, R.A. (2000), *Archaeology and the social history of ships*. Cambridge.

Gounaris, A.P. (1998), 'Poleodomia kai teichi tis archaias poleos Kythnou.' In Mendoni and Mazarakis-Ainian 1998, 381–435.

Graham, A.J. (1978), 'The foundation of Thasos.' *BSA* 73, 61–101.

——(1983), *Colony and mother city in ancient Greece*. 2nd edn. Chicago.

——(1992), 'Thucydides 7.13.2 and the crews of Athenian triremes.' *TAPA* 122, 257–70.

——(1998), 'Thucydides 7.13.2 and the crews of Athenian triremes: an addendum.' *TAPA* 128, 89–114.

Graindor, P. (1903), 'Mines anciennes en Grèce.' *MB* 7, 468–70.

——(1910), 'Fouilles et recherches à Tenos.' *MB* 14, 236–42.

Grandjean, Y., and Salviat, F. (1988), 'Décret d'Athènes, restaurant la démocratie à Thasos en 407 av. J-C.: IG XII, 262 complété.' *BCH* 112, 249–78.

Granovetter, M. (1985), 'Economic action and social structure: the problem of embeddedness.' *American Journal of Sociology* 91.3, 481–10.

Gray, V.J. (1980), 'The years 375 to 371 B.C.: a case study in the reliability of Diodorus Siculus and Xenophon.' *CQ* n.s. 30, 306–26.

Greco, E. (1999), 'Itanos (Crète Orientale).' *BCH* 123, 515–30.

Green, J.R., and Sinclair, R.K. (1970), 'Athenians in Eretria.' *Historia* 19 (5), 515–27.

Green, P. (1970), *Armada from Athens*. New York.

——(2003), 'Occupation and coexistence: the impact of Macedon on Athens, 323–307.' In Palagia and Tracy 2003, 1–7.

——(2006), *Diodorus Siculus, Books 11–12.37.1*. Austin.

Griffith, G.T. (1978*a*), 'Athens in the fourth century.' In Garnsey and Whittaker 1978, 127–44.

——(1978*b*), 'A note on Plutarch *Pericles* 17.' *Historia* 27 (1), 218–19.

Gruben, G. (1982), 'Naxos und Paros.' *AA* 1982 159–229, 621–89.

——(1997), 'Naxos und Delos.' *JdI* 112, 261–416.

——(2000), 'Marmor und Architektur.' In Schilardi and Katsonpoulou 2000, 125–38.

——and Koenigs, W. (1970), 'Der "Hekatompedos" von Naxos und der Burgtempel von Paros.' *AA* 1968, 135–53.

Guagliumi, B. (2005), 'Tra esilio e cittadinanza: il caso di Iulis.' In Angeli Bertinelli and Donati 2005, 419–25.

Guilmartin, J.F. (2003), *Gunpowder and galleys: changing technology and Mediterranean warfare at sea in the 16th century*. 2nd edn. London.

Haas, C. (1985), 'Athenian naval power before Themistocles.' *Historia* 34/1, 29–46.

Habicht, C. (1957), 'Samische Volksbeschlüsse der hellenistichen Zeit.' *MDAI* 72, 152–274.

——(1995), 'Buleuten und Beamte der Athenischen Kleruchie in Samos.' *MDAI* 110, 273–304.

——(1997), *Athens from Alexander to Antony*. Cambridge, Mass.

Hackens, T., and Moucharte, G. (eds.) (1993), *Actes du XIe Congrés international de numismatique organisé à l'occasion du 150e anniversaire de la Société royale de numismatique de Belgique. Bruxelles, 8–13 septembre 1991*. Louvain-la-Neuve.

Hadermann-Misguich, L., and Raepsaet, G. (eds.) (1982), *Rayonnemont grec. Hommages à Charles Delvoye*. Brussels.

Haggett, P., Cliff, A.D., and Frey, A. (1977), *Locational analysis in human geography*. London.

Hamilton, C.D. (1979), *Sparta's bitter victories: politics and diplomacy in the Corinthian War*. Ithaca.

Hammond, N.G.L. (1967), *A history of Greece*. Oxford.

——and Griffith, G.T. (1979), *A history of Macedonia*. Vol. II. Oxford.

Hansen, M.H. (1985), *Demography and democracy. The number of Athenian citizens in the fourth century B.C.* Herning.

——(1995), *Sources for the ancient Greek city-state. Acts of the Copenhagen Polis Center 2*. Copenhagen.

——(1997), *The polis as an urban centre and as a political community. Acts of the Copenhagen Polis Center 4.* Copenhagen.

——(2006*a*), *The shotgun method: the demography of the ancient Greek city-state culture.* Columbia, MI.

——(2006*b*), *Studies in the population of Aigina, Athens, and Eretria.* Copenhagen.

——and Nielsen, T.H. (2004), *An inventory of archaic and classical poleis.* Oxford.

——and Raaflaub, K. (eds.) (1996), *More studies in the ancient Greek polis. Historia Einzelschriften 108.* Stuttgart.

Harding, P. (1995), 'Athenian foreign policy in the fourth century.' *Klio* 77, 105–25.

——(2008), *The story of Athens: the fragments of the local chronicles of Attika.* London.

Harris, B.F. (ed.) (1970), *Auckland classical essays presented to E. M. Blaiklock.* Wellington.

Harris, D. (1995), *The treasures of the Parthenon and Erechtheion.* Oxford.

Harris, E.M. (2000), 'The authenticity of Andokides' *De Pace*, a subversive essay.' In Flensted-Jensen, Nielsen, and Rubinstein 2000, 479–505.

——(2006), *Democracy and the rule of law in classical Athens: essays on law, society, and politics.* Cambridge.

Harris, W.V. (2005), 'The Mediterranean and ancient history.' In W. V. Harris (ed.) *Rethinking the Mediterranean.* Oxford, 1–42.

Harvey, D., and Wilkins, J. (eds.) (2000), *The Rivals of Aristophanes: studies in Athenian Old Comedy.* London.

Hasebroek, J. (1933), *Trade and politics in ancient Greece.* Trans. L.M. Fraser and D.C. MacGregor. London.

Hatzopoulos, M.B. (2000/3), '*Νέο ἀπότιμα ἀπὸ Ἄφυτι τοῦ ἀττικοῦ ψηφίσματος περὶ νομίσματος σταθμῶν καὶ μέτρων.*' *Horos* 14–16, 31–43.

Hauben, H. (1974), 'An Athenian naval victory in 321 B.C.' *ZPE* 13, 61–4.

Head, B.V. (1991), *Historia numorum.* 2nd edn. Oxford.

Healy, J.F. (1978), *Mining and metallurgy in the Greek and Roman world.* London.

Heckel, W., and Sullivan, R. (eds.) (1984), *Ancient coins of the Graeco-Roman world. Nickle Numismatic Papers presented at Calgary Oct.19–23 1981.* Waterloo.

Heftner, H. (2001), *Der oligarchische Umsturz des Jahres 411 v. Chr. und die Herrschaft der Vierhundert in Athen.* Frankfurt-am-Main.

Heikell, R. (1992), *Greek waters pilot.* St. Ives.

Henry, A.S. (1979), 'Athens and Chalcis: I.G. i^2 39, lines 52–57 yet again.' *ZPE* 35, 287–91.

Herbert, S. (1977), *Corinth.* Vol.7 part 4: *The red-figure pottery.* Princeton.

Herbst, R.E. (1935), 'Naxos.' *RE* 16.2, (2079–80.

Herman, G. (1987), *Ritualized friendship and the Greek city*. Cambridge.

Herrmann, K. (2000), 'Zur verwendung des Parischien Marmors im heiligtum von Olympia.' In Schilardi and Katsanopoulou 2000, 379–89.

Herrmann Jr., J.J. Herz, N., and Newman, R. (eds.) (2002), *ASMOSIA 5: interdisciplinary studies on ancient stone*. London.

Hintzen-Bohlen, B. (1997), *Die Kulturpolitik des Eubulos und des Lykurg: die Denkmäler- und Bauprojekte in Athen zwischen 355 und 322 v.Chr*. Stuttgart.

Hodder, I. (ed.) (1978), *The spatial organization of culture*. London.

Hodgson, G.M. (1998), 'The approach of Institutional Economics.' *Journal of Economic Literature* 36, 166–92.

Hodkinson, S. (2000), *Property and wealth in classical Sparta*. London.

Hohlfelder, R.L., and Vann, R.L. (2000), 'Cabotage at Aperlae in ancient Lycia.' *IJNA* 29, 126–35.

Holladay, A.J. (1978), 'Athenian strategy in the Archidamian War.' *Historia* 27, 399–427.

Holloway, R.R. (1962), 'The crown of Naxos.' *ANSMN* 10, 1–9.

Homolle, T. (1884), 'Documents nouveaux sur l'Amphictyonie Attico-Delienne', *BCH* 8, 282-327.

——(1902), *Fouilles de Delphes. Vol.3*. Athens.

Hope Simpson, R., and Dickinson, O. (1979), *A gazetteer of Aegean civilization in the Bronze Age*. Göteborg.

Hopper, R.J. (1953), 'The Attic silver mines of the fourth century B.C.' *BSA* 48, 200–55.

——(1979), *Trade and industry in classical Greece*. London.

Horden, P., and Purcell, N. (2000), *The corrupting sea*. Oxford.

————(2005), 'Four Years of Corruption: A Response to Critics,' in Harris 2005, 348–76.

————(2006), 'The Mediterranean and "the New Thalassology",' *AHR* (111.3), 722–40.

Hornblower, S. (1982), *Mausolus*. Oxford.

——(1991), *A commentary on Thucydides*. Vol.1. Oxford.

——(1996), Vol.2. Oxford.

——(2008), Vol.3. Oxford.

——(2011), *The Greek world, 479–323 BC*. 4th edn. London and New York.

How, W., and Wells, J. (1975), *A commentary on Herodotus*. 2 vols. Oxford.

Howgego, C.J. (1995), *Ancient history from coins*. London and New York.

Hoyle, B. (1999), 'Islands, transport, and development.' In Biagini and Hoyle 1999, 137–58.

Humphreys, S.C. (1970), 'Economy and society in classical Athens.' *ANSP* 39, 1–26.

——(1985), 'Lycurgus of Butadae: an Athenian aristocrat.' In Eadie and Ober 1985, 199–252.
Hunt, P. (2006), 'Arming slaves and helots in classical Greece.' In Brown and Morgan 2006, 14–39.
——(2010), *War, peace, and alliance in Demosthenes' Athens.* Cambridge.
Hunter, V. (1982), *Past and process in Herodotus and Thucydides.* Princeton.
——and Edmondson, J. (eds.) (2000), *Law and social status in classical Athens.* Oxford.
Isager, S., and Hansen, M.H. (1975), *Aspects of Athenian society in the fourth century B.C.* Copenhagen.
Jackson, A.H. (1969), 'The original purpose of the Delian league.' *Historia* 18, 12–16.
——(1973), 'Privateers in the ancient Greek world.' In Foot 1973, 241–53.
Jameson, M.H. (1983), M.H. Jameson. 'Famine in the Greek world.' In Garnsey and Whittaker 1983, 6–16.
——(1987), 'Agriculture and Greek inscriptions: Rhamnous and Amorgos.' *Praktike tou H' Diethnous Synedrion Ellenikes kai Latinikes epigraphikes.* 2.290–2. Athens.
——(2000–3), 'Athens and Phaselis, *IG* I^3 10 (EM 6918).' *Horos* 14–16, 23–9.
——Runnels, C.N., and van Andel, T. (1994), *A Greek countryside: the southern Argolid from prehistory to the present day.* Stanford.
Jeffery, L.H. (1976), *Archaic Greece: the City States c.700–500 B.C.* New York.
Jehne, M. (1994), *Koine Eirene: Untersuchungen zu den Befriedungs- und Stabilisierungsbemühungen in der griechischen Poliswelt des 4.Jahrhunderts v. Chr.* Stuttgart.
——(2004), 'Überlegungen zu den Auslassungen in Xenophons *Hellenika* am Beispiel der Gründung des zweiten athenischen Seebunds.' In Tuplin 2004, 463–80.
Jigoulov, V.S. (2010), *The social history of Achaemenid Phoenicia.* London.
Jockey, P. (1996), 'Le sanctuaire de Délos à l'epoque archaïque.' *Topoi* 6, 159–97.
Johnston, A.W. (1979), *Trademarks on Greek vases.* Warminster.
Jones, A.H.M. (1957), *Athenian democracy.* Baltimore.
Jordan, B. (1975), *The Athenian navy in the classical period: a study of Athenian naval administration and military organization in the fifth and fourth centuries B.C.* Berkeley.
Kagan, D. (1961), 'The economic origins of the Corinthian War.' *La Parola del Passato* 80, 321–41.
——(1969), *The outbreak of the Peloponnesian War.* Ithaca.
——(1974), *The Archidamian war.* Ithaca.
Kallet, L. (2001), *Money and the corrosion of power in Thucydides: the Sicilian expedition and its aftermath.* Berkeley.

Kallet, L. (2004), 'Epigraphic geography: the tribute quota fragments assigned to 421/0–415/4 B.C.' *Hesperia* 73, 465–96.

——(2009), 'Democracy, empire, and epigraphy in the twentieth century.' In Ma, Papazarkadas, and Parker 2009, 43–66.

Kallet-Marx, L. (1993), *Money, expense, and naval power in Thucydides' History 1–5.24*. Berkeley.

Kallet-Marx, R.M. (1985), 'Athens, Thebes, and the foundation of the Second Athenian League.' *CA* 4 (2), 127–51.

Karwiese, S. (1980), 'Lysander as Herakliskos Drakonopigon.' *Numismatic Chronicle* 140, 1–27.

Keaveney, A. (1988), 'The attack on Naxos: a "forgotten cause" of the Ionian revolt.' *CQ* 38 (1), 76–81.

Keen, A.G. (1993), 'Athenian campaigns in Karia and Lykia during the Peloponnesian War.' *JHS* 113, 152–7.

——(2000), 'Grain for Athens.' In Oliver, Brock, Cornell, and Hodkinson 2000, 63–73.

Kiechle, F.K. (1979), 'Korkyra und der Handelsweg durch das adriatische Meer im 5. Jh.v.Chr.' *Historia* 28/2, 173–91.

Kim, H.S. (2002), 'Small change and the moneyed economy.' In Cartledge, Cohen, and Foxhall 2002, 44–51.

Kingsley, B.M. (1986), 'Harpalos in the Megarid (333–331 B.C.) and the grain shipments from Cyrene.' *ZPE* 66, 165–77.

Kinzl, K.H. (1976), 'Miltiades' Parosexpedition in der Geschichtsschreibung.' *Hermes* 104 (3), 280–307.

Kirigin, B. (1990), 'The Greeks in central Dalmatia: some new evidence.' In Descoeudres 1990, 296–302.

——(2006), *Pharos: the Parian settlement in Dalmatia.* BAR International Series 1561.

Knapp, A.B. (1990), 'Paradise gained and paradise lost: intensification, specialization, complexity, collapse.' *Asian Perspectives* 28, 179–214.

Kokkorou-Alevras, G. (1992), '*Τα ἀρχαία λατομεία μάρμαρου τής Ναξίου.*' *ArchEph* 101–27.

——(2000), 'The use and distribution of Parian marble during the Archaic period.' In Schilardi and Katsanopoulou 2000, 143–53.

Kolb, F. (1996), 'Stadt und land im antiken Kleinasien: der Testfall Kyaneai.' In Strubbe, Tybout, and Versnel 1996, 97–112.

Kolodny, E.Y. (1974), *La population des îles de la gréce.* Aix-en-Provence.

Kondoleon, N.M. (1963), 'Archilochus und Paros.' *Entretiens Hardt X: 'Archiloque'26 août- 3 septembre 1963*. Geneva.

——(1963/5), "*Οί Ἀειναῦται τής Ερετρίας.*' *AE* 1963 [1965], 1–45.

Korres, M. (2005), 'The tower of Agia Triada on Amorgos.' In Yeroulanou and Stamatopoulou 2005, 173–94.

Kostopoulou, S. (1999), 'Transport network access and degrees of insularity.' In Biagini and Hoyle 1999, 171–94.

Kourayos, Y. (2005), 'Despotiko Mandra: a sanctuary dedicated to Apollo.' In Yeroulanou and Stamatopoulou 2005, 105–33.

Kraay, C.M. (1976), *Archaic and classical Greek coins.* London.

Krentz, P. (1989), *Xenophon Hellenika I-II.3.10.* Warminster.

Kretschmer, K. (1909), *Die italieneschen Portolane des Mittelalters.* Berlin.

Kreutz, B.M. (1988), 'The ecology of maritime success: the puzzling case of Amalfi.' *Mediterranean Historical Review* 3, 103–13.

Kroll, J.H. (2006), 'Athenian tetradrachms recently discovered in the Athenian Agora' *RN* 162, 57-64.

——(2009), 'What about coinage?' In Ma, Papazarkadas, and Parker 2009, 195–209.

——(2011), 'The reminting of Athenian silver coinage, 353 B.C.' *Hesperia* 80.2, 229-59.

Kurke, L. (2002), 'Money and mythic history: the contestation of transactional orders in the fifth century BC.' In Scheidel and von Reden 2002, 87–113.

Laidlaw, W.A. (1939), *A history of Delos.* Oxford.

Laing Jr, D.R. (1966), *A new interpretation of the Athenian naval catalogue IG II^2 1951.* Ann Arbor.

Lalonde, G.V., Langdon, M.K., and Walbank, M.B. (1991), *Agora XIX: Inscriptions. Horoi, poletai records, and leases of public lands.* Princeton.

Lambrinoudakis, V. (2005), 'A new early Archaic building on Naxos: some thoughts on the Oikos of the Naxians on Delos.' In Yeroulanou and Stamatopoulou 2005, 79–86.

Länni, A. (2006), *Law and justice in the courts of Classical Athens.* Cambridge.

Lanzilotta, E. (1987), *Paro: dall'eta arcaica all'eta ellenistica.* Rome.

——and Schilardi, D. (eds.) (1996), *Le Cicladi ed il mondo egeo: seminario internazionale di Studi, Roma 19–21 novembre 1992.* Rome.

Larsen, J.A.O. (1968), *Greek federal states: their institutions and history.* Oxford.

Lätsch, F. (2005), *Insularität und Gesellschaft in der Antike.* Stuttgart.

Lattimore, S. (1997), 'Art and architecture.' In Tritle 1997, 249–82.

Lavelle, B.M. (1992), 'The Pisistratids and the mines of Thrace.' *GRBS* 33, 5–23.

——(2005), *Fame, money, and power: the rise of Peisistratos and 'democratic' tyranny at Athens.* Ann Arbor.

Lawall, M. (1998), 'Ceramics and positivism revisited: Greek transport amphoras and history.' In Parkins and Smith 1998, 75–101.

Lazarides, D.I. (1976), '*Επίγραμμα παρίων ἀπὸ τήν Ἀμφίπολιν.*' *AE* 1976, 164–81.

Lazenby, J.F. (2004), *The Peloponnesian war: a military study*. London.
Leahy, D.M. (1957), 'The Spartan embassy to Lygdamis.' *JHS* 77 (2), 272–5.
Legon, R.P. (1972), 'Samos in the Delian League.' *Historia* 21 (2), 145–58.
——(1981), *Megara: the political history of a Greek city-state to 336 B.C.* Ithaca.
Lepper, F.A. (1962), 'Some rubrics in the Athenian quota lists.' *JHS* 82, 25–55.
Le Rider, G. (1966), *Monnaies crétoises du* V^{e} *au* Ier *siècle av. J.-C.* Paris.
Lewis, D.M. (1954), 'Notes on Attic inscriptions.' *BSA* 49, 17–50.
——(1962), 'The federal constitution of Keos.' *BSA* 57, 1–4.
——(1975), Review of Coupry. *Gnomon* 47, 717–19.
——(1994), 'The Athenian tribute-quota lists, 453–450 BC.' *ABSA* 89, 285–301.
Lewis, J.D. (2009), 'Xenophon *Poroi* and the foundations of political economy.' In Gish and Ambler 2009, 370–94.
Lewis, S. (ed.) (2006), *Ancient tyranny*. Edinburgh.
Liampi, K. (1998), "*Οι νομισματίκες εκδοσεῖς τῶν Κυκλαδῶν καὶ η κυκλοφορία τους*.' In Mendoni and Margaris 1998.
Liata, E.D. (1987), *Η Σέριφος κατά την τουρκοκρατία*. Athens.
Littman, R.J. (2001), 'Dor and the Athenian empire.' *AJAH* 15.2, 155–76.
Lodwick, M.V. (1996), *The monumental architecture of the Cyclades in the Classical and Hellenistic periods: Volume I*. PhD diss. Oxford.
Lohmann, H. (1993), *Atene: Forschungen zu Seidlungs- und Wirtschaftsstruktur des klassichen Attika*. Cologne.
——(1999), 'Survey in der chôra von Milet.' *AA* 3, 439–73.
Loomis, W.T. (1992), *The Spartan war fund, IG V 1,1 and a new fragment*. Stuttgart.
Lotze, D. (1964), *Lysander und der Peloponnesische krieg, Abhandlungen der Sächsischen Akademie der Wissenschaften zu Leipzig. Phil-hist. Klasse 57*. Berlin.
Low, P. (ed.) (2008), *The Athenian empire*. Edinburgh.
Ma, J. (2000), 'Fighting *poleis* in the Hellenistic world.' In van Wees 2000, 337–76.
——Papazarkadas, N., and Parker, R. (eds.) (2009), *Interpeting the Athenian empire*. London.
McCormick, M. (2001), *Origins of the European economy: communications and commerce AD 300–900*. Cambridge.
MacDonald, B.R. (1979), *The distribution of Attic pottery from 450 to 375 B.C.: the effects of politics on trade*. PhD diss., University of Pennsylvania.
——(1981), 'The Phanosthenes decree: taxes and timber in late fifth-century Athens.' *Hesperia* 50, 141–6.
——(1982), 'The authenticity of the Congress Decree.' *Historia* 31 (1), 120–3.

——(1984), '*Λῄστεια* and *Ληιζομαι* in Thucydides and in *IG* I^3 41, 67, and 75.' *AJP* 105, 77–84

MacDowell, D.M. (2009), *Demosthenes the orator*. Oxford.

McGregor, M.F. (1982), 'Athens and Hestiaia.' In *Studies in Attic epigraphy, history and topography presented to Eugene Vanderpool. Hesperia Suppl. 19.* Princeton. Pp. 101–11.

——(1987), *The Athenians and their empire*. Vancouver.

McKechnie, P. (1989), *Outsiders in the Greek cities in the fourth century BC*. London.

McPhee, I. (1997), 'Part II: Attic pottery.' In White 1997, 67–108.

Maier, F.G. (1958), 'Stadtmauern auf Keos.' *AM* 73, 6–16.

——(1959–61), *Griechische Mauerbauinschriften*. Heidelberg.

Malitz, J. (2008), 'Der Preis des Krieges. Thukydides und die Finanzen Athens.' In Burrer and Müller 2008, 28–45.

Malkin, I., Constantakopoulou, C., and Panagopoulou, K. (eds.) (2009), *Greek and Roman networks in the Mediterranean*. London and New York.

Mallett, M.E., and Hale, J.R. (1984), *The military organization of a Renaissance state: Venice c.1400 to 1617*. Cambridge.

Mansfield, J.M. (1976), *IG XII. 9, 1273/1274: the Eretrian laws*. MA. thesis, University of California, Berkeley.

Marangou, L. (2006), 'Céramique attique à Amorgos: données archéologiques et tradition littéraire.' In de La Genière 2006, 69–74.

Marek, C. (1984), *Die Proxenie*. Frankfurt-am-Main.

Markoe, G. (2000), *Phoenicians*. Berkeley.

Marr, J.L., and Rhodes, P.J. (2008), *The 'Old Oligarch': the Constitution of the Athenians attributed to Xenophon*. Warminster.

Marshall, F.H. (1905), *The second Athenian confederacy*. Cambridge.

Martin, T.R. (1985), *Sovereignty and coinage in classical Greece*. Princeton.

Matthaiou, A.P. (2000), '*Ἀττικὸ ψήφισμα πρὸς τιμὴν Πολυπείθους Σιφνίου*.' In Zervoudakis 2000, 239–48.

Matthäus, H. (1988), 'Thasos in Altertum.' In Wagner and Weisgerber 1988, 13–39.

Mattingly, H.B. (1966), 'Periclean imperialism.' In Badian 1966, 193–233.

——(1987), 'The Athenian Coinage Decree and the Assertion of Empire.' In Carradice 1987, 65–71.

——(1992), 'Epigraphy and the Athenian empire.' *Historia* 41, 129–35.

——(1993), 'New light on the Athenian Standards Decree.' *Klio* 75, 99–102.

——(1996), *The Athenian empire restored: epigraphic and historical studies*. Ann Arbor.

——(1999), Review of Figueira, 1998. *AJA* 103, 712–13.

——(2002), 'The Athenian decree for Chalcis (*IG* I^3 .40).' *CQ* 52.1, 377–9.

Mazarakis-Ainian, A. (1993), '*Επιφανειακὲς ἔρευνες στὴ νῆσο Κύθνο: Τὸ τεῖχος τῆς ἀρχαίας κύθνου*.' *ArchEph* 132, 217–53.

Mazarakis-Ainian, A. (1996), 'Ricognizioni archeologiche nell'isola di Kithnos.' In Lanzilotta and Schilardi 1996, 245–73.

——(1998), 'The Kythnos survey project: a preliminary report.' In Mendoni and Mazarakis-Ainian 1998, 363–79 and 397–435.

——(2005), 'Inside the adyton of a Greek temple: excavations on Kythnos (Cyclades).' In Yeroulanou and Stamatopoulou 2005, 87–103.

Meadows, A., and Shipton, K. (eds.) (2001), *Money and its uses in the ancient Greek world*. Oxford.

Meiggs, R. (1966), 'The dating of fifth-century Attic inscriptions.' *JHS* 86, 86–98.

——(1972), *The Athenian empire*. Oxford.

——(1982), *Trees and timber in the ancient Mediterranean world*. Oxford: Clarendon.

——and Lewis, D. (1989), *A selection of Greek historical inscriptions to the end of the fifth century BC*. Oxford.

Meikle, S. (1995), *Aristotle's economic thought*. Oxford.

Mellor, R., and Tritle, L. (eds.) (1999), *Text and tradition. Studies in Greek history and historiography in honor of Mortimer Chambers*. Claremont, Calif.

Mendoni, L.G. (1985), '*Αρχαιολογικές έρευνες στην Κέα. Αρχαία Καρθαία.*' *Arkhaiognosia* 4, 149–84.

——(1994), 'The organization of the countryside in Kea.' In Doukellis and Mendoni 1994, 147–61.

——(1998), '*Αρχαιοι Πυργοι στις Κυκλαδες*.' In Mendoni and Margaris 1998, 471–83.

——and Margaris, N. (eds.) (1998), *Κυκλαδες: Ιστορια του τοπιου καὶ τοπικες ιστοριες*: Απο *το φυσικο περι·αλλον στο ιστορικο τοπιο*. Athens.

——and Mazarakis-Ainian, A. (1998), *Kea-Kythnos: history and archaeology. Proceedings of an international symposium, Kea-Kythnos, 22–25 June 1994. Meletemata 27*. Athens.

——and Mourtzas, N.D. (1990), 'An archaeological approach to coastal sites: the example of the ancient harbour of Karthaia.' *Parnassos* 32, 387–403.

Meritt, B., Wade-Gery, H.T., McGregor, M. (1939), *The Athenian tribute lists-Vol.III*. Cambridge, Mass.

Merker, I.L. (1968), 'The harbor of Iulis.' *AJA* 72, 383–4.

——(1970), 'The Ptolemaic officials and the league of the islanders.' *Historia* 19, 141–60.

Meyer, E. (1924), 'Die Wirtschaftliche Entwicklung des Altertums.' *Kleine Schriften* 81–168. Halle.

Migeotte, L. (1984), *L'emprunt public dans les cités grecques*. Paris.

——(1992), *Les souscriptions publiques dans les cités grecques*. Geneva and Quebec.

——(2009), *The economy of the Greek cities: from the Archaic period to the early Roman empire.* Trans. J. Lloyd. Berkeley.
Miller, M. (1971), *The thalassocracies: studies in chronography II.* Albany.
Miller, M.C. (1997), *Athens and Persia in the fifth century BC: a study in cultural receptivity.* Cambridge.
Millett, P. (1991), *Lending and borrowing in ancient Athens.* Cambridge.
Milton, M. (1979), 'The date of Thucydides' synchronism of the siege of Naxos with Themistokles' flight.' *Historia* 257–75.
Mirhady, D., and Lee Too, Y. (2000), *Isokrates I.* Austin.
Mitchell, F.W. (1970), *Lykourgan Athens 338–322 BC.* Cincinnati.
——(1973), 'Lykourgan Athens: 338–322'. In C.G. Boulter, D.W. Bradeen, A. Cameron, J.L. Caskey, and A.J. Christopherson (eds.), *Lectures in memory of Louis Taft Semple.* Norman, OK, 163–214.
——(1984*a*), 'The assessment of the allies in the second Athenian league,' *EMC* 28, 23–37.
——(1984*b*), 'The rasura of *IG* II^2 43: Jason, the Pheraian demos, and the Athenian league.' *AncW* 9, 39–58.
Mitchell, L., and Rubinstein, L. (2009), *Greek history and epigraphy: essays in honour of P.J. Rhodes.* Swansea.
Moggi, M. (1976), *I sinecismi interstatali greci*: vol.1. Pisa.
Möller, A. (2000), *Naukratis. Trade in archaic Greece.* Oxford.
——(2007), 'Classical Greece: distribution.' In Scheidel, Morris, and Saller 2007, 362–84.
Momigliano, A. (1929), 'Le cause della spedizione di Sicilia.' *RFIC* 7, 371–7.
Moreno, A. (2007), *Feeding the democracy: the Athenian grain supply in the fifth and fourth centuries BC.* Oxford.
——(2009), '"The Attic neighbour": the cleruchy in the Athenian empire.' In Ma, Papazarkadas, and Parker 2009, 211–21.
Morley, N. (2006), 'Narrative economy.' In Bang, Ikeguchi, and Ziche 2006, 27–46.
——(2007), *Trade in classical antiquity.* Cambridge.
Morricone, L. (1950), 'Cronaca, scavi e ricerche a Coo (1935–43): relazione preliminare.' *Bolletino d'Arte*, 54–75.
Morris, I. (1994*a*), 'The Athenian economy twenty years after the *The Ancient Economy.*' *CP* 89, 351–66.
——(1994*b*), ed. *Classical Greece: ancient histories and modern archaeologies.* Cambridge.
——(1999), 'Forward.' In Finley 1999, ix–xxvi.
——(2009), 'The greater Athenian state.' In Morris and Scheidel 2009, 99–177.
——and Manning, J.G. (eds.) (2005*a*), *The ancient economy: evidence and models.* Stanford.

Morris, I. and Manning, J.G. (2005*b*), 'The economic sociology of the ancient Mediterranean world.' In Smelser and Swedborg 2005, 131–59.

——and Scheidel, W. (eds.) (2009), *The dynamics of ancient empires: state power from Assyria to Byzantium.* Oxford.

Morris, S.P., and Papadopoulos, J.K. (2005), 'Greek towers and slaves: an archaeology of exploitation.' *AJA* 109.2, 155–225.

Morrison, J.S. (1987), 'Athenian sea power in 323/2 B.C.: dream and reality.' *JHS* 57, 88–97.

——Coates, J.F., and Rankov, N.B. (2000), *The Athenian trireme: the history and reconstruction of an ancient Greek warship.* 2nd edn. Cambridge.

Morton, J. (2001), *The role of the physical environment in ancient Greek seafaring.* Leiden.

Mossé, C. (1973), *Athens in decline, 404-86 B.C.* Trans. Jean Stewart. London and Boston.

Mosshammer, A.A. (1979), *The* Chronicle *of Eusebius and Greek chronographic tradition.* Lewisburg.

Motzo, B.R. (1947), *Il compasso de navegare.* Cagliari.

Müller, C. (1855), *Geographi Graeci minores* 2. Paris.

Munn, M.L.Z. (1983), 'Corinthian trade with the West in the Classical period.' PhD Diss. Bryn Mawr College.

Murray, O. (1966), '*Ο αρχαιος δασμος*.' *Historia* 15, 142–56.

——(1993), *Early Greece.* 2nd edn. Cambridge, Mass.

——and Price, S. (eds.) (1990), *The Greek city from Homer to Alexander.* Oxford.

Myres, J.L. (1906), 'On the "list of thalassocracies" in Eusebius.' *JHS* 26, 84–130.

——(1953), *Herodotus, father of history.* Oxford.

Nafissi, M. (1989), 'Distribution and trade.' In Stibbe 1989, 68–88.

——(2004), 'Class, embeddedness and the modernity of ancient Athens.' *Comparative Studies in Society and History* 46, 378–410.

——(2005), *Ancient Athens and modern ideology: value, theory, and evidence in historical sources, Max Weber, Karl Polanyi, and Moses Finley.* London.

Neer, R.T. (2003), 'Framing the gift: the Siphnian treasury at Delphi and the politics of architectural sculpture.' In Dougherty and Kurke 2003, 120–49.

——(2004), 'The Athenian treasury at Delphi and the material of politics.' *CA* 22, 63–93.

Newell, E.T. (1934), *A hoard from Siphnos: NNM 64.* New York.

Nicolet-Pierre, H. (1988),'Remarques sur le monnayage de Naxos (Cyclades) à l'époque classique.' *Praktika tou XII Diethnous Klasikis Archaiologias.* Athens. 159–62.

——(1997), 'Naxos (Cyclades) archaïque: monnaie et histoire. La frappe des "canthares," de la fin du Vie siècle à c.470 av. J.-C.' *Numismatica e Antichita Classiche* 26, 63–121.

Nielsen, T.H., and Roy, J. (1999), *Defining ancient Arkadia*. Copenhagen.

Nieto, X. (1997), 'Le commerce de cabotage et de redistribution.' In Pomey 1997, 146–59.

Nigdelis, P.M. (1990), *Politeuma kai Koinonia tōn poleōn tōn Kykladōn kata tēn ellenistike kai autokratorike epochē*. Thessaloniki.

Nixon, L., and Price, S. (1990), 'The size and resources of Greek cities.' In Murray and Price 1990, 137–70.

Ober, J. (1996), *The Athenian revolution*. Princeton.

——(2008), *Democracy and knowledge: innovation and learning in classical Athens*. Princeton.

Ohnesorg, A. (2005), 'Naxian and Parian architecture: general features and new discoveries.' In Yeroulanou and Stamatopoulou 2005, 135–52.

Oliva, P. (1981), *The birth of Greek civilization*. London.

Oliver, G.J. (2007), *War, food, and politics in early Hellenistic Athens*. Oxford.

——Brock, R., Cornell, T.J., and Hodkinson, S. (eds.) (2000), *The sea in antiquity*. Oxford.

Oliver, J.H. (1936), 'Inscriptions from Athens.' *AJA* 40, 460–5.

Ormerod, H.A. (1924), *Piracy in the ancient world; an essay in Mediterranean history*. Liverpool.

Osborne, M.J. (1974), 'Two Athenian decrees for Delians.' *Eranos* 72, 168–84.

——and Byrne, S.G. (1996), *The Foreign residents of Athens*. Leuven.

Osborne, R. (1987), *Classical landscape with figures: the ancient Greek city and its countryside*. London.

——(1988), 'Social and economic implications of the leasing of land and property in classical and hellenistic Greece.' *Chiron* 18, 279–323.

——(1991), 'Land use and settlement in hellenistic Keos: the epigraphic evidence.' In Cherry, Davis, and Mantzourani 1991, 319–25.

——(1996), 'Pots, trade, and the archaic Greek economy.' *Antiquity* 70, 31–44.

——(1999), 'Archaeology and the Athenian empire.' *TAPA* 129, 319–32. Reprinted in Low 2008, 211–24.

——(2000*a*), *The Athenian empire. LACTOR 1*. 4th edn. London.

——(2000*b*), 'Religion, imperial politics, and the offering of freedom to slaves.' In Hunter and Edmondson 2000, 75–92.

——(2004), 'Demography and survey.' In Alcock and Cherry 2004, 163–72.

——(2009), 'The politics of an epigraphic habit: the case of Thasos.' In Mitchell and Rubinstein 2009, 103–14.

——and Byrne, S.G. (2001), *The foreign residents of Athens: an annex to the Lexicon of Greek Personal Names: Attica*. Leiden.

Ostwald, M. (1982), *Autonomia: its genesis and early history*. Chico, Calif.
——(2002), 'Athens and Chalkis: a study in imperial control.' *JHS* 122, 134–43.
O'Sullivan, L. (2009), *The regime of Demetrius of Phalerum in Athens, 317–307 BCE*. Leiden.
Owen, S. (2003), 'Of gods and men: Archilochus, archaeology, and the Greek settlement of Thasos.' *PCPS* 49, 1–18.
Palagia, O., and Herz, N. (2002), 'Investigation of marbles at Delphi.' In Herrmann, Herz, and Newman (2002, 240–49.
——and Tracy, S.V. (2003), *The Macedonians in Athens, 322–229 B.C.* Oxford.
Paleothodoros, D. (2009), 'Commercial networks in the Mediterranean and the diffusion of early Attic red-figure pottery (525–490 BCE).' In Malkin, Constantakopoulou, and Panagopoulou 2009, 158–75.
Palmer, H. (1964), 'Part IV: the Classical and Roman periods.' In Blegen, Palmer, and Young 1964, 65–327.
Papadopoulos, J.K., and Smithson, E.L. (2002), 'The cultural biography of a Cycladic Geometric amphora: islanders in Athens and the prehistory of metics.' *Hesperia* 71, 149–99.
Papageorgiadou-Banis, Ch. (1993), 'Koinon of the Keians? The numismatic evidence.' *RBN* 139, 9–16.
——(1997), *The coinage of Kea: Meletemata 24*. Athens.
Papalas, A.J. (1999), 'Polycrates of Samos and the first Greek trireme fleet.' *Mariner's Mirror* 85, 3–19.
——(2000), 'The Parian expedition and the development of the Athenian navy.' *AHB* 14.3, 107–19.
Papazarkadas, N. (2007), 'An honorific decree from classical Siphnos.' *REA* 109, 137–46.
——(2009), 'Epigraphy and the Athenian empire: reshuffling the chronological cards.' In Ma, Papazarkadas, and Parker 2009, 67–88.
Parke, H.W. (1930), 'The development of the second Spartan empire.' *JHS* 50, 56–77.
Parker, V. (1997), *Untersuchungen zum Lelantischen Krieg und verwandten Problemen der frühgriechischen Geschichte*. Stuttgart.
Parkins, H., and Smith, C. (eds.) (1998), *Trade, traders, and the ancient city*. London.
Parlama, L., and Stampolidis, N. (2001), *Athens: the city beneath the city: antiquities from the Metropolitan Railway excavations*. Athens.
Parmeggiani, G. (2011), *Eforo di Cuma: studi di storiografia graeca*. Bologna.
Partida, E. (2000), 'Architecture in Parian marble at Delphi.' In Schilardi and Katsonopoulou 2000, 355–63.
Paschali, D. (1925 [repr. 1995]), *Ιστορια τῆς νεσου Ανδρου*. Athens.

Pébarthe, C. (1999), 'Thasos, l'empire d'Athènes et les *emporia* de Thrace.' *ZPE* 126, 131–54.
——(2000), 'Fiscalité, empire athénien et écriture: retour sur les causes de la guerre du Péloponnèse.' *ZPE* 129, 47–76.
——(2005), 'La perception des droits de passage à Chalcis (*IG* I^3 40, 446 A.C.).' *Historia* 54.1, 84–92.
——(2008), *Monnaie et marché à Athènes à l'époque classique.* Paris.
Pečirka, J. (1966), *The formula for the grant of enktêsis in Attic inscriptions.* Prague.
——(1982), 'Athenian imperialism and the Athenian economy.' *Eirene* 19, 117–25.
Pedley, J.G. (1976), *Greek sculpture of the archaic period: the island workshops.* Mainz.
Peppa-Papaioannou, E. (2000), 'Parian marble and the Asclepieion of Epidauros during the 4th c. B.C.' In Schilardi and Katsanopoulou 2000, 364–72.
Perlman, S. (1964), 'The causes and outbreak of the Corinthian War.' *CQ* 14 (1), 64–81.
Perlman, P. (1995), '*Θεωροδοκουντες εν ταις πολεσιν*: Panhellenic *epangelia* and political status.' In Hansen 1995, 113–64.
——(2000), 'Gortyn: the first seven hundred years (Part 1).' In Flensted-Jensen, Nielsen, and Rubinstein 2000, 60–89.
——(2004), 'Crete.' In Hansen and Nielsen 2004, 1144–95.
Pettegrew, D. (2001), 'Chasing the classical farmstead: assessing the formation and signature of rural settlement in Greek landscape archaeology.' *JMA* 14, 189–209.
Petzold, K.-E. (1994), 'Die Gründung des delisch-attischen Seebundes: Element einer "imperialistischen" Politik Athens?' *Historia* 43 (1), 1–31.
Phillipps, D.D. (2004), *Athenian political oratory: 16 key speeches.* New York.
Phillippson, A. (1959), *Die griechischen Landschaften IV: Das Aegaeische Meer und seine Inseln.* Frankfurt.
Photos-Jones, E., Cottiers, A., Hall, and Mendoni, L.G. (1997), 'Kean Miltos: the well-known iron oxides of antiquity.' *BSA* 92, 359–71.
——Hall, A.J., Atkinson, J.A., Tompsett, G., Cottier, A., and Sanders, G.D. R. (1999), 'The Aghia Kyriaki, Melos Survey: prospecting for the elusive earths in the Roman period in the Aegean.' *BSA* 94, 377–413.
Picard, O. (1979), *Chalcis et la confédération eubéenne: étude de numismatique et d'histoire, IVe-Ier siècle.* Athens and Paris.
Piérart, M. (1984), 'Deux notes sur la politique d'Athènes en mer Égée (428–425).' *BCH* 108, 161–71.
Placido, D. (1980), 'La ley atica de 375/4 a.C. y la politica ateniense.' *Memorias de Historia Antiqua* 4, 27–41.

Pleket, H.W. (1963), 'Thasos and the popularity of the Athenian empire.' *Historia* 12 (1), 70–7.
——(2008), 'Epilogue.' In Alston and van Nijf 2008, 181–96.
Polanyi, K. (1944), *The great transformation*. New York.
Pomey, P. (ed.) (1997), *La navigation dans l'antiquité*. Aix-en-Provence.
Porten, B., and Yardeni, A. (1993), *Textbook of Aramaic documents from ancient Egypt*, vol.3: *literature, accounts, lists*. Jerusalem.
Potter, D. (1984), '*IG* II^2 339; evidence for Athenian involvement in the war of Agis III.' *BSA* 79, 229–35.
Pouilloux, J. (1954), *Recherches sur l'histoire et les cultes de Thasos I, de la fondation de la cité à 196 avant J.-C.* Paris.
——(1982), 'La foundation de Thasos: archéologie, literature, et critique historique.' In Hadermann-Misguich and Raepsaet 1982, 91–101.
Powell, A., and Hodkinson, S. (eds.) (2002), *Sparta beyond the mirage*. London.
——and Meidani, K. (eds.) (forthcoming), *The eyesore of Aigina: anti-Athenian attitudes in Greek, hellenistic, and Roman history*.
Prent, M. (2005), *Cretan sanctuaries and cults*. Leiden.
Price, M.J., and Waggoner, N.M. (1975), *Archaic silver coinage. The Asyut hoard*. London.
Price, S., and Nixon, L. (2005), 'Ancient Greek agricultural terraces: evidence from tests and archaeological survey.' *AJA* 109, 665–94.
Pritchett, W.K. (1953), 'The Attic stelai: part I.' *Hesperia* 22 (4), 225–99.
——(1972), 'Lucubrationes epigraphicae.' *CSCSA* 5, 164–9.
——(1991), *The Greek state at war. Vol. V*. Berkeley.
——(1995), *Thucydides' Pentekontaetia and other essays*. Amsterdam.
——and Pippin, A. (1956), 'The Attic Stelai: Part II.' *Hesperia* 25, 178–328.
Prost, F. (2001), 'Sparte et les Cyclades au Ve siècle: à propos d'*ID* 87.' *REA* 103.1–2, 241–60.
Pryor, J.H. (1988), *Geography, technology, and war: studies in the maritime history of the Mediterranean, 649–1571*. Cambridge.
Psarras, S.E. (1994), '*Αρχαίες ελληνικές επιγραφές και τοπωνυμία η περιπτώση της Τήνου*.' *Onomata* 14, 29–42.
Purcell, N. (2005), 'The view from the customs house.' In Harris 2005, 200–32.
Purpura, G. (1985), 'Il regolamento doganale di Cauno e la lex Rhodia in D.14.2.9.' *Annali del Seminario Giurdico della Università di Palermo* 38, 273–331.
Quinn, T.J. (1964), 'Thucydides and the unpopularity of the Athenian empire.' *Historia* 13 (3), 257–66.
——(1981), *Athens and Samos, Lesbos, and Chios 478–404 B.C.* Manchester.
Rainbird, P. (1999), 'Islands out of time: towards a critique of island archaeology.' *Journal of Mediterranean Archaeology* 12.2, 226–34.

——(2007), *The archaeology of islands.* Cambridge.
Randall, R.H. (1953), 'The Erechtheum workmen.' *AJA* 57, 199–210.
Raue, H.O. (1937), *Untersuchungen zur Geschichte des korinthischen Bundes.* Würzburg.
Rauh, N.K. Townsend, R.F., Hoff, M., and Wandsnider, L. (2000), 'Pirates in the bay of Pamphylia: an archaeological inquiry.' In Oliver 2000, 151–79.
Rawlings III, H.R. (1977), 'Thucydides on the purpose of the Delian League.' *Phoenix* 31, 1-8. Reprinted in Low 2008, 49–57.
Rawlings, L. (2010), 'The Carthaginian navy: questions and assumptions.' In Fagan and Trundle 2010, 253–87.
Reber, K., Hansen, M.H., and Ducrey, P. (2004), 'Euboia.' In Hansen and Nielsen 2004, 643–63.
Reed, C.M. (2003), *Maritime traders in the ancient Greek world.* Cambridge.
Reger, G. (1992), 'Athens and Tenos in the early Hellenistic age.' *CQ* 42, 365–83.
——(1994*a*), *Regionalism and change in the economy of independent Delos, 314–167 B.C.* Berkeley.
——(1994*b*), 'The date and historical significance of IG XII v 714 of Andros.' *Hesperia* 63, 309–21.
——(1997), 'Islands with one *polis* versus islands with several *poleis.*' In Hansen 1997, 450–92.
——(1998), 'The historical and archaeological background to the disappearance of Koresia and Poiessa on Keos.' In Mendoni and Mazarakis-Ainian 1998, 633–41.
——(2004), 'The Aegean.' In Hansen and Nielsen 2004, 732–93.
——(2007), 'Hellenistic Greece and western Asia Minor.' In Scheidel, Morris, and Saller 2007, 460–86.
——and Risser, M. (1991), 'Coinage and federation in hellenistic Keos.' In Cherry, Davis, and Mantzourani 1991, 305–17.
Reiter, H.A. (1991), *Athen und die Poleis des delisch-attischen Seebundes: die Proxenoi und Euergetai des attischen Demos in den Poleis des delisch-attischen Seebundes im Licht der attischen Proxenie- und Euergesiebeschlüsse des 5.Jahrhunderts v. Chr.* Regensburg.
Renfrew, C. (1975), 'Trade as action at a distance: questions of integration and communication.' In J.A. Sabloff and C.C. Lamberg-Karlovsky (eds.), *Ancient civilization and trade.* Albuquerque.
——(1977), 'Alternative models for exchange and spatial distribution.' In Earle and Erickson 1977, 71–90.
——and Cherry, J.F. (eds.) (1971), *Peer-polity interaction and socio-political change.* Cambridge.
——and Peacey, J.S. (1968), 'Aegean marble: a petrological study.' *ABSA* 63, 45–66.

Renfrew, C. and Wagstaff, M. (eds.) (1982), *An island polity: the archaeology of exploitation on Melos*. Cambridge.

Rhodes, P.J. (1985), *The Athenian empire. GaR Survey no.17.* Oxford.

——(1992), 'The Delian League to 449 BC.' *CAH*² V, 34–61.

——(1993), *A commentary on the Aristotelian* Athenaion Politeia². Oxford.

——(2000), 'Oligarchs in Athens.' In Brock and Hodkinson 2000, 119–36.

——(2008), 'After the three-bar *sigma* controversy: the history of Athenian imperialism reassessed.' *CQ* 58.2, 500–6.

——and Osborne, R. (2003), *Greek historical inscriptions: 404–323 BC.* Oxford.

Richter, G.M.A. (1929), 'Silk in Greece.' *AJA* 33, 27–33.

——(1960), *Kouroi: archaic Greek youths.* New York.

Rickman, G. (1980), *The corn supply of ancient Rome.* Oxford.

Robbins, F.E. (1918), 'The cost to Athens of her second empire.' *CP* 13, 361–88.

Robert, L. (1960), *Hellenica* 11–12, 505–41.

Robertson, N. (1980*a*), 'Timocreon and Themistocles.' *AJP* 101, 61–78.

——(1980*b*), 'The true nature of the "Delian League".' *AJAH* 5, 110–33.

——(1987), 'Government and society at Miletus 525–442 BC.' *Phoenix* 41, 356–98.

Robinson, E.W. (1997), *The first democracies: early popular government outside Athens. Historia Einzelschriften 107.* Stuttgart.

Rocco, G. (2010), 'Il ruolo delle officine cicladiche nella trasmissione di modelli architettonici tra tardoarcaismo e protoclassicismo.' In Adornato 2010, 159–69.

Roebuck, C. (1950), 'The grain trade between Greece and Egypt.' *CP* 45.4, 236–47.

Roisman, G. (1987), 'Alkidas in Thucydides.' *Historia* 36(4), 385–421.

Rostovtzeff, M. (1941), *The social and economic history of the hellenistic world.* Vol.1. Oxford.

Royle, S.A. (2001), *A geography of islands: small island insularity.* London.

Rubensohn, O. (1901), 'Paros II: Topographie.' *AM* 26, 157–222.

——(1902), 'Paros III: Die Asklepieion.' *AM* 27, 199–238.

Rubincam, C. (1987), 'The Organization and Composition of Diodorus' Bibliotheke.' *EMC* 31, 313–28.

Ruschenbusch, E. (1982), '*IG* XII 5 609. Eine Bürgerliste von Iulis und Koresia auf Keos.' *ZPE* 48, 175–88.

——(1983*a*), 'Das Machtpotential der Bündner im ersten Athenischen Seebund (überlegungen zu Thukydides 1,99,2).' *ZPE* 53, 144–8.

——(1983*b*), 'Tribut und Bürgerzahl in ersten athenischen Seebund.' *ZPE* 53, 125–48.

——(1984), 'Modell Amorgos.' *Aux origine de l'hellénisme: la Crète et la Grèce: hommage à Henri van Effenterre*. Paris, 265–9.

Rutishauser, B. (2000), 'Siphnos and the Kyklades under the second Athenian league.' In Zervoudakis 2000, 249–56.

——(2005), 'A case of Siphnian *stasis*: the *Aiginitikos* of Isokrates.' In Zervoudakis 2005, 297–304.

——(2007), 'A dark wine in the wine-dark sea: production, trade, and Athenian policy in the northern Aegean.' *REA* 109, 465–73.

Ruzicka, S. (1988), 'War in the Aegean 333–331 B.C.: a reconsideration.' *Phoenix* 42, 131–51.

——(1998), 'Epaminondas and the genesis of the Social War.' *CP* 93(1), 60–9.

Ryder, T.T.B. (2000), 'Demosthenes and Philip II.' In Worthington 2000, 45–89.

Sackett, L.H. (1992), *Knossos: from Greek city to Roman colony. BSA Suppl. 21*. London.

Sacks, K.S. (1990), *Diodorus Siculus and the first century*. Princeton.

Sallares, R. (1991), *Ecology of the ancient Greek world*. Ithaca.

Saller, R. (2002), 'Framing the debate over growth in the ancient economy.' In Scheidel and von Reden 2002, 251–69.

Salmon, J.B. (1984), *Wealthy Corinth: a history of the city to 338 B.C.* Oxford.

Salomon, N. (1997), *Le cleruchie di Atene: caratteri e funzione*. Pisa.

Samons III, L.J. (2000), *Empire of the owl: Athenian imperial finance*. Stuttgart.

Sánchez, P. (2001), *L'Amphictionie des Pyles et de Delphes. Recherches sur son rôle historique des origines au IIe siècle de notre ère. Historia Einzelschriften 148*. Stuttgart.

Sancisi-Weerdenburg, H. (ed.) (2000), *Peisistratos and the tyranny: a reappraisal of the evidence*. Amsterdam.

Sarikakis, Th. Ch. (1986), 'Commercial relations between Chios and other Greek cities in antiquity.' In Boardman and Vaphopoulou-Richardson 1986, 121–31.

Sauciuc, T. (1914), *Andros: Untersuchungen zur geschichte und topographie der Insel*. Vienna.

Scheidel, W., Morris, I., and Saller, R.P. (eds.) (2008), *The Cambridge economic history of the Greco-Roman world*. Cambridge.

——and von Reden, S. (eds.) (2002), *The ancient economy*. Edinburgh.

Schepens, G. (1993), 'L'apogée de l'*archè* spartiate comme époque historique dans l'historiographie grecque du début du IVe s. av. J-C.' *Ancient Society* 24, 170–204.

Schilardi, D.U. (1975), '*Ἀρχαιολογικαὶ ἔρευναι ἐν Πάρῳ*.' *Praktika* 197–211.

——(2000*a*), 'Paros and the export of marble sarcophagi to Rome and Etruria.' In Schilardi and Katsanopoulou 2000, 537–53.

Schilardi, D.U. (2000*b*), 'Observations on the quarries of Spilies, Lakkoi, and Thapsana on Paros.' In Schilardi and Katsanopoulou 2000, 35–58.
——and Katsanopoulou, D. (eds.) (2000), *Paria lithos: Parian quarries, marble and workshops of sculpture: proceedings of the First International Conference on the Archaeology of Paros and the Cyclades, Paros, 2–5 October 1997.* Athens.
Schmitz, W. (1988), *Wirtschaftliche Prosperität, soziale Integration und die Seebundpolitik Athens: die Wirkung der Erfahrungen aus dem Ersten Attischen Seebund auf die athenische Aussenpolitik in der ersten Hälfte des 4. Jahrhunderts v. Chr.* Munich.
Schönert-Geiss, E. (1974), 'Die Geldzirkulation Attikas im Jahrhundert v. u. Z.' In Weiskopf 1974, 531–50.
Schönhammer, M. (1993), 'Some thoughts on the Athenian coinage decree.' In Hackens and Moucharte 1993, 187–91.
Schubert, C., and Laspe, D. (2009), 'Perikles' defensiver Kriegsplan: eine Thukydideische Erfindung?' *Historia* 58.4, 373–94.
Schuller, M. (1985), 'Die dorische Architektur der Kykladen in Spätarchaischer Zeit.' *JDAI* 100, 319–98.
——(1991), *Der Artemistempel im Delion auf Paros.* Berlin.
Schuller, W. (1974), *Die Herrschaft der Athener im Ersten Attischen Seebund.* Berlin.
——(1981), 'Über die ἰδιῶται–Rubrik in den attischen Tributlisten.' *ZPE* 42, 141–51.
Schütrumpf, E. (ed.) (1982), *Xenophon. Vorschläge zur Beschaffung von Geldmitteln oder über die Staatsseinkünfte.* Darmstadt.
Schweigert, E. (1939), 'Greek Inscriptions 4.' *Hesperia* 8, 10–14.
Schwenk, C.J. (1985), *Athens in the age of Alexander: the dated laws & decrees of 'the Lykourgan era' 338–322 B.C.* Chicago.
Scott, L. (2000), 'Were there *polis* navies in Archaic Greece?' In Oliver 2000, 93–116.
Scott, M. (2010), *Delphi and Olympia: the spatial politics of panhellenism in the archaic and classical periods.* Cambridge.
Seager, R. (1967), 'Thrasybulus, Conon, and Athenian imperialism 396–386 B.C.' *JHS* 87, 95–115.
——(1969), 'The Congress Decree: some doubts and a hypothesis.' *Historia* 18 (2), 129–41.
Sealey, R. (1966), 'The origin of the Delian League.' In Badian 1966, 233–55.
——(1993), *Demosthenes and his time: a study in defeat.* New York.
Seaman, M.G. (1997), 'The Athenian expedition to Melos in 416 BC.' *Historia* 46, 385–418.
Shaw, B. (2001), 'Challenging Braudel: a new vision of the Mediterranean.' *JRA* 14, 419–53.

Sheedy, K.A. (1985), 'Three vase-groups from the Purification Trench on Rheneia and the evidence for a Parian pottery tradition.' *BSA* 80, 151–90.

——(1996), 'The origins of the Second Nesiotic League and the defence of Kythnos.' *Historia* 45, 423–49.

——(1998), 'Keian federations and Keian coinage.' *NC* 158, 249–57.

——(2000), 'Archaic Parian coinage and Parian marble.' In Schilardi and Katsanopoulou 2000, 117–20.

——(2006), *The archaic and early classical coinages of the Cyclades.* London.

——and Papageorgiadou, Ch. (1998), 'The coinage of Kythnos.' In Mendoni and Mazarakis-Ainian 1998, 649–54.

Sheehan, M. (1996), *The balance of power: history and theory.* London.

Sherratt, S., and Sherratt, A. (1993), 'The growth of the Mediterranean economy in the early first millennium BC.' *World Archaeology* 24 (3), 361–78.

Sherwin-White, S. (1978), *Ancient Cos: an historical study from the Dorian settlement to the imperial period.* Gottingen.

Shipley, I.G. (1987), *A history of Samos, 800–188 B.C.* Oxford.

——(2011), *Pseudo-Skylax' Periplous: the circumnavigation of the inhabited world. Text, translation, and commentary.* Exeter.

Shipton, K. (2000), *Leasing and lending: the cash economy in fourth-century BC Athens.* London.

Simms, R.R. (1989), 'Isis in classical Athens.' *CJ* 84, 216–21.

Sinclair, R.K. (1978), 'The King's Peace and the employment of military and naval forces 387–378 B.C.' *Chiron* 8, 29–54.

Sippel, D.V. (1986), 'Tenos and the Nesiotic League.' *Ancient World* 13, 41–6.

Slot, B.J. (1982), *Archipelagus turbatus: les Cyclades entre colonization latine et occupation ottomane c.1500–1718.* Istanbul.

Smarczyk, B. (1986), *Bünderautonomie und athenische Seebundspolitik im Dekelischen Krieg.* Frankfurt.

Smart, J.D. (1977), 'The Athenian empire.' *Phoenix* 31, 245–57.

Smelser, N.J., and Swedborg, R, (eds.) (2005), *The handbook of economic sociology.* 2nd edn. Princeton.

Smith, R.E. (1948), 'Lysander and the Spartan empire.' *CP* 43, 145–56.

——(1954), 'The Opposition to Agesilaus' Foreign Policy 394–371 B.C.' *Historia* 2, 274–88.

Snodgrass, A.M. (1987–89), 'The rural landscape and its political significance.' *Opus* 6–8, 53–70.

——(2006), *Archaeology and the emergence of Greece.* Ithaca.

Soetens, Sarris, and Vansteenhuyse (2002), 'Defining the Minoan Cultural Landscape by the use of GIS.' *Proceedings of the conference 'Space Applications for Heritage Conservation', Council of Europe & International Space University, Strasbourg 5–8 November (2002* (CD Rome).

Sordi, M. (1958), *La lega tessala fino ad Alessandro Magno.* Rome.

Sparkes, B.A. (1982), 'Production and exchange in the Classical and Roman periods.' In Renfrew and Wagstaff 1982, 228–35.

Spence, I.G. (1990), 'Perikles and the defence of Attika during the Peloponnesian War.' *JHS* 110, 91–109.

Sprawski, S. (2006), 'Alexander of Pherai: *infelix* tyrant.' In Lewis 2006, 135–47.

Stadter, P. (1983), 'The motives for Athens' alliance with Corcyra (Thuc. 1.44).' *GRBS* 24, 131–43.

——(1989), *A commentary on Plutarch's* Pericles. Chapel Hill.

Stampolidis, N. (2003), 'A summary glance at the Mediterranean in the Early Iron Age (11th-6th c. B.C.).' In N. Stampolidis, ed., *Sea routes . . . from Sidon to Huelva: interconnections in the Mediterranean 16th-6th c. B.C.* (Athens), 41–79.

Stanford, W.B., and Finopoulos, E.J. (eds.) (1984), *The travels of Lord Charlemont in Greece and Turkey 1749, from his own unpublished journals.* London.

Starr, C. (1962), *The origins of Greek civilization.* London.

——(1989), *The influence of sea power on ancient history.* Oxford.

Steinbrecher, M. (1985), *Der delisch-attische Seebund und die athenisch-spartanischen Beziehungen in der kimonischen Ära (ca. 478/7–462/1).* Stuttgart.

Stewart, A.F. (1977), *Skopas of Paros.* Park Ridge, NY.

——(1990), *Greek sculpture: an exploration.* New Haven.

——and Martin (2005), 'Attic imported pottery at Tell Dor: an overview.' *BASOR* 337, 79–94.

Stibbe, C.M. (1972), *Lakonische Vasenmaler des sechsten Jahrhunderts v. Chr.* Amsterdam and London.

——(1989), *Laconian mixing bowls: a history of the* krater Lakonikos *from the seventh to the fifth century B.C.* Amsterdam.

Strassler, R.B. (ed.) (1998), *The Landmark Thucydides.* New York.

——(2009. *The Landmark Xenophon's Hellenika.* New York.

Strauss, B.S. (1986), *Athens after the Peloponnesian War: class, faction, and policy 403–386 B.C.* Ithaca.

Stroud, R.S. (1974), 'An Athenian law on silver coinage.' *Hesperia* 43, 157–88.

——(1998), *The Athenian grain-tax law of 374/3 B.C. Hesperia Suppl. 29.* Princeton.

Strubbe, J.H., Tybout, R.A., and Versnel, H.S. (eds.) (1996), *ENERGEIA: studies on ancient history and epigraphy presented to H.W. Pleket.* Amsterdam.

Stumpf, G. (1986), 'Ein athenisches Münzgesetz des 4. Jh. V. Chr.' *JNG* 36, 23–40.

Stylianou, P.J. (1998), *A historical commentary on Diodorus Siculus, Book 15*. Oxford.

Sutton Jr, R.F. (1991), 'Ceramic evidence for settlement and land use in the Geometric to Hellenistic periods.' In Cherry, Davis, and Mantzourani 1991, 245–63.

Swiny, H.W., and Katsev, M.L. (1973), 'The Kyrenia shipwreck: A fourth-century B.C. Greek merchant ship.' In Blackman 1973, 339–59.

Symeonides, S. (1990), *Istoria tes Siphnou*. Athens.

Talamo, C. (1996), 'Le cicladi e l'anfizionia di Delos.' In Lanzilotta and Schilardi 1996, 229–43.

Talbert, J.A. (ed.) (2000), *The Barrington Atlas of the Greek and Roman world*. Princeton.

Tandy, D.W. (1997), *Warriors into traders: the power of the market in early Greece*. Berkeley.

——(2001), *Prehistory and history: ethnicity, class, and political economy*. Montreal.

Tausend, K. (2006), *Verkehrswege der Argolis: Rekonstruktion und historische Bedeutung. Geographica Historia 23*. Berlin.

Tenenti, A. (1967), *Piracy and the decline of Venice 1580–1615*. Trans. by Janet and Brian Pullan. Berkeley.

Thiry, S. (2001), 'Aspects geopolitiques de l'histoire des îles ioniennes aux époques classique et hellenistique.' *Historia* 50/2, 131–44.

Thomas, D. (2009), 'Introduction.' In Strassler 2009, ix–lxvi.

Thomassen, L.A. (1984), 'The Aegean war of Alexander the Great 333–331 B. C.' PhD diss. Pennsylvania State University.

Thompson, W.E. (1979), 'A view of Athenian banking.' *MH* 36, 224–41.

Tiverios, M. (2008),. 'Greek colonization of the northern Aegean.' In Tsetskhladze 2008, 1–154.

Tod, M.N. (1962), *A selection of Greek historical inscriptions, vol. 2: from 403 to 323 B.C.* Oxford.

Tomber, R. (1993), 'Quantitative approaches to the investigation of long-distance exchange.' *JRA* 6, 142–66.

Tomlinson, R. (2000), 'Towards a distribution pattern for Parian marble in the architecture of the 6th c. B.C.' In Schilardi and Katsanopoulou 2000, 139–42.

Tournefort, J.P. de (1718), *A voyage into the Levant: performed by command of the late French king*. London.

Tracy, S.V. (1995), *Athenian democracy in transition: Attic letter-cutters of 340 to 290 B.C.* Berkeley.

——(2003), 'A major Athenian letter-cutter of the late 5th and early 4th centuries B.C.: the cutter of *IG* II^2 17 (dates:409/8–386/5).' In Bakewell and Sickinger 2003, 351–63.

Tréheux, J. (1948), 'Les dernières années de Délos sous le protectorat des amphictions.' *Mélanges d'archéologie et d'histoire offerts à Charles Picard.* Paris, 1008–32.

Treuil, R. (1983), 'Prospection archéologique à Naxos en 1981.' In Dalongeville and Rougemont 1983, 59–66.

Tritle, L. (ed.) (1997), *The Greek world in the fourth century.* London.

——(2010), *A new history of the Peloponnesian War.* Wiley-Blackwell.

Trundle, M. (2010), 'Coinage and the transformation of Greek warfare.' In Fagan and Trundle 2010, 227–52.

Tsetskhladze, G.R. (1998), 'Trade on the Black Sea in the Archaic and Classical periods. Some observations.' In Parkins and Smith 1998, 52–74.

——(ed.) (2008*a*), *Greek colonisation: an account of Greek colonies and other settlements overseas. Vol. 2. Mnemosyne Suppl.* 193. Leiden/Boston.

——(2008*b*), 'Grain for Athens.' In Alston and van Nijf 2008, 47–62.

Tuplin, C.J. (1993), *The failings of empire: a reading of Xenophon* Hellenica *2.3.11–7.5.27.* Stuttgart.

——(2004), *Xenophon and his world: papers from a conference held in Liverpool in July 1999.* Stuttgart.

Urban, R. (1991), *Der Königsfrieden von 387/6 v. Chr.: Vorgeschichte, Zustandekommen, Ergebnis und politische Umsetzung.* Stuttgart.

Urso, G. (2003), *Moneta, mercanti, banchiere. I precedenti greci e romani dell-Euro.* Pisa.

van Alfen, P.G. (2005), 'Problems in ancient imitative and counterfeit coinage.' In Archibald, Davies, and Gabrielsen 2005, 322–54.

van Berchem, D. (1991), 'Commerce et écriture. L'exemple de Délos à l'époque hellenistique.' *MH* 48, 129–45.

van Effenterre, H. (1948), *La Crète et le monde grec de Platon à Polybe.* Paris.

van Wees, H. (ed.) (2000), *War and violence in ancient Greece.* London.

——(2002), 'Herodotus and the past.' In Bakker, de Jong, and van Wees 2002, 321–49.

——(2008), '"Diejenigen, die segeln, sollen Sold erhalten": Seekriegführung und -finanzierung im archaischen Eretria.' In Burrer and Müller 2008, 128–150.

——(2010), '"Those who sail are to receive a wage": naval warfare and finance in archaic Eretria.' In Fagan and Trundle 2010, 205–26.

Vanderpool, E. (1962), 'Studies in Attic epigraphy.' *Hesperia* 31, 399–401.

——and Wallace, W.P. (1964), 'The sixth-century laws from Eretria.' *Hesperia* 37, 381–91.

Vélissaropoulos, J. (1980), *Les nauclères grecs: recherches sur les institutions maritimes en Grèce et dans l'Orient hellénisé.* Paris.

Vial, C. (1984), *Délos indépendante. BCH Suppl. X.* Paris.

Villard, F. (1993), 'La localisation des ateliers cycladiques de céramique géométrique et orientalisante.' In Dalongeville and Rougemont 1993, 143–65.

von Gaertringen, H (1906), *Die Inschriften von Priene*. Berlin.

von Reden, S. (2003), *Exchange in ancient Greece*. 2nd edn. London.

——(2007), 'Classical Greece: consumption.' In Scheidel, Morris, and Saller 2007, 385–408.

Wagner, G., Gentner, W., Gropengiesser, H., and Gale, N.H. (1980), 'Early Bronze Age lead-silver mining and metallurgy in the Aegean; the ancient workings on Siphnos.' In Craddock 1980, 63–85.

Wagner, G.A., and Weisgerber, G. (1979), 'The ancient silver mine at Ayos Sostis on Siphnos (Greece).' *Archaeophysika* 10, 209–22.

————(eds.) (1985), *Silber, Blei, und Gold auf Siphnos, prähistorische und antike Metallproduction*. Bochum.

————(eds.) (1988), *Antike Edel- und Buntmetallgewinnung auf Thasos*. Bochum.

Walbank, M.B. (1978), *Athenian proxenies of the fifth century B.C.* Toronto and Sarasota.

——(1986), 'Athens and Stymphalos: *IG* II^2 , 144 + .' *Hesperia* 55, 319–54.

——(1987), 'Athens grants citizenship to a benefactor: *IG* II^2 398a + 438.' *AHB* 1, 10–12.

Walek, T. (1924), 'Les opérations navales pendant la guerre Lamiaque.' *RPh* 48, 23–30.

Walker, K.G. (2004), *Archaic Eretria: a political and social history from the earliest times to 490 BC*. London.

Wallace, M.B. (1984), 'The "reduced Euboio-Attic" coin weight standard.' In Heckel and Sullivan 1984, 19–37.

——and Figueira, T.J. (2010), 'Notes on the island *phoros*.' *ZPE* 172, 65–9.

————(2011), 'Athens and Euboea in the fifth century: toward a new synthesis.' In Rupp and Tomlinson 2011, 233–59.

Wallinga, H.T. (1964), 'Nautika I.' *Mnemosyne* 17, 3–40.

——(1984), 'The Ionian revolt.' *Mnemosyne* 37 (3–4), 401–37.

——(1991), 'Naval installations in Cilicia Pedias: the defence of the *parathalassia* in Achaemenid times and after.' In Courtils, Moretti, and Planet 1991, 277–81.

——(1993), *Ships and sea power before the Great Persian War*. Leiden.

——(2000), 'The Athenian *naukrarioi*.' In Sancisi-Weerdenburg 2000, 131–46.

——(2005), *Xerxes' Greek adventure: the naval perspective*. Leiden.

Waltz, K.N. (1959), *Man, the state, and war. A theoretical analysis*. New York.

Wankel, H. (1976), *Demosthenes Rede für Ktesiphon über den Kranz*. Heidelberg.

Weber, M. (1976 (1924)), *The agrarian sociology of ancient civilizations.* Trans. R.I. Frank. London.

Weiskopf, E.C. (1974), *Hellenische Poleis: Krise, Wandlung, Wirkung.* Berlin.

Welwei, K.W. (1977), *Unfreie im antiken Kriegsdienst II.* Wiesbaden.

West, A.B. (1929), 'The tribute lists and the non-tributary members of the Delian league.' *AHR* 35, 267–75.

Whitbread, I.K. (1995), *Greek transport amphorae: a petrological and archaeological study.* Athens.

Whitby, M. (1998), 'The grain trade of Athens in the fourth century B.C.' In Parkins and Smith 1998, 102–28.

White, D. (ed.) (1997), *The extramural sanctuary of Demeter and Persephone at Cyrene, Libya.* Vol. 6. Philadelphia.

Whitehead, D. (1976), 'IG I^2 39: "aliens" in Chalcis and Athenian imperialism.' *ZPE* 21, 251–9.

——(1977), *The ideology of the Athenian metic.* Cambridge.

Whitelaw, T.M. (1991), 'The ethnoarchaeology of recent rural settlement and land use in NW Keos.' In Cherry, Davis, and Mantzourani 1991, 403–54.

——(1998), 'Colonisation and competition in the polis of Koressos: the development of settlement in north-west Keos from the archaic to the late Roman periods.' In Mendoni and Mazarakis-Ainian 1998, 227–58.

——and Davis, J.L. (1991), 'The *polis* center of Koressos.' In Cherry, Davis, and Mantzourani 1991, 265–84.

Wilhelm, A. (1940), 'Vier Beschlüsse der Athener.' *AbhBerl* 22 (1939), 3–29.

Wilkes, J.J., and Fischer-Hansen, T. (2004), 'The Adriatic'. In Hansen and Nielsen 2004, 321–37.

Will, E. (1954), 'Trois quarts de siècle de recherches sur l'économie grecque antique.' *Annales* 9, 7–22.

Willemsen, F. (1963), 'Arcaische Grabmalbasen aus der athener Stadtmauer.' *AM* 78, 104–53.

Wilson, J.B. (1981), 'Strategy and tactics in the Mytilene campaign.' *Historia* 30, 144–63.

——(1987), *Athens and Corcyra: strategy and tactics in the Peloponnesian War.* Bristol.

Winterscheidt, H. (1938), *Aigina: eine Untersuchung über Gesellschaft und Wirtschaft.* Würzburg.

Woodhead, A.G. (1962), 'Chabrias, Timotheus, and the Aegean allies, 375–373 B.C.' *Phoenix* 16, 258–66.

Woodhead, G. (1971), 'The "Adriatic empire" of Dionysius I of Syracuse.' *Klio* 52, 503–12.

——(1997), *Agora XVI: Inscriptions. The Decrees.* Princeton.

Worthington, I. (ed.) (2000), *Demosthenes: statesman and orator.* London.

——(2008), *Philip II of Macedonia.* London and New Haven.

——(2009), '*IG* II^2 236 and Philip's Common Peace of 337.' In Mitchell and Rubinstein 2009, 213–23.

Yeroulanou, M., and Stamatopoulou, M. (2005), *Architecture and archaeology in the Cyclades: papers in honour of J.J. Coulton*. BAR International Series 1455. Oxford.

Zelnick-Abramovitz, R. (2004), 'Settlers and dispossessed in the Athenian empire.' *Mnemosyne* 57 (3), 325–45.

Zervoudakis, M. (2000), *Πρακτικα Ἄ Διεθνους Σιφναικου Συμποσιου. Σιφνος 25–28 Ιουνιου 1998*. Athens.

——(2005), *Πρακτικα Β Διεθνους Σιφναικου Συμποσιου. Σιφνος 27–30 Ιουνιου 2002*. Athens.

Ziebarth, E. (1929), *Beiträge zur Geschichte des Seeraubs und Seehandels im alten Griechenland*. Hamburg.

Zimmermann Munn, M.L. (2003), 'Corinthian trade with the Punic West in the Classical period.' In Bookidis and Williams 2003, 195–217.

Index Locorum

General Index